Freshest Advices

FRESHEST ADVICES

Early Provincial Newspapers in England

By R. M. Wiles

Ohio State University Press

"It must . . . be confessed, that these things have their use, and are, besides, vehicles of much amusement. . . .

—Crabbe, "To the Reader,"
The Newspaper (1785)

Preface

WHEN Princess Anne was crowned Queen of her several realms in 1702, there were only two provincial newspapers in England to report the coronation; when, two generations later, another Archbishop placed the crown on the head of George III, there were local weekly newspapers in twenty-nine English towns. It is the purpose of this book to give an account of that interesting development in English journalism, and to confute the common assumption that early provincial newspapers were wretched little smutchy sheets containing only borrowed reports and notices of runaway apprentices.

For such a study as this the only "primary sources" are the original issues of the newspapers themselves and any surviving contemporary records which have a bearing on the early efforts to give English readers not living in London a regular budget of freshest advices, foreign and domestic. The sheer bulk of the material is enormous, and it is understandable that in examining such vast quantities of matter one's notes become voluminous. Excision of non-essentials has been the chief difficulty in dealing with so complex a subject, but if details have kept thrusting themselves in for their own sake instead of for the legitimate purpose of establishing perspective, perhaps some of those details have helped to redeem the following chapters from unconscionable dullness.

My search for original issues of early country newspapers began precisely thirty years ago, when I went as a graduate student from Harvard to explore the British Museum, the Bodleian, the Devon and Exeter Institution, and other haunts of scholars. During the past decade, I have revisited the great libraries of the United Kingdom and North America, and I have examined literally tons of early newspapers now to be found in those repositories and in the local libraries, museums, and newspaper offices of sixty English towns. These visits have taken me from the Yale University Library in New Haven, Connecticut, to the Black Gate in Newcastle-upon-Tyne, from the Morrab Gardens in Penzance to the Vicarage at Mottram-in-Longdendale, Cheshire.

In all this searching and finding I have been immeasurably assisted and encouraged by a host of librarians, newspaper officials, university people, archivists, curators of museums, and private owners of early newspapers. To name them individually would be to fill two pages of this Preface; the list would reveal inadequately the extent both of my indebtedness and of my gratitude. Their help was so graciously offered that it would be presumptuous to suppose I could pay my debt by naming them in a formal schedule of acknowledgments. Among them are men of authority in newspaper offices in Chester, Coventry, Reading, Salisbury, and Stamford, the general manager of an engineering firm in Kendal, the treasurer of an ancient Sussex town, the administrative head of a printing firm in Nottingham, a former mayor of the City of York, the chancellor of a great minster, a member of the B.B.C. staff, a retired professor who lives in Cornwall, the curator of books and manuscripts in the greatest Shakespeare library in North America, and scores of librarians in places as far apart as Charlottesville in Virginia and Whitehaven in Cumberland. I remember with happiness all their names and their acts of kindly assistance.

Yet to impose total anonymity upon these numerous

encouragers of research would be ungracious; I shall mention some whose kindness symbolizes that of many more. One of them is a book-loving Churchman, the Rev. Douglas G. Matthews, whose generosity has gone far beyond the giving of permission to examine his splendid file of the *Sussex Weekly Advertiser;* another is Horace Sanders, Esq., who generously gave me the enviable privilege of membership (for a time) in the Press Club, St. Bride's House, London, E.C.4. Three others, whose conversations have been as stimulating and as helpful to me as their fine collections of early newspapers, are W. B. Morrell, Esq., of London, Kenneth Monkman, Esq., also of London, and Sydney R. Turner, Esq., of Cheam, Surrey, England. To these and the hundred others who opened their doors and their treasures to me I offer warmest thanks.

For permission to use the illustrations and the manuscript material which appear in this book my thanks are also gratefully offered to the Yale University Library, to the Trustees of the British Museum, to the Bodleian Library, to the Controller of H.M. Stationery Office (through the Secretary of the Public Record Office), to the Northampton Public Libraries Committee, to the City Librarian of Liverpool (Brown, Picton, and Hornby Libraries), to the Archivist of Coventry and the Director of the City of Coventry Libraries, Art Gallery, and Museums, to the Royal Institution of Cornwall, to the Northamptonshire Record Office, to the City Librarian and Administrative Officer of Carlisle, to the City Librarian of Nottingham, to the Lincolnshire Archives Office, to the Somerset Archaeological and Natural History Society, to the City Librarian of Newcastle-upon-Tyne, to the City Librarian of Gloucester, to the City Librarian of Bristol, to the York Minister Library, to the City Archivist of Chester, and to the Senior Archivist in the Norfolk and Norwich Record Office.

Formal thanks are also offered to the Board of Governors of McMaster University for a year's leave of absence, which gave me leisure to gather material for this book, and to the Canada Council for a senior fellowship, which not only added distinction to my project but kept me supplied with food and ink while I set about it.

I am happy to record here my sincere appreciation of the editorial procedures of Weldon A. Kefauver, Director of the Ohio State University Press, and of Thomas E. Sheahan, the Editor. Their tactful patience has been infinitely reassuring; their standards of typography are responsible for whatever is attractive in the format of this book.

By a pleasing convention one may in this rather public fashion thank one's wife for her helpful forbearance during the crucial prenatal months of a coming book. My wife has shown a devotion far beyond the call of duty by engaging in that virtuous exercise quaintly called holding the tongue. If there is praise for this book it will be owing to Olwen's three thousand hours of silence.

R. M. W.

Hamilton, Ontario, Canada
November, 1964

Note on the Dating
of Early Newspapers

Until September, 1752, the printers of newspapers in England, like the writers of letters, often, but not invariably, changed the year date on 25 March instead of on 1 January. For that reason it is necessary to check the date of any newspaper printed in England during the first fifty-two years of the eighteenth century if that date falls within the eighty-three (in leap years, eighty-four) days from 1 January to 24 March inclusive. Checking the dates of newspapers is very simple, for there are usually two unmistakable guides: if the serial numbers of two papers dated 19 March 1734 and 26 March 1735 are consecutive, it is clear that the papers appeared just one week apart; even without serial numbers, the day of the week is a sure guide, for if a paper is dated Monday, February 3, 1734, one can be sure that it belongs to 1735, since 3 February was a Sunday in 1734 but fell on Monday in 1735. The volume number is also helpful, if a new volume began in January.

In this book and in the Register (Appendix C), all dates are given according to the pattern which includes January, February, and March within the same calendar year as the April which followed immediately. Thus the issue of the *Oxford Gazette: and Reading Mercury*, number 16 is dated "Monday, March 3, 1745," but (a) from the serial number in relation to those that precede and follow, (b) from the day of the week, and (c) from news of the rebels printed in the paper itself, it is perfectly obvious that the year is 1746, and in this work the issue is silently dated 3 March 1746. Some eighteenth-century printers recognized the possibility of confusion and put in the date line such a form as "Monday, February 22, 1747-8," or "Thursday, February 10, 1714-15," or "Friday, January 25, 172⅔." Such dates are in this book given as "Monday, 22 February 1748," "Thursday, 10 February 1715," and "Friday, 25 January 1723."

The millions of people who use English every day have different ways of writing dates, and each of us is ready to support his own favorite mode by invoking logical principles, sometimes heatedly, always ineffectually. Some like the cryptic form "6: 12: 47." Others find "6: XII: 47" perfectly obvious. Many write "October 15th, 1963," or "October 15, 1963." Just as many save a comma and write "15th October 1963," or "15 October 1963." In the text of this book the form "15 October 1740" is used, with a further reduction in the Register, where brevity and clarity are combined in the form "15 Oct 1740."

One other simplification should be pointed out. Some printers of newspapers gave the most explicit information in their date lines. The *Manchester Journal,* number 22, for instance, has in its date line "From TUESDAY August the 17th, to TUESDAY August the 24th, 1736." Cataloguers often give only one of the two dates but sometimes quite unaccountably select the earlier of the two instead of the later, which was obviously the nominal, if not actual, date of publication. In this book only the second date is given, even where the interval between successive issues was regularly less than a full week. Thus the *Maidstone Mercury,* number 25, which has in its date line *"From* MONDAY MAY 24. *to* THURSDAY MAY 27. 1725," is here dated simply 27 May 1725.

Contents

Illustrations

Chapter I

To *the* PUBLICK.

M R. B R Y A N having lately declin'd printing
T H E
Worceſter Journal,

It is now undertaken by *H. BERROW*, (who ſerv'd a
regular Apprenticeſhip in LONDON) and will be conducted in ſuch Manner, and contain ſuch a Variety of
News, Miſcellaneous Pieces, &c. as ſhall render it, in
all Reſpects, very uſeful and entertaining.

T H I S Paper is publiſh'd (every *Thurſday)* ſeveral
Hours ſooner than uſual; and all proper (tho' *expenſive)*
Means are taken to extend its Circulation, in order that
the Intention of *Advertiſing* therein may be the better
anſwer'd:----Upon theſe Conſiderations, it is hop'd, the
Publick will favour this Undertaking with Encouragement; whilſt, to oblige them to the utmoſt, it ſhall be
the conſtant Endeavour of

Their Humble Servant,
H. BERROW.

Note, Having purchas'd all Mr. BRYAN's Materials,
I carry on the *Printing Buſineſs,* in all its Branches, at
my Office in *Gooſe-Lane,* near the *Croſs,* WORCESTER.

Weekly Intelligence for Country Readers

WILLIAM COWPER was right when he declared in the fourth book of *The Task* that a newspaper was one kind of publication that not even critics would take the trouble to criticize; for no matter how eagerly a newspaper is read, after a few minutes it is thrown aside as heedlessly as a bus ticket and is as soon forgotten. To historians, however, a bundle of old newspapers—really old ones— is precious, and the reason is clear: the passage of two or three centuries can make a twopenny newspaper invaluable, not just because of its scarcity but because it discloses so much about the people who first read it and about the earlier developments of journalism.

Many years before the first regular local newspaper was established in an English provincial town, there were numerous corantos and newsbooks which, though printed in London, undoubtedly reached readers in the country.[1] During the Civil War period, all England cried out for news, and many a *Perfect Diurnall* or *Mercurius* or *Intelligencer* came into being on both Royalist and Parliamentary sides. Then, for a number of years, it was only the *London Gazette*—for a few early issues printed in Oxford and called the *Oxford Gazette*—that brought news to

FIG. 1—Hervey Berrow's announcement in 1748 that he had taken over the printing business of Stephen Bryan. (Used by permission of the Trustees of the British Museum.)

Englishmen living in the country. In the last twenty years of the seventeenth century, sporadic attempts were made to provide more bulletins of news from London, and (in addition to Sir Roger L'Estrange's *Observator*) there were competing papers with such titles as *Domestick Intelligence* or *True Protestant Mercury;* but it was not until George Ridpath's *Flying Post* and Abel Roper's *Post Boy* began to appear in 1695 that English readers in London and the country could count on seeing unofficial newspapers regularly every week, year in and year out, in addition to the *London Gazette.* By 1702, London had a daily paper, the *Daily Courant,* which in course of time had rivals in the *Daily Post,* the *Daily Journal,* the *Daily Advertiser,* the *London Daily Post,* and was followed in 1735 by the *Daily Gazetteer.* Those first decades of the eighteenth century saw also the establishment of numerous weekly, twice-weekly, and thrice-weekly papers in London—among them Defoe's *Review,* the *Evening Post,* George Read's *Weekly Journal; or, British Gazetteer,* the *St. James's Post,* Nathaniel Mist's *Weekly Journal; or Saturday's Post, Parker's London News,* the *Whitehall Evening Post,* the *London Journal,* the *British Journal,* the *Craftsman* (from number 45 called the *Country Journal; or, The Craftsman*), the *London Evening Post,* the *Universal Spectator,* the *Grub-Street Journal,* the *General Evening Post*—all of these and many other papers doubtless having some circulation in the country, as did the monthly *Gentleman's Magazine* and the *London Magazine.* As the eighteenth century advanced, any country reader willing to pay the cost of having newspapers brought or sent to him had his choice of a rapidly increasing number of London journals. Some papers, enjoying the benefits of subsidies and franking provided by the government, actually reached country readers free of charge.

Some of the London papers seem by their titles to have been intended primarily for circulation among readers in the rural areas or in provincial towns. John Houghton, F.R.S., clearly expected country readers as well as city readers to be interested in his *Collection of Letters for the Improvement of Husbandry and Trade* (published irregularly from 8 September 1681 to 16 June 1684) and in his weekly *Collection for Improvement of Husbandry and Trade* (from 30 March 1692 to 24 September 1704). Other papers printed in London and apparently intended for distribution in the provinces were the short-lived *Countrey Foot-Post* (1644), the *City and Countrey Mercury* (1667), and the *County* [*sic*] *Gentleman's Courant* (1685). Even after local papers began to appear in provincial towns, there were London newspapers which were designed for distribution in rural areas: J. Morphew's *Country Gentleman's Courant: or, Universal Intelligence* (1706-1707), *Country Gentleman* (1726), Dormer's *Country Tatler* (1736),[2] the *Country Magazine: Or, Weekly Pacquet* (1739),[3] and T. Cooper's *Country Oracle: A Weekly Newspaper, Containing Answers to All Questions in All Sciences* (1741). There were some London printers of news who used the word "Oxford" in the title or subtitle, implying (quite misleadingly) some connection with the university city.[4]

It is a fact that the proprietors of several London newspapers made special efforts to get their papers into the hands of readers outside of London. There is, at the Press Club in London, a single issue—number 2 (2 November 1646)—of a paper entitled *The Military Actions of Europe, as also the Councels made publique Relating thereto; with such other particulars as happen,* and its title is followed by the words, "Collected weekly for the Tuesday POST." The emphasis given to that last word suggests that Giles Calvert and his printer, J.M., "at the sign of the Black-spread Eagle at the West end of Pauls," expected sales in the country to be considerable. It was stated in the colophon of Houghton's later *Collection,* mentioned above, that the papers were sold not

5

only by the hawkers and by certain named venders in London but also by George Rose in Norwich; and in number 11 (14 May 1692), Houghton suggested that customers could receive the paper by post, or that local booksellers and coffee-men might arrange for carriers to bring regular supplies every week; " . . . or Carriers themselves may gain well," he added, "if they'll serve the Country Gentlemen. And any such Bookseller, Coffee-man, or Carrier that will apply themselves to me, shall have good Encouragement with liberty to return those that won't sell." One of the several papers called the *London Post,* in its issue of 9 May 1705, prefaced the news with a statement beginning, "since this Paper is Published every Night, to go into the Several Parts of England. . . . " George Ridpath, author of the *Flying Post,* announced in number 776 (30 April 1700) that although the paper came out early on the three days of publication, there would be added "for the conveniency of the Country" a postscript which would include all the domestic and foreign news arriving late in the day. A few proprietors went so far as to prepare special country editions of their London papers. Three times a week, two consecutive issues of the *Daily Courant* (1702-1735) were combined into a Tuesday-Thursday-Saturday country paper, and there was also a country edition of the later *Daily Gazetteer.*

It is worth noting, moreover, that London papers were sometimes advertised in country newspapers, a good example being the announcement in the *Gloucester Journal,* number 296 (5 December 1727), that one week later the first issue of R. Nutt's thrice-weekly *London Evening Post* would appear. No reference was made in the advertisement to the cost of sending the *London Evening Post* to subscribers in or near Gloucester, nor was there any list of agents from whom it might be obtained.[5] More explicit information on the provincial circulation of London papers is to be found in the advertisements in various

6

local papers in July, 1757, announcing the first issues of *Lloyd's Evening Post*: "It will be published in the Evening of every Monday, Wednesday, and Friday, and circulated thro' great Part of the Kingdom by the Post which now sets out on what were called the Bye Nights to all the trading Cities, and all the Sea Ports of Note." [6] Long before 1757, as may be seen from Treasury records of the 1730's, the government paid substantial sums annually to the authors and printers of the "double" *Courant*, the *Corn Cutter's Journal*, the *London Journal*, and the *Free Briton*, which were "sent to the Post Office every Post day" for distribution by the clerks of the roads. The publisher of the *British Apollo* advised persons living in the country to have friends in town send them the paper. [7] The printers of some country newspapers offered to take in subscriptions for London papers. [8]

The man who made the most remarkable efforts to induce country people to buy newspapers printed in London was Robert Walker, the address of whose shop was at various times given as (1) at Shakespeare's Head in Turn-again Lane, Snowhill, (2) in Exchange Alley, Cornhill, (3) next the White Horse Inn, Fleet Street, (4) at the British Oil Warehouse in Fleet Lane, (5) at the corner of Seacoal Lane, next Fleet Lane, and (6) at the corner of Elliott's Court in the Little Old Bailey. From one or another of these establishments Walker issued various newspapers bearing the names of provincial towns or counties: the *Warwick and Staffordshire Journal* (1737 and following years), the *Shropshire Journal* (1737), the *Derbyshire Journal* (1738), and the *Lancashire Journal* (1738-1741), all printed in London except the later issues of the *Warwick and Staffordshire Journal*. From his Fleet Lane shop he also issued several editions of the *London and Country Journal*, one series of which was intended (without change of title) to circulate in the Bristol area, and another, with title altered to *Northamptonshire Journal* but not otherwise different, for dis-

7

tribution in a country region.[9] It is possible that the concurrent but differing issues of *All-Alive and Merry* in 1741 represent a similar attempt to produce an edition for circulation in the provinces as well as the regular city edition.

More than one London printer of newspapers regularly left space at the end of the third page of his paper for use by customers who might wish to add written communications when they sent the newspapers to friends or relatives in the country, the fourth page being left blank so that the paper might be folded and addressed like an ordinary letter. According to Alexander Andrews,[10] Ichabod Dawks announced in an early issue of his printed *News-Letter* (1696) that it would be "done upon good writing-paper, and blank space left that any gentleman may write his own private business." No copy of this issue has survived. The *Evening Post*, number 10 (16 September 1709), had on its first page the statement that "being chiefly design'd for the Country" it would always be printed on fine paper "with a Blank to write on." Issues of the *Evening Post* now at the British Museum have written messages sent to Gabriel Walter of Chatham in Kent by his "ever dutyfull and obedient Son, Will: Walter," or to William from his brother Thomas. The letter in number 155 (10 August 1710) is from Thomas to William, who was then at home:

D^r. Bro^r:

after ye worst Passage that I ere had, did arrive at London, ab^t: Ten a Clock last night, & this morning was wth: Capt: Cleasby, to whom I delivered ye Pay List. M^r: Redman Called on me this Day, & I let him Know that had his piece of Holland wch he'll send for tomorrow; You may See p^r this paper what an alteration there is In Bank Stock Since I left you, If can get it at 108 or thereat tomorrow I will purchase; Pray let my Mother Know that have sent by ye Carrier this Day those things she desired. wth: my Due Respects to all I am

D^{rs}: Bro^r: y^r: Most Affect. Loving Bro^r:

Thos Walter.

The title of another London paper suggests that this unprinted space left for personal messages was regarded as a postage-saving feature: the *London Post, with the best Account of the whole Week's News, Foreign and Domestick; with Room left to write into the Country without the Charge of Double Postage.*[11] Issues of the *Evening General-Post* in All Souls' Library are addressed on the unprinted fourth page to the Rev. Dr. Kennett, Dean of Peterborough, at Peterborough in Northamptonshire. One of them number 51 (10 July 1716)—has a long written letter in the unprinted lower part of the third page and in the inner margin. Hasty and informal communications scrawled in the margins of some other London newspapers show that personal postscripts were commonly added for readers in the country even when space was not provided by the printer for the purpose.

Although the history of newsletters wholly in manuscript has not yet been written, it is well known that during the seventeenth century there were several series of hand-written bulletins of news, prepared in comparatively small quantities by men living in London, where great affairs took place or were discussed, and sent to regular subscribers in the country for a suitable annual fee. They began with "Sir" or "My Lord" and were addressed on the back to the recipient, as ordinary private letters were. The effect intended, ostensibly, was that of direct correspondence between individuals, one a city dweller, the other a man eager to hear early reports and rumors of what was going on. A full year's run of a manuscript newsletter sent from London every Tuesday, Thursday, and Saturday from 26 March 1723 to 24 March 1724 will serve as example. The letters, now in the British Museum,[12] are uniformly written on the first three pages of small folio sheets (12 by 15 inches) folded once, the fourth page being left blank for the address and the last few items being carried over from the bottom of the third page to the left margin of that page, from there to the left margin of the second page, and from there

9

to the left margin of the front page. It is clear from their regularity and from the opening words of the first letter— "In order to inform our Readers . . . "—that these are not private letters but were professionally prepared and copied for more than one person. These particular copies all begin with "My Lord," and several of them have on the back page the recipient's address:

To

The Right Honble the

Lord Viscount Percivall

To be left at ye Post House

in Bath.

Doubtless other copies of these same letters were addressed to other recipients.

Manuscript newsletters do not represent a temporary transitional stage in the emergence of the printed newspaper, for they increased rather than diminished in number and popularity during the first half of the eighteenth century, those of Wye, Stanley, and many others being frequently quoted in provincial newspapers as more informative or more trustworthy than the London "prints."

Prompted, one supposes, by a feeling for tradition and not by a desire to deceive anyone, the proprietors of certain early printed newspapers ordered special script type as a means of perpetuating the form of handwritten letters and, at the same time, producing more copies than even a large corps of scriveners could turn out. Most interesting of these quasi-manuscript news journals is *Dawks's News-Letter*, already mentioned. This was printed entirely in script type and began with the vocative "Sir" or S^r" on the date line.[13] *Dawks's Letter*, as it was at first called, continued to appear for at least twenty years (1696-1716). The same effect of a personal communication was suggested by the use of the salutation "Sir" at the head of the news in *Sam. Farley's Bristol*

Post Man (1715) and a few other newspapers printed in ordinary roman and italic type. Peter Motteux's *Gentleman's Journal* (1692-94) had as subtitle, "By Way of Letter to a Gentleman in the Country." A similar intention may be observed in the name given by Roger Adams to his *Manchester News-Letter* in 1719, though Adams made less effort to make his paper appear to be a personal communication than Francis Leach did in the *London News-Letter. With Foreign and Domestick Occurrences,* which he printed thrice weekly in 1696. The term "newsletter" was retained for over half a century in the subtitle of the *Kentish Post: or, the Canterbury News-Letter* (1717-68).

The printed and written bulletins of news from London were available to all country readers who could afford them, but delivery by post to distant places was slow and costly. The author of the *Country Gentleman's Courant* emphasized these disadvantages when he announced in the first issue (12 October 1706) that *his* paper would contain all that was of moment in the other newspapers published in London, "which many gentlemen and others have not the opportunity of seeing or perusing, either because of their distance from this City of London, or . . . by reason of the charge of the several newspapers and postage, which is very considerable." The author of the *Evening Post* made a similar observation in his attempt to procure regular subscribers in the country, pointing out in his first issue (6 September 1709) that "there must be 3 or 4 £ per annum paid by those gentlemen that are out of town for *written news.*" From the point of view of a printer living in a town or city many miles from London, it must have seemed reasonable, once official restrictions had been removed, to hope that a local paper would be supported by readers in the area, even though some of them would probably continue to receive a London paper by post.

It might seem justifiable to declare that the *Oxford*

Gazette, number 1 of which appeared on 16 November 1665, was the first provincial newspaper. There are two good reasons why this opinion is unacceptable. For one thing, the *Oxford Gazette* was not a local enterprise but the official publication of the government, temporarily removed from London because of the plague; in the second place, it was not the earliest English newspaper printed outside of London. The statement made in 1827 by Eneas Mackenzie that "A newspaper, in post quarto, was printed by Robert Barker, at Newcastle, in 1639 . . . "[14] suggests that Barker produced the first provincial newspaper. Barker, the King's printer, was apparently in Newcastle only about two weeks in May, 1639, and while there he printed certain proclamations, a sermon which had been preached before the King at Durham on 5 May, and a set of military regulations.[15] If he also printed one or two bulletins of news during that fortnight, he cannot on that account be credited with establishing a provincial newspaper. The same Robert Barker later also set up his press in York and other provincial towns, and he may have run off occasional bulletins of news in those places. J. R. Phillips asserted in *Memoirs of the Civil War in Wales and the Marches* (2 vols.; London, 1874), I, 118, that "packets of news" were printed on the King's press at Shrewsbury; but no specimens have survived, and in any case they could hardly be looked upon as regular newspapers.

Concerning one other seventeenth-century publication the claim has been advanced that it marks the actual beginning of provincial journalism. This is the news book called at first the *Oxford Djurnall: Communicating the Intelligence, And Affaires of the Court, to the rest of the Kingdome,*[16] printed weekly in Oxford by Henry Hall for William Webb from the beginning of 1643 until the first week of September, 1645. The first words of the title were soon altered to *Mercurius Aulicus,* and it is under this title that the publication is usually listed. A case has been made by Mr. Varley[17] for looking upon this as "the earliest regular English newspaper." That it *was* a newspaper, issued weekly, and that it *was* printed in Oxford cannot be denied, and to refuse to call *Mercurius Aulicus* the first provincial newspaper may, therefore, seem to be cavilling. Yet, like the later *Oxford Gazette,* already mentioned, this paper was published in Oxford only because the Court was there, and it was in no sense a local paper; it reported only the war news and other matters affecting the Royalist cause. When the "siege" was raised and "the mock-show at Oxford" was over, the paper ceased to be printed.[18] Provincial journalism cannot be said to have begun at Oxford in 1643 just because news was printed there during a temporary national emergency.

There is also scant reason to regard the *Colchester Spie* (1648) as a genuine provincial newspaper. Its two issues give remarkably vivid accounts of conditions within the besieged city in August, 1648; but it was probably printed in London. No printer is named in the imprint, which reads simply, "Printed in the Yeere, 1648." The provincial press had not yet become established.

For any private printer to set up a press in a provincial town and issue a newspaper would, indeed, have been as much as his life was worth; for, in spite of John Milton's magnificent plea in 1644 for the removal of restrictions on printing, there remained for many years after *Areopagitica* a strict limitation of the number of printing presses permitted in London and elsewhere. In 1680, a royal proclamation was issued forbidding all persons whatsoever to print or publish any news book or pamphlet of news not licensed by His Majesty's authority. From the Restoration until after the Revolution of 1688, the distributing of news, whether written or printed, was under the control of the secretary of state.[19]

When government control of news was relaxed through the lapsing of the Licensing Act in 1695, it was naturally Londoners who took the lead in starting rivals to the official *London Gazette;* and in that very year the coffee-house politicians in city and country were reading several new papers printed in London. There is no evidence that a regular country newspaper was established before 1701. The notion that there was a paper in Stamford earlier than the *Stamford Post* (1710–1712–?) continues to be mentioned locally, but it has long been recognized as unsupported conjecture based on the mistaken assumption that the early volume numbers of the *Stamford Mercury* (1713-32) were changed annually.[20] The claim that provincial journalism began in 1690 in Worcester is based entirely on a vague statement (not verified elsewhere) made over a century later.[21] The earliest first issue of a provincial paper to have survived is number 1 (7 December 1706) of Henry Cross-grove's *Norwich Gazette*; but Cross-grove had been preceded by another Norwich printer by five years, and papers had also been established earlier than December, 1706, in two—possibly three—other towns.

It is not surprising that it was in Norwich and Bristol and Exeter—all progressive cities over a hundred miles from London—that the first weekly newspapers in the provinces were started. Two printers from London, Francis Burges at Norwich and William Bonny at Bristol, share with Sam. Farley of Exeter the honor of being the pioneers in English provincial journalism. It would be more satisfactory to ascribe full and exclusive honors to one or another of these three instead of making them share the distinction; but until more issues of the *Norwich Post,* the *Bristol Post-Boy,* and *Sam. Farley's Exeter Post-Man* come to light, it is possible to calculate the starting dates only by counting back from issues printed long after number 1. That practice is not trustworthy.

No issue of the Norwich paper or of the Exeter paper is known to be extant earlier in date than number 91 of the *Bristol Post-Boy* (Saturday, 5 August, to Saturday, 12 August 1704). If there was no error in numbering and if there was no irregularity in weekly publication, the first issue of the *Bristol Post-Boy* must have been dated 21 November 1702. There is no particular reason for supposing that there was any irregularity in the publication of the first ninety issues of this paper; but errors in serial numbering occur frequently in newspapers of the eighteenth century. There is a disparity of two weeks (or two serial numbers) between number 91 of the *Bristol Post-Boy* and the next issue to have survived, number 281, dated Saturday, 13 March, to Saturday, 20 March 1708; by normal reckoning the paper issued on 20 March ought to have been numbered 279. At any rate, certainty about the conjectured date of the first issue is hardly possible.

Was that first issue of the *Bristol Post-Boy* earlier than number 1 of Francis Burges' *Norwich Post?* By the same process of counting back from the earliest issue extant— number 287 (3 May 1707)—one may conjecture that Burges' paper began its life span on 8 November 1701. This reckoning makes the *Norwich Post* the first country newspaper of England. Yet there is a greater probability of error in the numbering of a series of 287 weekly issues than in a series of 91, and there are obvious irregularities in the numbers of the nine issues of the *Norwich Post* known to have survived. The next extant issue after number 287 is dated nine weeks earlier than its number, 348, would lead one to expect and, in relation to the date of number 413, number 594 is out by nearly four months. Forty years ago, A. D. Euren suggested [22] that the additional identifying numbers and letters—"14 K" in number 349, for example—printed at the left of the title indicated the half-yearly volumes and the successive issues in the respective volumes; but most of these special designations neither match the regular serial numbers nor fit into any recognizable sequence of dates. Irregularities in the numbering of both the *Bristol Post-Boy* and the *Norwich Post* compel one to leave the question of priority unsettled; the available evidence in inconclusive.

Whatever may have been the dates of the first issues of the *Norwich Post* and the *Bristol Post-Boy*, Burges and Bonny stand in the records among the first men known to have published country newspapers in England. Deserving to share the special distinction here accorded to Burges and Bonny is Sam. Farley of Exeter. Various members of the Farley family appear in the imprints of West Country newspapers,[23] but Sam. was the man who made Exeter one of the first three provincial cities of England to have a newspaper. Once again the date of the first issue is conjectural, and the uncertainty is still greater. If *Sam. Farley's Exeter Post-Man; or, Weekly Intelligence* was a weekly paper from the beginning, the serial number, 556, of the only issue to survive, dated 10 August 1711, suggests a beginning in December, 1700; but a passage in the *Boston News Letter* dated 9 April 1705[24] makes it seem probable that the starting date was sometime in 1704. In either case, Sam. Farley is in the front rank of venturesome provincial printers.

It is possible that the next in priority was a Welshman, Thomas Jones of London and Shrewsbury, but evidence is scanty. Of a paper said to have been published by him in Shrewsbury in 1705, no copy has survived. The only hint that such a paper ever existed is in a note published in a Shropshire newspaper in 1881. In May of that year, a correspondent, T. W. Hancock, sent to the *Oswestry Advertiser* a statement[25] describing a two-page paper which he said he had seen "some years since" entitled *A Collection of all the Material News,* with the imprint, "Printed and sold by Thomas Jones at his house in Hill's Lane, near Mardol. Price 1*d*." A paragraph of news which Hancock remembered concerning the Duke of Marlborough's visit to Woodstock in order to "give his last instructions about building his palace" suggests that the only recorded issue of the Shrewsbury *Collection of all* *the Material News* was dated sometime after 14 March 1705, the date on which the Queen gave formal assent to the bill for granting to Marlborough the honor and manor of Woodstock. There is no particular reason why the existence of a local paper in Shrewsbury as early as 1705 should be doubted; but until a copy with serial number comes to light, it is impossible to do more than place it among the first four. In any case, Thomas Jones (1647-1713), Shrewsbury's first regularly established printer, should be remembered for another reason: he was the man who made the earliest recorded attempt to establish a newspaper in the Welsh language.[26] While he was in London, he announced in his *Almanack* for 1691 that he proposed to print a monthly bulletin of news for Welsh readers. A year later he announced that the plan had proved unacceptable; the Welsh distributors of his *Almanack* had been unable to induce their customers to subscribe to the projected newspaper, their reasons being that the Welsh people said there was no need to spend money for news from London when there were plenty of local people who could concoct sufficiently interesting news free of charge.[27]

Burges, Bonny, Farley, Jones—the list is growing. The first man to establish a newspaper in *any* town or city ranks as a pioneer, and it is proper to celebrate in their turn Stephen Bryan of Worcester, the proprietor of the *Stamford-Post,* Joseph Button of Newcastle, and John Collyer of Nottingham, all of whom started newspapers in their respective communities before the end of the year 1710. By the time Parliament decided to raise money by imposing duties on soap, paper (now including newsprint), pamphlets, and newspaper advertisements, the provincial "press" had well begun. Thereafter it never faltered in its steady and at times swift development.

If only four of the fifteen provincial papers established before 1712, the year of the first Stamp Act, can be shown to have continued thereafter—*Sam. Farley's Exeter Post-*

Man, the *Norwich Gazette,* the *Worcester Post Man,*
and the *Newcastle Courant*—ten others came into being
within three years after the tax was imposed. Several of
those earlier papers may well have ceased publication
before the tax was imposed. The Shrewsbury *Collection*
mentioned above, if, indeed, it continued for more than
a few weeks, certainly expired long before 1712. The
latest known issue of the *Bristol Post-Boy* is dated 26
August 1710; there is no evidence that it continued to
appear long enough to collapse under the weight of a
stamp a hundred weeks later. There is a reference to
Thomas Goddard's *Norwich Post-Man* in February, 1710,
but not thereafter; did it live on for another two and a
half years, only to be taxed out of existence? Since the
latest surviving issue of *Jos. Bliss's Exeter Post-Boy* is
dated 17 August 1711, who can say whether it ceased to
exist a year later or lived on until Bliss decided in September, 1715, to bring out a paper with a different format
and title? These examples show that no one can be sure
he is right if he asserts that most of the papers in
existence in 1710 were killed off by the Stamp Act of 1712.

It is easy to exaggerate the blighting effects of the Act
for laying several Duties upon all Sope and Paper made
in Great Britian . . . ; and upon certain printed Papers,
Pamphlets, and Advertisements (10 Anne, c. 19). Those
who have deplored the government's lack of wisdom and
foresight in imposing what they call a "tax on knowledge"
have said nothing about the equally discouraging consequences of the tax on washing. It is still commonly
asserted that the tax was imposed in order to suppress
adverse criticism of the government; but surely the main
intention was to raise money. A government does not
stamp out libel by making people pay a little more for
their newspapers, any more than it stops people from
smoking tobacco or drinking beer by taxing those commodities. The purpose of taxing newspapers and soap was
to bring in revenue; and the very fact that the Act of

10 Anne, c. 19, imposed a tax on newspapers is itself evidence that by 1712 they were firmly enough established in common use to be regarded—like soap—as a substantial and continuing source of revenue; they were there to stay. It is not to be denied that the government, so far as it was able to do so, continued to exercise strict control over certain kinds of news, but this control was exercised through *sub rosa* subventions to favored printers and by direct arrests of offending printers and venders.

This point is worth exploring, for it bears directly on the history of the provincial newspaper press. Addison, it will be remembered, expressed in *Spectator*, number 445 (31 July 1712), the day before the Stamp Act became effective, his fear that "this great Crisis in the Republick of Letters" would cause many a newspaper to collapse "under the Weight of a Stamp," but he added that several journalists who had resignedly taken farewell of the public would presently reappear, "tho' perhaps under another Form, and with a different Title." And Addison's forecast proved true. His tone, moreover, implied no great concern over restrictions on printing. In *Spectator,* number 488 (18 September 1712), he reported that he and a soap boiler both regretted having to charge higher prices for their respective wares and were both suffering a slight slump in sales. Jonathan Swift in his *History of the Four Last Years of the Queen*, written in 1713 but not printed until 1758, emphasized Queen Anne's desire to have effective measures taken for preventing the publication of "False and Scandalous Libels, such as are a Reproach to any Government," and went on to point out that in her message to Parliament the Queen had in mind "those Weekly and Daily Papers and Pamphlets, reflecting upon the Persons and Management of the Ministry"; but he gave it as his own opinion that the "Law for Taxing single Papers" had been quite unsuccessful in preventing the publication of reflections upon the government, for "the Mischiefs of the Press were too Exorbitant to be cured by such a Remedy as a Tax upon the smaller Papers." Moreover, he said, even though it must be acknowledged that "the bad Practices of Printers had been such, as to Deserve the Severest Animadversions of the Publick," there had hitherto always appeared "an unwillingness to Cramp overmuch the Liberty of the Press."[28] These are significant observations.

Further contemporary evidence supporting the opinion that the Stamp Tax was imposed to raise money rather than to restrict the liberty of the press in London and the provinces is to be found in John Toland's "Proposal for Regulating ye News-papers."[29] Toland did not attempt to decide whether the duties laid on newspapers had been intended to produce "a fund for the public service, or as a restraint upon the swarming of such papers, or for both these ends," but his own proposal was financial, not repressive. He simply recommended that the regulations requiring the use of stamped paper for printing news should be made tighter and more inclusive. True, he said, he "wou'd not have seditious insinuations spread abroad, . . . nor private persons, much less public ministers, abused with impunity"; but he did not advocate the suppressing of newspapers. At one point, on the contrary, he stated quite explicitly that Parliament, "intending the stamps for a duty, took at the same time all possible precautions not to discourage the sale of regular News-papers. . . . " And he insisted that the government's desires could be achieved "without incroaching in the least on the Liberty of the press (which ought to be sacred) or confineing to any one party the privilege of supplying the public with News. . . . "

Two or three other considerations suggest that, in the beginning at least, it was not determination to control the press that led the government to tax newspapers. For one thing, individual pamphlets were quite as offensive to Parliament as were the newspapers, yet the tax levied on pamphlets was much lower than that on newspapers;

the Treasury received from the printers of pamphlets only two shillings per sheet regardless of the number of copies printed, whereas the printer of a newspaper had to pay a tax of a halfpenny for *every* half-sheet he sold. On an octavo pamphlet of twenty-four pages (a sheet and a half), a printer paid a total of three shillings, even if he printed a thousand or two thousand copies; for a run of only seven hundred and twenty half-sheet newspapers, the printer paid ten times that amount in tax. It should be noted, furthermore, that the preamble of the Stamp Act itself (10 Anne, c. 19) indicates that the primary intention was to raise "large Supplies of Money to carry on the present War" and to defray the Queen's other extraordinary expenses. And it is to be observed that when the printers of newspapers were summoned to the House of Commons for violating the privilege of the House by printing in their columns matter which the members found offensive, there was no talk of increasing the tax as a means of stiffening control of the press.

When the government, moreover, after permitting artful dodgers to evade the newspaper tax for nearly thirteen years, formulated its law all over again in 1725, the printers complained only that their sales would be reduced; they did not protest against being muzzled. Even when the tax was increased in 1757, the printers said little about a tyrannical government's throttling of the public voice. "I will not presume to say," wrote Robert Raikes in his *Glocester Journal* on 4 July 1757, "that this Proceeding of the Legislature has its Rise in a Design to subvert the LIBERTY of the PRESS, on which every other Liberty of an Englishman in some Measure depends; or to suppress that Kind of Intelligence which all my Countrymen have a Right, and an Interest, to know." Raikes was perfectly confident that the tax would prove entirely ineffectual in subverting the liberty of the press. "However this be," he continued, "it is at present in the Power of my Readers to defeat any Attempt of this Kind, by continuing to take the GLOCESTER JOURNAL at the small Advance above-mentioned." Whatever hopes the government may have had of stifling libels by collecting a halfpenny for every half-sheet of news, two things are clear: the Stamp Tax did not put an end to bold censuring of the government, and in course of time it did bring in substantial revenue to the Crown. The retarding effects of the tax in 1725 and 1757 were certainly slight and temporary. There were a few casualties among both city and country papers, but in the provinces the momentum was quickly regained, as a glance at the chart in Appendix B will prove.

In any case, there were other reasons why newspapers proved short-lived. Some papers went down to defeat because the regional population was really too sparse to support a local paper; some were unable to overcome strong competition from papers printed in other towns of the region or brought in from London; some came to grief because another printer in the same town proved more aggressive in inducing people to buy his paper. Slender circulation and the lack of advertisements brought an early end to the *Ludlow Post-Man* in 1720; and it is probable that Thomas Hinton found the circulation of his *Cirencester Post* shrinking in 1723 because of the aggressive efforts of Raikes and Dicey to win a regional monopoly for their new *Gloucester Journal*, founded the year before. It is likely that Samuel Hodgkinson's second attempt to start a newspaper in Derby—the *British Spy: or, Derby Postman* (1727–1731–?)—was crowded out of business by Sam. Drewry's very successful *Derby Mercury*, which began in March, 1732.[30] Richard Lewis's *New Worcester Journal* (1753-54) was apparently hooted out of existence by the ebullient Hervey Berrow.[31] Sometimes even well-established papers were driven to the wall by relentless opponents. Robert Whitworth had been publishing his *Manchester Gazette* (with various changes of title) for nearly thirty years when he announced in number 3414 (25 March 1760) that, "finding the Profits not an Equivalent for the Trouble," he would print no more news in Manchester. He was, he said, fully satisfied that the interest of his newspaper had been "much hurt thro' the Opposition of a Party." The "Party" was doubtless Joseph Harrop and the supporters of his *Manchester Mercury*.

It will be noticed that the first ventures in the printing of local papers were made in towns on main roads far away from London—Norwich, Bristol, Exeter, perhaps Shrewsbury—and it is interesting to observe that the next five towns to make a beginning were also at a considerable distance—Worcester, Stamford, Newcastle, Nottingham, and Liverpool. Once established, the *Worcester Post-Man*, under various titles, throve, with Stephen Bryan as its editor for forty years, and then Hervey Berrow. The *Stamford Post*, the pioneer paper in Lincolnshire, after two or three years gave way to the *Stamford Mercury*, printed by Thomas Baily and William Thompson, who were also (until the death of Thompson in 1732) the joint printers of the *Suffolk Mercury: or, St. Edmund's-Bury Post*. Like Worcester, Stamford was not thereafter without a newspaper. The next towns to have papers were still farther north. The *Leverpoole Courant* (1712) did not find favor, or it was silenced by the Stamp Tax, and Liverpool had to wait forty-four years for its first successful paper. But at Newcastle-upon-Tyne there began in July, 1710, an activity in newspaper publishing which has never ceased to this day.[32] Nottingham was not far behind. The *Nottingham Post* began in October, 1710. The very year of the Stamp Tax saw the beginning of Ayscough's *Weekly Courant*, which kept going for half a century, during which time three other papers—the *Nottingham Mercury*, Collyer's second *Nottingham Post*, and *Creswell's Nottingham Journal*—came into being.

Meanwhile, within a period of five years—1715 to 1719

—Salisbury in the south, St. Ives in Huntingdonshire, Bury St. Edmund's in Suffolk, Canterbury in Kent, Plymouth in faraway Devon,[33] Cirencester in the west, Leeds, Manchester, and York in the north—all produced their own newspapers. By the date of the re-imposed Stamp Tax in 1725, there were or there had been "first" papers in Ludlow, Northampton, Ipswich, Derby, Chester, Gloucester, Reading, and Maidstone, as well as additional papers in Bristol, Exeter, and Norwich. Nor did the government's more effective taxing of newspapers from 1725 onward stem the onrush either of new papers or of the well-established ones.

During the next twenty years, one or more additional papers came into being in fifteen of the towns which already had a paper; and in seventeen other towns all over England, local papers were printed for the first time: Taunton, Yeovil, Sherborne, Bath, Hereford, Birmingham, Preston, Kendal, Whitehaven, Lewes, Eton, Colchester, Cambridge, Coventry, Lincoln, Hull, Durham.[34] Between 1745 and 1760, nine more towns—Oxford, Stratford, Leicester, Doncaster, Sheffield, Liverpool,[35] Warrington, Middlewich, and Halifax—began to have local papers.

The titles of most of these newspapers named only the towns in which they were printed; but there were several papers whose proprietors added the name of the county or the names of adjacent towns. It is, perhaps, hope rather than evidence of extensive circulation that one sees in such titles as the *Suffolk Mercury: or, St. Edmund's-Bury Post*, the *Kentish Post; or, the Canterbury News Letter*, the *Cirencester Post; or, Gloucestershire Mercury*, the *Essex Mercury; or, Colchester Weekly Journal*, and the *Sussex Weekly Advertiser, or Lewes Journal*. When each of those papers began, there was no other paper in the town named, and no other paper printed elsewhere in the shire; it is to be assumed that the whole county was expected to regard the paper as the journal of the region. Circulation beyond the bounds of a single community is implied in the change of the title of *Jopson's Coventry Mercury* for a time to *Jopson's Coventry and Northampton Mercury*. In 1742-43, a paper published in Bristol implied in its title that it circulated in an adjacent county: the *Bristol, Bath and Somersetshire Journal*. Still more inclusive in its ostensible coverage was a paper printed in Stratford-upon-Avon by James Keating in 1750 with the title *Stratford, Shipston, and Aulcester Journal*. Two years later, the title was expanded to *Keating's Stratford and Warwick Mercury; or, Cirencester, Shipston and Alcester Journal*. Many other papers served five towns; this is the only one whose title boasted that it did.

Merely enumerating the titles of newspapers and the towns named in those titles, however, is not a very sound way to estimate the true state of journalism. To say that there were one hundred and fifty newspapers in provincial England during the period 1701-60 is to conceal the fact that half of them did not last more than five years and that a quarter of the sixty towns and cities credited with having one or more newspapers in that period were actually without a local paper for fifty-odd years of that time. Nevertheless, as one looks at the scores and scores of newspapers which sprang into being in country towns all over England during the reigns of the first two Georges, one thing is apparent above everything else: a mighty struggle was in progress, the struggle of a force that burst its way into the open, thrusting aside all impediments, gaining momentum steadily, and bringing a new dimension into the life of England. It was a phenomenon of which few people at the time recognized the significance. Only now, two centuries later, is the magnitude of that emerging force becoming apparent. Even so astute an observer as Samuel Johnson saw only the fact; he did not perceive that what came to be called the fourth estate was in the making, even in the country. "Not many years ago the nation was content with one gazette," he wrote in his "Idler" paper, number 30 (11 November 1758),

25

"but now we have not only in the metropolis papers for every morning and every evening, but almost every large town has its weekly historian, who regularly circulates his periodical intelligence."

Samuel Johnson had his facts right. Had he glanced at a map showing the towns which had their own papers in 1758, he would not, perhaps, have been surprised to find that there were twenty-eight such towns, though the map would not have told him that five of those places—Liverpool, Manchester, Nottingham, Coventry, and Bath—had two papers each, and that Newcastle and Bristol each had three. He would be interested to observe that Yorkshire had papers in three of its busiest towns, York, Hull, and Leeds, that the two university towns each had a paper, that other towns not a hundred miles from his beloved London—Reading, Lewes, Canterbury, Ipswich—had papers, and that more distant places—Norwich, Sherborne, Exeter, Gloucester, Worcester, Chester—had their "weekly historians," as well as Stamford, Leicester, and Northampton. He would note with interest that in the town where he and Mrs. Porter had been married the *Derby Mercury* was still being printed by Sam. Drewry. Johnson would know that the paper in Birmingham was *Aris's Birmingham Gazette* and not Thomas Warren's earlier *Birmingham Journal,* to which he had contributed essays back in 1733. He would notice that Salisbury in Wiltshire had its own paper, though he would not know in 1758 that his friend Goldsmith's novel would later be printed on the same press as that on which Benjamin Collins produced his weekly *Salisbury Journal.* By 1758, there was no corner of England in which at least one attempt to found a local paper had not been made. Neither the government nor rivals nor the slow development of the market could keep the country newspaper from making itself felt as an instrument of information and opinion.

FIG. 2.—Map showing English provincial towns and cities that had local newspapers in 1758.

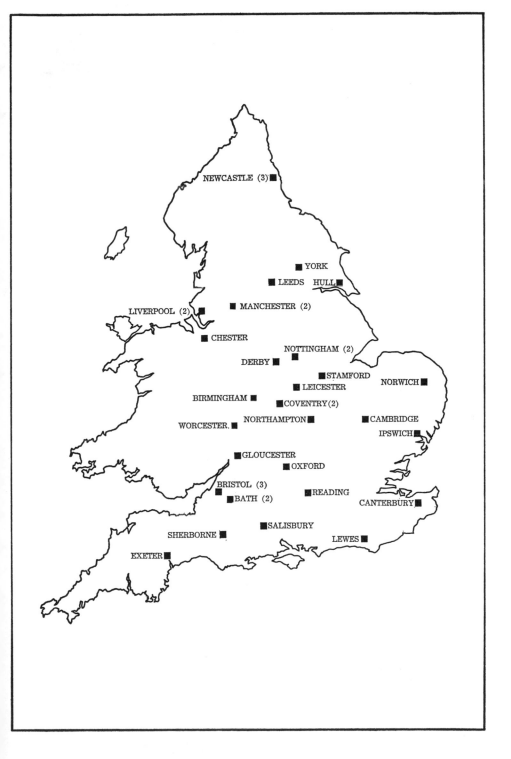

Certainly the founding of a newspaper demanded firm confidence and unquenchable hope. Again and again one finds the sturdiest kinds of resistance offered by established papers to those endeavoring to emerge. The efforts of William Cuthbert and Isaac Thompson to establish a new paper in Newcastle in 1739 were eminently successful in the long run, but they and their *Newcastle Journal* were jeered at mercilessly by John White, notably in White's *Newcastle Courant*, number 750 (8 September 1739). In their own paper on that same day, Cuthbert and Thompson referred to "the many ungrounded Charges and Misrepresentations" which had been "industriously spread round the Country" concerning both the *Newcastle Journal* and its publishers; they scorned to reply in kind to "the low squinting Scurrility" which had been thrown upon them. In November, 1755, John Gregory of Leicester and Samuel Creswell of Nottingham decided to undertake jointly the publication of a paper which up to then had been published by Gregory as the *Leicester Journal*. They gave the new paper a new title, the *Leicester and Nottingham Journal*, and in the first issue under this name (8 November 1755) they complained in large type about the "mean Artifices and bullying Gasconades" of the author of the *Nottingham Courant*, George Ayscough, "who like the Dog in the Fable wou'd neither eat Hay himself nor suffer the Ox to taste it; or in other Words refuses to furnish the Publick with a good News-Paper, and yet cannot bear others shou'd. . . . "

Particularly lively attacks were delivered upon rival newspapers by Robert Raikes and William Dicey, both from their office in Northampton, where they published the *Northampton Mercury*, and from their office in Gloucester.[36] In 1720, they took up cudgels in asserting their superiority over the *Stamford Mercury*, a paper which had been in existence seven years. Later on, when Dicey was alone as proprietor of the *Northampton Mercury*, equally vigorous attacks were delivered against the *Cam-*

bridge Journal; and there were occasional disparaging remarks against *Jopson's Coventry Mercury*. Nowhere else can one find such merciless abuse of a newcomer, however, than that which appeared in the *Northampton Mercury*, number 115 (9 July 1722), when Raikes and Dicey began their attack on James Pasham and the *Northampton Journal* which he was trying to start. With many a violent phrase they condemned "the new upstart Author who, bigotted in himself, and nurtur'd in his foolish Opinions by others," had "lavishly thrown away Money on a Press." They wrote of his "doating Brain," "his thick and stupid Crannium"; they called him a "noisy Animal" and an "Old Doatard"; they referred to the initial issue of the *Northampton Journal* as "his first Parcel of Bum-Fodder"; they described him and his assistants as "an opinionated Master, a Cypher of a Journey-man, and a Good-for-Nothing Sidesman." Raikes and Dicey did not extend the right hand of fellowship to rivals.

The *Northampton Journal* succumbed; but the shouting of insults did not always bring a rival to his knees. One of the most voluble of the several Norwich printers, Henry Cross-grove, tried more than once to dishearten Elizabeth Burges, printer of the *Norwich Post* after her husband died; and he also delivered heavy blasts against the *Norwich Post-Man,* printed by William Chase for Thomas Goddard. It must be admitted that Cross-grove was not unreasonable in insisting that in a city of about thirty thousand inhabitants[37] there was hardly room for three local newspapers; but his tone was invariably peevish and uncompromising. It irked him that he could not crush either of his rivals.

In these contentions Cross-grove was apparently only the agent of the *Norwich Gazette*'s real owner, Samuel Hasbart, perhaps the "Mr. Hasbart, Distiller, in Magdalen-street" who frequently advertised in the *Gazette*.[38] It was Samuel Hasbart, at any rate, who made repeated attempts to buy Mrs. Burges' paper, both before and after the first issue of the *Gazette* had been printed. No date was attached to Hasbart's letter to Mrs. Burges when it was published in the *Norwich Gazette* on 20 December 1707, but Cross-grove introduced it with a statement that proposals had been offered privately to Mrs. Burges "not only of late, but formerly before this Office was set up." The full text of the letter (for which see item 101 in the Register) indicates Hasbart's annoyance that Mrs. Burges was selling copies of her paper for too low a price and emphasizes his willingness to buy her out or to combine with her against their common rival. Mrs. Burges refused his offer with spirit and thereby evoked harsh words from Hasbart in "An Answer to the PRINTER of the NORWICH POST," printed in the *Gazette,* number 63 (10 January 1708).[39] Cross-grove, meanwhile, acting no doubt on orders from the proprietor, announced that the *Norwich Gazette* would thereafter be sold for a halfpenny and that advertisements would be printed free of charge.

Cross-grove triumphed temporarily, for both the earlier *Norwich Post* and the *Norwich Post-man* came to an end within a few years; but William Chase and Thomas Goddard ultimately provided irrepressible opposition in the form of a paper at first defiantly announced in 1713 as *Transactions of the Universe* and eventually known by its more modest name, the *Norwich Mercury*. It enlivens the pages of both the *Norwich Gazette* and the *Norwich Mercury* that both editors frequently shouted over the wall at each other; and they kept on shouting until both men died in 1744.

In spite of opposition from other printers, there were many enterprising men who saw opportunities for starting new local papers and were undeterred by inexperience, financial risk, unexplored possibilities of sales, and other uncertainties or discouragements. A weekly paper "compos'd of such articles as deserve the Public Attention cannot fail of Encouragement," said James Keating hope-fully in the opening number of his *Stratford, Shipston, and Aulcester Journal* (5 February 1750). Equally confident of success were several printers who thought it was necessary only to assure the public that every effort would be made to please the readers. "It shall be the peculiar Aim," wrote the undertakers of the *Bristol Weekly Intelligencer* in their first issue (23 September 1749), "to take great Care, that neither *Pains* nor *Cost* shall be wanting, to entertain its Readers, in all Occurrences, with the utmost Impartiality, Perspicuity, and Correctness."

One of the most ingratiating printed statements of the proprietors' intentions as they attempted to found a new provincial newspaper is in the first issue of the *Northampton Mercury, or the Monday's Post. Being a Collection of the most Material Occurrences, Foreign & Domestick. Together with An Account of Trade.* The title itself indicates the broad scope of the proposed publication, but number 1 of the paper (2 May 1720) contained an introduction in which Robert Raikes and William Dicey repeated (presumably) much of what Dicey had printed in his *St. Ives Mercury* during the two previous weeks. "It is surprising to think that this famous, this beautiful, this polite Corporation, has not long ago been the Object of those many Printers who have establish'd Printing Offices in Towns of less note." After these flattering words to elicit attention, Raikes and Dicey indicated that they had received official permission from the mayor, the aldermen, and the common council to conduct the paper, and they said that "the Country" would be "entertain'd and accommodated every week with a Journal of the most authentick Advices, foreign and domestick, drawn from the best private and publick Intelligences from London." They added somewhat vaguely that the news they printed would be "continually interspers'd with some delightful and instructive Amusement." With this declaration by its founders, the *Northampton Mercury* entered upon its long life. It is now well into its third century.

The same combination of assurance and blandishment appeared in other papers. When William Parks, whose *Ludlow Post-Man* failed to find a good reception, came to Reading in 1723 to found, with David Kinnier, the first newspaper in Berkshire, he and his partner addressed an enthusiastic paragraph "To the Gentlemen of Berkshire, and Counties adjacent; more particularly, To the Right Worshipful the Mayor, the Worshipful the Aldermen, and the rest of the Worthy Members of the Ancient Borough of READING." The art of printing, they said, had flourished for many years in London, York, Bristol, Norwich, Worcester, and other cities, and the success of printers in those larger places had encouraged the setting up of presses in smaller places, "as Cirencester in Gloucestershire, St. Ives in Huntingdonshire, Gosport in Hampshire,[40] and several other Places." This development of newspaper presses in the smaller towns made it a matter of wonder that Reading—"a Place of far greater Note than any of the last-nam'd"—should for so long have been slighted.

> We have, however, pitch'd our Tent here, induc'd by the good Character this Country bears, for Pleasure and Plenty, and intend, with your Leave, to publish a Weekly News Paper, under the Title of The READING Mercury, or Weekly Entertainer; . . . . And when a Scarcity of News Happens, we shall divert You with something Merry. In a few Words, we shall spare no Charge or Pains to make this Paper generally Useful and Entertaining, since we find ourselves settled in a Place, which gives all the encouraging Prospects of Success; . . . .

Like the *Northampton Mercury*, the *Reading Mercury* had the initial benefit of a bold manifesto; and as it turned out, both papers had merit enough to deserve and to receive continued encouragement.[41]

Success was doubtless the consequence of aggressive

management, but modesty had its place, too. It is pleasant to read Joseph Harrop's engagingly frank address "To the Publick" in the first issue (3 March 1752) of his *Manchester Mercury*. Having been "greatly encouraged" to publish a weekly newspaper, said Harrop, he had procured a new set of types and announced his intention to proceed with the plan, promising to abide by the stipulations in his printed proposals.

> . . . Though in a Time of general Peace a greater Dearth of foreign Advices may be urged as a Discouragement to my Undertaking at this Juncture; yet the friendly Excitement that I have had, and the honest Desire of Employment in my proper Calling, in the Place of my Nativity, are Motives, excusable at least, for attempting, in a private Station, to bespeak the Encouragement of the Public; to whom I purpose to give all the Satisfaction that I can, and no just Cause of Offence whatsoever. . . .

It is gratifying to record that this forthright, unpretentious local printer was entirely successful in establishing his new paper, even though two other weekly newspapers were being published in Manchester at the time.

Among all the printed prospectuses and introductory addresses to the public,[42] there is not one which sets forth so comprehensively the objectives of a country newspaper as the statement circulated by the proprietors ten weeks in advance of the first issue of the *Newcastle Journal* in 1739. On 22 January of that year, Isaac Thompson and William Cuthbert announced their intention to publish a new paper; and in the successive paragraphs of their *Proposals,* they set forth their objectives; the *Newcastle Journal* was to be attractive in its presswork, varied in its substance, comprehensive and trustworthy in its news reports, extensive in its circulation ("we are already assured of several Subscribers in Seven different Counties"), and, above all, non-partisan.

We declare we have no Design to enter into the Service of

a Party, nor to set our selves up in Opposition to any present Paper, or Publisher of News; but only to carry on an Affair, in a Manner as useful and entertaining to the Publick in general as any thing of its Kind extant. We shall therefore cautiously avoid the Rancour and Ill-nature of all Factions, Sects, political Distinctions, and particular Interests; tho' we shall make an impartial Use of every Side and Party to come at the Truth, and omit nothing in our Power, either of Information, or agreeable Amusement.

In their attempt to make the paper "as useful in general, as the Nature of the Thing will admit," Thompson and Cuthbert pledged themselves "honestly to apply all the Diligence, Skill and Care" they were capable of.

It will be convenient to keep these objectives and these pledges in mind as an attempt is made in the following chapters to answer such questions as these: What was the shape and what was the size of the provincial newspapers? What was in them? How were the contents arranged? How widely did they circulate? When and to what extent did local newspapers become significant in the history of journalism? And what is the interest or the value of early provincial newspapers to twentieth-century readers?

1. The most detailed account of these early news books is Joseph Frank's *The Beginnings of the English Newspaper 1620-1660* (Cambridge, Mass.: Harvard University Press, 1961).

2. Listed in a manuscript (AO3/952) at the Public Record Office.

3. Advertised in the *Reading Mercury,* number 96 (5 November 1739).

4. Examples are these: the *Oxford Post: or, the Ladies New Tatler* of 1718-19 (printed by and for Francis Clifton in Little Wild Street, London); *Clifton's Oxford Post. Or the Ladies New Tatler Reviv'd,* number 46 of which was published by Francis Clifton, near Scotch Hall, Water Lane, in Blackfriars, London, with the date 24 October 1723; and William Rayner's *Compleat Historian, or the Oxford Penny-Post* (1733).

5. From number 301 (9 January 1728) the *Gloucester Journal* regularly quoted the *London Evening Post.*

6. The passage is quoted from *Williamson's Liverpool Advertiser,* number 58 (1 July 1757).

7. See William F. Belcher, "The Sale and Distribution of the *British Apollo*," in Richmond P. Bond (ed.), *Studies in the Early English Periodical* (Chapel Hill, N. C.: University of North Carolina Press, [1957]).

8. The taking in of subscriptions to newspapers published elsewhere was apparently not regarded by some printers as jeopardizing the circulation of their own papers. All the extant issues of George Ayscough's Nottingham *Weekly Courant* from 1737 to 1754 have in the imprint the statement that at his printing shop in Bridlesmithgate subscriptions would be received for *all* the weekly and monthly papers. Elizabeth Jopson of Coventry went one better. In 1759, she advertised in her *Coventry Mercury* that at the desire of several gentlemen she was going to take subscriptions of half a guinea per annum from those who, at no additional charge, would like to read at her shop the *London Gazette,* the *London Chronicle,* and other papers which came from London on post days (Monday, Thursday, and Saturday), and "during the Time the Machine shall continue to Fly, in One Day," the *Daily Advertiser* and *Lloyd's Chronicle* on the three other days. Non-subscribers could enjoy the same privilege by paying a penny "upon every Perusal of the Papers."

9. For details about these several papers published by Robert Walker, see items 6, 75, 76, 77, 78, 86 in the Register at the end of this book.

10. *The History of British Journalism* (London: Richard Bentley, 1859), I, 87.

11. This particular *London Post* is now represented only by the title page of its first issue (7 January 1716), in the Bodleian Library.

12. Additional MS 27,980. There are many other written newsletters at the British Museum, and extensive collections are in the Bodleian Library, the Folger Shakespeare Library, and the library of the University of Minnesota. There are some interesting ones in the library of the Press Club in London.

13. See Stanley Morison, *Ichabod Dawks and his News-Letter* (London: Cambridge University Press, 1931).

14. *A Descriptive and Historical Account of . . . Newcastle upon Tyne* (Newcastle-upon-Tyne: Mackenzie and Dent, 1827), II, 727. Note also the statement by J. Collingwood Bruce in *A Hand-Book to Newcastle-on-Tyne* (Newcastle-upon-Tyne: Reid, 1863), pp. 148 f.: "The earliest instance of the printing of a newspaper in any provincial town in Great Britain occurred in Newcastle, during the sojourn of Charles I in the North, in 1639. He was attended by Robert Barker, the royal printer, who issued a news-sheet from time to time."

15. See Richard Welford, "Early Newcastle Typography, 1639-1800," *Archaeologia Aeliana,* Ser. 3, III (1907), 16.

16. This is the title of the issue for the first week (from Sunday, 1 January, to Saturday, 7 January 1643), now in the Yale University Library. The imprint of this eight-page pamphlet is: "Printed by Henry Hall, for VVilliam VVebb. An. Dom. M.DC.XLII."

17. Frederick John Varley, *Mercurius Aulicus* . . . (Oxford: Blackwell, 1948).

18. *Mercurius Aulicus* was not the only news book printed in Oxford in the first half of the seventeenth century. The Huntington Library has copies of a *Mercurius Academicus,* apparently printed in Oxford, published weekly between mid-December, 1645, and mid-March, 1646. For notes on this and other early bulletins of news printed in Oxford see F. Madan, *Oxford Books* (Oxford: Clarendon Press, 1912), and Derek Hudson, "Three Hundred Years of University Journalism," *Oxford,* VII (1940), 54-64.

19. For details see Peter Fraser, *The Intelligence of the Secretaries of State & Their Monopoly of Licensed News 1660-1688* (London: Cambridge University Press, 1956).

20. The volume numbers were changed semiannually. See Joseph Phillips, "The First Local Newspaper," *Notes and Queries,* Ser. 5, IX (16 March 1878), 214 f., and A. Adcock, *Notes and Queries,* Ser. 11, VII (14 June 1913), 471 f.

21. See item 142 in the Register at the end of this book.

22. *The First Provincial Newspaper: A Brief Survey of the Earliest Norwich Newspapers* (Norwich: *Norwich Mercury* Office, 1924).

23. See items 3, 9, 11, 16, 17, 22, 42, 47, 50, 128 in the Register.

24. Dr. G. A. Cranfield in his *Hand-List* has drawn attention to the passage. See the note in item 42 of the Register.

25. Reprinted as "The First Shrewsbury Newspaper" in *Bye-Gones relating to Wales and the Border Counties 1880-1* (Oswestry: Caxton Works, n.d.), p. 240.

26. An earlier item in the record of Welsh journalism is a paper dated 5 December 1643 and entitled *Mercurius Cambro-Britannus, The Brittish Mercury, or the Welch Diurnall, Communicating remarkable Intelligences, and true Newes to awle the whole Kingdom.* A copy is in the University of Texas library.

27. For information about Jones see *Journal of the Welsh Bibliographical Society,* I (1914), 239-45, and II (1918), 97-110; also Llewelyn C. Lloyd, "The Book-Trade in Shropshire," *Transactions of the Shropshire Archæological and Natural History Society,* XLVIII (1935-36), 65-142, 145-200.

28. See *The History of the Four Last Years of the Queen,* ed. Herbert Davis, Introduction by Harold Williams (Oxford: Blackwell, 1951), pp. xxii, 103-6. Under the heading "The Secret Reasons for first laying a Duty upon News-Papers," the whole section of this work dealing with official control of the press was reprinted in the *Ipswich Journal,* number 1003 (1 April 1758), shortly after the whole work had been printed in London by Andrew Millar.

29. British Museum, Additional MS 4295, fol. 49 f.

30. Hodgkinson's earlier paper, the *Derby Post-Man,* may have collapsed because of the re-imposed Stamp Tax in 1725, but no issue later than that dated 18 May 1721 has survived.

31. See the passage quoted in item 143 of the Register.

32. A comprehensive account of the early newspapers in Newcastle is Richard Welford's "Early Newcastle Typography, 1639-1800," in *Archaeologia Aeliana,* Ser. 3, III (1907), 1-134.

33. Browne Willis's observation in *Notitia Parliamentaria,* II, 292, that there were two printing houses at Plymouth in 1716, both of which subsisted "chiefly by publishing News-Papers," is puzzling, for there is no other record of newspapers printed in Plymouth before W. Kent established the *Plymouth Weekly-Journal* in 1718.

34. For evidence that there actually was a *Durham Courant,* see item 40 in the Register. It is probable that all references to a Boston paper are really to a paper printed in Massachusetts rather than in Lincolnshire. *Henry's Winchester Journal* (item 141 in the Register) was printed in Reading, not in Winchester. *The Oxford Journal: Or The Tradesman's Intelligencer,* advertised in 1736, was probably printed in London. For reference to a printing press in Gosport and possibly to a newspaper printed there, see above, page 32 and note 40.

35. The short-lived *Leverpoole Courant* (1712) was mentioned above.

36. Examples of their animosity against printers of newspapers are the attack upon Sam. Farley of Bristol in the *Gloucester Journal,* number 8 (28 May 1722) and the following number, and upon Stephen Bryan of Worcester in number 53 (8 April 1723).

37. William Chase on 29 August 1752 printed in his *Norwich Mercury* "A Parochial List of the Number of Houses and Inhabitants within the City of Norwich . . . Taken in the Month of July, 1752 . . . ; To which is annexed . . . the Number of Inhabitants in the said City, . . . in the Year 1693." According to this list, the number of souls in Norwich in 1693 was 28,881; the number given for 1752 was 36,169.

38. In the *Norwich Gazette,* number 63 (10 January 1708), Hasbart denied Mrs. Burges' charge that he was a periwig-maker.

39. The full text of this letter is reproduced in facsimile by Mr. M. Payne in *The Norwich Post: Its Contemporaries and Successors* (Norwich: [Norfolk News Co.], 1951), p. 10, and most of the text of Hasbart's letter in the *Norwich Gazette* of 20 December 1707 is reprinted there.

40. Although Parks and Kinnier seem to be referring to newspaper presses, no evidence has emerged to confirm the implication that Gosport had its own newspaper.

41. William Parks subsequently crossed the Atlantic. The story is told by Lawrence C. Wroth in *William Parks, Printer and Journalist, of England and Colonial America* (Richmond, Va.: William Parks Club, 1926).

42. Three of the most detailed are the introductory paragraphs in *Williamson's Liverpool Advertiser,* number 1 (28 May 1756), the separately printed prospectus of the *Union Journal: or, Halifax Advertiser* (1759), and the declaration of policy in the first issue of John Grabham's *Bristol Chronicle* (5 January 1760).

Chapter II

Vol. II.

Numb. XIX.

THE

Exeter Mercury:

OR,

Weekly Intelligence

Being an IMPARTIAL

ABSTRACT of all the *News Papers* of Note.

Containing the MATERIAL OCCURRENCES

FOREIGN and *DOMESTICK*;

With a Particular Account of what BOOKS
and PAMPHLETS are Publiſh'd in *Great
Britain, France, Holland,* &c. Now publiſh'd
every *Tueſday* and *Friday.*

From FRIDAY *November* 25. to TUESDAY *November* 29. 1715.

EXON:

Printed by PHILIP BISHOP at his Printing-Office in St. *Peter's Church-yard,* 1715.

Deliver'd to all Subſcribers in this City at 13 s. *a Year. Seal'd and
Deliver'd to Country Subſcribers at* 15 s. *a Year, they paying
Carriage. And at my own Houſe Deliver'd at* 3 *Half-Pence each
Paper.*

Format and Press Time

Only persons who have seen and handled the original files of early newspapers can know how firm they are to the hand, how convenient in size, how comfortable to the eye—at least those printed before 1760, by which time the printers had begun to use smaller type in all their columns. Readers unaccustomed to eighteenth-century print will, on first looking at the *Leeds Mercury* or the *Salisbury Journal,* be puzzled to read that the firft Poft had brought Word of a fmart Engagement in which fome Pruffians had furrendered to the Auftrians; but they will soon recognize that what looks like ƒ (and is here printed as ƒ) is really the old tall *s*, for it lacks the serif near the top. It will be noticed, too, that many common nouns are printed with initial capitals, that italic type is used for names of persons and towns as well as for emphasis, and that some words—"compleat" and "Musick," for example —have an antiquated look because of the spelling. Once these slight peculiarities become familiar, one can read with the greatest ease a newspaper printed while Samuel Johnson was still a schoolboy. With few exceptions, newspapers two hundred and forty years old are much

Fig. 3.—Title page of an unstamped six-page newspaper printed on a sheet and a half and showing subscription rates. (By permission of the Keeper of Printed Books, Bodleian Library.)

less frail than newspapers printed forty years ago with machine-made type on machine-made paper.

Some early eighteenth-century papers, regrettably, have not been preserved at all, not because the sturdy hand-made paper has crumbled, but because all the copies were used to wrap fish or light fires or were put to more ignominious household uses. There are splendid files of the *Northampton Mercury,* the *Gloucester Journal,* the *Birmingham Gazette,* and a dozen other papers which continued to appear decade after decade, but many other papers have survived only in broken runs or odd issues, and at least twenty known to have existed have disappeared without a trace. Several bundles of early papers have been rescued only by the merest chance. For instance, some of the early issues of the *Sussex Weekly Advertiser* may now be examined at the Brighton Public Library only because a sharp-eyed journalist who saw a village butcher using those unique and irreplaceable sheets for wrapping chops was able to get them in exchange for ordinary wrapping paper; and the three earliest surviving issues of *Adams's Weekly Courant* (Chester), discovered some years ago to have been used in binding a volume of the parish register at Mottram in Longdendale, Cheshire, may still be seen at the Mottram Vicarage. There are twenty-one provincial papers of the period 1701-60 which have survived in only a single copy of each.

Regrettable though the disappearance of so many of these early newspapers is, it is a fact that tens of thousands of copies remain to show their distinctive features. They differ from present-day newspapers in size, in number of pages and columns, in having no headlines, in having (certainly after the end of April, 1725) a red stamp impressed on a corner, in having the news arranged in three batches—the latest news being printed at the end, not on the front page—and in having practically no pictures except (in some papers) a panoramic view of the city or simple rectangular wood-blocks flanking the title.[1] The blocks or "ear-pieces" usually depict a bringer of news, such as a ship in full sail, a rider with a horn, or a figure of Mercury. Occasionally there is a seated Britannia, a St. George and the dragon, or the city arms with the official motto or such a phrase as *"Fama volat."* These blocks, like the elaborate "factotum" used in the first column of many papers, add to the attractiveness of the front page, for some of them exhibit considerable skill in the fashioning of the details. More attractive still are the panoramic "prospects" of the respective places of publication, used in at least fifteen papers, among them the *Norwich Gazette,* the *Newcastle Courant,* the *Northampton Mercury,* the *Ipswich Gazette, Farley's Bristol Newspaper,* and the *Derby Mercury.*

By comparison with most twentieth-century newspapers, those published two hundred or two hundred and fifty years ago all seem small, though some were much smaller than others. Many of the twelve-page papers published between 1712 and 1725 had pages only a little broader than the pages of this book and not quite so tall. The four-page papers printed before August, 1712, and after April, 1725, had larger pages; and by the middle of the century, the pages of provincial newspapers were commonly 11 by 16½ or 17 inches—very little smaller than a page of the *Times Literary Supplement.* These differences in the dimensions of pages were brought about as a direct consequence of the Stamp Tax, which, of course, also affected the selling price.

Before the texts of the three Stamp Acts (1712, 1725, 1757) are examined to see how their provisions affected the size and shape of newspapers, it is useful to note that early newspapers were not printed on endless rolls of machine-made newsprint but on single sheets or half-sheets of paper in sizes that could be produced one by one on the paper-making frames. Until there was a tax on newspapers, the printers used either an unfolded half-sheet (two pages) or a whole sheet folded once to make four pages, with two columns on each page. Of the fifteen provincial papers which began before the Stamp Act of 1712 was passed, seven or eight were printed on unfolded half-sheets with two columns to the page—the *Bristol Post-Boy, Sam Farley's Exeter Post-Man, Jos. Bliss's Exeter Post-Boy,* the *Norwich Gazette* in its earliest issues, the *Nottingham Post,* the Shrewsbury *Collection of all the Material News,* and the *Leverpoole Courant.*[2] Another paper which used a half-sheet, but set so as to make four pages instead of two, was John White's *Newcastle Courant* in 1711 and 1712.[3] The *Stamford-Post* survives in only two issues, each printed on a single half-sheet. This paper deserves attention as the first provincial newspaper to have three columns to the page. The issue dated 7 April 1712 contained an announcement that thereafter the paper would fill a whole sheet, with the news on one half-sheet and a variety of entertaining pieces of prose and verse on the other half-sheet.[4] Five other newspapers—and from 29 March 1707, the *Norwich Gazette* also—were printed on a whole sheet, folded once to make four pages, each with two columns. That is the format of the earliest provincial newspaper, the *Norwich Post* (at least from 3 May 1707), of the *Norwich Post-Man,* presumably of the *Yarmouth Post* and the *Yarmouth Gazette* (local editions of two Norwich papers), and of the *Newcastle Gazette* by 19 April 1712.

If one wishes to ascertain the size of the sheet used for printing these fifteen newspapers prior to the first day of August, 1712, when the tax brought about changes, one has only to measure surviving issues that have not been cropped in binding. The single half-sheets range from 7½ by 12½ inches to 8½ by 14 inches, so that the whole sheet before cutting must have measured 12½ to 14 inches in width by 15 or 16 or 17 inches in length. Roughly, then, the provincial newspapers printed before the 1712 Stamp Act came into effect were run through the presses on stock more or less equal in dimensions to what has since the beginning of the eighteenth century been called "foolscap," which is 13½ by 17 inches, or else they were printed on pieces of paper equal to half a foolscap sheet. The paper could have been obtained— and much of it probably was obtained—from the nearest paper mill.[5]

Readers of this book who are not bibliographers may see the question "How large is a sheet of paper?" as only an idle Alice-in-Wonderland conundrum; but it became a matter of vital concern to all who printed newspapers. Curiously, the question was apparently never faced squarely by the government; and when Parliament decided in 1712 to impose a tax on newspapers, the Act at no point defined "sheet" and "half-sheet." This is really incredibly stupid (or careless), for the statute (10 Anne, c. 19) stipulated that the rate of tax was a penny per "sheet" and a halfpenny per "half-sheet." No thought, apparently, was given to the possibility that a newspaper might be printed on a large half-sheet carrying a half-penny stamp just as well as on a small whole sheet with a penny stamp. Failure to define the permitted dimensions cost the government much of the revenue that might have been derived from the tax. The Lords of the Treasury rejected the proposal submitted by Edmund Curll[6] that Parliament should regulate the size of paper on which newspapers could be printed. The consequence of this inadvertency or neglect was that the size of the sheet used for newspapers was increased;[7] newspapers grew larger and larger, but used only folded half-sheets bearing, until 1757, halfpenny stamps.[8]

It was suggested in Chapter I that the Stamp Act of 1712 did little permanently to discourage printers of provincial newspapers and that new papers soon took the place of any that were unable to continue publication because of the tax. The government may have hoped that newspapers would collapse under the burden of taxation; it may, on the other hand, have hoped that newspapers would continue to be published and would, therefore, send substantial revenue to the Crown. Neither hope was fulfilled in 1712, for one very good reason: the shrewd English printers found a loophole in the law and enjoyed immunity from the tax for thirteen years.

It is expedient at this point to see precisely what the Stamp Act of 1712 required. With the usual particularity of language, the effort was made in section CI to set forth the details:

> And be it enacted by the Authority aforesaid, That there shall be raised, levied, collected, and paid, to and for the Use of her Majesty, her Heirs and Successors, for and upon all Books and Papers commonly called Pamphlets, and for and upon all News Papers, or Papers containing publick News, Intelligence or Occurrences, which shall, at any Time or Times within or during the Term last mentioned [i.e., 32 years beginning 1 August 1712], be printed in *Great Britain*, to be dispersed and made publick, and for and upon such Advertisements as are herein after mentioned, the respective Duties following; that is to say,
>
> For every such Pamphlet or Paper contained in Half a Sheet, or any lesser Piece of Paper, so printed, the Sum of one Half-penny Sterling.
>
> For every such Pamphlet or Paper (being larger than Half a Sheet, and not exceeding one whole Sheet) so printed, a Duty after the Rate of one Penny Sterling for every printed Copy thereof.
>
> And for every such Pamphlet or Paper, being larger than one whole Sheet, and not exceeding six Sheets in Octavo, or in a lesser Page, or not exceeding twelve Sheets in Quarto, or in twenty Sheets in Folio, so printed, a Duty after the Rate of two Shillings Sterling for every Sheet of any kind of Paper which shall be contained in one printed Copy thereof.

The Act also imposed a tax of one shilling on every advertisement in "the *London Gazette,* or any other printed Paper, such Paper being dispersed or made publick weekly, or oftener." The penalty for infringement was set at ten pounds plus the costs of suit; and it was directed that "Pamphlets containing more than one Sheet of Paper" should be registered within six days after printing (in London or Westminster) or fourteen days (elsewhere in Britain).

What did the printers do? John White's *Newcastle Courant* was unlike most other early provincial newspapers in having been published (from its beginning in August, 1711) three times a week, and, as was noted above, in being printed in four pages on a folded *half*-sheet. When the Stamp Act became operative on 1 August 1712, White continued for several weeks to publish his *Courant* in exactly the same format, but now used paper bearing a halfpenny stamp. Then it must have occurred to White that there was no need for him to collect an extra halfpenny for every copy of his *Courant* which he sold, nor did he need to have stamped paper transported all the way from London to Newcastle. With a degree of shrewdness which surpassed that of the country's legislators, White saw how to evade the tax. The act required half-sheet papers of news to be printed on paper bearing a half-penny stamp and whole-sheet papers to be printed on paper bearing a penny stamp, but nothing was said about newspapers filling a sheet and a half; they could be printed on unstamped paper and would be classed as pamphlets, chargeable only with the duty of two shillings for each sheet required for one copy, no matter how many sheets were printed in the whole impression. Instead of paying twenty shillings for the stamps on 480 half-sheets brought from London, White could buy paper wherever he wished to and stretch each issue to fill a sheet and half, registering the *Courant* as a pamphlet and paying only three shillings. That is precisely what he did. Until number 171 (1 September 1712)—perhaps longer—the *Newcastle Courant* was printed on stamped half-sheets; then, sometime between that issue and the next which is now extant—number 208 (26 November 1712)—White made the change. From that date until 1725, when the Stamp

Tax was reimposed with stricter terms, White's *Newcastle Courant* appeared as a twelve-page single-column paper printed on a combined sheet and half-sheet of unstamped paper with a page approximately 5½ by 7½ inches. By 1720, it had become a weekly paper and the slightly larger paper gave pages 6½ by 8 inches.

With the exception of some issues of the *Norwich Gazette,* of the *Newcastle Courant,* and perhaps of the *Worcester Post-Man,* no provincial newspaper published between the first Stamp Act (1712) and the second Stamp Act (1725) was printed on either a single sheet or a single half-sheet. During these intervening years, practically all provincial printers of newspapers used an unstamped sheet *and* an unstamped half-sheet for every copy of their papers. Many of them doubtless paid the duty of two shillings per sheet, and in fact several papers —Stephen Bryan's *Worcester Post-Man* and William Cooke's *Chester Weekly Journal,* for example—have on the title page a statement that the paper had been licensed and entered in the Stamp Office.[9] So long as a sheet and a half were used in printing a single copy of a newspaper, the printer simply entered his paper as a pamphlet and handed over three shillings. The paper could be printed in six pages—four on the sheet, two more on the half-sheet—or in twelve pages—eight on the sheet, four more on the half-sheet—without affecting the classification. Until the government enacted a statute in 1725 putting a stop to this device for getting around the law, no fewer than twenty provincial newspapers appeared in twelve pages, most of them with a single column each. Ten others regularly appeared with six pages, usually with two columns to the page.

As before, if one wishes to estimate the average size of the sheet used in printing these six-page and twelve-page papers published between 1712 and 1725, it is easily done by measuring the pages of surviving copies which have not been cropped for binding. Henry Cross-grove

used an unusually large sheet—about 13 by 20 inches—
for his six-page *Norwich Gazette* from the beginning of
January, 1723, to the last issue in April, 1725, but the
usual range in other papers was from 11 by 14 inches to
13½ by 16 or 17 inches. The figures for the twelve-page
papers are not substantially different, though the extra
fold meant a very small reading surface on each page.
Most of the papers in this format had pages 6 or 6½
by 8 or 8½ inches, typical examples being the *Chester
Weekly Journal*, which in 1724 had twelve pages 6¼ by
8 inches, uncropped, and the *Suffolk Mercury*, which in
1719 had pages 6½ by 8¼ inches, uncropped. On the
average the sheets used in the twelve-page newspapers
were about 13 by 17 inches.

The measurements thus far given are appropriate for
papers printed before the end of April, 1725. Then, at
last, the government recognized that many thousands of
pounds in revenue were being lost annually because the
printers had found a way of evading the tax demanded
by the Act of 10 Anne, c. 19. The Act of 11 George 1,
c. 8—"An Act for continuing the Duties upon Malt, . . .
and for explaining a late Act in relation to Stamp-Duties
on News-Papers"—deplored the misinterpretations of the
Act of 1712, declared that newspapers printed on a sheet
and a half-sheet would not for the future be taken as
pamphlets, and provided that from and after 25 April
1725 the individual sheets and half-sheets of newspapers
would be subject to the respective penny and halfpenny
taxes, here specified again in detail, during the remainder
of the term (thirty-two years) mentioned in the Act
of 1712.[10]

The effect in town and country was immediate and
spectacular. The six-page and twelve-page papers ceased
over night to appear. Thereafter for many years English
provincial newspapers were printed on a single half-sheet
of stamped paper. In announcing the reduced number of
pages and the increased selling price, the printers quoted

passages of the Act, forestalled some of the expected criticism of their customers by complaining—as Andrew Brice of Exeter did—of the *"blushing Blood-colour'd* Mark of the *wholesome Severity* lately stamp'd upon us," and promised not to reduce the amount and variety of substance in the new series of papers. Brice said that he would give his former *Post-master* a new name and that the *Journal* would thereafter consist of a half-sheet; "yet I have taken Care," he added, "to procure it so *large,* and the Print shall be so *fine* and *curious,* that it shall contain rather more than it has done ordinarily, in a Sheet and Half of this *small* Size."

It was the same story everywhere. In number 358 (5 April 1725) of the *Northampton Mercury,* Raikes and Dicey filled the verso of the title page with an announcement of their desire to alter the *Mercury* from a sheet and a half of small paper to one half-sheet of "very large Paper," promising to use "a good and legible Character" but assuring subscribers that the half-sheet would "contain as much Matter as the three half Sheets do now." Stephen Bryan began immediately to use a stamped half-sheet of moderate size for his *Weekly Worcester-Journal,* the four pages being 7½ by 10½ inches each with a printed area of 6 by 8⅜ inches; but in number 828 (7 May 1725), he said he had "given Orders for the stamping of a Parcel of Paper of a prodigious Size." Bryan's large paper enabled him to increase the total printed area of the four pages from 195 square inches to 275. From number 831 (28 May 1725) onward, the page measured not less than 9 by 11¼ inches even after being cropped in the binding, with a typed area of 7¼ by 9⅞ inches.

This sort of change confronted the readers of all provincial newspapers published on or after 25 April 1725, though it should be noticed that the printers of two papers, the *Stamford Mercury* and (until sometime between March, 1729, and August, 1730) the *Suffolk Mercury,* preferred to set the half-sheet in eight pages instead of the standard four. The size of the sheet was not uniform all over the country; though from 1725 onward, no half-sheets smaller than 10½ by 17 inches were used. Generally speaking, there was a marked increase in the size of the half-sheet in the succeeding decades, as one perceives at a glance when standing in front of a case containing the bound volumes of such a paper as the *Northampton Mercury,* the *Gloucester Journal,* or the *Weekly Worcester-Journal;* and gradually the provincial papers advanced from two columns to three.[11] Papers which in 1725 had used a half-sheet measuring 10½ by 17 inches were thirty years later printed on half-sheets measuring 16 or 17 by 22 inches. In other words, the size of the half-sheet doubled during the first thirty years the Stamp Tax was really in effect. New papers which began to appear during those thirty years adopted the current size of paper and later both widened and lengthened the columns. Thus Griffith Wright's *Leedes Intelligencer* began in 1754 with a printed surface of 9⅛ by 13¾₁₆ inches on each page; six years later, the printed surface of the page measured 9¾ by 14¹¹⁄₁₆ inches.

Statistics need not be numerous to indicate the universal increase in the size of the half-sheet after 1725. The changes in the dimensions of the *Weekly Worcester-Journal* in thirty-five years are typical, though some other papers were slower in enlarging their columns. By 1732, Stephen Bryan's "prodigious" half-sheets had grown to provide his readers with a page 9½ by 13 inches, each with a printed surface 8⅝ by 11 inches. From July, 1736, the pages were 1¾ inches taller, and the expansion continued. Readers of the *Weekly Worcester-Journal* in 1742 found the page 10¾ by 16 inches. By 1749, the page had become 11 by 17 inches, with a printed surface of 9½ by 14½ inches, and these continued to be the dimensions until March, 1760, when the page became 18 inches tall and the printed surface became quarter of an inch taller than before. All these figures are for uncropped pages.[12] The extra halfpenny which was added to the Stamp Tax in 1757 produced no marked change in size or format;

whatever resistance the public offered was entirely on the score of price.

Sometimes there was a purely accidental change in the size of paper. William Cooke assured readers of his *Chester Weekly Journal* in number 6 of Volume XXXI (10 May 1732) that the supply of paper just received from London was not according to specifications and that the change was only temporary:

> Being disappointed of Paper in the usual Size, I am obliged to make use of this; but in a Fortnight or three Weeks it will be as large as before.

With number 8, two weeks later, the usual size was resumed. The size and the quality of paper which the printer preferred were doubtless specified in the orders which he sent periodically to London, but the warehouse-keepers were not always able to send what was required. Thomas Cotton, printer of the *Kendal Weekly Courant*, offered profuse apologies in number 22 (27 May 1732) because an inferior sort of paper had been sent to him: " . . . the Stationer at *London*, did either by Mistake or Imposition send me down this Paper, tho' my orders were for much Finer, . . . I cannot Return it without more Loss than your Benevolence can wish or my Fortune afford. . . . " It was over six months before Cotton's stock of thick, dark paper was used up.

Other printers were evidently less concerned about the quality of the paper. The printers of the twice-a-week *Kentish Post* regularly used coarse paper without apology. Joseph Bliss of Exeter found some of his readers objecting to the coarseness of the paper used for his *Protestant Mercury* in 1716 and decided to print two editions, one on coarse paper, one on fine, charging more for the latter:

> *.* By reason many Complaints have been made of the Badness of my Paper, which makes the Print appear the worse, and most Persons that buy my News being rather inclin'd to pay the price for better. . . . This is therefore

to give Notice, That next Week I shall print on very Fine Paper, Price Single Three Half-Pence; but to those who take it Quarterly, at the rate of 10s. per Annum.

Thereafter, for nearly a year, Bliss's imprint clearly indicated the two prices: "Fine Paper, three Half-Pence; Coarse Paper, One Penny." Specimens of both have survived. Except when shipments of bad paper brought annoyance to printer and readers alike, most of the newspapers here being considered were printed on good stock, and most surviving copies are still firm and perfectly legible.[13]

Legibility depends partly on the size and quality of the type. In general, the quality was good, and in many printing shops completely new fonts of type were purchased specifically for use in printing the newspaper.[14] The *Gloucester Journal* introduced new types in 1724. In 1725, Henry Cross-grove brought about a general improvement in the appearance of his *Norwich Gazette* by using better types, better paper, and an engraving of the "New Prospect of the City nicely contracted for a Head-Piece"; and in 1742, Cross-grove acquired two new fonts of type. When John Gilfillan took over the proprietorship of the *York Courant*, of which he had for seven years been the printer, he announced in number 470 (10 September 1734) that in order to improve the paper he had sent for "a Set of curious Types." In the final "Nota Bene" of their proposals announcing the new *Newcastle Journal* in 1739, Isaac Thompson and William Cuthbert drew particular attention to the "compleat Set of new Types" which they had ordered from London. Earlier that same year, when William Craighton established his *Ipswich Journal*, he began with old types— perhaps taken over from John Bagnall, whose *Ipswich Gazette*, printed with blunt types on poor paper, had apparently ceased publication—but he told his readers that the paper would be printed in a neater manner as soon as new types could be procured. Other papers introduced new types—usually smaller[15]—in course of time. As is only to be expected, some papers were unattractive because the paper was coarse and the types old and battered; but it would be quite wrong to assume that the provincial newspapers were usually printed with inferior or second-hand types.[16]

Most provincial printers had available for printing the regular columns of their newspapers at least three sizes of types, and some of them four, both roman and italic. The range of type size may be indicated—not very accurately—by noting that the most commonly used types occupied approximately seven lines to the inch, but on occasion—and more frequently after 1725—the smaller types were used, a common size after 1750 being nine and a half lines to the inch. In other words, the types most frequently encountered are approximately of the size known as pica, but one often finds small pica. Long primer and bourgeois were in most shops by the middle of the century and even brevier was used for long articles or advertisements of extraordinary length. Bold face was not used in the regular columns of news, but many shops had black letter and larger roman and italic in sufficient quantity to set advertisements and elaborate title pages in a considerable variety of type sizes. In shops where job printing was regularly done, such as John White's in Newcastle,[17] there would, of course, be several fonts of type in addition to those regularly used for the newspaper.

Partly to catch the eye or to give emphasis, partly to avoid running out of some letters of roman, the printers of provincial newspapers normally used italic type for the names of persons and places, and it is clear that some printers regularly used italic for matter set from manuscript. It must always be recognized that in the days of hand-set types a printer's stock of types in any one font might be inadequate for use in the whole paper, and he would use two or three different fonts of roman and as much italic as he could in order to avoid running out of

a much-used character.[18] Shortage of types may have
been the reason why Jacob Ilive and John Akers used
four sizes of type in printing their *Maidstone Journal*
in 1737.

There were usually better reasons for having a variety
of types in any one issue. In the first place, a change of
type size gives relief to the eye. There is a bleak monotony
in a sequence of closely printed pages, particularly if there
are few captions to break up the columns. Many country
newspapers make easy reading now—the *Reading Post*
in 1732, for example, and the *York Gazetteer*—because
of a good use of types. Again, one of the best ways of
giving prominence to an item of news or a particular
advertisement is to use larger type than in the surrounding matter. A notable instance is Henry Cross-grove's
using of large type to announce on the second page of
his *Norwich Gazette*, number 4 (28 December 1706), the
suicide of a member of Parliament; another is an item
of local news on the third page of Jos. Bliss's *Protestant
Mercury*, number 13 (13 September 1717):

> *EXON.* On Friday last, *Ralph Edmunds* was executed at
> *Heavytree* for shooting at and killing one Mr. *William
> Ayres* of *Kentsbere*. He confess'd, That he went with a
> Design to Pilfer; and that he aim'd his Picce directly at
> the said *Ayres,* with a Design to mischief him. About 6
> the next Morning a Reprieve came for him, about 4 hours
> after Execution. . . .

Another reason for varying the type size is the psychological effectiveness, still operative in twentieth-century
newspapers, of printing the first lines of a news story in
large type and then reducing the size of type in one or
two stages lower down in the column. Something like this
was done in *Orion Adams's Weekly Journal; or, The
Manchester Advertiser* in 1752, which usually had its first
article in larger type than the remainder of the paper.
In the same year, *Whitworth's Manchester Magazine* used

large type for the first page, smaller type on the second and third pages.

More often than not, however, the use of smaller type was dictated by a shortage of time or of space. The six-page papers using a separate half-sheet for the last third of their space could be issued as soon as that half-sheet was printed; and that could be done most quickly if only one side of the half-sheet was required. The result was that between 1712 and 1725 such a paper as the *Worcester Post-Man* often appeared with page five crowded and page six blank. The same sort of thing might happen in the setting up of a four-page paper. When press-time drew near, the second of the two unprinted pages might use larger type because too little matter had arrived to fill the space left for it (as in *Norris's Taunton-Journal* in 1725), or the last "copy" to be set might prove so extensive that smaller type was required to get all the matter into little room. A good instance of such crowding is in the *Weekly Worcester Journal*, number 1319 (4 October 1734), in which the printer found at the last minute that after putting into the first column of his fourth page seven short paragraphs from the latest post (the second and third columns being already filled with paid advertisements), he had less space than he required to print an especially interesting bit of news about the drowning of three "transports" en route (via Bristol) to the plantations in America. Bryan might have reduced the "copy" by one-quarter and it then would have gone into the available space, but he or his man[19] used regular type for the first nineteen lines (151 words) and then used smaller type so that the remaining 88 words could be crowded into little space.

This crowding of *local* news, it is to be observed, was quite normal, though in four-page papers the usual spot for crowding was in the third column of the third page, and the whole passage, not just the last few lines, was commonly set in smaller type than the rest of the news.

One soon becomes accustomed to looking there for news *not* taken from London papers.[20]

One extraordinary use of ordinary type should be noticed before anything is said about captions and other uses of larger types: it is startling to find occasionally in the *Salisbury Journal*—number 711 (2 September 1751), for example—and in several issues of *Farleys Bristol Advertiser* in 1744 that news for which there was no room in the regular columns was printed in an outer margin at right angles to the regular lines. In *Farleys Bristol Advertiser,* number 19 (14 April 1744), the third page has four additional paragraphs—a total of 178 words—set in shallow (five-line) columns of the usual width but printed side by side in the margin, at right angles to the regular columns. That was one way of drawing attention to late news; few readers could resist the temptation to see what could have deserved such special treatment.

Today, of course, one looks to the headlines to see what exciting news the paper contains; eighteenth-century newspapers had no headlines in the sense of short, eye-catching phrases giving the gist of the paragraphs below. There were captions to distinguish the London dispatches from foreign news and to set apart such divisions as "American News," "Thursday Night's Post," "The Low Countries," "Dartmouth, May 26th," and "Country News," but anything in the nature of a headline referring to a particular piece of news occurs very seldom. The prominence given by display types in advertisements is almost never found heading a paragraph of news. It is true that the account of a local fire in the Exeter *Protestant Mercury*[21] used capitals for the word "FIRE" in the first line of the report itself; and in the *Norwich Gazette,* number 1107 (23 December 1727), a title standing at the head of two columns of fine print promised an exciting piece of reading for the Christmas season: "The Tryal of Mr. Savage, Mr. Gregory, and Mr. Merchant, for the Murder of Mr. Sinclair." A descriptive caption in the

True British Courant (Preston), number 11 (22 March 1745), is too long by thirty words to be called a headline, but it does use capital letters for the most important word: "A full and true Account of the late terrible HURRICANE that happen'd at Jamaica; brought in by two Ships from Boston in New-England, and from Charles-Town in South-Carolina, (now arrived at Liverpool)." A heading spread across two columns in the *Leedes Intelligencer,* number 216 (22 August 1758), was set entirely in italics in order to report the local excitement aroused by a dispatch from London:

> On Sunday Evening, about Seven o'clock, arriv'd at Leedes, by an Express, to the excessive Joy of every True Briton, the following GAZETTE EXTRAORDINARY, containing the Account of the Taking of Cape-Breton: On which Occasion the Bells were set a-ringing, and continu'd 'till late at Night. And Yesterday several Vollies were fired by the Gentlemen Independents, and the whole Day dedicated to Mirth and Jollity by all Ranks of People.

But how can a passage running to seventy-two words be called a headline?

A closer approach to what a twentieth-century editor might write as a heading for an item of news is to be seen in the *Gloucester Journal,* number 1629 (25 September 1753), which had in the third column of its first page a paragraph taken from the *London Evening Post,* number 4033 (18 September 1753). The editor of the *Gloucester Journal* slightly modified the text and decided to use italics for more of the words than were so distinguished in the original, but his chief alteration was to add a heading that gave a hint of his own opinion concerning an issue in which he knew his readers were interested:

> *Somewhat to be* LAUGHED *at.*
>
> We hear, by a Letter from *Nottingham,* dated the 13th Instant, that Mr. Creswel, a Bookseller there, was, the Day before, summoned to appear before the *worthy* Magis-

trates of that Corporation, and rebuked for selling the *Leicester Journal*; in which, they say, are very severe Reflections on the Ministry for promoting the late *Jewish Naturalization-bill*, greatly tending to create Fears and Jealousies in his Majesty's *good* Subjects, and to promote *Sedition* and *Rebellion*, by persuading the People *they were in Danger of losing their Liberties*: When offering to *defend himself*, he was *threatened* to be sent to Gaol, unless he found securities for his good Behaviour. At last, however, he was discharged, on consideration that he sold no more of those Papers *reflecting* on the *Jews*, who are now to be incorporated amongst us, as they are a *good Sort of People,* and meet with great Encouragement from the above *very worthy Magistrates.*——

Here the heading gave no hint of what the following paragraph was about, but Robert Raikes obviously felt that by using a label he would attract particular attention to what at first glance would otherwise have appeared to be a very ordinary piece of news.

It is much easier to find exciting local or national news for which there ought to have been a headline and was not. Things like the death of the Queen, the declaration of war, the execution of Dick Turpin, the murder of a townsman, the robbing of the mail, a disastrous flood, a sharp rise in the local incidence of smallpox—these and a hundred other events received no more typographical emphasis than the most ordinary biting of a man by a dog. The headline had not yet been invented.

Perhaps the absence of headlines simply indicates a difference in reading habits. In our century people allow themselves to be guided by the large-print labels devised by the newspaper editors; two centuries ago, the reader, especially if he lived in the country and waited seven days for his newspaper, was ready to read *all* the news, deciding for himself (after he had read it) what interested him most.

The freshness of a country newspaper's "intelligence" depended on four time-consuming operations: (1) getting the news from its source to the printer; (2) getting the

"advices" set up in type; (3) getting two sides of the
paper printed; (4) getting the printed sheets into the
readers' hands. If the news came from abroad, the first
of these operations sometimes took many weeks. It took
four months for news of English victories in India to reach
England, and ordinarily it was many weeks before events
in North America were reported in English newspapers.
News came more promptly from Lisbon, Vienna, Prague,
and St. Petersburg, but nevertheless it took the couriers
many days and nights of travel, even if they came "Post
Haste" and even though the eleven days' difference between English Old Style and Continental New Style
seemed to reduce the time gap. If one forgets this difference in the calendar, it is really startling to find a dispatch dated at the Hague on 5 July 1712 printed in the
Norwich Post of that very date. A still "fresher" dispatch
dated at the Hague on 7 July was printed in the *Salisbury
Journal* of 6 July 1730. Adverse winds in the Channel
might delay the ship many hours; and after the first ship
bearing expected or unexpected news reached port, there
was still much galloping over English roads before printers
could set to work with types, composing sticks, ink balls,
and blank sheets of paper.

One of the best accounts of quick conveyence of news
to London was reported in *Adams's Weekly Courant*
(Chester), number 51 (14 November 1733), in which
there is much about the preparations for the arrival of
the Prince of Orange for his marriage with the Princess
Royal. The Prince arrived at Greenwich about noon on
Wednesday, 7 November, attended by Horatio Walpole,
and was taken in one of the King's barges to the Tower
of London and thence to Somerset House; but there had,
of course, been advance news about the progress of the
Fubbs yacht as it moved into the estuary long before
reaching Greenwich:

> The Person who brought the first News of the Prince's
> being seen off Margate, was one who keeps a publick House

there, who, upon seeing the Yatchts immediately took his Horse and rode to Canterbury, where he took Post Horses, and came to St. James's at 11 o'Clock on Monday Night. Her Majesty ordered him twenty Guineas, and Sir Robert Walpole gave him Five. The Twenty he has since laid out on a Silver Tankard, on which his Majesty's Arms are engrav'd.

For many a year this anonymous but enterprising publican must have pointed proudly at the well-polished trophy in his Margate house of cheer.

From Margate to London, by way of Canterbury, was a journey of about seventy-two miles, and the alert Margate man deserved his reward for a long, swift ride with news for his sovereign. News from the Orkneys would in the best of times have taken a whole week's hard riding, even after it reached the northern mainland; but in 1746, when postal services were interrupted because of bad weather or rebels, a letter dated at Stromness on 27 January did not reach London until 1 March, though readers of the *Oxford Gazette: and Reading Mercury* saw it shortly afterwards, in their paper dated Monday, 3 March 1745 (i.e., 1746):

> We have been for this Week or more under great Uneasiness, on account of a French Ship lying at Flotta Bay. By the surest Advices we have, she mounts 14 Ninepounders, is full of Swivels, and has 130 Men, commanded by an Irishman, bound to Caithness, with Arms, Ammunition, and Officers. . . . As the Communication by the Post is now stopp'd, I am obliged to send this by Sea, by a New-England Ship.

By the time the transatlantic ship reached her southern port, the authorities could do nothing to relieve the anxiety in Stromness, but they may have been much interested in the message nevertheless.

Ships from New England had long enough crossings in those days without calling at places like Stromness in the Orkneys, and the time lag between events in North

America and news thereof in England's towns was often considerable. A voyage which usually took less than two months sometimes lasted some weeks longer. Readers of the *Western Flying Post; or, Sherborne and Yeovil Mercury,* number 358 (5 January 1756), saw among the "Fresh Advices from America" a brief report dated at Boston on 13 October: "Last Week the several Carpenters who went from hence to Oswego returned here, having, as we understand, compleated the building of the several armed Vessels, designed for the Security of the Lake Ontario, in about 28 Days from the cutting of the Trees." It took more than three times as long for the news to reach Dorset and Somerset readers as the men from Boston took to fell the trees and construct the ships. Advices from over the sea could hardly be "fresh."

That there were special London "correspondents" who were employed to transmit news to country editors is apparent (if there were no other evidence) from statements made by printers in Birmingham, Worcester, Stamford, Halifax, and other towns. When William Thompson, printer of the *Stamford Mercury,* died in 1732, a new *Mercury* was started by Francis Howgrave. In defending himself against charges of having treated Thompson's widow unfairly, Howgrave quoted (in number 6, 20 July 1732) a letter from John Hannis of Goose Alley in Sea-Coal Lane, near Snow Hill, London, "who used to send Mrs. Thompson's News." Ten years later, *Aris's Birmingham Gazette* regularly had a column or more headed "From our London Correspondent,"[22] the articles being variously dated from Exchange Alley, Dick's Temple-Bar, Bolt-Court Coffee-House, Fleet Street, and "From my own Chambers." The *Sherborne Mercury* sometimes had two or three columns with the heading "From our London Correspondent." In 1758, the proposals of the new *Union Journal: or, Halifax Advertiser* included the usual statement that the *Journal* would be collected from all the London papers, and then referred to "a peculiar Advantage" in that a correspondent in London would supply the printer from time to time with "the earliest Intelligence, after the Evening Papers come from the Press."

Another "advantage" was possible: the news could be personally conveyed from London. Many printers arranged, presumably at considerable cost, for a special "express" (that is, a man on a horse) to bring the news over the shortest roads and trails. Direct conveyance of dispatches was not in every case satisfactory, as is apparent from a statement in *Berrow's Worcester Journal,* number 2072 (6 April 1749), addressed "To the Kind Encouragers of this Paper." Berrow said flatly that the special courier was less dependable than the regular post which arrived some hours later: " . . . we therefore intend, for the future, waiting the Arrival of our Intelligencies [*sic*] by the ordinary Post; But tho' this will consequently delay the Publication some Hours, yet, we hope, our Readers will dispense with it, since they will have a greater Quantity and Variety of News, &c. . . . " Unsatisfactory experience with special couriers convinced Berrow that the greater punctuality of the post would enable him to publish his paper with a minimum of irregularity.[23]

It is not surprising that in a period distinguished for its bad roads and its highwaymen there were delays in the securing of news from London, whether it was the postboy or a private courier who was unpunctual. Bliss's *Protestant Mercury* (Exeter), number 4 (25 January 1717), was published on its usual day, Friday, but the sixth page lacked its usual Thursday night news; "the Post Boy being robb'd of his Mail, between London and Staines," said Bliss, "there was no News or Letters came in by last Night's Post." The serious illness of one of the postboys bringing mail from London delayed publication of the *Western Flying Post; or, Sherborne and Yeovil Mercury,* number 88 (8 October 1750). December and January were particularly hard months for the carriers of news. The *Gloucester Journal,* number 196 (4 January 1726), was late in being printed and distributed, the reason being the lateness in the arrival of the packet from London: "the Post Boy alledges, that he was nine Hours in coming about a Mile, occasioned by the great Rains and sudden Frost." At the end of the news in the same paper on 13 December 1726 was a prominent notice:

₊ P.S. We hope our Readers will excuse our Messengers coming so late, by reason the Post did not come to Gloucester till after 4 this Evening: The Snow being very deep, several Distributors could not perform their Stages, especially to Burford, Farringdon, Wantage, Stow, &c.

Hazards of travel delayed both those who brought news to the printing office and those who later set out on their rounds with bundles of printed newspapers.

When storms, highwaymen, and sudden illness did not interfere, the local printers of newspapers would normally be able to keep to a fairly tight schedule as the established day of publication approached. Both the day of the week and the time set for publication on that day would depend on the usual time of the arrival of the post or of the special courier. Though some regions had a more frequent service,[24] the mail started along most of the great roads from London every Tuesday, Thursday, and Saturday night. The time of arrival in the provincial towns would naturally depend on the distance over which the mailbags had to be brought. Andrew Brice, of Exeter, indicated with very helpful precision the times at which the news from London reached him. In *Brice's Weekly Journal,* number 243 (Friday, 31 October 1729), for instance, his first two and one-half columns are headed "Substance of the Advices we receiv'd on Saturday Night." That Saturday was 25 October, and the articles were dated "London, Oct. 23." There followed three columns headed "The Articles following came last Monday Night" (that is, 27 October); they were dated "London,

Oct. 26." The third batch of news, dated "London, Oct. 28," has the heading "Between 3 and 4 o'Clock this Morning we receiv'd these further Advices."

Normal times of arrival of the London news are often indicated in notices of delay. *Norris's Taunton Journal* had an announcement in the issue dated Friday, 9 December 1726, that "The London Post who was expected here last Night, came in this Day about Noon." Obviously Norris usually had his final batch of news in his hands sometime Thursday night. On Saturday, 9 October 1731, Anne Ayscough of Nottingham declared that that day's post, which usually arrived "about 8 or 9 o'Clock in the Morning," had not come until nine o'clock that night.

On what principle did the publisher of a provincial newspaper decide which day was the most suitable for publication? It was certainly not the general practice to publish on the local market day, though that was done in some places. Nor was any one day of the week universally favoured. Saturday was the most popular, Monday being a close second. Friday was preferred in Exeter, Plymouth, Ludlow, Preston, Liverpool, and (while Stephen Bryan was the printer) Worcester; Tuesday was the day for the *Leeds Mercury* and the *Leedes Intelligencer,* for the earlier *Newcastle Gazette,* for most of the York and Manchester papers, for the *Hereford Journal,* the two Sheffield papers, the *Doncaster Flying Post,* and the papers in Warrington, Middlewich, and Halifax. Wednesday was undoubtedly the least popular, though William Cuthbert's *Newcastle Gazette* and the *Newcastle Intelligencer,* which took its place in 1755, were both published on that day. One paper, *Adams's Weekly Courant* in Chester, which for the first few years appeared on Wednesdays, eventually changed to Tuesday. On the other hand, another printer, William Cooke, moved his publishing day back to Wednesday after having brought out his *Chester Weekly Journal* on Thursdays for ten years. Cooke also chose Wednesday for publishing his other newpapers, the *Industrious Bee* (1733-34) and the *Chester Weekly Tatler* (1734).[25]

The most clearly defined reason for selecting one day as better than the others appears in a Worcester newspaper of 1753. Remembering that the three-days' news sent into the country from Lombard Street on Tuesday nights would be greater in bulk than the two-days' accumulations that went out on Thursdays and Saturdays, one realizes that a printer might well decide to issue his paper on the day which brought him the largest assortment of dispatches. Such was Hervey Berrow's reasoning. In November, 1753, Richard Lewis tried to start a *New Worcester Journal* in opposition to *Berrow's Worcester Journal*, but he did not achieve any advantage either by his aggressive methods [26] or by his bringing out the new paper on Wednesday, the day before Berrow's. The notice at the foot of the third page in number 234 (8 November 1753) of Berrow's paper and prominently spread across the front page of the following issue indicates that, whatever might be done elsewhere, the established Worcester printer recognized the expediency of publishing his paper as soon as the advices leaving London on Tuesday night were available:

> . . . It may likewise be necessary to observe, That a News-Paper, publish'd in Worcester on a Wednesday, cannot obtain the News from those Papers that are publish'd in London on a Tuesday Night, and which arrive in Worcester on a Thursday Morning; whereas, this Journal, being publish'd on a Thursday, always contains the News of those London Papers.

Thursday was preferred also in Stamford and (until 1743) in Derby. Manchester's first paper, Roger Adams's *Manchester News-Letter,* was published on that day, as were also the papers in Maidstone, Eton, and Whitehaven.

It is natural to suppose that the day regularly specified in the date line was the normal day of publication, and that only the non-arrival of news or of stamped paper would delay publication beyond that customary day; but careful examination reveals some anomalies not at first apparent. It can easily be seen that the Nottingham *Weekly Courant,* which year after year bore Thursday dates under its title, actually came from the press on Saturday. How otherwise could Anne Ayscough have possibly printed in her *Weekly Courant* dated Thursday, 29 July 1725, items of news from *Jones's Letter* and the *London Evening Post* of that same date? And how came it that these pieces, like similar paragraphs in most other issues, were placed under the caption "Saturday's Post"? This inconsistency is demonstrated in the issue of the *Weekly Courant* dated Thursday, 8 December 1726, in which there are blank spaces at the bottom of the two columns on the fourth page, with a note in place of the usual caption: "Saturday, Dec. 10. This Day's Post is not yet come in." Anne Ayscough's readers looked for their Thursday paper on Saturday, and she could not keep them waiting; number 31 came out on time! It is perhaps being too utterly logical to insist that a Thursday paper should be published on Thursday.

For reasons not always made clear, some printers deliberately changed the regular day of publication. The *Sherborne Mercury* in its earliest years came out on Monday; by 1740, its day of publication had been altered to Tuesday; then, from 3 February 1746, the day was moved back to Monday, and that was the accepted day after the amalgamation with the *Western Flying Post, or Yeovil Mercury* in 1749. Although the *Lancashire Journal* apparently started on Thursday, it soon began to come out regularly on Monday; the surviving issues from number 66 to number 72 bear Tuesday dates, but thereafter the day of publication was again Monday.[27] Sometimes the change was made at the particular request of readers. The *Birmingham Journal* had for over six months been appearing on Monday when, in number 28

(21 May 1733), the printer explained that certain encouragers of the paper had recommended altering the day of publication to Thursday. According to the only surviving issue of Edward Ward's *Bristol Mercury*, number 24 (Thursday, 20 October 1748), Thursday was not the most acceptable day, for Ward's city and country friends had repeatedly told him that the paper would circulate much farther and be of more service to the public if he published on Saturday. He said he would make the change at once.

The most frequent change was that from Saturday to Monday or vice versa. The lively and long lasting *Salisbury Journal,* which began on 27 November 1736, fluctuated between these two days. The first four issues appeared on Saturdays; but during the early weeks of 1737, the paper appeared as often with Monday dates as with Saturday dates. From the beginning of April, 1737, the day named in the date line was regularly Monday, but a notice in number 43 (Monday, 19 September 1737) makes it clear that Collins had developed the practice of publishing his paper *before* the day specified in the date line:

. The publishing this Paper as usual, on Saturday Evening, being attended with many Inconveniences, the same will be published, after the last day of this Month, on every Tuesday Morning, so that the freshest Intelligence by Monday's Post will by that means be inserted, and the same sooner and better conveyed to our Readers.

In spite of this declaration, the day of publication given in the date line did not change to Tuesday until early in 1739. With number 426 (17 March 1746), the day was moved back to Monday.

It is apparent from the many satirical observations in the *Salisbury Journal* and a dozen other papers that within the limits of a particular region the strongest point of rivalry was the question of whose news was the latest.

William Collins wrote scathingly in his *Salisbury Journal* of Monday, 22 May 1738, about the "stale Stuff" in the *Gloucester Journal*. Raikes and Dicey aggressively declared in an early issue of their *Gloucester Journal*— number 4 (30 April 1722)—that their paper included the latest news, and was not like some other newspapers in which all the news of the last post was kept over to the next week, with the result that the most material part of the news was a week old before it came out. This was a controversy which showed up in various parts of the country. Every surviving issue of the *Sussex Weekly Advertiser* in its first ten years carried at the top the confident assertion that readers would find in this Monday paper the news from Saturday's *London Gazette*, which could not otherwise reach them until two or three days later. The argument was stated with more particularity in Elizabeth Jopson's *Coventry Mercury*, number 924 (19 March 1759):

> *⁎⁎* Some News-Writers having affirmed, in Favour of some *Weekly Papers*, published on a SATURDAY, that they contain as many Articles of early Intelligence as THIS which is published on a MONDAY; in order that the Publick may no longer be imposed upon, by *false* Assertions, we think it proper to inform them, that the Paragraphs of News, inserted in the *last* Post of such Papers, are all copied from those published in London on a FRIDAY; whereas our *Monday Morning's Post*, is taken from the *London Gazette* and other Papers published on a SATURDAY EVENING; so that THIS contains a NIGHT *and* DAY'S *more Intelligence of important Events.*

This is a much more explicit statement, and probably closer to the truth, than the emphatic claims advanced by some other printers.

No one was so absurdly insistent upon the freshness of his news as Robert Walker, whose reports in the *London and Country Journal* and other papers were either long out of date or not dated at all. He and his partner, William Jackson, changed the day of publication of their *Oxford Flying Weekly Journal* from Saturday to Monday, they said, because they wished to include the news of Saturday's *London Gazette.* "Our Readers are desired to observe," they remarked in number 71 (11 January 1748), "that this Gazette News and our other early Advices cannot appear in the Northampton Mercury till the Week after." This hostility against the *Northampton Mercury,* which had for many years appeared on Monday, probably had its root in a vigorous attack leveled by the *Northampton Mercury* on 27 May 1745 against the *Cambridge Journal,* of which Walker (along with Thomas James) was a proprietor. The attack on the *Cambridge Journal* was apparently deserved, for in the issue of Saturday, 16 March 1745, and later issues was a statement that by means of the "great Expedition" used in procuring news, they were two days before the Northampton paper and "all Sunday's Post before the Ipswich Paper."

It is quite possible that Walker and his partner really did conduct their business with "Expedition" and engaged special messengers to gallop from London to Cambridge and to Oxford on Saturday, bringing news which would not ordinarily reach either town until the post arrived on Sunday. Walker could probably have had a G.P.O. "express" to either place for about a pound.[28] He had assured readers of the *Cambridge Journal,* number 52 (Saturday, 14 September 1745), that "no Care, or Expence, no Diligence or Attention" would be spared to procure the earliest intelligence. But when he asserted, as he did repeatedly, that news printed in his Saturday paper actually contained extracts from "the London Evening Papers" which did not reach Cambridge until Sunday afternoon, he was obviously trying to convince his readers that he was referring to London papers published on Saturday. It was egregious deception. In their number 37

(Saturday, 1 June 1745), Walker and James declared that all persons living in Cambridge or coming to the market could be supplied with the *Cambridge Journal* "after Seven o'Clock every Saturday Morning"; and three months later the hour was announced as "after Six o'Clock every Saturday Morning." It is small wonder that the *Northampton Mercury* and Charles Micklewright's *Oxford Gazette: and Reading Mercury* [29] poked fun at the fantastic claim to "great Expedition" in the printing of weekend news in the two university towns. There was not enough money in all England to pay for the conveying of a Saturday evening London paper to Cambridge (or even to Oxford) fast enough for Walker to print its news before seven o'clock that morning.

Every weekly newspaper contains what Collins of Salisbury called "stale Stuff," for its earliest advices are at least a week old before they are in the hands of readers. "Freshest" means "as fresh as can be managed." Walker was too ready to claim that his papers were miracles of promptitude. Most other printers made real efforts to gather the news without delay.

Delays in procuring the news were sometimes unavoidable; delays in getting the news into type and onto paper could be minimized if care, diligence, and attention were exercised during that time of most critical urgency in a newspaper office—the hour or two before blank paper begins to be fed into the moving press, whether it is a whirring modern giant, all wheels and rollers, or a simple flat-bed press worked by hand. That critical hour was sometimes four or five o'clock in the morning. We have observed Robert Walker's claim to have his Cambridge paper ready for customers by six o'clock on Saturday mornings. Sam. Farley announced on the title page of his *Salisbury Post Man*, number 1 (27 September 1715), that if he could get two hundred regular subscribers his paper would be delivered to any private or public house in town every Monday, Thursday, and Saturday morning, "by

Eight of the Clock, during the Winter-Season, and by Six in the Summer." Two months later, the same man, or another man of the same name, assured readers of *Sam. Farley's Bristol Post Man* that his paper would be "constantly Publish'd every Saturday Morning, Two Hours after the London Post comes in." Just over ten years later, *Farley's Bristol News-Paper*, number 69 (27 August 1726), had an extended subtitle which included the phrase, " . . . and Publish'd every Saturday Morning soon after the London Post comes in."

It must be kept in mind that the time of going to press depended entirely upon the arrival of the London news. There was no waiting for advertisements. The allowed interval between the deadline for the receiving of paid notices and the time of going to press varied from one paper to another and changed also with the developing efficiency of the shop, but most editors insisted on a gap of two or three days.[30] This request was not unreasonable; the printer had to make up and print half or more of the paper well in advance. The reason why persons advertising in the *Sherborne Mercury*, published on Tuesday, had to have their notices at the printing office on the preceding Thursday was that the first side of the paper was set up and started through the press that day or on Friday. In 1737, the *York Courant*, likewise published on Tuesday, asked its advertisers to send in their notices on Saturday in the forenoon; by 1741, the same paper had shortened the interval, the note in number 835 (13 October 1741) urging that advertisements be sent in on Monday morning "by Ten o'Clock at farthest" or they could not possibly be inserted until the following week. Caesar Ward's notice in the *York Courant*, number 1104 (9 December 1746), makes the arrangement perfectly clear. Advertisements carried over from the preceding issue and enough new ones to fill the available space would be made up with the other matter of page 4. That page, together with the first page, was printed on Saturday afternoon.

As the Number of Courants *now printed is so very great, that we are oblig'd to go to Press with one Side of the Paper on* Saturday; *and it's frequent to order an Advertisement to be continued till forbid; our Correspondents are desir'd to send in their Orders of Discontinuance before that Day at Noon, otherwise their Advertisements cannot be taken out.*

Ward also said that new advertisements could be received as late as Monday if they were put into the hands of Benjamin Lund in Tadcaster (was he the typesetter?) so that they and the latest news could be set together. The arrangement could hardly have been better.

With careful planning, then, the greater part of the type-setting would already have been done before the final post arrived, and half the printing would have been completed, too.

Accidents could happen in the printing office to delay the final putting to bed of the type for the second side. In the *Cambridge Journal,* number 309 (18 August 1750), there was a mournful note about pied type:

⁎.⁎ We hope our Readers will excuse the Newsmen serving the Cambridge Journal so late this Week; it being occasion'd by a Misfortune happening just as the Paper was going to Press, whereby one whole Page of the Paper was broke to Pieces.

With two masters to serve—Robert Walker and Thomas James—some poor "devil" must have had both his ears boxed for being so awkward. But aside from such regrettable accidents and storms which delayed the news carriers after the paper was printed, the provincial purveyors of "freshest advices" in the reign of George II were usually able to get the news into their customers' hands before the reports were much more out of date than when the printers received them.

It is expedient now to consider the whole operation of a country printing office, or at least that part of the business concerned with getting out the paper. There will remain many uncertainties, for there is little evidence about the ink used, about the number of men usually employed in a country printing office, about their wages and the length of their working day, about the number of sheets or half-sheets that could be printed off (one side) in an hour,[31] about the number of printing presses, if indeed there were more than one, in particular printing shops, and about the matter of second, third, or fourth editions or impressions of a particular weekly number.

What went on in the shop of a country printer of news can only be conjectured, but the general practices are obvious enough. Once the preceding issue was off the press and the types had been distributed, the preparations could go forward for the next issue. In a well-conducted shop there would be an adequate supply of paper, for the printer would not have forgotten to order enough for his needs. The title-heading or separate title page would be all ready set in large types, sometimes with the characteristic "news-bringer" wood blocks—a ship, a mercury, a mounted postman—or a view of the city. If a factotum block was customarily used at the top of the first column, it was easy to insert the appropriate initial.[32] The standard captions would be ready;[33] if page numbers and running titles—such as "PILBOROUGH'S NEWS" or "Crossgrove's News"—were used, these could be transferred from the previous setting of the type; the colophon would remain as already composed or be slightly altered if a new agent had to be named; the serial number and the date could be changed immediately from those of the week before; uncancelled advertisements could remain intact.

The procedure is best understood if one examines the standard layouts of representative papers. The pattern in a pre-1712, two-page, half-sheet weekly paper is illustrated by number 556 (Friday, 10 August 1711) of *Sam. Farley's Exeter Post-Man; Or, Weekly Intelligence, From*

Holland, France, Spain, Portugal, &c. With General Oc-currences both Foreign and Domestick. Flanking this five-line title are woodcuts, one showing a ship in full sail, the other showing a gate in a city wall. Under the date line, which contains the serial number as well, are two columns of badly printed news, introduced by the statement, "Since our last, we have receiv'd Three Mails from Holland, and Three from Flanders with the following Advices." The first caption, "Geneva, August 3, N.S.," is the only one on that page. The news, which on the front page is mostly foreign, continues on the second page, where there are short items dated "Falmouth, Aug. 6," "Plymouth, Aug. 7," "Bristol, Aug. 4," and "London, August 7"; but most of the space on the second page is occupied by thirteen advertisements,[34] each having the first line in type larger than that of the body. The only caption on the second page is the word "Advertisements." The colophon is simply "Printed at my House near the New Inn."

When the Stamp Act in 1712 drove printers to use a sheet and a half for each copy of their papers, there was plenty of space, and it was common for the first page of these six-page or twelve-page papers to be used exclusively for the title and the imprint. Long titles and wordy descriptive subtitles were preferred, and types of several sizes were used lavishly. In some of the papers the front page had a large oblong cut showing a panoramic view of the town, or had a pair of square woodcuts flanking the upper lines of the title. Display types in titles were most flamboyant in rival papers in the same town. From his printing office in St. Peter's Churchyard, Exeter, Philip Bishop in 1715 sent out his six-page newspaper with a title of forty-two words and an ampersand:

The / Exeter Mercury: / or, Weekly Intelligence / of / News: / Being A Faithful / abstract of all the News Papers of Note. / Containing the Material Occurrences / Foreign and Domestick; / with a Particular Account of what Books / and Pamphlets are Publish'd in Great / Britain, France, Holland, &c.

Using a similar pair of woodcuts to adorn the page and duplicating Bishop's large interlaced monogram for good measure, Jos. Bliss sent out his paper from "the NEW PRINTING-HOUSE near the London-Inn, without East-gate," with a title longer than Bishop's, but only because he added eleven defiant words after his ampersand: " . . . So that no other can pretend to have a better Collection." In substance these competing papers were similar, though Bliss used more prominent headings for the news of the three posts than Bishop did. Both used two columns to the page. Other six-page papers of the 1712-25 period were set in much the same fashion as these two Exeter papers, but some of them were in single columns and some used only part of the front page for the title. That was the layout of the *Worcester Post Man* after the Stamp Act of 1712. The full title (sixteen words), the two wood-blocks, and the date line filled only one-third of the front page.

From 1725 onward, as was indicated earlier in this chapter, all provincial newspapers were printed on the two sides of a single half-sheet, all but two of them—the *Stamford Mercury* for a time and the *Suffolk Mercury*— being set so as to be folded once into a four-page paper with two or three columns to the page.

Since in most towns the bulk of the news arrived with the post from London three times a week, a few pioneers in the printing of local papers believed that they should publish their papers three times a week, each issue offering only the news that came in the current batch. This was the practice of the first two Newcastle papers, both of them published on Monday, Wednesday, and Saturday. The *New-castle Gazette*, number 65, for example, printed news selected by J. Button or his printer, J. Saywell, from dispatches received in Newcastle between Saturday, 23

December, and Monday, 25 December 1710. As soon as Saywell reached the catchword in setting his first page, he printed as many copies of that page as he required, then turned the paper and printed his second page, which (unless Saywell was both compositor and pressman) would have been set in type while the first page was being run off.

If the paper came out once a week, the printer might make up his paper in one of two ways. He could fill the first third of the available space with items of news selected from the first batch, then fill another third with pieces from the second set of dispatches, and leave enough space to print selected parts of the last lot of advices when they arrived near the end of his week. That would produce a paper which in effect would be three successive bulletins of news issued at one time. The other way would be to let the selected items accumulate until all three posts had come in and then to rearrange the material so as to bring together all the foreign news, all the American news, all the country news, and so on, in the several recognized categories. This procedure might make an orderly grouping of items, but it would have one serious disadvantage: no part of the paper could be printed until the whole thing was ready for the press. The problem would be the same whether the printer used twelve, eight, six, four, or two pages. It is easy to see why almost all printers preferred to make up the paper with three separate sections of news; by this arrangement they could get ahead with the printing and bring out the paper with minimum delay after the final news arrived in the shop.

Yet there were two papers in which the whole week's news was presented in one lot rather than in three. One of these, the six-page *Plymouth Weekly Journal,* had a title filling the first page, with the verso blank, and only four pages of news and advertisements. The third page, headed "FOREIGN AFFAIRS," was set up and printed first, followed by page 4 (the other side of the half-sheet).[35] A second caption, "LONDON," with the date, was inserted at the appropriate place in the series of paragraphs, with no other interruption to the end of the sixth page. By 1724, the news was being set up in three batches, and a rigid allotment of space for each batch had been established. Invariably page 2 (now no longer blank) had "Sunday" as its first word, followed by foreign news and such captions as *"PORT NEWS"* and *"LONDON."* Page 4 regularly had at the head of its first column an ornamental band and some such statement as this: *"Friday, Oct. 9. Arrived three Mails from Holland, two from Flanders, and one from France."* [36]

The principle that the setting of the news in a single batch was superior found most emphatic utterance in a special note under the date line of the four-page *Oracle: Or, Bristol Weekly Miscellany*, which began to appear in April, 1742: "Some of our Readers, accustomed to the vulgar Division of the News into Mondays, Thursdays and Saturdays Posts, think it strange that we deviate from the common Practice." What follows was intended to "obviate this Popular Prejudice." The *Oracle's* manner of reducing every article under its proper general head was believed to be "less confused, more laborious and more useful," and was justified because the *Oracle's* foreign news was directly transmitted from abroad and could therefore be set up in type well in advance of the posts bringing the news via London. One might understand from this explanation that all reports from Germany were to be grouped together under one heading. That simple arrangement was apparently not feasible; instead, there are in number 3 (17 April 1742), not one, but several sections headed "GERMANY." These sections, separated by others headed "FRANCE and SPAIN," "LOW COUNTRIES," "ITALY," give the news from Newhauss, Vienna, Ratisbon, and Frankfort in chronological order it is true, but one must still search the columns before finding all the news from one area. The setting of news in three batches would certainly have been less "laborious" for the readers.

Special circumstances may have made it seem reasonable for the proprietors of the *Oracle* in Bristol to depart from "the general Mode," but other printers uniformly preferred to dispense the news in three batches, even after the posts began to arrive more often than thrice weekly. And the principle which kept them doing that was nowhere so directly stated as in Henry Cross-grove's *Norwich Gazette,* number 27 (10 May 1707), in answer to a question ostensibly submitted by a "Constant Peruser," who asked, "Why you constantly divide your News into three Days Intelligence, and not make it one continued Story?" Cross-grove's reply is illuminating:

> . . . the reason why I pursue that Method is this, because I would not impose upon my Customers, and in particular those that live in the Country; I do not therefore run it all together, to take the Advantage of picking a Saturday's Account out of the old Intelligence, but particularize each Day's Account, that the Buyers may be satisfied they have the Whole Week's News.

Cross-grove, like practically every other printer of news, continued the practice of setting it up in three batches, both before and after the change of design from six pages to four in 1725.[37]

It takes a twentieth-century reader a little time to accustom himself to look at the *end* of a paper for the latest news, but the eighteenth-century reader had no reason to look elsewhere for it. Philip Bishop, printer of the *Exeter Mercury,* used a special heading at the top of page 6 in the issues of late 1714 and early 1715: "By the last Nights Post we had the following Advices," and he drew particular attention to his plan of keeping that page exclusively for late news: "'*•*' N.B. The last Page of this Paper, in which has usually been inserted all that comes in the Thursday Nights Post . . . , shall for the

future be entirely reserv'd for the News of that Post."
Other printers refrained from making such a declaration,
knowing that all readers would automatically turn to the
end of the paper for the freshest advices. Certainly if
anyone perused the six-page *Worcester Post-Man,* number 267 (Friday, 6 August 1714), only as far as page 4
he would see on that page that the ailing Queen Anne,
after suffering "a Fit of Convulsions, others say the Appo-
plexy," had been given "much Relief by Blisters"; only
on page 5 of that same issue would the reader discover
that the Queen had died on Sunday, 31 July.[38]
With two-page, four-page, and eight-page papers the
printer had to decide which of the two sides to print first.
The pages were, of course, set one at a time, column by
column; in a four-page paper, the pages were printed two
at a time, pages 1 and 4 first, unless it was the printer's
preference to put his latest news on page 4, in which case
he ran off pages 2 and 3 first. Many four-page papers have
freshly-set catchwords showing unmistakably the order
in which the pages were set; and there are other signs
indicating what was the customary order of printing in
any one shop. In eight-page papers, four pages were
printed at a time, pages 2, 7, 6, and 3 on one side, 8, 1, 4,
and 5 on the other.
The standard threefold sequence of news groupings in
four-page papers with the latest news on page 3 may be
seen in the *Oxford Gazette; and Reading Mercury,* number 16, published on Monday, 3 March 1746: at the head
of the first column stands the caption, "Wednesday's
Post"; two-thirds from the top of the first column of the
second page is the caption, "Friday's Post"; and the third
page begins with the heading, "Sunday's Post." The Reading news comes in the third column of that third page,
followed by the weekly list of bankrupts, prices of stocks,
London bills of mortality, and prices of commodities on
various markets. The fourth page is filled with advertisements. This being so, the printer would naturally first

work off the "outer" side of the paper, containing pages 1 and 4. Page 2 would be standing ready in type when the compositor received the material for his page 3. Then the types of pages 2 and 3 would be locked in the chase and the half-printed sheets would be put through the press a second time. This was the most common procedure.[39] Other printers also set page 1 first, but preferred to hold it until page 4 could be set with the final batch of news or—as in the *Salisbury Journal*, the *Derby Mercury*, and the *Ipswich Journal*, for example—to insert on the fourth page a short section of late news from London, sometimes labelled "Postscript," on the model of such London papers as the early *Flying Post* and the *St. James's Evening Post* in the early months of 1735. In such cases, obviously, it was the "inner" side of the paper that went through the press first.

This keeping of limited space at the bottom of the last column to be set up in type makes one think of the common twentieth-century practice of reserving space on the first or last page for the inserting of special bulletins concerning sporting results, political crises, new rockets to the moon, or any other exciting development reported after the edition has been run off; but eighteenth-century provincial news printers did not do that. News, letters, and advertisements which came in after the printing of the second side of the sheet had begun were ordinarily held over until the next week's issue. There were exceptions. One of these is seen in *Norris's Taunton Journal,* a four-page paper which appeared on Tuesdays and Fridays. Norris had three fresh pages of news in the Tuesday issues but used as page 1 the last page of the preceding Friday's issue. Friday's paper reprinted (as pages 1 to 3) the previous Tuesday's latest news, only the final page being new. Norris's customers regularly got the whole week's news whether they took the Tuesday or the Friday edition, but the Tuesday customers got three times as much "fresh" news as those who took the Friday edition. Ten years earlier, Jos. Bliss of Exeter had provided the same sort of twice-a-week news service, the subtitle of his *Protestant Mercury* indicating that "for the Convenience of those that will take the same but Once a Week, it is so order'd, that every Friday's Paper will contain three Posts; or, the whole Week's News." The *Protestant Mercury* had six pages, not four, but the title filled page one in both editions, and in the Tuesday paper the second page was blank. The bulk of the week's fresh news appeared in the last four pages of the Tuesday paper; the Friday paper reprinted everything that was in the Tuesday paper of that week, adding only a page at the end containing the news which had arrived by Thursday's post. Philip Bishop's *Exeter Mercury* for a time appeared in the same way on Tuesdays and Fridays. These three newspapers were, in effect, weekly papers published on Tuesdays, with an extra edition on Friday containing one additional page of late news.

If the word "extra" is to be reserved for supernumerary issues brought out unexpectedly to spread news too exciting to be held over for the next regular issue, it is appropriate to apply the term to extraordinary editions of two Liverpool newspapers in the period of the Seven Years' War. As early as 1712, John White brought out a sheetful of news between numbers 96 and 97 of his *Newcastle Courant,* but this was rather by way of a continuation of the first of these than an "extra." It was pointed out near the beginning of this chapter that in number 95 (8 March 1712) of his paper, White used eight pages instead of four because of developments at Utrecht. He decided not to do that in the issue of 10 March, preferring to print his usual four pages and announcing that additional pages would be published later: "The remainder of the News coming by this Post, together with the Specifick Demands of the States-General, delivered in at the Congress at Utrecht, which being very large, could not be comprized in this Paper, will be Published a few Hours after the

Publication of this Paper, in a *Supplement to the* New-castle *Courant.*" The supplement has four pages, is dated 10 March 1712, and bears the same serial number (96) as the regular paper of that date.

Forty-six years later, both Robert Williamson and John Sadler occasionally printed "extraordinary" editions of their respective Liverpool papers between one regular Friday edition and the next. These extra editions were unnumbered, and were distributed free of charge to all the regular customers who could be reached. While the news carriers were still going their rounds distributing the issue of *Williamson's Liverpool Advertiser* published on Friday, 18 August 1758, news of the surrender of Louisburg reached London and was announced in an "extraordinary" issue of the *London Gazette.* Williamson lost no time. On Monday, 21 August, he brought out his own *Liverpool Advertiser Extraordinary,* reprinting on one side of a leaf the full text of the exciting announcement. In the next regular issue (Friday, 25 August 1758) he explained that it had, of course, been impossible for him to send this special news to every one of his customers, "the Hawkers not being returned"; he therefore put the whole account of the Louisburg capitulation on the front page, with a note expressing the hope that those already served would excuse the repetition. He then found that by the time he had selected articles from Sunday's and Tuesday's posts there was room in the last column and a half of the third page (the fourth page being filled with advertisements) for only an extract of a letter received from New York by a local man, and details of Monday's celebration in Liverpool—with the help of six barrels of ale. Readers were assured that advertisements and "Particulars" not inserted in that day's paper "for Want of Room, on Account of the agreeable and welcome News" would be printed in the next regular issue. In the following months there were several other "extraordinary" issues of this paper and of John Sadler's *Liverpool*

Chronicle, a few being published even on Sunday.[40] These special efforts by White and by Williamson and by Sadler to get important news into circulation as early as possible represent what has since become the primary impulse of the journalist.

Haste could cause errors, and some of the mishaps now detectable in extant copies make one feel very close to the original operation. Errors in typesetting could easily be made, particularly if the compositor was inexperienced or very young. "Thro' Haste in my little Boy's composing the Dissenter's Address, an ugly Omission happened in His Majesty's Answer, which those that have bought are desired to correct, and read thus. . . . " So wrote Jos. Bliss of Exeter in the *Protestant Mercury* dated 15 March 1717. Or the error could be in the arranging of the form. In the *Worcester Post,* number 755 (13 December 1723), Stephen Bryan, the printer, put a notice on page 5 asking his readers to be guided by the page numbers on the inside of the main sheet, pages 2 and 3 having unfortunately been printed in reverse order. Apparently the whole of the first sheet, both sides, had been run off before the error was noticed. Sometimes the pressman was at fault. The Hendon copy of the *Ipswich Journal,* number 378 (11 November 1727), has pages 2 and 3 upside down; so has the Newcastle Reference Library copy of the *Newcastle Courant,* number 604 (20 November 1736). The copy of the *York Courant,* number 1422 (16 January 1753), in the York Public Library has the second and third pages blank.

More exciting than these minor slips by the pressman are the several typographical flaws which were perceived too late to be corrected but were noted elsewhere in the same paper. If an error on page 2 or page 3 is mentioned on page 4, obviously page 4 was set up after the type for the inner surface of the half-sheet had been locked in the chase, and there are many examples of this kind of emendation. Of special interest are several references to such errors caught and corrected while the faulty page was being run through the press. John White's *Newcastle Courant,* number 499 (9 October 1714), has on page 12, just before the advertisements, "*Erratum.* In some of our last, Page 11. Line 14. for Matthew read Roger." This clearly implied that the mistake was observed and corrected after some copies has been printed. The same is true of the *Weekly Worcester Journal,* number 1340 (28 February 1735), which has on the fourth page this note: "*Pag.* 2, Col. 3, *Line* 20, *for* that *read* the. *Line 67, for* Treasures *read* Measures. *This happen'd only in some few Papers of this Impression.*"

If printers were careful to point out errors perceived only after an issue had gone through the press, it is reasonable to assume that they normally made efforts to detect mistakes in typesetting before the half-sheets were given to the pressmen for the actual running off. One of the most interesting examples of proofreading and correcting of the press is to be seen by comparing the office copy of William Chase's *Norwich Mercury,* dated 17 November 1750—it is in the British Museum—with a corrected copy in the Norwich Public Library. The first column on the fourth page in the British Museum copy has fourteen errors marked for correction. The proofreader's eye saw (among other things) that a letter was missing from "threatned," that two letters were transposed in "overboadr," that "Southwaod" and "Fdge" had wrong letters, and that there was an unnecessary letter in "haveing." The copy in Norwich shows that the alterations proposed by the proofreader were made, but several other flaws, not marked for correction, remained: a redundant "of," a misspelled "partad," several omissions, and six punctuation marks that were either missing or wrong. William Chase, or the man who read proof for him, could see that there was something wrong with the word "Intepredity" in the account of a fearless rescuer of a drowning man, but he could think of no other way to put it right than to insert another "r"; the typesetter obeyed his instructions and the word—bigger if not better—now reads "Intrepredity." A glance at these proofreader's marks and at the corrections leaves one with a strong sense of ink-stained fingers fumbling with individual pieces of type in Chase's printing shop in the Cockey Lane. The same sort of effort was probably made by the printers of other provincial newspapers.

Sometimes the changes were not typographical but substantial. On at least one occasion there were two differing editions of the *Gloucester Journal,* in one of which a later report was substituted for an erroneous early report which had appeared in the other edition. The *Gloucester Journal,* number 672 (11 March 1735), has in the place usually reserved for local news this declaration:

> *.* It having been inserted in some of our last Papers, that Sir *W^m. Keyt* and *W^m. Bromley,* Esq; were voted duly elected for Warwick; the Mistake was owing to the Thursday's Post, with which those Papers were printed off, before that of Saturday arrived to contradict it, which brought Word, that the Petitioners, *Thomas Archer* and *Henry Archer,* Esqrs. were the Gentlemen voted duly chosen for the said Town.

This surely means that what some readers found in number 671 was not the same as what others found in their copies.[41] Presumably Saturday's post arrived before all the required copies of the *Gloucester Journal,* number 671, had been run off. It would not be expedient to incorporate all the fresh news that came in Saturday's post, since that would be used in the next week's paper, but a patent error could certainly be corrected if it meant only altering two lines of type in the third column of the front page.

There is evidence that one paper on several occasions had to be reprinted immediately because the sale proved greater than had been expected. *F. Farley's Bristol Journal* and *Farleys Bristol Advertiser* (published on alternate Saturdays) apparently sold so well that the first impression was soon exhausted and more had to be printed. The *Journal*, number 71 (18 May 1745), had on the third page an announcement which began, "N.B. *The Demand for our Papers is so great, that last Saturday there were no less than* THREE *Impressions of that Day's* Paper. . . . " On 5 October 1745, *Farleys Bristol Advertiser*, number 84, had a similar notice: "N.B. This Paper is so universally receiv'd, that it had no less than *three extraordinary* Impressions last Saturday." That seems to mean that after they had finished the normal run of his paper Farley's pressmen went back to the press three more times. There is no knowing how many additional copies were run off in these extra impressions, and it is not clear why *one* extra running should not have served. The increased demand in October, 1745, might be attributed to the growing excitement over the Jacobite Rebellion, but similar claims were made long after the battle at Culloden. On 18 April 1747, Farley said there had been "no less than Three Impressions" on the preceding Saturday, and precisely three months later he used italics and capitals to shout forth his triumph: "*N.B. This Paper had* AGAIN *Three Impressions last Saturday*. . . . " Unless several copies of one issue can be compared, there is no way of knowing the extent to which (if any) these "impressions" differed.

There are other aspects of this matter of multiple impressions which will bear looking into, but here it is enough to observe that there were several papers which may be said to have been printed in more than one "impression" or "edition," though sometimes the variation was slight. *Henry's Reading Journal* was also issued with the title *Henry's Winchester Journal;* the *London and Country Journal* was issued with other titles; the *Salisbury Journal* was also issued with the title *Portsmouth and Gosport Gazette;* the *Public Advertiser (Sheffield)* seems to have appeared in several different "impressions," each with precisely the same matter as the others but each having a different agent (or perhaps proprietor) named under the title. (See item 131 in the Register.) Genuinely differing editions of the *York Courant* in 1741 are extant, with extensive variations in the substance on the "inner" side of the paper; but the involved relationships between the two editions cannot be discussed here. What matters is that before the reign of George II came to an end there were local newspapers all over England; and whether each came out in several impressions or only one, the total weekly output must have been tens of thousands. How they were put into the hands of waiting readers will be considered in the following chapter.

1. In a few instances diagrams and maps were attached to items of news concerning naval and military operations, usually to show the disposition of British and enemy forces at such places as Portobello, Carthagena, Chagre, Louisburg, Culloden. The *York Courant,* number 729 (2 October 1739), had on the front page "A Plan of the City of Belgrade, as it stood, when besieged by the Turks, in 1739, Drawn by the Hon. Brigadier General Douglas of York." Occasionally other subjects were illustrated: the *Norwich Gazette,* on 12 February 1737, had an illustration concerning the approaching eclipse of the sun; and the first issue of the *Western Flying-Post; or, Sherborne and Yeovil Mercury* (30 January 1749) had its front page filled with a sketch of the stupendous firework used in London to celebrate the Peace of Aix la Chapelle a few weeks earlier. Reference will be made in Chapter IV to the use of small cuts of houses, ships, and horses as a means of classifying advertisements.

2. Since no copies of the last two in this list have survived, I have taken the evidence of the nineteenth-century historians who saw copies of these papers which were then extant. See items 72 and 133 in the Register.

3. Because White wished his readers to have the text of an official communication concerning the proposed congress at Utrecht to discuss a general peace, the *Newcastle Courant,* number 95 (8 March 1712), was double the usual size, being a whole sheet printed in eight pages of the regular dimensions.

4. See item 134 in the Register.

5. See A. H. Shorter, *Paper Mills and Paper Makers in England, 1495-1800* (Hilversum, Netherlands: Paper Publications Society, 1957) and D. C. Coleman, *British Paper Industry, 1495-1860* (London: Oxford University Press, 1958).

6. See below, pp. 157-58.

7. See details hereafter, and Graham Pollard, "Notes on the Size of the Sheet," *The Library,* Ser. 4, XXII (1941), 105-37.

8. I have examined thousands of provincial newspapers of the period 1700-1760 but have yet to see one bearing a penny stamp. When the tax was increased by a halfpenny in 1757, the additional amount was indicated by a band inscribed "HALFPENNY" attached to the lower part of the former design of the stamp, which still rather inconsistently had as its motto the words *"semper eadem."* For an excellent account of the mechanical process by which the half-sheets were stamped, see Sydney R. Turner, *The Newspaper Tax Stamps of Great Britain: The First Issue, 1712-1757* ([Cheam] : Sydney R. Turner, [1936]).

9. The British Museum copy of the *Ipswich Journal,* number 19 (24 December 1720), has on the first of its six pages a written receipt, signed by John May, "for duty upon this Paper 3ᵈ. and for one advertisement one Shilling," but the duty on a sheet-and-a-half pamphlet would be three shillings; "3ᵈ." must be an error for "3ˢʰ."

10. In 1744, the year in which the term of thirty-two years mentioned in the Act of 1712 came to an end, nothing was done officially to continue the Stamp Tax, printers and government alike apparently assuming that once the tax was established it would remain in effect until altered by Act of Parliament. There was passed in 1743 an act—16 Geo. 2, c. 26—which included a section imposing a penalty on the venders of unstamped newspapers, but the next formal legislation dealing with taxes on newspapers was the Act of 1757—30 Geo. 2, c. 19—which added a halfpenny to the tax assumed to be still in effect.

11. The printing of four columns to the page began in provincial newspapers about 1762.

12. *Berrow's Worcester Journal* continued to expand. By 1778, the pages, now in four columns, measured 11½ by 18¼ inches; and by 1813, the pages had five columns and measured 15½ by 21 inches.

13. Subsequent mishandling interferes with the legibility of some copies still extant, as is obvious in some issues of the *York Courant* in the York Minster Library, which are covered with clippings from later newspapers, and some issues of *Adams's Weekly Courant* in the Chester Public Library, which are badly stained with what appears to be the juice of red currants; some of the currants are still stuck to the paper.

14. Thomas Boddely announced in a prominent advertisement in his *Bath Journal* on 26 November 1750 that he had placed an order for "several new Fonts of Caslon's Types"; but it is clear that he intended to use these in printing books.

15. It was the *smallest* of the new types that Thompson and Cuthbert said they would use in their *Newcastle Journal* in 1739. The new types which the *Weekly Worcester Journal* began to use in 1742 were smaller than had been used before. The *Norwich Mercury* had used small but clear type in 1727; by 1743, the standard type was even smaller, and smaller still in 1751. By 1751, *Adams's Weekly Courant* was using smaller

type than before. The *York Courant* used distressingly small type from 1754 on. In 1755, both the *Newcastle Journal* and the *Newcastle Courant* used very small type, much smaller than that being used in the *Newcastle Intelligencer,* obviously because they both had twice or three times as many advertisements as the *Intelligencer.*

16. A few of the earliest papers were carelessly set—the *Manchester News-Letter,* for example—and in some shops the types were dirty. In the only surviving issue of the *Salisbury Post-Man,* the printer asked his readers not to take notice of "the foulness of the Character," but he explained that the types had been damaged in transit and would take some time for cleaning.

17. In the second issue of his *Newcastle Courant* (4 August 1711), John White announced that his shop was "furnish'd with great Variety of Letters and Presses" and that he had "all requisite help and Assistance." He said he was prepared to print books, subpoenas, watch warrants, certificates for burying in woolen, "Pennances, &c."

18. In the *Ipswich Journal,* number 415 (27 July 1728), John Bagnall's compositor used *vv* instead of *w* on the last page.

19. Bryan was sometimes not in his shop while the compositor's work was being checked, and he often had to apologize for errors. In number 1430 (19 November 1736), for example, he inserted this note: "N.B. Our Readers are desir'd to to correct several literal Mistakes in the 2d and 3d Pages of this Paper, that happen'd yesterday in the Printer's Absence, and overlook'd by his Men."

20. One of the few instances of local news printed on the first page instead of on the third page of a four-page paper is to be seen in the *Colchester Journal,* number 334 (17 August 1739). There, after one and a quarter columns of foreign affairs, the first page has eight separate paragraphs under the prominent heading, *"COLCHESTER, Aug. 17."* See also note 39 in this chapter.

21. See below, p. 256, for reference to the use of large type for a caption in this paper.

22. Aris had declared in his first issue (16 November 1741) that he would spare no pains to make the paper agreeable, "having settled the best Correspondence I possibly could in London for that Purpose."

23. On the other hand, William Jackson, in 1753, drew special attention to the fact that his *Oxford Journal,* published on Saturdays, contained news headed "Saturday's Post [Received by an Express from London]." See above, p. 70, for claims made earlier by Jackson and his partner Robert Walker that Saturday's news from London reached them with "great Expedition."

24. The *Gloucester Journal,* number 999 (Tuesday, 23 June 1741), printed the postmaster-general's official announcement, dated at London, 10 June 1741, that the post would "pass and repass every Day in the Week, (Sundays excepted) between London, Norwich and Lynn, and between London and Yarmouth, and all the intermediate Towns in those Roads." A similar daily service was announced between London and

Bristol, the route passing through Oxford, Abingdon, Cirencester, Gloucester, and Bath. A thrice-weekly service between Bristol and Salisbury was also announced to begin "at midsummer next."

25. See below, pp. 108-9

26. Berrow alleged in his paper, on 15 November 1753, that Lewis had tried to obstruct the sale of *Berrow's Worcester Journal* by circulating a report in Bewdley, Kidderminister, and Stourbridge that Berrow's newsmen had left his service, and "at Pershore, Evesham, Campden, &c. a like Report was as industriously spread."

27. It is possible that, like the *London and Country Journal,* this paper was issued in two parallel series. The earliest recorded issue, number 3 (Thursday, 20 July 1738), was reported by J. P. Earwaker in *Local Gleanings of Lancashire & Cheshire,* I (1876), 236-37, as having been used as stuffing in the binding of the first volume of the parish register at Mottram-in-Longdendale, Cheshire. The copy, badly cropped but otherwise in good condition, is still in the library of the Vicarage at Mottram.

28. According to *The Traveller's Pocket Book* . . . (1763), pages 219-20, the charge for a post rider on any of the post roads was "Three Pence British Money for each Horse-hire for every English Mile and Four-pence for the Guide of every Stage."

29. Some derisive stanzas by "Philalethes" were printed in the *Oxford Gazette* in October, 1746, when the *Oxford Flying Weekly Journal* was still being published on Saturday. Under the title "Sunday's Post on Saturday Morning" the versifier declared that in the view of learned men miracles no longer took place.

> Say then, from whence their wondrous Skill
> Does *Walker* and his Partner borrow,
> That they *To-day* their Page can fill
> With all the Tidings of *To-morrow.*

All that Walker and Jackson needed, said "Philalethes," was credulity among their readers. The principle was simply this: *Si populus vult decipi, decipiatur.*

30. In 1752, C. Micklewright said that notices sent in after Saturday noon would not appear in the following Monday's *Oxford Gazette,* unless they concerned "Robberies, Losses, or other extraordinary Cases."

31. On the strength of Timperley's *Dictionary of Printers and Printing* (London: Johnson, 1839), modern historians suggest that two men could handle 250 sheets an hour. See Ellic Howe, *The London Compositor* (London: Bibliographical Society, 1947), p. 95; see also D. Nichol Smith, "The Newspaper," *Johnson's England,* ed. A. S. Turberville (2nd ed.; Oxford: Clarendon Press, [1952]), II, 334, and Robert L. Haig, *The Gazetteer 1735-1797* (Carbondale, Ill.: Southern Illinois University Press, [1960]), p. 32. A heading block in *Harrop's Manchester Mercury,* number 9 (28 April 1752), shows two men working a press.

32. Because a careless compositor noticed too late that he had neglected to change the initial in the factotum block of the *Salisbury*

Journal, number 62 (3 April 1739), it was necessary to add this request to the fourth page: *"In the first Word of the first column of this Paper for ROHN read JOHN."*

33. In the *Worcester Post-Man,* number 335 (25 November 1715), one of the standard captions was inadvertently left in place when it should have been removed. Above the first line of news are these three lines:

> From the News-Letter and other Intelligence.
> Saturday's and Monday's Post.
> The Foreign Mails bring us the following Advices.

But there is no foreign news in this issue of the paper.

34. One of these lists as to be sold or to be let for a term of years "the House that Sam. Farley, Printer now lives in."

35. The inserted half-sheet, which normally had the serial number of the issue at the top of the third page, is missing from many surviving issues of the *Plymouth Weekly Journal.*

36. Page 5 in number 136 (10 July 1724) of the *Plymouth Weekly Journal* has the usual catchword, "Friday's," but in the copy at the Plymouth Proprietary Library the sixth page is blank. Perhaps the final batch of mail arrived so late that the printer decided to go to press without it; or this particular half-sheet was missed in the printing of its second side.

37. As long as the *Norwich Gazette* had six pages, the second page invariably had at the bottom the catchword "Thursday" and the fourth page invariably had the catchword "Saturday." Obviously the fifth page was set last, for the sixth page (as well as the second column of the fifth page) was filled with advertisements, which could be set and printed before the last post arrived. When final press time came, then, Crossgrove had only to run off one side of one half-sheet.

38. In this and other issues of the *Worcester Post-Man* the fourth page regularly had the catchword "Thurs-." To save time, page 5 was set in smaller type than was used on the first four pages so that all the late news could be printed on that one side of the half-sheet.

39. A less common arrangement is seen in the *Kentish Post,* which for many years had its earliest news on the second and third pages, with a catchword connecting the two. The next dispatches to come from London went on page 1 and the latest of all on the fourth page, which also carried the Canterbury news. Advertisements were distributed on the first, third, and fourth pages, this distribution apparently being the one that was most convenient for a paper that appeared twice a week. If the fourth page was fully occupied by advertisements, the latest and the local news went on the first page.

40. For example, *Williamson's Liverpool Advertiser Extraordinary* was published on Sunday, 21 October 1759.

41. The copy of number 671 at the Gloucester Public Library has the corrected statement: "Thomas and Henry Archer, Esqrs. Petitioners, are voted duly Elected for Warwick."

Chapter III

VOL. II.

NUMB. 30.

THE Northampton Mercury.

The Southwest PROSPECT

Kingsthorpe

MONDAY, *November* 20, 1721. [*To be continued Weekly.*]

NORTHAMPTON:

Printed by *R. Raikes* and *W. Dicey.* Of whom may be had Land Tax Receipts, Affeffors Warrants, Funeral Affidavits, &c. Likewife all manner of Stationary Wares, as Shop-books, Pocket-books, Paper, Pens, Ink, Wax, &c. Likewife Dr. *Bateman's* Pectoral Drops. and *Radcliffe's* Purging Elixir : The firft fam'd for the Colic, Pains in the Limbs and Joints, Agues, and all Ailments of the Breaft and Bowels. The fecond is the very beft of purging Medicines ; witnef the many Certificates we daily receive from our Readers and their Friends. Thefe Medicines are fold at 12 *d.* the Bottle, with printed Directions how to take them, and Certificates of their Cures.

(Price of the Mercury Three Half Pence.)

Distribution and Profits

WILKINS MICAWBER might find happiness in a favorable difference of sixpence between annual income and annual expenditure, but no printer of newspapers could sleep at night with so narrow a margin between solvency and misery. One of the most puzzling things about the early weekly newspapers is this: how could a newspaper selling for three halfpence a copy yield a livelihood to those who produced it and a profit to those whose investment and enterprise got it started? The investment must have run into many pounds. Even at its barest minimum, the publishing of a newspaper in any eighteenth-century English country town required space in a building, a printing press with fonts of type and a few cuts, supplies of paper and ink, and enough practised hands to attend to all operations in the process of producing a paper once a week or oftener—gathering the news and other matter to fill the columns, setting the type, making up the forms, running the paper twice through the manually operated press, folding the sheets, carrying the printed copies to those wishing to buy them, and sorting the type for use in printing the next issue. It is conceivable that in a small

FIG. 4.—Title page with list of commodities sold by the printers of the *Northampton Mercury*. (By permission of the Northampton Public Libraries Committee.)

shop one man with a boy to help him could do all these things, but what profit could there be unless he sold thousands? Did both E. Verral and W. Lee make money week by week from their *Sussex Weekly Advertiser*? What income from the *Salisbury Journal* reached the unnamed members of the firm of Benjamin Collins and Company? What profits reached the pockets of Mr. Akenhead and "the rest of the Partners" who controlled the *New-Castle Weekly Mercury*? The *Newcastle Journal* was printed by John Gooding from November, 1742; the four proprietors of that paper were identified in the issue of 24 September 1743 as Isaac Thompson, Jonathan Walker, Peregrine Tyzack, and Robert Thorp. Did all five of these men make enough to live on from the paper? Unless the proprietor of a country newspaper was a perennial granter of subsidies to a losing enterprise, most of the papers enumerated in the Register at the end of this volume must have sold at the rate of many hundreds, probably thousands, weekly.

There is little evidence to indicate how many copies of any one issue of a provincial newspaper were printed in the period 1700-1760. The Rev. Thomas Tanner, who later became Bishop of St. Asaph, observed to a correspondent in 1706 that Francis Burges, printer of the *Norwich Post,* cleared nearly fifty shillings every week, selling "vast numbers to the country people." [1] In 1715, Joseph Bliss, printer of the *Protestant Mercury* in Exeter, made the confident assertion in the twelfth issue (dated 10 February) that his paper "circulated Forty Miles round, and several hundreds dispers'd every Week." At the end of the *Northampton Mercury*'s first year, the printers asked their readers to excuse a delay of an hour or two in the publishing of that particular issue (number 52 of volume I, 24 April 1721), "since the prodigious Increase thereof demands a longer time than usual for the Press." It was the same two printers, Raikes and Dicey, who at precisely the same stage in their next

paper—the *Gloucester Journal,* number 53 (8 April 1723)
—thanked their readers for enabling them "in the Space
of Twelve Months, to print some Hundreds (Weekly)
more . . . than the paper printed at *Worcester.*" In 1732,
William Cooke declared in a note under the date line of
his *Chester Weekly Journal* that the paper, by then over
ten years old, was carried through nine counties and that
"some Thousands" were sold each week. A firmer figure
stands in number 15 (14 July 1739) of the *Newcastle
Journal,* in which Isaac Thompson and William Cuthbert
declared that they were by then selling "nearly 2000 of
these Papers weekly"; and in *Whitworth's Manchester
Magazine,* number 3136 (13 June 1755), the statement
was made that eleven hundred copies of the preceding
week's issue of that paper had been printed ("a larger
Number than is printed of any other News Paper
published near this Place . . . ").

These figures and such terms as "vast numbers" and
"some Thousands" would be more convincing if paper-
stock ledgers or other business records of the printers
survived to confirm or elucidate them. If Tanner's figure
is trustworthy, the *Norwich Post* must have sold very
well to clear nearly £2 10s. from the sale of each issue.
If the *Norwich Post* sold for a penny, the gross return
from the sale of one thousand copies would amount to
only £4 3s. 4d. Out of that would have to come the
paper-maker's charge for five hundred whole sheets of
paper, the wages of all who had a hand in the printing and
distributing of the *Post,* and a proper share of the annual
payments for rent, candles, heat (if any), and deprecia-
tion of equipment. Could Burges have managed to realize
a profit of £2 10s. unless he sold many more than a
thousand copies?

Several early papers give no indication of their selling
price, but generally speaking the country newspapers sold
for three halfpence up to 1725, for twopence from 1725
to 1757, and for twopence halfpenny from 1757 until the

next increase in the stamp tax. There were exceptions, for some early papers are known to have sold for a penny, and at least six papers in the 1725-57 period sold for three halfpence. As late as 1748, Ward's *Bristol Mercury* was marked "Price ONE PENNEY." A few printers thought it expedient to offer the first issue or two *gratis,* so that people might be lured into taking it regularly. Even after eight months of publication, the *Doncaster Flying-Post* in 1755 carried at the foot of its first page the note: "This Paper is given Gratis." Possibly the proprietor was receiving financial support from a political party, but in any case he escaped the halfpenny tax by not charging for the paper.

When Henry Cross-grove announced in January, 1707, that any postmen or letter carriers who were willing to sell his *Norwich Gazette* in the towns and villages along their regular routes would be supplied with copies at threepence a dozen, he did so presumably in order that the papers might be sold for a halfpenny instead of a penny, for two months later he said that "the Ingenious and Generous Encouragers" of the *Gazette* had advised him to "raise it to its former Price." At the end of that year, as was mentioned in Chapter I, Cross-grove again reduced the price to a halfpenny, but this time he and the proprietor, Samuel Hasbart, suffered the loss of income because they were determined to squeeze the proprietor of another Norwich paper into bankruptcy or enforced partnership. Perhaps here again there was financial backing by a political party, for Cross-grove wrote with vigor and tenacity in support of the Tories. When the Stamp Tax was firmly imposed in 1725, the price became three halfpence, and it remained so for the next quarter-century. Perhaps it was assistance from the same party that enabled Cross-grove's successor, R. Davy, to charge the same low price for his *Norwich Journal,* of which only one issue, dated 2 June 1753, remains.

With or without the aid of subventions provided by a

political party, the printer's income rose as circulation increased and fell if anything caused the circulation to shrink. Buyers' resistance to the newspaper stamp tax affected adversely the circulation of most papers both in 1725 and in 1757, as the printers' complaints testify. Andrew Brice, of Exeter, may not have been the greatest sufferer, but he was certainly the most eloquent in expressing his dissatisfaction over the tax and its effects on his income. In number 23 (15 October 1725) of his *Weekly Journal,* established in April, 1725, to replace the former *Post-master,* he tried to put a touch of whimsicality into his observations about the "wide Sweep of the fatal Besom," but it is clear that his sales and therefore his profits had been considerably reduced by the tax. Brice could not evade the tax; he resolved to make greater efforts than ever to please the customers he still had, though he had been relieved of "above Half the Burthen of former Profit" and no longer had "the Fatigue of serving so many Customers." It was a plain and disturbing fact that a vast number would not pay "the imposed What-d'ye-call-it; as perhaps not seeing the great Necessity thereof in time of profound Peace." Brice had warned his readers in advance that the price would be increased by sixpence a quarter, and declared that "according to a moderate Computation" the amount he would have to pay in duty to the King would be "above 100 £ per Annum more than ordinary." The figure is only approximate, but it gives a hint about the normal circulation of the *Post-master.* Brice had presumably been registering his *Post-master* as a sheet-and-a-half pamphlet, paying three shillings for each week's whole issue, or nearly eight pounds per annum. If his "moderate Computation" was at all realistic, he expected to have to transmit to the Commissioners of the Stamp Office more than £108 a year, or well over two pounds a week. At a halfpenny per copy that round figure implies an average weekly edition of nearly a thousand copies. If there were a thou-

99

sand customers, an increase in the selling price of sixpence a quarter—two shillings per annum—would wipe out the expected deficit of £100.

The tax could not, of course, be absorbed by the printer; it had to be added to the price charged, not because the law required it, but because no margin of profit could absorb a tax amounting to one third or one quarter of the selling price. It was simple arithmetic, exasperating but inescapable. The shift of price resulting from the tax is seen in the *Newcastle Weekly Courant,* which sold for three halfpence while it was an untaxed twelve-page paper, and for two pence when it changed to a four-page paper bearing a halfpenny stamp. In 1757, the extra halfpenny of tax raised the price again by just that much. Some printers tried to keep to a basic price of one penny plus tax, but few could continue long at that rate. The price of the earlier *Stamford Mercury,* unlike that of most other pre-1725 papers, remained at three halfpence in spite of the 1725 tax, and that was the selling price set by Francis Howgrave when he started his own *Mercury* in the same town in 1732; but after four years, Howgrave found that he had to increase the price to twopence. *Adams's Weekly Courant* likewise sold for three halfpence, and this price was raised only in 1757, when Elizabeth Adams, the proprietor, apologetically informed her readers, in number 1263 (5 July 1757), that the price would thereafter have to be twopence. From that date onward, one whole penny had to be paid in advance for the stamp on each half sheet. The paper itself cost one farthing, she said, and the newsmen were allowed one halfpenny for each copy they disposed of. It plainly appeared from these figures that there was "no more than One Farthing to defray the great Expence of Printing, procuring Intelligence, &c. &c." Behind that double ampersand lurked also Elizabeth Adams's profits, which can hardly have paid for her cups of tea. How could anyone run a newspaper on a farthing?

This same question must have caused Thomas Aris of Birmingham many a sleepless night. For nearly a year and a half after starting his *Birmingham Gazette* in 1741, Aris had struggled to overcome his persistent and resourceful rival, Robert Walker, who from the first had irritated him by printing his *Warwick and Staffordshire Journal* in Birmingham [2] before Aris's shop was ready for occupancy and annoyed him still more by selling his paper for three halfpence. Believing that the local people would not pay more than that for his *Gazette* but hoping that eventually they would recognize the superiority of his paper, Aris set his price at three halfpence and lost money week after week. By the end of June, 1743, it was clear to both Aris and Walker that their contest was profitable to no one except the buyers of their newspapers. The price had to be raised. In *Aris's Birmingham Gazette*, number 86 (4 July 1743), Aris assured his customers that he had already lost a considerable sum by selling the paper for three halfpence. Then came his summary analysis of the costs of producing and distributing it:

> That a great deal of Money may be sunk in a very little Time by a Publication of this Nature, cannot seem strange to anyone who considers, that out of every Paper one Half-penny goes to the Stamp-Office, and another to the Person who sells it; that the Paper it is printed on costs a Farthing; and that consequently no more than a Farthing remains to defray the Charges of Composing, Printing, London News Papers, and meeting, as far as Daventry, the Post; which last Article is very expensive; not to mention the Expence of our London Correspondence.

Once again, how could a newspaper be profitably produced for a farthing?

Aris's margin of profit was minute. So, for that matter, was Walker's; but at this time Walker was making a good income from the sale of books in weekly fascicules, often using these in combination with his various newspapers.[3] The two rivals agreed that one paper in Birmingham was enough, and that three halfpence was not enough to charge for it. "The Truth is," wrote Aris, "I had no Design originally of attempting the printing a News-Paper for Three Half-pence; but another Paper being publish'd at that Price by Mr. Walker, obliged me to submit to the same Terms; tho' now we are both sufficiently convinced that we were in the wrong, and think it high Time to drop the Opposition, and unite both Papers in one." Thereafter, for many years, *Aris's Birmingham Gazette* was the only Birmingham newspaper, the imprint no longer reading "Printed by T. Aris . . . " but "Printed by T. Aris and Comp. . . . " [4] The price was two pence.

Set forth in tabulated form, the inescapable out-of-pocket expenditures for producing a thousand copies of *Aris's Birmingham Gazette* or any other four-page newspaper of the time would be these:

1. A due proportion of the annual "overhead" for premises and equipment.

2. The wages of the type-setter, pressman, and helpers.

3. The cost of 1,000 half-sheets of paper.

4. £2 1s. 8d. for the stamps impressed on these half-sheets.

5. The carriage charges for bringing the stamped paper from London.

6. The cost of procuring news (subscriptions to London and other newspapers, fees paid to special correspondents in London and perhaps elsewhere, charges for riding to meet the post).

7. The fees or allowances to distributors.

From the sale of one thousand copies of *Aris's Birmingham Gazette* at three halfpence, there would be a gross return of only £6 5s. 0d. For the stamped paper alone, exactly half of this sum had already been paid before a single piece had been put into the press.

This paying in advance for stamped paper was required of all printers of newspapers, whether their printing shops were in London or in the country. It undoubtedly caused special hardship to Aris and other printers living many miles from the only source of supply, the London warehouse of the Commissioners of Stamps. A London printer of newspapers had only to send a boy with a barrow to the warehouse in Serle Court, Lincoln's Inn, and he did not need to buy more than he expected to use in a week or a fortnight. A provincial printer would not only have to pay higher carriage charges than the Londoner; he waited longer for his shipments and had to lay in a much larger stock or run the risk of finding himself without paper when press time came. For country printers of newspapers there was the additional embarrassment of having to ship back to London any unsold copies in order to claim a rebate on the stamps. The London printer could easily and immediately and at negligible cost get a credit for the stamps on his left-over copies by having one of his boys take them back to the Stamp Office in Lincoln's Inn Fields.[5]

Whether the fault was the printer's in not ordering the paper soon enough, or the London warehouseman's in not having adequate stocks on hand, or the carrier's in not traveling swiftly enough, it happened repeatedly that the printer's paper cupboard was bare when press time came. What was he to do? Postpone or cancel the issue? Pay the tax in a lump sum? Brief postponement seemed reasonable to William Norris of Taunton, whose *Journal* in its fifty-first week came out on Saturday, 7 May 1726, one day later than usual. In the *Leeds Mercury*, number 726 (8 January 1740), the printer, James Lister, explained that "being disappointed of a Parcel of Stampt Paper for the News, which should have come to hand by Samuel Fenton, the London Carrier, on Saturday the 29th past," he had printed the *Mercury* on unstamped paper, and that since it was illegal to sell unstamped newspapers he was giving the paper *gratis*. Thomas Aris announced in number 16 (1 March 1742) of his *Birmingham Gazette* that, having been disappointed in the receipt of stamped paper from London, he was using unstamped stock and added that he had informed the distributor of stamps, "to whom an Oath will be taken of the Quantity sold and the Duty paid accordingly." This practice was followed in other towns.

It is greatly to be regretted that not one of these sworn statements about the "quantity sold" has as yet come to light, for there could be no more convincing evidence of the circulation of the papers concerned. It is probable that copies of such statements, with exact figures—certainly they would not be exaggerated—are hidden among the papers in various local solicitors' offices, for it was undoubtedly to the local officer, not to the Commissioners in London, that payments and affidavits were sent. It is reasonable to assume that Aris paid the due amount to John Smith, the distributor of stamps in the Birmingham area in 1742. A reference in the *Norwich Mercury,* on 9 April 1757, clears up any doubt, for in that issue William Chase, Jr., stated that instead of waiting for a supply of paper with the extra stamp impressed on it, he would be permitted to make use of what "Half-Penny Stamps" he had in stock, "on making Affidavit of the Number, and paying the additional Duty to the Distributor of the Stamps in this City."

Probably not many London printers of newspapers filed such affidavits, for they would undoubtedly be able to procure stamped paper if they wished to use it. On this supposition the Audit Office figure showing the gross produce from the duty on unstampt newspapers for the year ending 2 August 1742 [6] may be taken to cover only Thomas Aris's payment and similar payments from a few other provincial printers who during the fiscal year from 2 August 1741 to 2 August 1742 had filed statements that they had on one or more occasions used unstamped paper.

The amount recorded for the whole year was only £16 6s., representing payment in lieu of halfpenny stamps on 7,824 copies. It is impossible to conjecture how many of these were Aris's. The figures for the year ending 2 August 1758 are no more helpful, though they show that the new additional halfpenny tax had brought in £25 3s. 1/2d. (representing 12,073 copies) and that the former half-penny tax had brought in £19 7s. 8d. (representing 9,304 copies) from printers who either had no stamped paper at all or had to use paper with only the original halfpenny stamp. Again there is no way of discovering which particular papers are represented in these figures, though on at least two occasions within this period (on 11 November 1757 and on 10 February 1758) the *Liverpool Chronicle* was published on unstamped paper.

Among the provincial printers caught unprovided with paper bearing the double stamp in July, 1757, was William Craighton, of Ipswich, who had on hand "near 10,000 Half-penny Stamps"—over thirty pounds' worth, if the cost of the paper is included—a figure which probably shows the normal stock of stamped paper in a flourishing provincial newspaper office. Craighton had been advised by a friend in London to use up these ten thousand half-sheets bearing halfpenny stamps; but he said in number 965 (9 July 1757) that the officer in the country had received no instructions about the matter. He said that with some difficulty and extraordinary expense he had procured a parcel of paper with double stamps for that week's issue of the paper, but was "several Hundreds" short of the number he would have been willing to print in spite of expected shrinkage in circulation because of the increased price. In the same issue Craighton reprinted with approval one sentence from a letter signed "Britannicus" in the *London Evening Post* of 19 May foretelling that because of the increased tax "many of the News-Papers in Town, and most, if not all, in the Country, would be dropp'd." "Britannicus" and Craighton were both wrong. While circulation was undoubtedly affected, not a single country newspaper known to have been appearing regularly in June, 1757, ceased publication within the next six months; thirty-seven of those which were being issued in 1757 were still appearing three years later, and most of them continued from many years after that.[7]

Craighton's anxiety about not having enough paper with double stamps to supply his regular subscribers was experienced by other printers of newspapers, but several of them did not hestitate to go on using their stocks of single-stamped paper, paying the difference in a lump sum. Joseph Harrop raised the price of his *Manchester Mercury* to twopence with number 278 (12 July 1757), but he did not begin using paper with the double stamp until number 281 (2 August 1757). On that same date the *Gloucester Journal* carried at the foot of its front page the note that, "This Journal being printed with the Old Stamp," the additional duty would be paid "on Oath."

Naturally there were strong objections to the paying of the additional duty. Hervey Berrow in his *Worcester Journal,* number 2446 (30 June 1757), requested all readers to pay the new price, $2\frac{1}{2}d.$, regularly every week, adding that the "great Loss and Inconvenience" caused by the additional duty would not permit him to continue the practice of making some allowance to those who paid for the newspaper by the quarter. Berrow made a strong point of his having to pay in advance:

> And it may be necessary to observe, as a material Argument for its being paid for Weekly, that the Stamp'd Paper (which will come to near Three Fifths of the Money the Newspaper is to be sold for) must be purchased in a Quantity sufficient for several Weeks' Sale, and the whole of it paid for before any Part of it will be deliver'd from the Stamp Office in London.

This probably represents the special anxiety of most of

the provincial printers whose papers nevertheless survived the extra burden of tax in 1757.

Many a printer in towns far distant from London must
have felt tempted to use plain paper for at least part of
each issue, running the risk of detection and a heavy
fine.[8] In earlier years unstamped papers were sold in
defiance of the law both in London and in the country.
Those who sold them ran great risks, and there were
many arrests, as notices in the newspapers testify.[9] This
particular illegal traffic became so extensive that in 1743
an act was passed (16 George 2, c. 26) imposing a penalty
of three months' imprisonment and offering twenty shillings reward to informers.

In spite of the risk, provincial printers themselves were
occasionally guilty of evading the tax by using unstamped
paper for all or part of the weekly issues.[10] Samuel Worrall, the distributor of stamps in Gloucestershire, must
have had a particular reason for publishing in the *Bristol
Oracle* of 27 June 1747 a warning against the selling of
unstamped newspapers. According to a statement by
Frederick Leary in an article entitled "Manchester Journalism in the Eighteenth Century,"[11] Robert Whitworth,
printer of an important Manchester newspaper, "pleaded
guilty at Lancaster assizes in 1735 to an indictment for
uttering counterfeit stamped paper." This may not have
had anything to do with Whitworth's newspaper, for it
is difficult to see how he could counterfeit the newspaper
tax stamp on hundreds of copies, unless he went to the
trouble of copying the design on copper or wood.

The original records of Whitworth's case remain hidden;
but the search for them led to the discovery of official
records concerning earlier charges against William Cooke
of Chester, not for uttering counterfeit stamped paper,
but for selling two different newspapers, neither of them
bearing stamps. The several charges were laid by Roger
Adams and his son John. Roger had been the founder
and printer of Manchester's first newspaper, and, from

1732 onward, was the printer of *Adams's Weekly Courant* in Chester. The details of the charges against the well-established Cooke are set forth with the utmost clarity in documents now in the Public Record Office in Chancery Lane and among the archives at the Town Clerk's Office in Chester.

Because these records of conviction reveal the existence of two hitherto unknown provincial newspapers, and because they probably represent the kind of tax dodging that was tried in other places, it is worth noting the developments of the two cases. The files of the Portmote Court at Chester for the year 1733-34 contain a declaration[12] signed by Roger Adams on 18 February 1734 that on 28 November 1733 Cooke had sold or exposed to sale number 17 of a newspaper contained in two unstamped half-sheets of paper and entitled *The Industrious Bee, or Weekly Entertainer. Containing Something to hit every Man's Taste and Principles Being more in Quantity than any Thing of the Kind Published at the Price.* Number 17 was dated "From Wednesday November 21 to Wednesday November 28, 1733." Citing the earlier of the two Stamp Acts (10 Anne, c. 19), Adams petitioned the mayor and the recorder of Chester, who were justices of the peace, to issue a summons to Cooke and warrants for the calling in of witnesses. A note dated "23rd ffeby. 1733" at the foot of the page indicates that the defendant was acquitted. But Roger Adams persisted, guided perhaps only by an honest desire to have Cooke's dishonesty halted, perhaps by a determination to make his rival obedient to the same law as bound himself, perhaps by a yearning to receive half the fine, as the Act promised. On 30 March 1734, he renewed the charge, citing two later issues of the *Industrious Bee*—numbers 22 (2 January 1734) and 23 (9 January 1734)—and declaring that Cooke should be made to pay ten pounds for *each* offense, as the Act provided, plus the costs of suit. Accordingly the summons was issued, and Cooke appeared on 20 April 1734. The court found him not guilty of printing, selling, or exposing to sale the issue numbered 22, but did find him guilty of exposing to sale number 23. They reduced the fine to fifty shillings, half to go to the King, half to Adams as informer, together with costs amounting to £4 2s. 2d. Cooke, not satisfied with this unaccountable leniency, appealed to the next sitting of the court, but the original judgment was confirmed, Cooke being required to pay as well a second bill of costs amounting to £4 7s. 7d.

The other unstamped newspaper which William Cooke was accused of selling[13] was entitled *The Chester Weekly Tatler. Containing the Freshest Advices foreign and Domestick, with a New Voyage round the world.* This time the charge was laid by Roger Adams's eldest son, John,[14] who asserted that on 18 September 1734 Cooke had sold a paper with this title. The record of the indictment, now in the Public Record Office,[15] indicates that the summons was issued and was served on Cooke by Elias Williams on Wednesday, 12 February 1735. The justices heard the charge and Cooke's defense on the following Saturday and declared that in their judgment Cooke was guilty. He was ordered to pay a fine of £10 and costs of twenty shillings.[16] These shady efforts can hardly be excused on the ground that the saving was to be passed on to the customers; Cooke apparently found his margin of profit too small and in a quiet effort to make a dishonest pound he lost many times the amount he hoped to gain.

More honorable and usually more successful methods of increasing the net income from the sale of a newspaper were aimed at extending its circulation by making it easier for people to get the paper or by making it more worth the getting. The substance of a newspaper naturally had a good deal to do with its success or failure; if the news was both fresh and accurate, if there was information about prices, books, bankrupts, births, deaths, marriages, preferments, shipping, public health, entertainments, if there were special features such as serialized matter or anagrams or problems in trigonometry, if there were contributed essays in prose and verse, if there were controversial exchanges and editorial observations, if the paid advertisements were numerous and diverting, the paper would have good reason to succeed. Either because the quality of the regular elements left something to be desired or because competition made it imperative to seek extraneous means of keeping the circulation from dropping, some proprietors offered their regular customers a "premium" or else supplied a detachable supplement which could be kept, week by week, and bound into a book.[17]

These inducements or rewards were sometimes offered at a reduced charge or were limited to enrolled subscribers, much as subscribers to a modern newspaper may purchase life insurance for a few extra pennies per week. In February, 1744, William Dicey of the *Northampton Mercury* offered "to constant Readers only" a map of Dunkirk at the low price of threepence. Sometimes the "premium" was supplied gratis. William Carnan advertised in the *London Evening Post,* number 1370 (28 August 1736), that his *Reading Mercury; Or, the London Spy* would regularly have a portion of Ned Ward's popular work on its front page, and that along with each issue would be delivered a sheet containing an account of the history and antiquities of Berkshire, "printed on a superfine Paper, and in such manner as to be fit to bind up." In 1749, R. Davy gave readers of the *Norwich Gazette* a cumulative gift of music and drama, announcing in number 2222 (23 September 1749),

> Next Saturday, to oblige my Friends, [I] shall give with this Paper half a Sheet of Songs, and to continue weekly 'till Christmas, at which Time will be deliver'd an Act of a Play, weekly, 'till compleated, then half a Sheet of Songs, 'till Lady [Day], the whole Collection being of the newest and celebrated Songs now extant, and sung at the Playhouses and publick Gardens in London.

That sort of thing was done by printers in other towns. These special offers undoubtedly cost the printers something, at least for paper; the expense was probably justified as a means of extending the circulation or maintaining it in the face of competition.

The issuing of detachable supplements was a device used frequently by Robert Walker to make his customers think they were getting wonderfully good value for their pennies each week. Some of Walker's supplements were nominally free; others had a price on them. When Walker and T. James established the first newspaper in Cambridge in 1744, they delivered portions of *The Life and Reign of her late Majesty Queen Anne,* "given **Gratis,**" charging twopence for the newspaper. With issues of their *Oxford Flying Weekly Journal* (1746-49), Walker and William Jackson delivered free of charge octavo half-sheet portions of Francis Midon's *History of . . . Masaniello,* of Lillo's *London Merchant,* of Fielding's *The Mock Doctor,* and of J. Nalson's *Trial of King Charles the First.* As usual, Walker gave in order to gain. His most widely issued supplement was Laurence Clarke's *History of the Holy Bible,* which was attached to the *London and Country Journal* and to at least five other papers, practically identical except in title, intended for circulation in Shropshire, Derbyshire, Warwickshire, Staffordshire, Lancashire, and Northamptonshire. With one exception, all of these "provincial" papers were printed in Walker's London shop, and the cost of production was thereby kept to a minimum, since the supplements, like the works issued independently in fascicules, could be run off in large quantities at times when the press was not being used for printing news.

In an earlier venture than the papers printed by Walker in Oxford and Cambridge, this enterprising man quite frankly used his newspapers as bait to lure people to buy the weekly numbers of the many books he published in that form. Notices in the *Warwick and Staffordshire Journal* show that at one period, if not throughout its existence, this paper was issued merely as a wrapper for the weekly quarto sheet of a work named in the subtitle. In number 148 of the Thursday series (1 June 1740), for example, the initial weekly numbers of the *Works* of Josephus and of Laurence Clarke's *Compleat and Full History of . . . Jesus Christ* were announced as to appear the following week. Then came this statement: "These Works will be separately publish'd, in Numbers, Weekly, At the Price of Two Pence. . . . Each Number will be stitch'd in Paper, on which will be printed the Whole Week's News, Foreign and Domestick, of the [latest?] Date; stamped in the same manner as has been done. . . ."

Three years earlier, Walker had clung to the hope that the Commissioners of Stamps would look upon these printed covers as not subject to the regular newspaper tax because they were not sold separately as newspapers. For a time he issued his free half-sheet of news without stamps. The issue of the *Warwick and Staffordshire Journal* dated Saturday, 29 October 1737, had a note addressed "To the Customers of this Work [*The History of the Holy Bible*]":

> There having been some Talk made by Persons as that this Work would not be finish'd, and that it would be oblig'd to be dropt on Account of its not being stamp'd on the News Part. This is therefore to assure my Customers, that the said Report is scandalous, and without Foundation; and farther to assure them, that it is publish'd in London in the like Manner; and in no ways molested by the Commissioners of the Stamp Duties. . . .

It was not until ten months later that the Commissioners of the Stamp Office succeeded in compelling Walker to use stamped paper for his news-covers.

Survival in business depends on many things; in newspapers the *sine qua non* is circulation. Competition was serious in eighteenth-century London where, as the century advanced, dozens of different papers were offered for sale on the streets and in the shops every week. In the country the competition was less keen, but only because the area was so much greater, and this gave country printers a specific item of expense which did not trouble the London printer of newspapers. As Craighton of Ipswich said in 1757, the London printers sent no hawkers to distant places. It is important to remember that. Without wide distribution, regional rather than purely local, few provincial newspapers could carry on, and no one's territory was exclusive.

Yet lists of towns and counties served can hardly be accepted as convincing evidence of large circulation, for bluffing and window-dressing are normal resources of competitors, no matter what their trade and no matter in what century they practice it. One need not take too literally the good-natured exchange of boasting by the proprietors of the *Stamford Mercury* and the *Northampton Mercury* shortly after the latter was established in 1720. In their fourth issue, dated 24 May 1720, Robert Raikes and William Dicey, who had given over their newspaper ventures at St. Ives, announced to readers of their new Northampton paper that they were not in the least disturbed to hear of the neighboring editor's enmity over their having spoiled his circulation: " . . . as for Mr. Stamford, we fear him not. . . . And we must let him know that our Paper will serve for the end, after Reading, which his is scarce fit for before since his Sense is so little, and the Paper so bad." In their next issue Raikes and Dicey bluntly declared,

> This Paper goes further in length, than any other Country News-Paper in England, and takes weekly the Counties of Bedford, Berks, Buckingham, Cambridge, Derby, Essex, Hertford, Huntingdon, Leicester, Lincoln, Norfolk, Northampton, Nottingham, Oxford, Rutland, Stafford, Suffolk, and Warwick.

"But," they added, "we will not say it goes into Cheshire, Lancashire, Somersetshire, and Yorkshire, for fear we should romance, like our Stamford Neighbour, who gives out that no other Country Paper extends itself into half the Counties that his does, tho' our one touches all that he has nam'd, except the four last mention'd, which, by the bye, his two Papers[18] never reach."

On this point it is worth noting that there is more than one opinion about the propriety of arguing that the localities from which a newspaper's advertisements come will indicate with certainty the areas in which the paper regularly circulates. "The Stamford Mercurist has lately given himself an Air of notifying to the Publick how far his Paper circulates, by the remote Places from whence he sometimes (by chance) receives an Advertisement." So wrote Raikes and Dicey in their *Northampton Mercury* of 25 July 1720. "But," they continued, "he might with as much Truth have exemplify'd this, by the different Parts, from whence his foreign Advices come. For his News as often goes to Constantinople, as to many Places from whence he receives Advertisements. And this may easily be prov'd. We ourselves have had Advertisements from within a Mile of London, and Towns equally distant another way: But are not so much Masters of the Faculty as to assert that our Mercury goes thither."

Whatever truth there may have been in the rival claims by the Northampton and Stamford printers, there is no doubt that they and the printers of newspapers in other towns could succeed only if they induced large numbers of people to become regular subscribers. One of the most effective ways of inducing people to become regular customers was certainly that of maintaining prompt and uninterrupted delivery, both in the town of publication and in the surrounding area. What the reader wished was to get his copy of the paper as soon as possible after it was printed; what the printer wished was to have a standing arrangement for the prompt dispersal of a large proportion of the copies printed, together with a little band of lively hawkers working hard to sell the copies not regularly subscribed for. Grace White and Thomas Hammond, founders of York's earliest newspaper, obviously hoped to enlarge the solid body of regular subscribers to the *York Mercury* by pointing to early delivery as a clear advantage over casual buying of the paper. In the ninth issue of their second volume (18 April 1720), they invited all who were willing to take the paper quarterly to send in their names, "and they shall have 'em deliver'd every Monday Morning, before they are Cry'd about the City by the Hawkers." They also took care to indicate to possible buyers and subscribers that they had agents in twenty-seven other towns and villages in the surrounding district. All their agents are named, as are the agents of many other newspapers throughout the period.[19]

There should have been no difficulty in providing prompt distribution of a weekly paper within the limits of the town in which it was printed. The least aggressive printers could simply let it be known that interested persons could call in at the printing shop on press day and buy copies for themselves, paying cash over the counter, as is still done in many local newspaper offices. Or the printer could send bundles of each week's papers to two or three booksellers' shops in the same town; there the people who wished to take the paper regularly would soon discover that they could pick up their papers on publication day.

But it would be a very stupid and inert printer, indeed, who did not engage a corps of "mercuries" and hawkers to carry the papers through the town streets and into the public houses, bawling out the name and thrusting a copy into every outstretched hand, strictly for cash. On the faithful service of these hawkers depended to a large extent the commercial success of a local paper, and it must have been exasperating to printer and customer alike when the venders proved inefficient or untrustworthy. In the issue of his *Protestant Mercury* for 3 May 1717,

Joseph Bliss of Exeter printed some harsh words about one of his venders, whom he had had to discharge:

> One Dame Bedford (a Hawker that used to sell my News) being a very sottish and profane Person, and being weary of her continual Abuses, this is to give Notice that she sells the same no longer; and those that used to take it of her, may be supplied therewith for the future either by some other of my Hawkers, or by my Order.

Henry Cross-grove printed a similar notice in his *Norwich Gazette,* number 598 (22 March 1718): "Note, that the Fellow with the Crutches sells my News no longer, I having turn'd him out for several Abuses; therefore pray take Care of being deceiv'd." To find honest and reliable venders must have been difficult for the printers of most country newspapers.

The problem was much larger and certainly more difficult as the distribution extended along the roads outside the town and to other towns in the region. Here, as in the town of publication, there were two classes of buyer, the "customer," who had a standing order for the paper to be delivered at his house or left for him at a designated place, and the casual buyer, who was not a subscriber but walked to a shop for a copy of the paper or else bought it from a hawker on the street. Printers of newspapers were presumably eager to induce readers to become regular subscribers, but they would certainly wish also to dispose of many copies to casual buyers, who may in fact have been more numerous than those who paid for the paper quarterly. How did subscribers and casual buyers living six or sixteen or forty-six miles from Gloucester get their copies of the *Gloucester Journal?* This question, which may also be asked in respect of fifty other towns in which papers were printed, resolves itself into these alternatives: did the printer make use of delivery services already available, or did he entrust the distribution to his own employees? "Such Persons as think proper to take in the *York Courant* Quarterly," said Ward and Chandler in their number 692 (16 January 1739), "may have it sent, every Tuesday, to their Homes, at Two Shillings a Quarter." Whose hands actually carried the *York Courant* to the homes of the regular subscribers and sold copies to those who preferred to pay cash?

The answer to this question is often to be found in the imprints of the newspapers themselves, where agents are named. These names and addresses, placed in the imprint for the guidance of possible purchasers, now prove to be most valuable sources of information about distribution. Once the bundles of papers reached outlying towns, men and women of various trades acted as distributors. In 1723, the sellers of the *Leeds Mercury* included a grocer in Otley, a clockmaker in Skipton, a barber in Halifax, and a livery lace maker in Manchester. In 1743, the Sheffield agent of the *Derby Mercury* was Nicholas Hick, a schoolmaster. It titillates the fancy to imagine Master Hick operating a paper "route," as many schoolboys—but not schoolmasters—do in North America. But how were bundles of papers conveyed from Leeds to the Halifax barber and the Manchester lace maker?

Undoubtedly some country newspapers were sent to distant subscribers by post, and there is evidence that local postmasters assisted in the distribution. Even the earliest issues of the *Newcastle Journal* list eleven postmasters as distributors in a wide area: "Mr. Pattinson, Postmaster, in Carlisle, who also distributes to Brampton, Wigton, Annan, and Dumfries; . . . Mr. Fisher, Postmaster, in Cockermouth; . . . Mr. Birket, Postmaster, in Whitehaven, who also distributes to Workington; . . . Mr. Richardson, Postmaster, in Penrith, who also distributes to Hesket and Keswick; . . . Mr. Parkin, Postmaster, in Appleby; . . . Mr. Dalton, Postmaster, in Kirby-Steven; . . . Mr. Lamb, Postmaster, in Brough; . . . Mr. Holmes, Postmaster, in Bedale, who also distributes to Midlam, Askrigg, and Masham; . . . Mr. Grieve, Postmaster, in

Berwick, who distributes to Eymouth; . . . Mr. James Hunter, in Duns; . . . Mr. Maben, Postmaster, in Kelsoe."

The arrangements made with these postmasters in 1739 for the distribution of the *Newcastle Journal* were probably unofficial; an enterprising proprietor in Bristol was apparently able to make a firm arrangement with a man of considerable authority in the Post Office. In Andrew Hooke's *Bristol Oracle, and Country Intelligencer*, number 10 (14 May 1743), is a long statement announcing that in order to make the paper "the most extensive Country News-Paper in the three Kingdoms" Hooke had induced Ralph Allen, the proprietor of the cross-posts, to let him enjoy "the free Use of his Mails." Under Allen's patronage, said Hooke, the *Bristol Oracle* was being distributed "thro' all the Towns Westward and Northward from Exeter to Liverpool." By the following March the paper was "circulated Weekly by Post from Manchester in Lancashire to Leskard [*sic*] in Cornwall, throughout the Counties of Wilts, Hereford, Monmouth, and all South Wales." Nevertheless, in the eighteenth century the post was much less used for the conveyance of country newspapers than it was for the carrying of London newspapers (through the Clerks of the Roads), and much less than came to be the practice after low postal rates for all newspapers were granted in 1870.

There was one other established means of conveyance available to news publishers whose circulation was extensive. This was the local or the long distance "carrier," who on his regular trips transported goods of all sorts to people living along his route. Carriers were slow, but they were certainly numerous; the network of services in and out of the larger towns was really quite remarkable. For example, one whole page of *Felix Farley's Bristol Journal*, dated 17 August 1754, is given over to "A List of the Carriers that come into, and set out from, the City of Bristol. With the Days they keep, the Places they come from, and the Inns they put up at." The alphabetical index of places includes 162 cities, towns, and villages served by the hundred men and women who are named as operating carrier services from one or another of the twenty-five Bristol inns enumerated. In St. Thomas Street alone there were four inns—the Three Queens, the Three Kings, the White Lion, and the Bell—which served as calling stations for a total of twenty-nine services. A similar listing of the carriers serving Bristol in 1760 (in early issues of John Grabham's *Bristol Chronicle*) shows that many of the same men were still operating over the same routes and using the same inns as headquarters.

It is difficult to suppose that these carriers could have undertaken the delivery of newspapers one by one to houses along the way, since to do that would have caused intolerable delays, with no great financial gain to themselves. Carriers, nevertheless, are often mentioned in newspaper imprints. Three of the twenty persons listed in the *York Journal* on 19 April 1748 as sellers of the paper outside of York are specifically called carriers: "Mr. Bainbridge, Carrier, at Easingwold, Northallerton, Thirsk, &c., Mr. Jonathan Sweeting, Carrier, at Stoxley, Yarm, Guisbrough, Stockton, Sedgefield, Hartlepool, and other Places adjacent, and . . . Mr. John Newby, Carrier, at Halmsly." The printer concluded the list of venders with the statement that these twenty persons "and the other Carriers of this Paper" would accept advertisements and letters directed to him.

Evidently those "other Carriers" of the *York Journal* were men sent out expressly to deliver bundles of papers, and perhaps even single papers, to designated places. That inns or public houses served as local distributing stations is seen in the September and October, 1745, issues of *Whitworth's Manchester Magazine,* which have at the bottom of the fourth page the statement that "for the greater Expedition" the paper was carried to a large number of towns "by Men on Purpose," who called at twenty-eight places named, as well as many other small towns. Ten of the calling places were inns or public houses, among them the Black Bear at Chester, the Talbot at Ormskirk, and the Green Lattice at Warrington. In that same year Robert Walker and Thomas James regularly printed at the head of the first column in their *Cambridge Journal* a statement that they would make every effort to deliver the paper to all who sent their names and addresses. "All Persons living at a Distance from such Places as our Newsmen go thro'," they said, "may have them sent to Market Towns, or other Places where they shall appoint." The *Bath Advertiser* had been running for only a few months when the printer, Stephen Martin, explained in number 39 (10 July 1756) and following issues that country gentlemen who had asked him to send them his paper would have to let him know "how to have it directed, and where left for them, by the News-men, it being improper for the News-men to quit their regular Circuits, by turning out of their settled Paths."

At least one printer, Robert Goadby in Sherborne, tried to meet the demands of would-be customers "lying out of the Circuit of the News Carriers" by suggesting that they could be served regularly if one of their own number would pick up a supply at a nearby point:

> . . . This is to inform all such in the Counties of *Wilts, Dorset, Somerset, Devonshire,* and *Cornwall,* That the PROPRIETOR is ever willing to oblige even every single Person; but that it is impossible so to contrive the Circuits of the News Carriers, as to take in every House or Place: But if the Inhabitants of any such Parishes where this Paper is not at present carried, will be so kind as to send a Messenger to any Place where it is brought in its usual Circuit, for as many Papers as are wanted in the Parish, the PROPRIETOR will allow the Person who comes for them a Halfpenny on each Paper he takes, besides a further Allowance upon all the Pamphlets, Books, *&c.* which he can sell in the said Parishes.

Whether such do-it-yourself arrangements were found to be acceptable is not known, but that the printers themselves engaged "Men on Purpose" is made certain by numerous and unmistakable references in the newspapers themselves and in the printed proposals in which new papers were announced.

As early as 1721, John White, of Newcastle, had on the title page of his *Weekly Courant* a long list of regular venders in fifteen towns, and he announced that several persons had been appointed to "call the News" at Shields, Sunderland, Durham, Bishop Auckland, Barnard Castle, and some other places, where thenceforward no quarterly subscriptions would be accepted. Isaac Thompson and William Cuthbert, proprietors of another Newcastle paper, used every means of having their *Journal* conveyed to regular subscribers and to chance purchasers scattered over a large area. In addition to the eleven postmasters mentioned above (page 117), they had agents in Hexham, Kendal ("Mr. Robert Wharton, . . . who also distributes to Ambleside, Hawkshead, Ulverstone, Cartmell, Milthrop, and Burton"), Lancaster ("Mr. Isaac Rawlinson, . . . who also distributes to Hornby, Garstang, and Preston"), Kirby-Lonsdale, Sedbergh, Whitby, Morpeth, Felton, Alnwick, Belford, Wooler, Duns, Jedburgh ("Mr. Robert Winterup, . . . who distributes to Hawick"); their paper was sold by Mr. Andrew Spottiswood, bookbinder in Durham; it was handled by Mr. Emmleton, the Warkworth carrier; it was delivered by "the News-Carrier to Sunderland and Shields," by "the News-Carrier to Bishopauckland, Raby, Staindrop, and Bernardcastle," and by "the News-Carriers to Darlington, Richmond, Rippon, Thirsk, Northallerton, Stoxley, Gisbrough, Yarm, Stockton, Norton, and Sedgefield"; it was, of course, also sold by the booksellers in Newcastle-upon-Tyne, and by the publishers at the new printing office on the Head of the Side.

The prospectus announcing the *Union Journal: or, Halifax Advertiser* in December, 1758, included the statement that the new paper would be published every Tuesday morning and "dispatch'd immediately by proper

Messengers, with all Expedition, to a great number of
Towns, and country Places for many Miles round." Forty
other printers were doing that in 1759, and "proper Messengers" had been used for many years before that time.
In the second issue of the *Ludlow Post-Man* (16 October
1719), the printer, William Parks, announced that he
needed an honest man who could "walk well, and be
constant 2 or 3 days in the Week." Speedier distribution
seems indicated in *Farley's Bristol News-Paper,* for the
aggressive Samuel, insisting that "After all Ignorant and
Fruitless Attempts of Pretenders,[20] no other News-Paper
is Printed in this City; This Circulates above 50 Miles
round," announced that every Saturday morning, soon
after the London post came in, he would regularly send
the paper abroad "by Two or Three Running Footmen
. . . For Conveniency of People in the Country." These
newsmen, said Farley, would take the paper as far as
Devizes, Westbury, Sherborne, Shafton, Taunton, Bridg-
water, "and most other Towns and large Villages between
those Places and Bristol. They'll be at Bath every Saturday about Twelve or One o'Clock." Twenty years later,
another Farley, in number 1590 of *F. Farley's Bristol
Journal* (21 November 1747), commended with great
cordiality his man Christopher Wilkinson, who had been
engaged as the constant vender of the paper in Bath
("every Saturday, as soon as possible in the Afternoon")
and along the Bristol-Bath road. He was, said Farley,
"a Man of a sober, honest Character, no way given to
Drinking or Idleness." During the next forty years, the
numbers of honest walkers and agile runners increased
steadily all over England, though many of the newsmen
working outside the towns went on horseback rather
than on foot, at a considerable increase of speed.

There was no better mode of delivering the papers
and of collecting the quarterly charges than by sending
one's own "proper Messengers." John Rawson, printer of
the *Hull Courant* for many years, for a time thought to

save money for some of his Lincolnshire readers by agreeing to let their helpful neighbors carry the papers to them; but these volunteers proved most unsatisfactory. Almost incoherent with indignation, Rawson denounced this carelessness in large italic type at the top of his first column in the issue for 20 March 1759:

> As several Country People, who have been desired to call for this Paper, to carry home for their Neighbors, has frequently, and does still continue to break open the same, particularly in our Lincolnshire Circuit, who reads and dirty it, and afterwards keeping it the best part of a Week by them, before the Delivery of the same, to the great Prejudice of the Printer hereof; Therefore, it is requested, that such ill Practice be laid aside for the future, without any further Notice.

Rawson, who might have sold more copies of his *Hull Courant* if he had sent his own carrier on the Lincolnshire circuit, no doubt echoed the annoyance of his customers in that area; but it was surely a wonderful recommendation for the *Hull Courant* that, once the obliging men of Lincolnshire had it in their hands, they would not surrender it to the subscribers who would be paying for it at the end of the quarter!

Accidents and bad weather sometimes delayed even the experienced and trustworthy newsmen. On one occasion a regular distributor simply disappeared, the printers of the *Sherborne Mercury,* number 16 (7 June 1737), spreading the sensational announcement right across the front page above the date line, not quite in the manner of a modern headline but none the less eye-catching:

> *Whereas* JAMES ARNOLD, *one of the Hawkers of this* Mercury, *set out last Week from* Sherborne *for* Taunton *as usual, with his Number of Papers for that Walk, and has not since been heard of, 'tis fear'd he is either dead, or come to some Misfortune: 'Tis therefore hoped, that such of our kind Readers as have been disappointed thereby, will excuse the Proprietors for an Accident against which no one can*

guard. And whoever shall give Intelligence what is become of the said James Arnold, *to the Printers of this Paper, shall be gratefully rewarded for their Trouble.*

If hawker Arnold ever did return, all readers of the *Sherborne Mercury* along his "Walk" must have welcomed him with more than usual cordiality and have demanded an account of his temporary disappearance.

The unexpected disappearance of a hawker of newspapers was, as the printers of the *Sherborne Mercury* said, an accident against which no one could guard, but when two Northampton newsmen and a quantity of goods disappeared at the same time, the incident clearly had in it less of accident than of design.

> Whereas John Chambers, a Tall, Thin, Black Man, about 6 Foot high, or better, who used to Travel with the Northampton Mercury to Leicester; and Thomas Moss, a short well sett Fellow, very much Freckled in the Face, and Limps with his right Leg, who also travelled the Road with the aforesaid Mercury from Northampton to Witney, are run away from their Masters Service, with a considerable Quantity of Goods. . . .

So begins an advertisement in the *Northampton Mercury*, number 40 (30 January 1721); and the printers offered a reward of ten shillings for the arrest of the two decamping newsmen. Their absconding must have interfered with the delivery of many copies of the Northampton paper; for between them, the six-foot Chambers and the limping, freckle-faced Moss traversed an extensive strip of country, and it would be difficult to replace them on short notice in midwinter.

Foul weather and a hawker's occasional disappearance being beyond control, it can be said that most printers made excellent arrangements to maintain and to increase circulation both among casual buyers and among those who could be prevailed on to take the paper weekly by subscription. A statement in number 86 (5 February

1746) of William Cuthbert's *Newcastle Gazette* shows that the network of distribution was being extended in the south:

> *∵* This Paper may, for the future, be had of Mr. Relph in Sedgefield, from which Place it will be distributed by John Hart, to Bishop-Auckland, Barnardcastle, Darlington, and all the Market-Towns adjacent to those Places; Also by John Robson, to Stockton, Yarm, Stokesly, Gisborough, and Places adjacent.

Cuthbert's announcement reveals unmistakably the actual steps taken to extend the circulation of a newspaper in its second year of publication. The details of the process deserve careful examination. A man living in a town twenty-seven miles away was put in charge of a distributing base, from which two other men were to carry the *Gazette* into areas still farther away from Newcastle. Hart had a long road to ride: a dozen miles through Rushyford to Bishop Auckland, fourteen more through Staindrop to Barnard Castle, sixteen from there to Darlington—unless he went by Watling Street to Scotch Corner—and a devious route back to Sedgefield through scattered Durham hamlets. Robson's circuit lay more to the east, for after his ten-mile journey to Stockton and six miles more to Yarm he worked his way along one side of the River Leven to Stokesley, then to Guisborough and "Places adjacent" before leaving Yorkshire, re-crossing the Tees, and going back to Sedgefield.

Such notices as the one just examined lift the matter of distribution out of the realm of surmise and settle at least some of the questions one asks about the methods of opening up new areas and about the extent of the separate circuits. Office records, if they were still extant, would clarify these matters further. Fortunately the newspapers themselves are often quite explicit in providing information about efforts to extend their circulation. When Robert Raikes and William Dicey had for many months been developing the circulation of their *Gloucester Journal,* they were very much concerned lest the change in size and the increase in price from three halfpence to twopence because of the Stamp Tax would cause a shrinkage in their sales. In their final six-page issue, published on Saturday, 24 April 1725, instead of on the regular day, Monday,[21] they made a highly illuminating statement about distribution. They informed all subscribers, advertisers, and others who might be interested in the continuance of the *Gloucester Journal* that it was distributed regularly in a very extensive area divided into thirteen divisions, in each of which a named agent had the responsibility of delivering the required copies.[22] The First Division was Gloucester itself, where John Chapman was in charge. The city of Bristol, thirty-five miles away, was the Second Division, the distributor being John Wilson, a bookseller in Horse Street, who had his own agents to carry the papers to various parts of that city. The eleven other divisions comprised 120 named towns, "besides Villages" in each division. Typical of the local areas thus designated as "Divisions" is the Ninth Division, embracing Newent in Gloucestershire, Ledbury and Leominster in Herefordshire, Bromyard and Tenbury in Worcestershire, Ludlow in Shropshire, "and several Villages." Taken together, the network of distributors in these thirteen divisions is impressive.

That the printers sent bundles of papers to their main local agents in nearby towns can safely be assumed, then, as a regular practice. Illuminating particulars of the practice are recorded in a communication from one of those agents, expressing his dissatisfaction at irregularities in the number of papers sent. The date is 1770, but the standing arrangements and the occasional difficulties alike were doubtless much the same in the earlier decades of the century. The agent's message to the printer was in the form of four short notes written in the lower margins of the four pages in a copy of the *Leicester and Notting-*

ham Journal, number 908 (Saturday, 28 July 1770), now at the Nottingham Central Library. The last two of these notes have to do with advertisements and mistakes in the prices charged for them. The others give illuminating evidence concerning the distribution of John Gregory's paper. The signature of the writer is no longer legible, because the lower edge of the fourth page is frayed; it was doubtless one of the agents named in Gregory's list under the date line of the paper, perhaps Mr. Saunders, who had shops in Derby and Ashbourne. "I rec.ᵈ an Additional Subscriber yesterday at Ashbourne," he wrote to the Leicester printer, "& promise of another soon so that my Quarterly Customers are now increas.ᵈ to 25." He complained that there had been an error in the invoice of the bundle received the day before: instead of the usual twenty-five papers and two "blanks,"[23] plus "Mr. Bladon's 16 & 1 Blank," he had received "45 Stamp.ᵈ Papers & only one blank." This sort of error had occurred before, and he was annoyed: "I must again earnestly caution ag.ᵗ the carelessness of your Servants," he added. He had a suggestion to make concerning the seventeen papers usually shipped along with his but sent on by him to James Bladon in Carter Street, Uttoxeter:

> I wish you would direct that Mʳ. Bladon's Papers be *always sent open* with mine as it is less trouble to me to take account of them so then [i.e., than] when separately packed. *P[lease] to observe this.*

The agent's note also confirms the conjecture that the quarterly subscription charges were collected by the local agent: "You will not advise me about unsettled Customers," he wrote. "Why will you not?"

It is understandable that here and there in the earliest stages of newspaper publishing and selling in the country a bookseller should find the handling of papers printed in other towns either troublesome or unremunerative and have refused to act as agent. A well-established bookseller in Daventry noted in the third volume of his daybook, "Aug. 11th 1746 began to sell yᵉ Newspapers at 1st . . . left of Nov. 10." Some years later this same bookseller—his name was John Clay and his account books are now at Delapré Abbey, Northampton—may have resumed the selling of newspapers, for he entered on 1 July 1758 that one Mr. Knightly had paid him two shillings eightpence halfpenny for one quarter's news, and on 31 July recorded payments received from two customers for advertisements which he had sent on their behalf to the *Northampton Mercury* and *Jopson's Coventry Mercury*.

Out of the foregoing discussion of distribution emerges one insistent question, a question which surely must have given deep concern to the provincial printers: how was it possible to pay for the distribution of country papers outside the towns in which they were printed? In those towns and near by, according to statements made in 1743 by Thomas Aris, of Birmingham, and in 1757 by Elizabeth Adams, of Chester,[24] the hawkers charged a halfpenny for every copy they disposed of.[25] What was the cost of sending papers to customers living far away? If the subscribers received the paper by post or by the commercial carriers, they would, of course, pay the charges. If obliging neighbours brought the paper from town, the only cost would perhaps be a delay of four or five days while the conveyers perused it. Back in 1715, when the competition between Philip Bishop and Jos. Bliss was becoming heated and both men were publishing twice a week instead of once a week as they should have been doing, Bliss said the subscription rate for his *Protestant Mercury: or, the Exeter Post-Boy* was ten shillings per annum, "seal'd for the Country." Bishop's rates were thirteen shillings per annum, delivered to city subscribers, fifteen shillings "Seal'd and Deliver'd to Country Subscribers . . . they paying Carriage."

Ordinarily a paper literally did not "pay its own way"; someone, either the proprietor or the purchaser who lived at a distance, had to pay for the delivery of the paper, whether by post, by commercial carrier, or by special newsmen, mounted or on foot. Presumably the greater the distance the higher the charges, particularly if more than one carrier was involved. Probably no country papers traveled farther than those received by the Rev. William Borlase, the distinguished Cornwall antiquary, naturalist, and historian, while he was rector of Ludgvan, three miles from Penzance. His account book, recording disbursements during the years between 1734 and 1772, is now at the Royal Institution of Cornwall in Truro. It shows numerous payments for the newspapers regularly supplied to him by Jabez Harris and (from 1741) Mr. Dickerson.[26] The entries clearly indicate that Borlase did not pay in advance, that payments were usually made for a half year ending at midsummer, at Michaelmas, or at Christmas, and that his average weekly expenditure for newspapers was ninepence. The money was paid over to Mrs. Fudge, or to her successor in 1758, Mrs. Clies, invariably in settlement of Mr. Harris's or Mr. Dickerson's bill. These two women may have been the persons who actually carried the papers to the Ludgvan rectory, Harris and later Dickerson being the newspaper printer's appointed agents for Cornwall. Most of the half-yearly payments from 1738 to the end of 1751 ranged from 18/3d. to 19/0d.; from 1752 onward, the amounts were larger, from £1 1s. 7d. to £1 12s. 5d. for two quarters. How much of the sums paid went for delivery charges cannot be determined, for there is no way of knowing what papers Borlase got, or how many. They probably came from Exeter or Sherborne, though the payment on 9 October 1735 to Jabez Harris "for news paper etc. in full to Mics. [Michaelmas] 1735 by bill on Mr. Smith" cannot have been for the *Sherborne Mercury* (subsequently the most popular paper in the West) for the good reason that its publication did not begin until February, 1737. It is clear from some of the later entries that the newsmen known as the Sherborne riders[27] came all the way to the Ludgvan rectory; but payments for newspapers continued to be paid to Mrs. Clies until the end of the account book in 1772.

Typical entries in the Borlase manuscript account book are these:[28]

11 Nov 1738	Pd Mrs Fudge for Jabez Harris Esq in full for news papers to Mics 1. 18. 4.
25 Jan 1740/1	Pd Mrs Fudge for J. E. and selfe ½ a year's newspapers to Xstmas 18. 9.
1 Aug 1741	Pd Mrs Sybi. Fudge for Dickerson, news papers for J. E. and selfe to Midsummer 1741 19. 0.
16 Jul 1752	Pd Mrs Fudge for news by Mr. Dickerson's order to Midsr 1752 1. 1. 7.
9 Feb 1760	to Mr Dickerson's acct of news to Xstmas 1759 to Mrs Clies 1. 11. 6.

These figures in the account book at the Royal Institution of Cornwall suggest that, like thousands of other subscribers to country newspapers all over England, the Rev. William Borlase paid the usual twopence or twopence halfpenny for each paper he received, plus something for delivery in a place far away from the town in which the papers were printed. Part of that delivery charge paid by the rector of Ludgvan went to Mrs. Fudge, part to Jabez Harris, and part to the man who carried the papers over the long miles from the printing shop in Exeter or Sherborne to Mr. Harris in Cornwall.

There is no escaping the question, nevertheless, of how it could possibly pay a man to ride 115 or 165 miles once a week to deliver a bundle of papers. To this question there is a good answer: The printer's own "proper Messengers" carried more than newspapers on their rounds. The printers saw to it that the men who started off with bundles of *Journals* or *Mercuries* carried a profit-making load of other things as well. It cost no more in time and shoe leather. The result was that the net returns from each trip paid both newsman and printer much more than if only newspapers were carried. It is not going too far to suggest that without this second string to their bows the printers of country newspapers could not have shot their arrows much beyond the limits of their own towns; provincial journalism developed rapidly because men on horseback or on foot could easily carry more than the weekly budget of news so joyously received by Cowper[29] in his rural retreat later in the century and by ten thousand other country dwellers in every year of Cowper's lifetime.

There were three distinct kinds of "payload": (1) parcels and letters brought to the newspaper office for delivery in other places by the newsmen; (2) various commodities from the shelves of local merchants who advertised in the paper that the newsmen would take orders and deliver goods in places along the regular paper routes; (3) printed forms, pamphlets, books, medicines, and an astoundingly varied assortment of merchandise sold by the printers at their own shops. For all three types of messenger work there is plenty of evidence, though it cannot be proved that *all* newsmen were parcel carriers and traveling salesmen as well. Certainly the newsmen employed by James Abree of Canterbury to deliver his twice-weekly *Kentish Post* carried parcels as well; for in the issue of 3 December 1726, it was announced that "Thomas Low goes every Saturday and Wednesday, with News or any Parcels, &c. to Barham, Elham, Folkstone, Hyth, Dimchurch, Romney, and Lydd." The request was made that the "Parcels, &c." be left at Low's house in St. Mildred's Church Gate or at Mr. Randall's at the White Hart in Castle Street by eight o'clock on Friday and Tuesday nights. Abree's announcement concluded with a special note pointing out that "Parcels, &c." for his other newsmen were also taken in at the said Mr. Randall's. A note in *Jopson's Coventry Mercury*, number

1000 (1 September 1760), makes one other point clear: the carrier actually took the papers, number books, the *Gentleman's Magazine,* and the parcels to the houses of subscribers:

> ☞ Thomas Clarke now carries this Paper to Lutterworth, Market-Harborough, Uppingham, and Stamford. My Customers are desired to give him Orders to leave it, as well as the Magazines, Numbers, &c. at their Houses. He also carries small Parcels to or from any Place on the Road: They are taken in for him at Coventry by Mr. Miller, Hackel-Maker, at Jordan-Well.

It should be remembered that Clarke was not the only delivery boy Elizabeth Jopson had.

The financial importance of this collateral business is indicated by Francis Howgrave's remarks in the first issue of *Howgrave's Stamford Mercury* (15 June 1732). In a front-page salute to the public, he outlined his plans and mentioned certain benefits which he said would ensue from the publication of his paper. In addition to the reading which it would provide, there would be wider advantages affecting the nation's economy: he mentioned the great quantity of paper required for each issue, the revenue paid to the Crown, and "the large Quantity of Goods which will be weekly carried out by the Persons which distribute this Mercury." This last, he said, would be "no small Advantage to the Trading Part of Mankind." It also gave Howgrave great satisfaction to think that many persons were profitably employed in the complex process of manufacturing paper from rags, printing the news, and distributing the finished product in many areas along with other goods.

> In short, when I trace in my Mind a Bundle of Rags, to a Quire of these Mercuries, I find so many Hands employ'd in every Step they take thro' their whole Progress, that while I am compiling a Mercury, I fancy my self providing Bread for a Multitude.

Howgrave was not performing a miracle of feeding five thousand when he sent his paper into the surrounding country; yet it is undeniable that in the process of distributing it much money changed hands, for the distributors conducted an extensive trade in various commodities and services in addition to their primary duty of delivering the newspapers to subscribers and casual buyers. That Howgrave's observations about the newsman's contribution to general trading were not the product of day dreaming is confirmed by statements in other newspapers, the most explicit being a lengthy note[30] at the head of the first issue of the *Oxford Flying Weekly Journal* (6 September 1746), concerning the advantages which its establishment would bring to the people of the region. Among the expected benefits was one which would appeal to "the Tradesman and even the meanest Mechanic": "for as we propose to employ Men to carry this paper round the Country, a weekly opportunity will be thereby afforded to extend Trade and Commerce, and dispatch all sorts of Business. . . . " The extent of that expansion of trade is suggested in William Dicey's request, in many issues of his *Northampton Mercury* in 1750, that orders for goods to be delivered by his news carriers should be in writing, "as it cannot possibly be expected that the News-Carriers should remember the many different Persons, Places, and particular Goods that are Weekly desired to be brought to the several Towns they pass through and send to."

Readers as well as printers of news had business to dispatch. Once a subscriber to a country newspaper came to know personally the man who delivered the newspaper every week it was natural that the newsman should be asked occasionally to perform errands en route, and equally natural that the newsman should perform those errands for a small gratuity or a gift at the year's end, provided that the errands were not too numerous nor too costly in time or effort. Among the entries in the Rev.

William Borlase's account book, mentioned above,[31] are references to just such transactions:

To the Sherborn for 6 pds of coffee	10. 0.
Pd Lobb the Sherborn man for a cheese salver from Mr Halse of Truro	6. 0.
Sent a present to Dr. B. of St Mewan by the Sherborne	5. 5. 0.
Sent money to son John by his order by Lobb the Sherborn	10. 0. 0.
To 3 handkerchiefs to the Sherborn	12. 6.
To Frank the Sherborn. New Year's Gift	5. 0.

These and many similar transactions were all recorded by Borlase between 1763 and 1769, but manuscripts from other parts of England show that such services were rendered by country newsmen earlier in the century. Two instances will serve. A letter[32] sent on 10 May 1727 by J. Wallace to Madame Whichcot at the home of John Maddison in Ketton, near Stamford in Lincolnshire, ends with the thoughtful observation, "I am sure You'l want Money, & therefore I must venture twenty Pounds again by the Newsman. . . ." The sending of money by a distributor of the *Stamford Mercury* was perhaps a "venture," but it was not the first time a considerable sum had been sent in that way by J. Wallace. A quarter of a century later, on 26 November 1752, Lawrence Dawes at Kibworth—that is to say, Kibworth Beauchamp, six miles or so northwest of Market Harborough in Leicestershire—wrote a letter to Sir John Heathcote of Normanton Park, between Stamford (Lincolnshire) and Oakham in Rutland, and added a postscript which shows that even letters were sometimes carried by newsmen.[33] Once again it was one of the men who carried the *Stamford Mercury* whose services were engaged as conveyor of a private message:

if at any time yo've Ocation to write your Leters will

come safe if sent to Mr. Bunning of Upingham directed to be sent by the Stamford News Man who comes to this place Every Friday morning.

It appears that the Stamford newsmen, like the later Sherborne riders, had among their customers a reputation for dependability.

That dependability is doubtless one reason why merchants who advertised their wares in the local newspaper often said that orders would be taken and goods delivered by the newsmen. Joseph Cooke, at the "Ball" on Pease Hill, Cambridge, advertised in the *Cambridge Journal,* number 29 (6 April 1745), for example, that the carriers of that paper would take orders for his fine cider (at a shilling per gallon), oysters, lobsters, pickled salmon, and other delectable foods. Somewhat different fare was available to readers of *Jopson's Coventry Mercury,* who saw in the issue dated Christmas Day, 1758, an advertisement of Dr. Waldron's worm-destroying cake, or "sugar plumb," sold constantly at Mr. Jones's shop opposite the Golden Horse in Bailey Lane, Coventry. Mr. Jones added, "Persons in the Country may be supply'd with these Genuine Worm-destroying Cakes, by giving their Orders to the Men who carry this Paper."

It was the sale of the wares on their own shelves, however, that kept the printers in business, no matter how slender the profits from the sale of their newspapers were. It is, of course, only natural that the printer of a weekly newspaper should keep his helpers employed all the time by having them run off all sorts of standard printed forms and do job printing whenever they were not busy with the newspaper. There is abundant evidence that this was commonly done. Roger Adams, printer of the earliest Manchester newspaper, indicated in the imprint of his *Manchester News-Letter* in 1724 that at his printing shop "at the lower End of the Smiby-door . . . Summons, Citations, Warrants, Commitments, Passes, Certificates

135

both relating to Settlements and Burials, are Printed and sold at reasonable Rates."[34] Benjamin Collins of Salisbury inserted a prominently displayed notice in number 736 (Monday, 24 February 1752) of both his *Salisbury Journal* and its twin the *Portsmouth and Gosport Gazette:*

> Gentlemen and others living in the Country may be supplied by the Newsmen, with all Sorts of New Books, Pamphlets, Maps, and Prints, as cheap as in London, from the Printing Office and Bookseller's Shop on the New Canal in Sarum, where Books are bound either plain, or Gilt and Letter'd, at reasonable Rates.

Other printers of country newspapers both listed the latest publications in London and printed the advertisements which London booksellers sent to them for insertion at the usual rates.

It is not here suggested that books were available in the provinces only through the printers of newspapers. Most towns had booksellers' shops, and townspeople or visitors from outside could see a good stock of books on the shelves or order from the bookseller any works in print. The extent of such ordering in even a small town is apparent in the day books, ledgers, and miscellaneous memoranda[35] of John Clay, a bookseller in Daventry who did an extensive trade in stationery and reading matter. These records show that, from 1717 onward, Clay sold all sorts of books, including works issued in weekly fascicules, regularly disposed of twenty-five or more copies of the *Gentleman's Magazine,* did a good deal of book binding for William Dicey and others, and procured from London booksellers many books ordered singly by his customers, among them "Odes by Wm Collings" and "Instruction for ye Hautboy wth a Reed for the same." Country people had opportunity to buy books every time they went to a market town; but even villagers who stayed at home could get books if they read the newspaper advertisements and placed their orders with the newsmen. Most of the publications so advertised were books printed in London; some were modest little threepenny or sixpenny pamphlets printed at the local newspaper office.

It would require considerable space to catalogue all the pamphlets printed in the shops from which came the early Georgian provincial newspapers, and the works themselves would prove to be for the most part an unimpressive lot. A few should be mentioned. Raikes and Dicey in 1722 printed a threepenny *Collection of . . . Amusements,* which they advertised as sold by themselves, by James Hunt of Hereford, Mr. Rogers in Ross, Mr. Wilde in Ludlow, and by "the Men that carry the Gloucester JOURNAL and the Northampton MERCURY." Many publications came from the same presses as printed these two newspapers. Robert Williamson, of Liverpool, was another news printer who ventured to publish other things. In May, 1757, he announced that a half-crown octavo pamphlet entitled *Secrets in Art and Nature,* by Thomas Lawrenson, engraver, was in the press and that orders would be taken by various agents at Chester, Manchester, Preston, Wigan, Warrington, Ormskirk, Prescot, Lancaster, Kendal, and by the distributors of the paper. Dozens of other titles could be cited if proof were needed that pamphlets were printed at newspaper offices and that they were sold by the newsmen.

One particular sort of publication, works issued in weekly or monthly "numbers" or fascicules, could very easily be distributed with desirable regularity all over England by men who, all told, traversed thousands of miles in all weathers and seasons, calling at weekly intervals at the houses of people who habitually read newspapers. The market was large and growing all the time; the means of contact were perfect. "Number books" are not likely to have been sold by itinerant peddlers whose calls were irregular and uncertain, but there is plenty of evidence that these fascicules, stitched in blue paper covers to protect them, were not only procurable at local book shops but were carried to subscribers by the newsmen from the offices of the provincial newspapers.

Most of the works published in weekly or monthly fascicules before the middle of the century were printed in London,[36] though it appears that a few provincial printers of newspapers—notably Benjamin Collins of Salisbury —had a financial interest in such publications. It is understandable that Caesar Ward and Richard Chandler, who were partners in several of the most successful "number" books published in London, should have continued to handle the weekly parts after they took over the *York Courant* in 1739. In their issue of that paper dated 4 May 1742, they gave a prominent place to this announcement, using plenty of capital letters and italic type:

> SUBSCRIPTIONS *for* CHAMBERS'S *Dictionary*; STACK-HOUSE'S *History of the Bible*; TILLOTSON'S *Works, &c. as publish'd Weekly, are taken in by* WARD *and* CHANDLER, *Booksellers in* Coney-street, YORK. *Such Gentlemen as please to subscribe to them for the same, may have the Numbers sent to them (free of Carriage) by the several News-Carriers in their respective Circuits.*

A similar offer to deliver without extra charge the weekly numbers of another work published in parts, Astley's *New General Collection of Voyages and Travels*, appeared in Benjamin Collins's *Salisbury Journal*, number 304 (22 November 1743): "Note, The Numbers will punctually be delivered Weekly, at any Distance, clean and free of any Expence by the Distributers of this Paper." Robert Walker, whose weekly publications were sold all over England, promised in the *Warwick and Staffordshire Journal*, number 52 (10 August 1738), that three sheets of Jacob Hooper's *True and Impartial History of the Rebellion . . . During the Reign of King Charles the First* would be delivered once a week for threepence, stitched up in covers, and that country farmers or others living at a distance could "have 'em left for them" so that they might take them home with them on market days.

The traffic in "number" books in the rural areas was heavy, and although not every country news-printer handled these fascicules, there was not a year from 1727 onward which did not see these weekly or monthly parts, covered with blue paper, carried by newsmen from Norwich, Reading, and Worcester, and later from Sherborne, Liverpool, Preston, and several other towns. This is not the place for enumerating the titles of these works published in "numbers," but it can be said that they included books of many kinds, among them Nicholas Tindal's translation and continuation of Rapin's *Histoire d'Angleterre*,[37] Smollett's *History of England,* Dr. John Hill's *British Herbal,* the autobiography of Hannah Snell, Milton's *Paradise Lost, A Description of the Maritime Parts of France,* Dr. Doddridge's *Family Expositor,* William Ryder's *New Universal English Dictionary,* John Torbuck's *Compleat Collection of Debates in the Parliament of England,* and various narratives, surely not authentic, of the "Young Chevalier."

Some of these works printed and distributed in "the new-fashion'd Weekly Way" were run off on the local printers' own presses. David Henry, printer of the *Reading Journal* and its twin *Henry's Winchester Journal,* published Samuel Boyse's *Historical View of the Transactions of Europe* in twopenny numbers in 1746 and 1747. No more convincing evidence of success in this sort of publishing by a provincial printer can be found than the notices inserted by R. Goadby in his *Western Flying-Post; or, Sherborne and Yeovil Mercury* in 1751. Number 119 of the paper (6 May) announced that on the following Monday would be published the first twopenny number of *The unhappy Voyage and long Captivity of Thomas Pellow, Of the Borough of Penryn, in the County of Cornwall.* It was Goadby's own publication, and he told his readers they could get it from his usual representatives (whom he named) in Weymouth, Somerton, Taunton, Exeter, Plymouth, St. Austell, and Penzance, as well as from his newsmen. Small wonder that the work took well; all red-blooded Englishmen in the south and west would naturally be interested in the Cornish sailor's twenty-three years' captivity in a strange land. Within a few weeks Goadby reported that the weekly numbers were being completely sold out and that in response to continuing demand they had been reprinted.

There is nothing incongruous in a printer's selling of books, pamphlets, "numbers," ink, pens, writing paper, lead pencils, sealing wax, music paper, printed forms, maps, and other articles for which one would now go to a stationer's shop. What seems surprising is that at a printing shop in any English town in the eighteenth century one could get a great variety of articles not very closely connected with newspapers. It would be convenient, perhaps, to buy spectacles at Verral's shop in Lewes in 1755, though it was not until later in the century that newspaper print became cruelly small, but why did he also sell fiddle strings, a "curious Hair-colouring Water," and an extract of lavender for beautifying the skin? These, with Bibles, prayer books, and a variety of stationery wares, were on Verral's shelves; and according to his advertisements, people living in the country might be supplied with any of these articles at their own houses by the men who carried the *Advertiser.* Griffith Wright, printer of the *Leedes Intelligencer,* on 11 July 1758 filled two columns of his paper with a descriptive list of thirty-six articles available at his "Wholesale Medicinal Warehouse at New-Street-End" in Leeds, adding, "Any of the above Articles may be had of the Persons who sell the Intelligencer." The list concluded with "Fine Spermacoeti CANDLES and TAPERS"; and if one looks eagerly over the list again to see whether Wright wholesaled sweetness as well as light, the list is found to include also "the much celebrated Volatile Essence, call'd Eau de Luce."

Spermacoeti candles and eau de luce were not the only

unexpected articles sold in newspaper offices two centuries ago. William Dicey, printer of the *Northampton Mercury,* announced in his paper on 2 November 1730 that he had purchased "a Choice and large Quantity of Violins," which he proposed to retail at the London wholesale price. Other printers advertised that they sold lemons,[38] chocolate, lottery tickets, corn salve, snuff,[39] wash balls, tooth powder, itch ointment, and forty other plasters, pills, ointments, powders, oils and elixirs, the very names of which are fantastic: Dr. Griffith's Tincture Asthmatica, Robert Twilington's Balsam of Life, Sydenham's Anti-Convulsive Powder, Bateman's Golden Spirits of Scurvy Grass, the Litholytick Drops of Paracelsus, the Transcendent Restrictive Electuary, and the Incomparable Cordial for the Gripes. What rattling of pills in packets, what gurgling of bottled elixirs there must have been as the newsmen galloped along country by-roads with their hundred papers and all.

Many papers have long lists of articles sold by the proprietors and their newsmen, and the variety is beyond belief. To reproduce in full even one of these lists would be unconscionably tiresome; it is enough to say that if, to choose a single example, the newsmen who distributed *Keating's Stratford and Warwick Mercury* carried a sample of every article—from mathematical instruments to hungary water—enumerated after the imprint in number 116 (23 March 1753), they would need broad-backed horses and ample saddlebags. These jacks-of-all-trades would have put Autolycus to shame. How much profit they made and how much clear gain their efforts brought to the printers whom they served cannot now be ascertained or even conjectured, since the business records have not been preserved. It is to be supposed that these transactions, like job printing, were profitable to the scores of men and women who printed newspapers in the period here considered; if not, the trade in commodities and services would not have continued.

There was, however, one source of direct profit to the

printers which can be measured with some exactitude—
the printing of advertisements in the columns of the newspapers. For each of these advertisements the printer
charged two shillings or more; and as the rates are usually
indicated, it is possible to calculate what income they
brought each week simply by counting the formal notices
in the paper. There were three or four newspapers in
which there were no advertisements, or only very few;
most papers had anything from a dozen to forty or more
in each issue, and although the printer's charge for each
insertion had to include one shilling in duty payable
immediately to the Crown—two shillings from 5 July
1757—the remainder of the fee was almost all clear gain.

On the basis of the figures given by Thomas Aris when
he said he was losing money by selling his *Birmingham
Gazette* at three halfpence, the profit on the sale of one
copy of a twopenny newspaper must have been less than
one halfpenny, if one leaves out of account the income
from advertisements. At that rate the shilling and sixpence left to the printer after he had subtracted the tax
on a half-crown advertisement exceeded the profit on the
sale of thirty-six copies; the net income from ten advertisements amounted to more than the sale of 360 copies
would bring. It is worth looking at a specific example.
Number 396 (27 September 1756) of the *Western Flying
Post* has fourteen advertisements on its second page,
fourteen on its third page, and fifteen on the fourth. At
two shillings and sixpence each, the minimum charge in
this paper, these forty-three notices brought in £5 7s. 6d.,
out of which Goadby the printer had to pay £2 3s. 0d.
in duty; the remainder, £3 4s. 6d., exceeded what he
could expect to clear from the sale of 1,550 copies, if it
is fair to estimate that apart from advertisements each
copy brought him a net profit of not more than a halfpenny; if the net profit per copy was only a farthing,
the profit on Goadby's forty-three advertisements would
equal the net gain from the sale of nearly 3,100 copies.
Advertising *paid*.

Some aspects of this strong sustainer of journalism will be considered in the next chapter.

1. Quoted by W. H. Allnutt, "English Provincial Presses," *Bibliographia*, II (1896), 295.

2. In the *Birmingham Gazette* on 16 November 1741, Aris declared, "Mr. Walker . . . came here and printed a News-Paper. . . . "

3. On 23 October 1738, it was announced in the *Lancashire Journal: With the History of the Holy Bible* that the *Journal* itself would be sold at a penny, the supplement at three halfpence, "or together at the usual Price, at Two-pence Half-penny." The earliest issues of this paper bear Walker's London imprint; by number 11 (11 September 1738), the imprint was "Manchester: Printed by John Berry, at the Dial near the Cross . . . ," but the supplement was still printed by Walker in London. Perhaps Walker retained full control of the *Lancashire Journal* and Berry was merely Walker's printer and local agent in Manchester.

4. Aris's communication "To the Readers of this Paper" in number 86 concluded with the statement that the books published by Walker in weekly fascicules would thereafter be sold "by the Men who carry this Paper; so that those Gentlemen who at present take in Mr. Walker's Numbers, may be assured of having their Books completed."

5. The *Grub-Street Journal,* number 148 (26 October 1732), refers to a group of printers' devils who were returning to their shops after having taken unsold papers to the Stamp Office to have the stamps cut off.

6. Public Record Office, A.O. 3/953.

7. The chonological chart in Appendix B shows at a glance which papers were in existence before and after 1757.

8. Copies printed for use in the newspaper office and not offered for sale could be printed on unstamped paper. Office copies of the *Leeds Mercury* now at the Reference Library in Leeds were printed on stock not only unstamped but quite different in size and quality from that used for the copies sold to the public.

9. The *Daily Advertiser* for 27 October 1741 reported that "Last Saturday Robert Beaumont was committed to the House of Correction in Bury, by Thomas Discipline Esq; Alderman of Bury, for hawking unstamped News-Papers." The *Reading Mercury* of 25 January 1742 reported as news received in Reading on that date that Mr. Woodman, "Distributor of the Stamps for the County of Hants," had taken up a person for hawking unstamped newspapers in Portsmouth and that the offender had been committed to Winchester jail.

10. Occasionally a printer found that he had not quite enough stamped paper for *all* the copies he wished to print and with complete honesty paid duty on those he printed on plain paper. In the *Western Flying-Post; or, Sherborne and Yeovil Mercury,* number 125 (10 June 1751), for

example, the printer inserted this notice at the foot of the first page: "*.* We being disappointed of Stamps, are oblig'd to print a small Number without them, the Duty of which shall be duly paid."

11. One of several articles in a manuscript volume at the Manchester Local History Library.

12. I am indebted to Miss Josephine L. Reid in the Archivist's office at Chester for her transcribing of the two documents in the Mayor's Files for 1733-34 and 1734-35.

13. Cooke was not directly charged with *printing* either paper, but it is reasonable to assume that they came from his press.

14. It is irrelevant but curious that by the terms of his will, dated 9 September 1741 and proved 22 February 1749, Roger Adams left his son John "One Shilling and no more for his abuse and Unmindfulness in cursing both me and his Mother in my life time."

15. KB 11/32/4.

16. I can find no record of payment or appeal; but the presence of the record of conviction among the King's Bench papers at the Public Record Office suggests that Cooke engaged a solicitor to appeal in hopes of having the decision quashed.

17. For a discussion of these supplements, see R. M. Wiles, *Serial Publication in England before 1750* (London: Cambridge University Press, 1957), pp. 61-74.

18. William Thompson and Thomas Baily were joint proprietors of both the *Stamford Mercury* and the *Suffolk Mercury: or, St. Edmund's-Bury Post.*

19. Representative lists of distributors are given in the Register of Newspapers in Appendix C.

20. His reference is probably to Henry Greep, proprietor of the *Bristol Weekly Mercury,* which may have come to an end shortly before Farley began, on 29 April 1727, to print after the subtitle of his paper the statement quoted above.

21. Publication on Monday was resumed in number 161 (3 May 1725), but the regular day of publication was changed from Monday to Tuesday with number 191 (31 November 1725), a few weeks after Dicey's name was dropped from the imprint.

22. The complete list of divisions and places served (in Appendix A) shows how widely the *Gloucester Journal* was distributed in 1725.

23. It is possible that a "blank" paper was one with no subscriber's name on it and therefore saleable to a casual purchaser. Yet the distinction made later in the passage quoted above between "45 Stamp.d Papers" and "one blank" seems to imply that an agent usually received one or two copies on unstamped paper. Did Gregory use unstamped paper for copies intended as free gifts for his agents? In this case it is hard to understand why any agent would wish to have more than one such free copy, since he could not sell it without breaking the law.

24. See above, pp. 100-101.

25. "Any Person who will take a Quantity, at Taunton, to serve another Town shall have them at an Whole-sale Price." So stated Jos. Bliss, of Exeter, in his *Protestant Mercury* on 27 January 1716; and on 4 May 1716, he announced: "Carriers, as all others, that take 3, 4, or more Papers, buying them at my House, shall have a Reasonable Allowance." Similar allowances were probably made to those who arranged to have several copies sent to them at distant places.

26. Borlase sometimes wrote "Dickenson," but the usual form is "Dickerson."

27. Because the *Sherborne Mercury* sold more widely in Cornwall than any other newspaper, the term "Sherborne rider" was apparently used throughout the West Country to designate the men who brought newspapers, wherever published, much as in the fifteenth century any mystery play, no matter where performed, came to be known as a "Coventry" play. For Borlase's references to "the Sherborn man" and "the Sherborn," see above, p. 134.

28. I am indebted to Mr. H. L. Douch, Curator of the Royal Institution of Cornwall, Truro, for his kindness in transcribing these and many other entries in the Borlase account book pertaining to newspapers.

29. It was a postman, however, not a newsman, whose twanging horn Cowper mentioned in *The Task,* Book IV.

30. Transcribed by a contemporary reader in a manuscript now at the Bodleian, MS. Top. Oxon. d. 247.

31. See p. 129.

32. This letter (Asw. 10/24/6) and the next one referred to (Anc. 7/15/12) are both in the Lincolnshire Archives Office.

33. There is more evidence on this point. As late as 1755, when the postmaster-general announced that the delivery of mail in a considerable area of England north and west of London would be extended from thrice weekly to six times a week, particular emphasis was laid on the complaint that "great Numbers of Letters" had hitherto been privately collected and delivered, "as well in these as in other Parts of the Kingdom, contrary to Law, to the great Prejudice of the Revenue of the Post-Office." According to the text of the announcement dated at Warrington on 13 September 1755 and printed in *Whitworth's Manchester Magazine,* number 3151 (23 September 1755), all persons detected in the illegal collecting, conveying, or delivering of letters would, after Friday, 10 October 1755, be prosecuted with the utmost severity, the penalty being five pounds for every letter collected or delivered contrary to law, and one hundred pounds for every week the practice was continued. Particular warning was given to several groups of past offenders, among them carriers, coachmen, watermen, wherrymen, and "dispensers of Country News Papers."

34. The address was "Smithy-Door"; the form "Smiby" continued to appear in Adams's imprint for many weeks; it may have been a jocose representation of local bi-labial pronunciation of the third consonant sound in "Smithy."

35. These manuscripts, mentioned above, page 129, are in the Willoughby (Daventry) collection in the Northamptonshire Record Office, Delapré Abbey, Northampton.

36. See the list in Appendix B of my *Serial Publication in England before 1750* (London: Cambridge University Press, 1957).

37. Many of the careful ink drawings made by the Rev. William Borlase in his work as a naturalist and antiquarian in Cornwall were mounted by him on the blue-paper covers of the successive weekly numbers of this popular work in its third edition, to which obviously Borlase was a subscriber in 1743 and 1744. The volumes containing these blue covers are at the Penzance Library in the Morrab Gardens, Penzance.

38. For example, Elizabeth Kent, who after the death of her husband printed the *Plymouth Weekly Journal,* inserted a notice in number 26 (30 March 1722) that at her printing house in Southside Street, near the new quay, interested persons would get "Lemons very Good, at Four Shillings a Hundred." At Ipswich, T. Norris included in the imprint of his *Ipswich Weekly Mercury* the statement that at his office in the Cross Key Street, near the Great White Horse corner, might be had "Lemmons by Wholesale and Retail."

39. John Collyer, printer of the *Nottingham Mercury,* advertised on 31 October 1723 that "the Best Tobacco Snuff, commonly called Killycrankey; or scotch Snuff, . . . approv'd of by Gentlemen and Ladies of the Greatest Quality and Figure" was sold at his shop, "and by the Men that carry the News Northwards."

Chapter IV

Advertisements.

Now fitting out with all Expedition,

For a Cruize againſt the French,

The PRIVATEER ISAAC,

A noted prime Sailor,

Under the Command of Captain David Clatworthy.

She mounts 16 Carriage Guns, and to have 130 Men ——All Gentlemen Seamen and able bodied Landmen, who are willing to enter on board her, will meet with ſuitable encouragement, by applying to Mr. R. Townſend, merchant, in King's-ſtreet.

On MONDAY the 16th Inſtant,

At Mr. Hardy's Dancing-School in the New-market,

Will be performed a CONCERT of MUSIC,

For Mr. PERKINS and SON,

Who will endeavour to pleaſe on the Hautboy.

The principal muſical performers in town will aſſiſt.

NOW in Mr. George Cowper's Warehouſe in Cleveland's Square, a Hogſhead of Sugar, black mark N P H Nº 136, which has been there by neglect ſince June laſt. Whoever produces a juſt title to the ſame, may have it by paying for advertiſing.

John Urmſton, *Upholſterer*,

AND

John *and* James Glover, *Cabinet-makers,*

From LIVERPOOL,

AT their ſhops in the Corn-market, Warrington, make and ſell all ſorts of Upholſtry and Cabinet Goods in the neweſt taſte, and at moderate prices.

Beſt Tobacco SNUFF,

Sold wholeſale at the Maker's price,

By W. BARKER, *GROCER, in Water-ſtreet.*

Advertising

PERSUADING people to buy something and pay for it is the basis of business, and no better means of bringing seller and buyer together can be devised than what the English-speaking world has for a long time called "advertising," itself now a big business. A man who "advertises" is simply giving notice, making a statement intended to influence others. For over three centuries English newspapers have provided a convenient medium for the issuing of such notices; and although newspapers are no longer the sole medium for persuading members of a community to part with money, it is beyond dispute that newspaper advertisements have accelerated the growth of trade in commodities of all kinds, including newspapers themselves. A dignified gentleman may feel annoyed that his newspaper gives more space to tradesmen's notices than to political news and editorial paragraphs, but he would pay guineas instead of pennies for his paper if it carried no advertisements. Advertisers say that he would pay more for everything else, too, if there were no advertisements.

The fact remains that in some circles advertising is frowned upon, and it was so in the eighteenth century.

FIG. 5.—Cuts used to classify advertisements in the *Liverpool Chronicle,* 6 May 1757. (By permission of the City Librarian, Brown, Picton, and Hornby Libraries, Liverpool.)

In the first issue of the *Liverpool Chronicle* (6 May 1757), the observation was made that not many years before that date "it was thought mean and disreputable in any tradesman of worth and credit to advertise the sale of his commodities in a public Newspaper." Mean and disreputable it may at first have been; but by the time that remark was printed in the *Liverpool Chronicle,* there were not only many London newspapers which were called "Advertiser" but nine country papers so called and fifteen others with the word in the subtitle. "Advertisements are now so numerous that they are very negligently perused. . . . " That statement could have been made this morning; the words were written two centuries ago by Samuel Johnson in one of his "Idler" essays. Johnson had London papers in mind, to be sure, but country papers had for many years been giving large portions of their space to notices intended to warn, persuade, or inform.

Because the advertisements in early provincial newspapers have been too negligently perused or not perused at all by those who have attempted to trace the development of advertising, it is commonly supposed and sometimes said in print that until the last decades of the eighteenth century the newspaper advertisements were few in number and were mainly about farms for sale, runaway servants, strayed horses, and quack medicines. That the public announcements were numerous, and that they dealt with every conceivable aspect of normal and abnormal life in English communities, can be seen at a glance if one picks up a copy of almost any English country newspaper from 1710 onward.

Before there were any provincial newspapers, the London papers of the seventeenth century had many notices either sent by or intended for readers in the country. Readers living outside of London who saw the *City and Countrey Mercury* (1667)[1] would be interested in its advertisements and its twice-weekly dialogues on economic conditions. Country people must also have read with delight—as who does not?—the friendly notices inserted by John Houghton, F.R.S., in his *Collection For Improvement of Husbandry and Trade* (1692-1703). "I know of several Estates to be sold," he wrote in number 11 of volume V (9 November 1694); and again, "I sell Chocolate made of the best Nuts, without Spice or Perfume, at 5 s. and 6 s. and with Vinelloes and Spice at 7 s. the Pound, which I know to be a great helper of bad Stomachs, and Restorative to weak People. I'll answer for their Goodness."

Once the provincial weeklies got started, advertisements soon began to appear in them. The earliest extant issue of a provincial newspaper—number 91 (12 August 1704) of the *Bristol Post Boy*—has at the bottom of its final column an advertisement offering the services of John Mitchell, "Licensed Physician and Chyrurgion," who lived at the Two Blue Balls in King Street, Bristol; and the first of the provincial newspapers to be established in the eighteenth century, the *Norwich Post,* had numerous advertisements, every surviving issue for 1708 and 1709 having seventeen or more, the offerings ranging from "very good Cart Greece" to "14 couple of good seized and well manag'd Beagles." One of the unusual opportunities advertised as available to Norwich people is announced in number 413 (23 July 1709) of the *Norwich Post*:

> This is to give Notice to all persons in this City, that over-against the Three Feathers in St. Peters Hungate, there is one lately come from London who teacheth all sorts of Pastry and Cookery, all sorts of Gellies, Greens and Pickles, also all sorts of Collering and Potting, and to make rich Cakes of all sorts and everything else of that Nature. She Teaches for a Crown down, and a Crown when they are fully learn'd, that her teaching so cheap may encourage very many to learn.

This anonymous London expert in "all sorts and everything else" was outdone in versatility, however, by a specialist in another art, according to a well-displayed advertisement inserted "By Permission" in the *Norwich Post*, number 594 (5 July 1712):

> These are to give Notice to all Gentlemen, Ladies and Others, That Mr. Clench of Barnet, who imitates the Horn, Huntsman and Pack of Hounds, the Sham Doctor, Old-Woman, Drunken-Man, the Bells, Flute, Double-Curtel, the Organ with Three Voices, by his own Natural Voice, to the greatest Perfection; (being the only Man that ever could attain so great an Art) Will perform the same this present Evening, at Mr. Bosley's Dancing-School.
>
> Beginning exactly at Six a Clock.
>
> Price One Shilling.   Vivat Regina.
>
> All Gentlemen and Ladies are desired to come exactly at the Hour, for later is not Convenient for the Performance or the Place.

Less than a month after Mr. Clench of Barnet emitted his assortment of noises in Mr. Bosley's Dancing School, the government imposed the first tax on newspapers and the first one-shilling levy on newpaper advertisements; but the temporary setback which resulted was followed by irrepressible expansion of both newspapers and the advertisements in them.

It is true that in the half-century before 1760 there were some country newspapers in which only a few advertisements appeared, and it will be noticed that several of these particular papers did not continue very long. Only one advertisement is to be found in the six surviving issues of *Sam. Farley's Bristol Post Man* (1713-16); several early issues of the *Reading Mercury* have no advertisements, or only one or two; and most of the extant issues of the earlier *Hull Courant* have no advertisements.

From the first decade of the century, on the other hand, one finds papers in which more than a quarter of the available space was occupied by advertisements. As early as 1709 and 1710, the *Norwich Gazette* had its fourth

page filled with advertisements, and thirty years later
that paper had an even larger proportion of its space
given over to advertising. It took Francis Howgrave a
few weeks to build up the advertising in the *Stamford
Mercury* which he started in 1732, but in the period 1736-
39 this paper had five full columns out of twelve given
over to paid notices. At the same time newspapers in
other towns regularly had their last three or four columns
filled with advertisements. Practically every issue of the
Newcastle Journal from 1739 onward had dozens of advertisements, and those printed in the *Newcastle Courant*
during its first half century number many thousands.
During the decade 1751-60, there were many papers which
regularly had six, seven, even eight columns out of twelve
filled with advertisements. It was an extensive business.

That newspaper advertisements were not scanty and
sporadic is to be inferred from the fact that Parliament
sought to raise money from them. By the Stamp Act of
1712 [2] a tax of one shilling was imposed on "every Advertisement to be contained in the *London Gazette,* or any
other printed Paper, such Paper being dispersed or made
publick Weekly, or oftener." Just as it is unthinkable that
the newspaper Stamp Tax was imposed with the expectation that it would stifle the press, so it is ridiculous to
suppose that a tax would be imposed on newspaper advertisements unless substantial revenue could be produced
thereby. The truth is that by the middle of the eighteenth
century there were tens of thousands of advertisements
in the London and country newspapers every year, and
from them the Treasury garnered thousands of pounds
annually.

Proof that this statement is not unwarranted is to be
seen in the Audit Office accounts in the Public Record
Office,[3] which show the amounts of advertisement tax
collected annually; and the *Journal of the House of
Commons* (XXVII, 369 ff.) has an account of the gross
produce (that is, including office charges) of the duty

on advertisements at one shilling each for the seven years from 2 August 1749 to 2 August 1756. The total for those seven years was over £52,585, the annual figures ranging from £6,113 in the year ending 2 August 1750, to £8,477 in the year ending 2 August 1756. The figure for the penultimate year in the period covered was £8,955, this being the duty collected on 179,100 advertisements. For the same number of advertisements in the year ending 2 August 1758, the duty collected would be £17,910, since the tax was doubled by the Act of 30 George 2, c. 19 [1757]. But let it be remembered that these figures include returns from the London as well as the provincial papers. The yield from the country papers was at first much smaller than that from London papers, but the proportion steadily increased, as Professor Aspinall points out.[4] The figures at intervals of ten years show the increase both in the totals and in the proportion that came from country papers. The figures here given show the amounts paid at the Head Office (A), the amounts paid to the collectors in the country (B), and the totals for the year indicated ending 2 August (C):

	A	B	C
1720 ...	£1,319 14s. 0d.	£136 7s. 0d.	£1,456 1s. 0d.
1730 ...	1,882 7 0	486 17 0	2,369 4 0
1740 ...	2,969 6 0	814 10 0	3,783 16 0
1750 ...	4,951 0 0	1,248 18 4	6,199 18 4
1760 ...	11,239 0 0	4,567 15 6	15,806 15 6
1770 ...	15,642 18 0	9,505 18 0	25,148 16 0
1780 ...	20,796 19 6	15,748 19 0	36,545 18 6

The sharp increases resulting from the doubling of the advertisement tax in 1757 are reflected in the figure for 1760, but it is to be noted that after 1757 the figures are larger for another reason: the Act of 30 George 2, c. 19 [1757], imposed for the first time a tax on advertisements in papers published at intervals longer than one week.

These totals have their usefulness as a graphic demonstration that advertising in newspapers increased rapidly, but they do not reveal what payments were made by any one newspaper for a given period. Fortunately that particular information is available to the utmost degree of accuracy. All one has to do to find out what amount of duty was payable on the advertisements in the *Gloucester Journal* for 1729 or the *Norwich Gazette* for 1742—or any other year—is to count the advertisements. Whether or not the proprietor ever felt tempted to cheat, he could not do so for there was no way of concealing the evidence.

That substantial sums were actually paid by the proprietors of provincial newspapers is shown by receipts written by the collector. The statute of 10 Anne, c. 19 (section cxviii) stipulated that the officer must "without any other Fee or Reward, . . . stamp with the proper Stamp, to be provided for that Purpose, one Copy of such Advertisement or Advertisements, or . . . give a Receipt for the Duty or Duties hereby charged thereupon, in Testimony of the Payment thereof." It does not appear to have been the practice of local collectors to use a "proper Stamp" as a means of showing that the duties on particular advertisements had been paid; and the reason is a perfectly good one: the stamp would have to be applied to every single advertisement.

The alternative method provided by the statute was much simpler. It may well be that some collectors wrote out a formal receipt on a separate slip of paper. Certainly some of the collectors preferred to write the receipt in the margin of one copy of the newspaper itself. Occasionally the note was made by the printer himself. Thus William Norris noted in his *Taunton Journal* on 1 August 1726: "I Paid Mr Greenway 0 – 16 – 0 for the Duty of 16 Advertisements on this and several former Journals, in full to that day." [5] But this is a memorandum, not a receipt. Ordinarily it was the collector who recorded the payment, as the office copies of several papers show. On 4 February 1729/30 Sam Worrall, the official distributor of stamps in Gloucestershire, wrote this statement at the foot of the front page of the *Gloucester Journal,* number 404 (30 December 1729), affixing his signature:

> Rec[d] Feb.[y] 4. 1729 of M[r] Rob[t] Raikes Eight pounds one shil[g] for one hundred Sixty one Advertisem[ts] from Sept. 30. 1729 Inst. to Dec.[r] 30 1729 Inst.[6]

In the fourteen issues of the *Gloucester Journal* from number 391 (30 September 1729) to number 404 (30 December 1729) there are actually 171 advertisements. Was Worrall being careless, or lenient, or did he close his eyes to the brief note by the printer in numbers 400 and 402,[7] and look upon eight notices by the Commissioners of Turnpikes as not subject to tax?

Samuel Worrall, of Gloucestershire, was certainly lenient in the matter of the time of payment. The statute required[8] that the duty on advertisements had to be paid "within the Space of thirty Days after the Printing or Publication of such . . . Advertisements," the penalty for failing to comply with this stipulation being the payment of "treble the Duties . . . chargeable thereupon." Worrall often let the thirty days go by without making any collection. The most striking evidence that he was dilatory is the receipt written by him in the bottom margin of the fourth page of *Felix Farley's Bristol Journal,*[9] dated 27 July 1754:

> Rec.[d] Oct.[r] 25. 1754 in account this day settled fifty four Pounds ten shillings in full for the duty of one thousand & Ninety Advertisements in this Journal from Aug.[t] 4. 1753 to this Paper both included
>
> Sam Worrall

Worrall had allowed a whole year to go by before receiving payment from Felix Farley.[10]

By Worrall's computation there were 1,090 advertisements in *Felix Farley's Bristol Journal* in the course of a

year, or an average of twenty-one in each issue. Receipts
written by William Wharton, the collector in Newcastle,
indicate that the average number of advertisements in
the *Newcastle Journal* in 1741 and 1742 was close to
thirty per week, as, of course, is obvious from a glance
at the papers themselves. Wharton made a practice of
writing his receipt in the space between the second and
third pages of the paper, and (with some difficulty,
because the papers are now bound in volumes) the
receipts can still be read. In number 156 (27 March
1742), for example, he wrote

> Reced of Mr Isaac Thomson & partners Eleaven pounds
> eighteen Shill^s for 238 advertisem^{ts}. inserted in their Jour-
> nalls from No 149 to & with No 156 both inclusive.
>
> Witness my hand
>
> Wm Wharton Coll^r.

Similar receipts are in the Newcastle Public Library
copies of several other issues before and after number 156.
These show that Wharton received payment for 255
advertisements on 27 June 1741, for 202 on 7 September,
for 659 on 15 February 1742, and for 298 on 4 June.
Payment for the 229 advertisements in numbers 166 (11
June 1742) to 174 (31 July 1742) was not made until 30
August, but the next payment, £18 13*s*. for 373 advertisements in numbers 175 (7 August 1742) to 187 (30
October 1742), was made more promptly, on 9 November
of that year. In the sixty-one issues of the *Newcastle
Journal* from number 127 to 187, there were 1,797 advertisements, for which the government ultimately collected
£89 17*s*. through William Wharton.

The government's revenue from advertisements might
have been much higher. Had the scheme proposed on 16
March 1731 by a disreputable London bookseller come
to anything, the development both of the newspaper and
of its advertising might have been very seriously impeded.

Recognizing that taxes on newspapers and the duty on advertisements were sources of revenue not fully utilized by the government, Edmund Curll pointed out to Sir Robert Walpole and the other Lords of the Treasury that the size of the sheet or half-sheet on which a newspaper might be printed was nowhere defined, nor was it officially laid down what number of words should be allowed as a maximum in any one advertisement. Restricting the size of paper might have forced newspapers to remain tiny or might have led to the use of whole sheets at a penny tax instead of half-sheets at a halfpenny tax; in the same way advertising might have been hampered by the restriction in size or by a sharp increase in the duty on advertisements exceeding the legal maximum permitted at the minimum rate. Curll estimated that if an inspector were appointed to enforce such restrictions as he proposed, there would be a gain in revenue amounting to more than ten thousand pounds per annum. Curll doubtless hoped he would receive the appointment. Wisely the Commissioners of Stamp Duties reported to the Lords of the Treasury on 1 June 1731 that there already was a qualified "Register" to collect the authorized duties and that they did not think it necessary to put the government to the expense of engaging an inspector of newspapers and advertisements.[11]

That newspaper advertising brought substantial revenue to the government cannot be disputed. But that was not the reason why the proprietors of country newspapers put notices in their columns; what they had in mind was increased income for themselves, and it was just a happy circumstance that the tax did not deter merchants and others from paying both the printer's fee and the government's duty. There were occasions when a printer announced that he was quite willing to print advertisements in his columns free of charge. That was easily done in the years before the advertisement tax was imposed in 1712. After having announced in his first two issues (7 and 14 December 1706) that advertisements would be inserted in the *Norwich Gazette* "at reasonable Rates," Henry Cross-grove apparently decided to strive for a local monopoly by inserting advertisements at no cost to the advertiser. Attracting particular attention by using a cluster of six asterisks and a large initial, he announced in number 129 (Saturday, 5 March 1709):

> Advertisements are still put into this Newspaper for Nothing, upon the following Conditions:
> 1. That they are put into no other *Norwich* Newspaper.
> 2. That each Advertisement exceeds not 70 Words.
> 3. That they be not about trifling impertinent Matter.
> 4. That they be sent in Writing before Friday Noon.
>
> But all Persons must pay for all such Advertisements as are not within the said Conditions, if inserted herein.

After the Act of 10 Anne, c. 19, came into effect on 1 August 1712, a printer might decide to collect no fee for himself, but the customer none the less was required to pay the duty on his advertisement. For a limited time William Parks and his partner in the *Reading Mercury* offered to print notices at no cost beyond the shilling duty, clearly as a means of doing what Parks had failed to do in Ludlow, namely, develop a clientele. Their third and fourth issues (22 and 29 July 1723) had this notice on the back page:

> N.B. Till Michaelmas next, Advertisements will be taken in to be incerted in this Paper gratis, paying only One Shilling each Time of Advertising, which by Act of Parliament we are oblig'd to pay to the Government: So that any Persons who have Houses or Estates to be Lett or Sold; or have lost Horses, Cattle, &c. or would have any Business made Publick 40 or 50 Miles round, may for a Shilling have it advertis'd in this Paper, by coming to the Printers hereof, or sending by the Persons who carry out this News.

It was not long before standard rates were established for advertising in the Reading papers.

Other reasons than a desire to build a business connection occasionally justified a printer in remitting the regular charge for an advertisement. Thus it was announced in *Williamson's Liverpool Advertiser,* number 27 (26 November 1726) and the next two issues, that a charitable subscription for the relief of the wives of men impressed into naval service had been opened at the bank near the Exchange; such an advertisement would normally have been inserted at a charge of half a crown, but the office copy bears the notation "gratis." Williamson apparently donated the space, but he undoubtedly had to pay the shilling tax. It is probable that a printer would be obliged to pay the shilling tax even on an advertisement that had been cancelled too close to press time for it to be removed. For instance, Caesar Ward may have had difficulty in collecting the full fee for an advertisement in the *York Courant,* number 1465 (13 November 1753), in spite of this statement set in small print on an inner page of that issue:

> *.* The new-built Dwelling-house at Knaresborough (advertised to be lett or sold in the last Column of the last Page) is lett. The Order for discontinuing it came too late.

Ward would doubtless be held responsible for the duty on the Knaresborough advertisement. The same is true of a facetious and fictitious advertisement which a reader of the *Bath Advertiser* sent in. The issue of 1 March 1760 has at the end of its last column this note:

> ☞ A humorous Advertisement of a new Magazine is received, but the Author, cannot expect to have it inserted at the Printer's Expence; the usual Dues remitted, it shall be inserted next Week.

The principle had to be explained again in the next issue:

> The Author of the Burlesque Advertisement will be pleased to remark that the inserting a Piece of Poetry has

no Duty to be paid to the Government for it; but an Advertisement, serious or not, has a Duty of Two Shillings charged on it. If the Author will give it another Form, instead of an Advertisement, (which must be paid for) we shall with Pleasure comply with his request.

The government did not try to stop advertising; but it did demand its shilling or two for each notice, whether the printer collected his own charges or not.

The government's demand of a shilling undoubtedly seemed equally annoying and ineludible; but tax-dodging, if morally deplorable, has its allurements for some people, and there were ingenious Englishmen who saw a way of evading the tax without breaking the law. John Newbery, of Reading, saw the way; Andrew Hooke and Felix Farley, of Bristol, actually tried it. The statute which imposed the shilling tax on newspaper advertisements explicitly limited itself to advertisements in papers dispersed or made public weekly, or oftener. It was not until forty-five years later that a duty of two shillings was levied on advertisements "contained in or published with any Paper or Pamphlet whatsoever, printed in Great Britain, to be dispersed or made publick yearly, monthly, or at any other Interval of Time exceeding one Week." [12] Now no one in the intervening years cared to establish a fortnightly newspaper in any country town; but John Newbery in 1740 realized that a weekly paper could be given an alternative *title* every second week and be therefore ostensibly a different paper, neither publication being "dispersed or made public weekly, or oftener." In his account of John Newbery, Charles Welsh quotes the following passage [13] from Newbery's private memorandum book:

> Let Mr. Micklewright print a *Reading Mercury and Advertiser* once a fortnight, and J. Carnan print a *Reading Mercury and Weekly Post* once a fortnight, and by that means save the duty of advertisements. Note, let the titles be *The Reading Mercury,* and *The Reading Courant.*

But the notion does not appear to have been carried into actuality in Reading. By the beginning of 1743, however, Andrew Hooke, of Bristol, perceived that he could avoid any payment of advertisement duty by publishing the *Bristol Oracle, and Country Intelligencer* on one Saturday and the *Bristol Oracle, and Country Advertiser* on the next Saturday, each paper having its own serial numbering. Hooke did precisely the same thing with two later papers, the *Bristol Oracle* and the *Country Advertiser,* which likewise appeared on alternate Saturdays. "The Variation in the Title," said Hooke above the date line of the *Country Advertiser,* number 2 (11 May 1745), "is in Consequence of a private Agreement that does not concern the Publick." Does this declaration imply willing connivance by Samuel Worrall, the Gloucestershire collector?

The same artifice, apparently, was used by another printer in Worrall's territory. This was Felix Farley, who from December, 1743, to the end of August, 1746, and for a time early in 1748 published on alternate Saturdays *F. Farley's Bristol Journal*—there were variations in the title—and *Farleys Bristol Advertiser.* All of this must have been confusing to subscribers; presumably it brought to Samuel Worrall a sufficient degree of obfuscation or satisfaction to insure his silence.

The other printers and proprietors of country newspapers found it simpler to collect the duty and pay it on demand to the local collector. What gave the printer greater concern was the possibility that the advertiser might neglect to send the duty along with the text of his advertisement; payment for the printing of the advertisement was expected in advance, too. Most printers insisted on "ready money" for advertisements. "As one Shilling Duty is paid to his Majesty for each Advertisement every respective Time it is inserted," said Ward and Chandler upon taking over the *York Courant* in 1739, "it cannot be expected that the Printer should give Credit for

Advertisements." Elizabeth Adams, of Chester, repeatedly insisted that no advertisements would be accepted for her *Weekly Courant* unless payment was made in advance. Bitter experience seems to lie behind the handwritten note in the office copy of number 549 (14 October 1749) of the *Newcastle Journal*: "NB. Mind that you take in no Adv^{ts} without money unless you know them to be good hands, but *never never* trust any of the running ons." Quite clearly some of the "running ons" in this and other papers were not paid for in advance. The office copy of the *Salisbury Journal* dated 30 October 1738 has in the margins (top and bottom) of the front page this note: "Rec^d of Mr. Sheerer one pound in full for Advertisements of Squire's Elixir to the 30th of Octr. Inclusive." William Collins, the printer of the Salisbury paper, could retain only part of that pound, since one shilling went to the Crown for every insertion of the advertisement. And the balance may not have been all his to keep. Contemporary manuscript notes on the office copies of some papers indicate that it was a common practice for a printer to allow his peregrinating newsmen a commission of twopence for each advertisement which they brought in. The clearest evidence of this is to be found in manuscript notes in the issues of the *Oxford Gazette: and Reading Mercury* for 1755-59 which are in the office of the present *Reading Mercury*.[14] Advertisements which came by post would bring in the full rate to the printer, for the printers always insisted that the postage be prepaid by the sender. Setting aside the duty, then, the printer retained every penny which he collected from the advertiser except what he agreed to pay his newsmen for bringing in advertisements.

There was one further reduction in the possible gross income from advertising, and that was the discount offered for repeated insertions. This discount was fair enough, since a continuing advertisement would not have to be reset for the second and subsequent printings.

William Norris charged three shillings and sixpence, without limit of size, in his *Taunton Journal,* but he said in his colophon on 1 October 1725 that he would "Continue them for Two Shillings per Week." This was a favorable rate, since his paper was issued twice a week. Felix Farley, boasting that the demand for his *Bristol Journal* was so great that he had been forced to print three impressions of number 70 (11 May 1745), offered a new low price on advertisements, both for first insertion and for repeated insertions: "the Price thereof will, after this Week be fallen to 3s. Entrance, and 2s. 6d Continuance, or 10s. for four Insertions, without any thing for Entrance." A few weeks later Farley made it clear that these rates applied to small advertisements only; large ones were to be charged "in Proportion." Twenty years earlier another Farley announced somewhat higher rates for advertising in his *Bristol News-Paper*: "Advertisements are Enter'd for 4s. If they don't exceed 10, or 12 Lines; and Continued for 3s. per Week after"; and these charges did not discourage advertisers, for with number 36 (8 January 1726) there were more notices and the paper itself was printed on larger half-sheets than before.

Prices charged for advertisements were not uniform throughout the kingdom. In the first issue of the *York Mercury* (23 February 1719), Grace White and Thomas Hammond, Jr., offered to insert advertisements at two shillings each. In the far southwest in the previous year, William Kent charged three shillings for inserting notices in his *Plymouth Weekly Journal,* and more than that if they exceeded ten lines in length. In David Henry's *Reading Journal* in 1748, the rate was half a crown for twenty lines. The printers of several other papers—the *True British Courant,* for instance, and the *York Courant* —gave half a crown as their normal charge, but were less definite about the maximum length which would be accepted for that sum. In 1747, Elizabeth Adams charged three shillings and sixpence for the first insertion of advertisements "of a moderate length" in her *Weekly Courant*.

The phrase "of a moderate length" is not much more specific than "as long as a piece of string." Some printers were much more definite. William Dicey placed under the date line of his *Northampton Mercury* in 1756 a plain statement of rates: for notices of twenty lines or less, the charge was three shillings and sixpence for the first insertion and half a crown for each subsequent insertion; for every four lines (or less) above twenty lines, the additional charge was sixpence. The office copy of C. Micklewright's *Oxford Gazette: and Reading Mercury* for 1753 and 1754 shows that Micklewright made weekly calculations of his income from advertisements, jotting down at the foot of the fourth page the number of paid notices in each issue—22, 34, 38, 32, and so on—and marking the price charged for each. Small advertisements were charged three shillings; those of thirty-six to forty-one lines were charged four shillings; one of forty-six lines was marked four shillings and sixpence, and one of seventy-seven lines, seven shillings. Another clear statement of a graduated scale is in the *Newcastle Journal*—number 378 (5 July 1746), for instance. For any advertisement containing up to one hundred and forty words the charge was half a crown the first time and eighteen pence thereafter; these charges were increased by sixpence for each hundred words in excess of one hundred and forty, and sixpence was also charged for "any Addition to, or Alteration in a running Advertisement, if under 100 Words." The charge for advertisements occupying two full columns or more is in most instances not known precisely.[15] Mr. K. G. Burton draws attention to the payment of two guineas for an advertisement occupying the whole of the second page of the *Oxford Gazette: and Reading Mercury*, number 743 (19 November 1759).[16]

Prices for advertisements rose by one shilling when the duty was increased by that amount in 1757; but the net profit to the printer was not affected unless the number of advertisements was reduced because advertisers refused to pay the extra charge. It did not take long for the new rates to be accepted. Both in 1757 and earlier the printers of provincial newspapers made strong efforts to overcome resistance to the duty.

In the attempt to develop the sale of a newspaper, the proprietor did everything he could to make it easy for people to get the paper; in the attempt to attract advertisers he had to make it as convenient as possible for people to put their advertisements into the printer's hands. This was easy enough if the advertiser lived in the same town as the printer of the paper, for the notice, with payment, could be brought right to the printing shop. Sometimes there were two or three places in town where advertisements could be left. For some months in 1749 and 1750, Edward Ward stated under the title of his *Bristol Weekly Intelligencer* that advertisements would be taken in at the printing office in Castle Street, by Messrs. Hickey and Palmer in Nicholas Street, and by T. Cadell in Wine Street. Andrew Hooke, author of the *Bristol Oracle,* hoped for printing work as well as advertisements when he announced that customers could leave orders and advertisements at his printer's shop at the sign of the Bible in Shannon Street, but said that he himself might be spoken with every day between the hours of twelve and two at St. Michael's Coffee House in Magdalen's Lane or at the London Coffee House in Corn Street.

Arrangements for the placing of an advertisement were less easily managed if the advertiser lived out of town; but many printers listed out-of-town agents who would receive advertisements and forward them to the printer. Anxious to secure all the advertisements his two alternating *Bristol Oracles* could carry, Andrew Hooke placed under the date line—in number 21 (22 October 1743), for instance—a notice which shows that he made arrangements to have postmasters all over the country receive paid announcements for him:

> Advertisements for this Paper, (which is at present circulated by Post to all the considerable Towns North and South, from Liverpool to Plymouth, throughout Wiltshire, Dorsetshire, and all South Wales, and is extending it self farther every Week) are taken in by the Deputy Post-Masters on all the Cross Roads throughout England, or they may be sent, (under Cover to Mr. Thomas Pyne Postmaster in Bristol) directly to the Author, who will take Care to insert them, according to Order, at the lowest Prices. To prevent Mistakes, all Advertisers are desired to give Directions in Writing how long they are to be continued.

The implications are clear: Hooke was not merely willing to accept advertisements; he made special efforts to obtain them.

Other printers of newspapers were equally keen, and most of them took the trouble to name their agents in distant places. Many papers have in the imprint or the colophon a lengthy list of booksellers and others who could take in advertisements. Forty such lists could be cited, but a few will have to suffice. The *Leeds Mercury,* number 897 (12 April 1743), named twenty-nine persons by whom the paper was sold and advertisements taken in, the places thus served numbering thirty-three; and in addition there were news carriers in eighteen other places, as well as the Derby and Bakewell posts. During the early months of 1744, the proprietors of the *Reading Mercury* attached to their imprint the statement that advertisements were taken in at the Bible and Crown in the Reading market place, and then added that they were also taken in at their warehouse without Temple Bar in London and by thirty-six named persons in towns all over the south of England from Bicester to Portsmouth and from Salisbury to Tenterden in Kent. The receivers of advertisements for the *Sherborne Mercury* in 1744 included nine named persons in nine towns, as well as the men that carried the *Mercury*. By 1747, the list had extended to twenty-four towns, in three of which there were two takers of advertisements, not just one. These twenty-seven collectors of advertisements for the *Sherborne Mercury* included booksellers, merchants, tavern keepers, three saddlers, a schoolmaster, a tobacconist, a farrier, and a jeweller—all in addition to the *Sherborne Mercury* newsmen and the printers themselves. After John Keene had taken over *Boddely's Bath Journal*—"one of the most Extensive Country Papers in the Kingdom"—the list of persons prepared to take in advertisements for Keene even included the printers of four other newspapers: Goadby in Sherborne, Collins in Salisbury, Raikes in Gloucester, and Berrow in Worcester.

There is probably no better inducement to advertising in a particular journal than firm assurance that the advertisements will be seen by a large number of readers. As the proprietors of the *Bristol Gazette* declared in 1774, the advantage of advertising in a successful journal is obvious: "the benefit arising therefrom is always in Proportion to the Number of Readers and Variety of Places into which a News-Paper is circulated." This is a point which modern advertisers and the proprietors of modern periodical publications alike insist upon; in our century the "net sworn circulation" largely determines the scale of charges for advertising space. This was so to only a very limited extent in the eighteenth century, for, as we have seen, the rates did not vary widely; but claims of wide distribution were made in emphatic terms.

Again and again throughout the eighteenth century the link between a newspaper's circulation and its usefulness as a medium for advertising was proclaimed. As early as 27 September 1715, when Sam. Farley launched his *Salisbury Post Man*, it was stated on the title page that the paper would be "made Publick in every Market Town Forty Miles distant from this City"—several would be sent as far as Exeter—and this wide distribution was declared explicitly to be for the encouragement of all those who might have occasion to "Enter Advertisements." Within a few years of its establishment, the *Gloucester Journal* gave prominence to the claim that it covered a larger circuit than any other country newspaper in England; and at the end of April, 1725, when the proprietors were concerned to keep the tax from affecting circulation, the confident assertion was made that the Gloucester paper was "of far greater advantage for Advertising any Business than any other News-Paper on this side the Country, by reason of the Number of Men employed to disperse them. . . . " Robert Williamson of Liverpool was only saying what many others might also have said when he referred in number 59 (8 July 1757) to his paper's wide circulation, "which has been daily manifested, by applications from different Parts of Great Britain and Ireland, to those who have favoured us with their Advertisements."

As was observed earlier, these claims of extensive circulation lack the irrefutable evidence which only firm and verifiable figures could give. Yet it is worth noting how frequently the printers said in their own words what William Cooke declared under the date line of his *Chester Weekly Journal* in 1732: "N.B. This Paper being carry'd through Nine Counties, and some Thousands Sold Weekly; all Persons may consider the Advantage of Advertising herein." Ward and Chandler said the same sort of thing in the *York Courant* in 1739;[17] H. Berrow in 1753, reporting that the sale of his *Worcester Journal* had increased considerably, declared that since the paper was distributed "in great Numbers, and with the utmost Dispatch" through several counties, "the Purpose of Advertising in it must, of Course, be sufficiently answer'd"; and in number 25 (3 April 1756) of the *Bath Advertiser*, Stephen Martin assured those who advertised in that paper that it was "constantly and regularly distributed through a Space of Country near Sixty Miles in one Direction, Westward; and above Seventy Eastward; and so in Proportion all around," being so well received that the demand for the paper was steadily increasing.

It is understandable that the printer of a country newspaper should assure those who advertised in it that they would have their notices read by people in all adjacent counties and perhaps in remote parts of the kingdom.[18] It is of particular interest that the printers of several country papers from 1750 onward made a point of sending copies regularly to London coffee houses, to the advantage (they said) of all who advertised in them. The benefits claimed for this practice are nowhere better stated than in the announcement printed in the *Western Flying Post*, numbers 87 (24 September 1750) and 112 (18 March 1751):

> All those who have Occasion to Advertise any Thing, are desired to take Notice, That the Proprietors of this Paper have now made a very great Improvement, for the Benefit of those who Advertise in it; for besides circulating it through all the Towns and Parishes of Dorsetshire, Somersetshire, Devon, Cornwall, and Part of Wiltshire, they now send regularly every Week, a Paper to each of the following much-frequented Coffee Houses, &c. in the Cities of London, Bristol, and Bath; viz. in London, at Batson's Coffee-House, Cornhill; Lloyd's, in Lombard-street; the Royal Exchange Coffee-House, Threadneedle-street; Sam's, near the Custom-House; Chapter Coffee-House, St. Paul's Church-yard; Richard's, in Fleet-street; George's, Temple Bar; Knight's, in Essex-street; Somerset-House Coffee-House, in the Strand; Forrest's, at Charing-Cross; Seagoe's, in Holbourn; Cocoa-Tree, Pall-Mall; the White-Bear-Inn, Piccadilly; the Bear and Ragged Staff, in Smithfield; and Hyde-Park Corner Coffee-House. At Bristol, the Exchange Coffee-House. At Bath, Morgan's Coffee-House; and the Booksellers Shops.
>
> *⁂* As by this Means the Advertisements are seen and read by Thousands in London, as well as in the Country, it cannot fail of being of considerable Advantage to those

who have Occasion to advertise Estates, Houses, Goods lost, Horses stolen, &c. And must in all Probability answer their Expectation in Advertising.

Anyone desiring wider coverage than the *Western Flying Post* afforded him could get it easily enough (at higher cost) by sending his advertisement to other papers published in London, in the eastern provinces, in the midlands, and in the north—there were thirty-five other provincial papers to choose from in 1750—but no other single paper could place an advertisement before the eyes of readers in thirteen London coffee houses and in the four western-most counties of England.

Both in the area to which the papers were distributed and in the area from which advertisements were received, then, the scope of advertising in provincial newspapers became very extensive indeed. There is one other respect in which, as has already been suggested, advertising became extensive, and that was in the space occupied in the columns of the newspapers. Printers who found that half their column space was filled with advertisements could hardly object, since those advertisements brought in half their net income; but after 1725, this congestion became a problem, for it was not possible to use more than a half-sheet of paper for each copy without having to pay a whole penny in tax instead of a halfpenny. Yet space was needed for news. The printers knew, of course, that they could conserve space by using small types. This now seems contrary to the principle that notices should be so legible that he who runs may read, but it is obvious from a glance at the newspapers of 1730 and later that printers sometimes preferred to use small type for paid notices. Ward and Chandler in 1739 said they were using paper of large size for their *York Courant* and had gone to the extraordinary expense of buying a new set of small type "purposely for Advertisements." The use of smaller types for long advertisements was common both in the

London and the provincial papers; for short notices most
printers used a variety of type sizes, often quite attrac-
tively displayed.

The pressure of space was none the less embarrassing.
In the *York Courant,* number 700 (13 March 1739),
Ward and Chandler admitted that they had on several
occasions felt obliged to hold back some advertisements
in order to make room for news. Some advertisements,
"which ought to have been inserted this Day," they said,
had been left out of that very issue. Other printers had
the same comfortless words for their advertisers. "Advertisements omitted this Week, will be in our next," said
Felix Farley in his *Bristol Journal* on 27 July 1754. The
problem became acute if advertisements came in close to
press time. The difficulty was genuine, for the printer had
to choose between the immediate income from paid notices
and the ultimate income from the extensive sale of an
acceptable newspaper. "I do not mean that it has been
absolutely impossible to insert them," wrote William
Craighton in his *Ipswich Journal,* number 914 (7 August
1756), but he requested an angry advertiser to recognize
that "a considerable Part of a News Paper ought to be
allowed for News, and also for many other things which
are equally agreeable to the Readers of it":

> . . . I might indeed make great Profit of this Paper for a
> single Week, if I should fill it with Advertisements from
> Beginning to End, without one Line of News; and this I
> cou'd easily do, by only taking in those that are offer'd me,
> relating to Books or Medicines; for which I shou'd be as
> well paid as I am for any others. But then, who wou'd buy
> the Paper the next Week? and the third Week, who wou'd
> think it worth their while to advertise in it?——and what,
> in a short Time, wou'd become of all the Pains that I have
> been taking, for many Years, to establish and extend it?

These words form part of a lengthy explanation offered to
Matt. Hopkin at the Brandon Black Bull, who, like a
thousand others, had taken it for granted that the printer

of a newspaper always had room for any number of advertisements that happened to be sent to him. For several years, said Craighton, there had not been one week in which he had not received many more advertisements than he could find room for. He had, in fact, actually set Hopkin's advertisement for the preceding issue but had been obliged to omit it and "above 20 others."

The earlier an advertisement could be sent in, the more likely it was to be in the next issue. There was another advantage in having the advertisement reach the printer early. In the *Cambridge Journal,* number 181 (5 March 1748), the proprietors promised to take the greatest care of advertisements, especially if they came in as early in the week as possible, "which means," they said, "we shall be enabled to oblige them with a good Place in the Paper." That the advertisers and the newspaper men—if not the readers—were conscious of the advantage which position might give to a notice is attested by a statement under the date line and also in the colophon of a London paper, the *Daily Journal,* number 4303 (1 November 1734): "Advertisements of this Paper, of a moderate Length, that require no Preference of Place, Character, or Disposition, are taken in at Two Shillings each." Psychologists may now be able to explain why particular spots in a newspaper are more advantageous to advertisers than other parts of the paper.

Generally speaking the advertisements in a country paper printed during the first decades of the eighteenth century were at the very end, whether the paper was set in two, four, six, eight, or twelve pages; but some of the four-page papers kept part of the last page for the latest news. It is not altogether uncommon to see single advertisements or groups of advertisements inserted between the second and third batches of news. Occasionally early twelve-page papers had notices on the verso of the title page, and the *Suffolk Mercury* in 1727—an eight-page paper—had the lower three-quarters of the title page itself occupied by the printer's own advertisements of writing ink and a cure for the itch. Until the middle of the century not many printers of four-page papers were willing to have advertisements on the front page,[19] but after 1750 some papers regularly used part of their front-page space for display advertisements. A good example is the *Bath Journal*, which, in number 31 of Volume VIII (21 October 1751), had more than half its front page filled with advertisements. What the printers of the *Cambridge Journal* meant by a "good Place in the Paper" was perhaps only the top or the bottom of a column, or the first or last place in a group of advertisements. In such positions a notice would more easily catch the eye than if it were smothered in the middle of a column. The lack of classification and of conventional sequence is probably not to be looked upon as evidence of the printer's carelessness or unconcern; it was doubtless recognized that readers would be more likely to scan the whole set of notices if there were no groupings.

The position of an advertisement is important; its typographical design is more so. We have seen that the printers of country newspapers made no more attempt than did their London brothers to choose display types to head important items of news; it was altogether different in the setting up of paid notices, at least from the third decade of the century onward. In early papers one sees a succession of short notices in type mainly of uniform size, each hardly distinguishable from those before and after; horizontal rules or spaces were used to separate consecutive advertisements, and there was usually a deep initial at the beginning, or a font of larger type was used for the whole of the first line. One could discover what the advertisements were about only by reading through the whole series. By 1725, some attempt was made in most papers to separate each announcement from the others by the use of a special caption—"To be SOLD," "To be LETT against Lammas next," "This Day is

Publish'd," "Notice is hereby given"—or by the use of a simple cut—a book, a keg, a dwelling house, a horse, a spouting whale, a ship in full sail.

These woodcuts enliven the page, but they had a particular purpose: they served to indicate instantly the theme of the advertisement. That is what Robert Goadby, the proprietor of the *Western Flying-Post*, had in mind when he announced on 26 November 1753 that he had gone to the expense of having eye-catching cuts made for the purpose of "distinguishing" the advertisements in his paper, and he added that the extra charge for notices so distinguished was only sixpence. These cuts were used to classify the notices, which were not (as now) grouped according to subject. It may be that in the eighteenth century there were people with time on their hands who read all the advertisements as a matter of interest. Advertisers were less concerned to keep these curious idlers occupied than to catch the eye of someone who might be induced to buy a mahogany voider, try a new cure for abdominal misery, attend the Three Choirs Festival, or take his family to Maryland.

The second phase of newspaper advertising was reached when printers began to use larger types for prominent words and phrases to compel the casual reader's attention. It is pleasant to find in early country newspapers a good deal of what can properly be called display advertising, in which, though limited in width to a single column, varied type sizes and fonts and symmetrical arrangement caught the reader's eye. The intricate visual, mathematical, aesthetic, and psychological aspects of types in advertising deserve the most careful study,[20] but here it is sufficient to note that in many papers the advertisements have a commendable degree of homogeneity in the types, yet there is enough variety of type size, of line length, and of spacing to attract attention. Large and varied types were used more lavishly in some papers than in others. William Cooke had well-set advertisements in his *Chester Weekly Journal* in 1732, for example, and excellent specimens are in the *Norwich Gazette* in 1741-42, the *Bristol Weekly Intelligencer* in 1750, *Felix Farley's Bristol Journal* in 1752-60, the *Bath Advertiser* in 1756, and the *Liverpool Chronicle* from 1757 onward. In spite of the wretched habit of using small type for the body of long advertisements, many a full page of notices in the eighteenth-century newspapers can be examined with greater ease and more immediate comprehension than those of the nineteenth century.

Printing an advertisement in large and legible type makes it easy for people to read it but does not guarantee that they *will* read it. One way to lure people into reading advertisements was to print the announcement in the form of news. It is a device still in use, though now the item so printed is usually set in a slightly different type from that used for the authentic news, and some printers insist on putting a tell-tale label ("Advt.") at the end. The collector of the advertisement tax may have been willing to ignore informal announcements included as pieces of news, and the printers may have accepted these announcements without charging the usual fee—though it is difficult to understand why they would do that. In any case, there are several good examples of professional men receiving effective publicity in what appear to be ordinary items of news.

This deceptive form of advertising through the medium of what is ostensibly news was commonly used by the managers of traveling companies of actors or other entertainers. The tone of this piece of regional "news" in the *Gloucester Journal*, number 1693 (5 November 1754), leads one to suspect that the statement was prepared by a member of the troupe as informal advertising:

> They write from Ledbury that, last Night, the Company of Comedians there left off Acting at that Place, where their Performances always met with the general Applause of a crouded Audience. Some Day next Week they are to open

at Hereford, from whence they will proceed to Leominster, Brecon, &c.—The Publick may be assured no Care nor Expence shall be wanting to make their Entertainment still more agreeable, and Mr. Ward takes this Method of informing them, that he has very lately purchased from London a large Quantity of Rich Modern and Roman Habits, that the Characters in the several Plays the Company perform may be properly dressed.

This sort of solicitation is sometimes quite startling— something like hearing "So-and-so's pills are just the thing" as the second line of "Hark, the herald angels sing." The *Cambridge Journal,* number 637 (11 December 1756), has a paragraph about the Reverend Mr. Sharpe's having been presented by the Bishop of Ely to the living of Trinity in Cambridge. That is news. Then comes a reference to the "very handsome" tribute drawn up in Latin (naturally) by the public orator in the name of the University and read in the Senate House as a compliment to the chancellor. That, too, is news. Then follows what looks exactly like another piece of news; but the theme is somewhat less academic:

> Mr. Powell the celebrated Fire-Eater, returns his humble Thanks to the Ladies and Gentlemen for the great Encouragement he has received during his Stay in Town; and begs Leave to inform them that this present (Friday) Evening, and To-morrow (Saturday) Evening will be *positively* the last Nights of his performing in this Town. ——He will perform on Monday Evening next at Newmarket.

Did the proprietors of the *Cambridge Journal* print this announcement free of charge in return for two complimentary tickets to the fire-eater's Saturday night farewell performance?

Advertisements in the form of news stories concerning remarkable cures of physical ailments are more numerous than those concerning actors and other people of the theater. There is in the single surviving issue of the *Man-*

chester Journal (24 August 1736) a report of Mrs. John Byrom's recovery from a painful illness (ischuria), but the astoundingly precise clinical details and the unctuous tone—"she is thro' Gods Help totally relieved by Roger Booth, Apothecary and Surgeon in the said Parish"— show that the "news" is no more than the cleverly designed advertisement of a local practitioner. Equally curious is the "news" of a remarkable cure by one Dr. Mohun, who made no acknowledgement of divine collaboration (Mohun shone by no reflected glory). The account is ostensibly an exciting piece of "front-page" news—though it occupies three quarters of the third column on the second page in the *Gloucester Journal,* number 217 (10 May 1726). A crude half-column cut of a man hanging from a gibbet draws attention to what begins like an ordinary piece of news headed "Gloucester, May 7."

> They write from Taunton in the County of Somerset, that one William Collard, Servant to Mr. Ayers of Streat, near Glastenbury, was Executed the 29th of March last, at Marshal's Elm, near the Place aforesaid and afterwards hang'd in Chains, for the barbarous Murder of his Dame, the Particulars whereof have been already related in our Journal of the 21st of December last.

As the *Gloucester Journal* had reported nearly five months before, Collard had also attacked his master's twelve-year-old daughter, cutting and beating her so fiendishly that he thought he had killed her. The reader of this subsequent report now learns that the girl has miraculously recovered, but only through the skill of a man who, whatever else may be said of him, clearly does not care to remain anonymous:

> . . . People presently coming in, and perceiving some breath in the Girl, Dr. MOHUN of Glastenbury (a most ingenious and admirable safe Practitioner in Physick and Surgery) being immediately sent for, strangely recovered her to Life. . . .

It is just as well, perhaps, that Dr. Mohun did not attempt to restore Collard to life.

These thinly disguised testimonials are crude in comparison with the clever and elaborate "press releases" concerning a man whose journeyings across the face of England for several decades were heralded by more "news" than ever marked the movements of the Duke of Marlborough or the royal family. This was John Taylor, esquire, who let it be known that he was "Doctor of Physick, Occulist to the King, Knight of the Order of Portugal, Fellow of the Imperial Academy, and of the Academies of France, Spain, Italy, Sweden, &c."[21] This was the man of whom Samuel Johnson said on 24 April 1779—seven years after Taylor's death—"Taylor was the most ignorant man I ever knew; but sprightly." Taylor's technique for building eager expectation in advance of his visits had all the marks of the professionally planned publicity campaign. "The celebrated Dr. Taylor" was reported in a dozen papers to have been surrounded by a "vast Concourse" of people wherever he went; he gave lectures on "the Make and Beauty of the Eye" to select audiences; he invited "the Gentlemen of the Faculty and Curious" to witness his operations; he saw to it that his published treatises on diseases of the eye—"so well receiv'd Abroad as to be translated into all the Neighbouring Languages"—were advertised in local papers as he moved about the country in one "Progress" or another; he announced his itinerary weeks in advance,[22] and sometimes had to inform his throngs of admirers that pressure of appointments delayed him. He even announced in the *Newcastle Courant*, number 2532 (3 July 1742), that persons who had previously been under his care or were "of inferior Circumstances" would be treated free of charge if they attended his clinic immediately after his arrival in town.

The items of Taylor's "news" which appeared in the *Newcastle Courant*, the *Weekly Worcester Journal*, the

York Courant, the *Norwich Gazette,* the *Cambridge Journal,* and other newspapers make delightful reading; they were probably all written by Taylor himself, and they make a bulky portfolio of self-advertisement. He liked to announce publicly that he had out-stripped his past achievements, and he sometimes listed persons cured by him. On one occasion "Chev." Taylor appears to have used more subtlety than was usual with him by arranging to have the account of his itinerary (in *Aris's Birmingham Gazette,* number 116, 30 January 1744) preceded by a ghastly story showing the regrettable consequences of being treated by a non-professional. It was reported that a Shropshire wagoner suffering from a dislocated shoulder "was prevailed on by a Farrier in his Neighbourhood to submit to an Operation of his," the procedure being that the farrier fastened the man to a post, tied cloths round his arm, and engaged stalwart helpers to apply their strength; but they "pull'd so violently, that they tore his Arm from his Body, and the Man died on the Spot." This, said the writer, "should be a Caution to Persons to make use of those Gentlemen only, whose Profession and Experience must render most serviceable." The next paragraph begins, "Dr. Taylor, Oculist to his Majesty. . . . " Ordinarily the itinerant eye-man simply drafted six or eight notices and sent them at appropriate intervals to the local papers before, during, and after his visit. John Taylor's horn-blowing to herald his approach and the trailing clouds of glory which followed his departure may have been entirely justified by phenomenal success in the restoring of sight; but even if he was an unmitigated quack, his advertising methods were superb.

There were ethical considerations which kept some advertisements from being printed, even in a century which accepted without a qualm all sorts of notices about horse breeding and cures for loathsome diseases. "We are sorry we cou'd not decently insert the advertisement receiv'd last Week," said J. Jopson in his *Coventry Mercury,*

number 887 (3 July 1758); "it's Wit is really too coarse
for our Paper: So wou'd recommend it to the Author to
have it carefully philter'd against some other Opportunity." In general the tone of advertisements is matter
of fact, sometimes detached and dull, occasionally personal and vivacious. If there is little of psychological
subtlety, there is a wide range of theme, and (as in a
good proverb) there is frequently a hint of dramatic
situation or forceful character.

William Cowper found himself amused by the advertisements in the newspaper which came to him on a
wintry night, and it is probable that a reader's amusement
in that "wilderness of strange / But gay confusion"[23] is
increased rather than diminished by an interval of two
centuries. Many an early newspaper proves to be diverting
just for the variety of its paid notices. One column has
advertisements of olive oil, beeswax, fustick, and organ
voluntaries; another invites readers to join the crew of
a privateer, attend an auction, subscribe to a lying-in
hospital, or enjoy a concert at which Mr. Perkins and his
son will "endeavour to please on the Hautboy"; the same
page has a grocer's announcement to peruke makers that
he has for sale hair of all kinds from a London warehouse,
a wholesaler's offer of molasses and English bar iron, and
the business card of James Stephenson, "Druggist and
Chymist" who sells "Colours of all sorts, for Faces, House,
or Ship Painting." One Liverpool flour merchant in 1757
offers at reasonable prices "Ten Pipes of Raisin Wine, a
Parcel of Bottled Cyder, and a Negro Boy." A Newcastle
man offers the unexpended provisions of two whaling
ships just back from Greenland. In 1755, Daniel Stainer
of Sherborne, trumpeter to the sheriffs of Dorset, Somerset, and Bristol, invites gentlemen of the best fortune to
visit the Mermaid Inn, which he has just taken over,
offering "civil Usage," stabling for fifty horses, and a
special attraction at no extra charge: "Music on the
Trumpet, French Horn, Violin, Bass Viol, &c. either singly

or in Consort." Besides farms, hats, harness, and Newfoundland codfish, one could buy drums, fishhooks, lottery
tickets, biscuits for funerals, does (a guinea each), a coal
mine, a spinet, artificial limbs, milch asses, and ready
made shrouds. In St. Ives, a grocer (friend of some modest
parson) said in 1718 that he had for disposal "a Choice
and Private Composure of Manuscript Sermons, in a
legible Hand, and never in Print." Here a pipe organ is
to be raffled; there a thousand oak trees are "expos'd to
sale," or "a Large, Beautiful Ox, six Years old" may be
acquired.

Then, as always, the buyer had to be on his guard. "If
Folks have their Senses," said Robert Whitworth in his
advertisement of the Original Cordial Elixir in 1741,
"there never was more Occasion to use them than now;
for almost every one cries up what he deals in, whether
he thinks it good or not, nay many use all Arts, however
scandalous they are, to promote their own Gain." This
was particularly true of the claims made for medicines
and services. There were in the eighteenth century no
"reduce now, pay later" advertisements, but there was no
imaginable ailment for which a cure was not proposed.
As was pointed out in the preceding chapter, the printers
themselves often sold medicines. It is no concern of ours
whether James Lister, printer of the *Leeds Mercury*, ever
swallowed the "Cordial Tincture for the Cholick and the
Gripes" which he advertised on 24 February 1741, but he
could hardly be blamed if he felt tempted to open a bottle,
since this concoction, his own advertisement stated, was
"of such a chearing, sweetning, warming, searching, cleans-
ing, friendly, balsamick, restorative Nature and Quality,
that it immediately pacifies the most severe and terrible
raking Pains, frees the Body from vicious Humours,
defends the Head from noisome Vapours, takes away
Dizziness and Megrims; being the most speedy and
effectual Remedy yet found out." Similar enthusiasm was
displayed by those who prepared and offered for sale a

hundred other mixtures. Someone ought to gather together a few of these advertisements of potent pills and medicines; they would make a diverting section in a volume compiled for holiday reading.

Entertainment of many kinds was available to contemporary readers of the eighteenth-century country papers. Our ancestors could drink the chalybeate waters "very lately discovered at Brosely in Shropshire"; they could venture to engage in sea bathing at Aldeburgh; they could gaze at five hundred pounds' worth of waxworks to the accompaniment of chamber organ music; they could watch—or participate in—wrestling, backsword ("No Head to be deemed broke unless the Blood runs an Inch"), and dancing competitions; they could visit a showing of auriculas in April, or set eyes on a female rhinoceros—"the real unicorn." There were numerous performances of plays to be enjoyed or endured: *Oroonoko, The Merry Wives of Windsor,* and unheard-of pieces by local playwrights; there was music in practically every town in the kingdom, from performances of the Three Choirs in Gloucester, Hereford, and Worcester to the celebrations of St. Cecilia's Day in various centers and the annual musical festival in Salisbury; there was even a moving-picture machine to be wondered at.[24] Not least attractive among the diversions frequently advertised in the country papers were the battling of cocks, horse racing, and bull baiting.

Few of these quaint and sprightly advertisements prove so stimulating to the imagination as those in which a turn of phrase or a hint of circumstances gives a glimpse of an individual human being. This is a quality which modern advertisers continue to strive for. One touch of nature serves. Perhaps the advertisement is no more than a notification that Mr. Curtis, "very old and weary with Trading," is going out of business in Bury St. Edmund's in 1726; or the announcement by Mr. Hughes of Plymouth in 1723 that his apothecary's shop "with a very Fashionable Set of Bottles" is to be disposed of; or a profuse apology by Thomas Wells of the Devizes in 1725 for having publicly called his neighbor's wife "an Old Pox'd Whore." The situation may be deplorable, or ludicrous, or both. Someone in St. Ives in 1718 decides to expose the fraudulent practices of "an Illiterate and Impudent Pretending Quack . . . a Person who stiles himself, Dr. Vulverstone." A journeyman nailer in Foregate Street, Worcester, beseeches his eloped wife to return because their young child, "which suck'd at her Breast," will die soon if the said breast does not come back. A lath cleaver in Framlingham challenges any other lath cleaver in Suffolk to match him in making a load of oaken rift into lath, "and the Lath as good, . . . let the Timber be great or small or twisted." A distant relative of a later poet fumes with rage in June, 1755, because "on Monday last some Person or Persons did cut off, or otherwise deprive of his Tail, a Hound, belonging to Bish Shelley, Esq.," and the reward for the discovery of the person or persons is to be five guineas. A disgruntled barber and periwig maker of York finds himself with a large stock of wax candles made, as usual, for the minster; but "by Reason he poll'd for Sir Miles Stapylton in the late Election," he has been disappointed in the sale and must sell them off at two shillings a pound. A spirited lady—likely to make herself heard in her community whether she remained in England or migrated to America—has a strong statement to make on a family matter in the *Gloucester Journal* of 10 May 1726:

> Mr. Richard Harwood being a Reproach to his Family, hath nothing to say for himself, but that Mrs. Lucy Stokes, his Aunt, hath defrauded him of an Estate: Therefore she declares she is ready to shew her Title to the said Estate, at Longford, and bids Defiance to any body that says she defrauded them.

This is gossip, and gossip is the most ephemeral of all

human communication; but the defiance of Lucy Stokes and the annoyance of Bish Shelley, like many of the wants and warnings and money-making efforts reflected in these old newspaper advertisements, have a charm which does not dwindle.

1. The first issue was entitled *True Character of Mercurius Urbanicus & Rusticus,* and from number 14 the title was *Mercury, publishing advertisements of all sorts: as of Persons run away, lost or spirited; horses, or other Things lost or stoln.*

2. 10 Anne, c. 19, An Act for laying several Duties upon all Sope and Paper made in Great Britain, or imported into the same, . . . And upon several Kinds of stampt Vellum, Parchment, and Paper; And upon certain printed Papers, Pamphlets, and Advertisements, for raising the Sum of Eighteen hundred thousand Pounds by way of a Lottery towards Her Majesties Supply. . . .

3. A.O.3/950 to 1026. The figures showing the gross produce of the advertisement duty in Great Britain for the years 1713 to 1798 have been assembled by Professor A. Aspinall in "Statistical Accounts of the London Newspapers in the Eighteenth Century," *English Historical Review,* CCXLVI (1948), 201-32.

4. *Op. cit.,* p. 204.

5. The authorities kept an eye on Norris. A month later he wrote on the front page of his paper, "Taunton, Septem 3rd. this Day Mr Hollis Inspector of the Stamp Duties was at my House in Taunton." The copies on which these notes were written are now in the library of the Somerset Archaeological and Natural History Society, Taunton.

6. The copy on which this receipt was written is in the Clifford Collection, deposited in the Gloucester City Libraries.

7. "A Chariot and one Pair of Harness to be sold, all little the worse for wear. Enquire at the Printing-Office in Gloucester."

8. 10 Anne, c. 19, section cxviii.

9. The office copy of this paper is in the Bristol Municipal Library.

10. Worrall's tardy habits appear also in the Audit Office accounts in the Public Record Office (A.O.3/952 to 954), which show annual unpaid balances usually amounting to more than two thousand pounds due to the receiver-general from the Gloucestershire collector. For the year ending 2 August 1755, for example, the outstanding balance due from Worrall for all kinds of duties was £2,197 17s. 5¼d. Of this total, the sum of £252 16s. 19½d. was owing for duties of "Several Kinds," including the duty on advertisements.

11. Curll's letter and the report of the Commissioners of Stamp

Duties are filed as Treasury Board Papers CCLXXVI, No. 14. See *Calendar of Treasury Books and Papers 1731-1734,* ed. W. A. Shaw (London: H. M. Stationery Office, 1898), p. 65.

12. 30 George 2, c.19 [1757].

13. Charles Welsh, *A Bookseller of the Last Century* (London, 1885), p. 12. The passage is also quoted by K. G. Burton in *The Early Newspaper Press in Berkshire (1723-1855)* (Reading: Privately Printed, 1954), p. 118.

14. Details have been assembled and interpreted by K. G. Burton, *op. cit.,* pp. 54-55, and 254.

15. An advertisement commending an edition of Churchill's *Collection of Voyages and Travels* occupies two and a half columns on the first page of the *Derby Mercury,* number 51 (2 March 1744).

16. *Op. cit.,* p. 50.

17. "We print every week several hundreds more than our Predecessors in the Printing Office ever did, which makes the Advantage of advertising in the *York-Courant* too obvious to require any Thing farther to be offered on this Hand."

18. London publishers frequently advertised their books in provincial newspapers before as well as after 1760.

19. Long before 1750, James Abree used pages one, three, and four for advertisements in his *Kentish Post: or the Canterbury News-Letter.*

20. Attempts to examine the subtle differences of type in continuous prose are set forth by Sir Cyril Burt in *A Psychological Study of Typography* (London: Cambridge University Press, 1959).

21. Taylor's titles became more glittering as time went on. In *Jopson's Coventry Mercury,* number 927 (9 April 1759), he was called "the Chevalier Taylor, Ophthalmiater (Oculist) to his present Majesty, to the Pontifical and Imperial Courts, and to the several other Crown'd Heads, &c." But back in 1732, the *Newcastle Courant,* number 349, declared that its earlier report of Taylor's having been "complimented with the Degree of Doctor" at the University of Edinburgh was false.

22. In *Aris's Birmingham Gazette,* number 35 (12 July 1742), there appeared as "news" the statement that Taylor would "return to London from Chester in the following Manner: Will arrive at Hull the 9th of this Month, 17 Lincoln, 20 Nottingham, 21 Derby, 23 Leicester, 24 Stamford, 27 Harborough, 28 Northampton, 29 Warwick, 31 Worcester, August 2d Hereford, 4th Gloucester, 6th Cirencester, 9th Bristol, and from thence by Bath for London."

23. *The Task,* IV, 78 f.

24. This was Mrs. Hurck's "Moving Paper Machine," exhibited at Shrewsbury in August 1742. It was reported in *Aris's Birmingham Gazette,* number 140 (16 August 1742), to be "the most curious and surprising Piece of Machinery . . . ever seen, every Figure resembling Life so near, and in their proper Motion, as not to fail raising the greatest Wonder and Satisfaction in the Beholder."

Chapter V

THE
Ipſwich Journal,
OR,
Weekly-Mercury:

The South Eaſt Proſpect of Ipſwich.

With the Freſheſt Advices Foreign and Domeſtick.

From SATURDAY *June* 3, to SATURDAY *June* 10. 1721.

From *Stanley*'s News-Letter, June 3.

Yeſterday the Committee appointed to Enquire who was the Author of the Traitorous Letter in Miſt's Journal of Saturday laſt, and other Affairs, ſat in the Speaker's Chamber and Examined Mr. Crawford Mareſhal of the King's Bench, and the Priſon Books in Relation to the Action of 500 l. laid againſt Miſt, as alſo a Stationer who is Plantiff in the ſaid occaſion, and ſome begin to ſay, that this Action is only a Sham and Contrivance to keep Miſt out of Newgate. This Committee is compoſed of the Lord Hinchenbroke, Chairman, and Mr. Walpole, the two Mr. Poultneys, Sir Richard Steel, Mr. Kelſoe, Mr. Stanhope, and 4 or 5 others.

The ſame Day the Committee of the Houſe of Commons gave the following Allowances to the Reſt of the late Directors, viz.

To Theodore Janſen 50000 l. on a Diviſion 134 againſt 118. Sir Jacob Jacobſon 11000 l. which is the whole of his Inventory. Arthor Ingram 2500 l. Sir John Lambert 5000 l. Sir Harcourt Maſter 5000 l. Mr. Morley 1800 l. which is the whole of his Inventory, except 69 l. 10 s. 3 d. Ambroſs Page 10000 l. Col. Raymond 30000 l. Samuel Read 10000 l. Thomas Reynolds 14000 l.

The further Conſideration of Publick Credit was deferred to Wedneſday, after ſome Debates, wherein a Controverſy happened between Mr. Walpole and Mr. Lechmere about

Proroguing the Parliament for a ſhort time, in Order the better to confirm the Reſolution of the Grand Committee, for remitting part of the 7 Millions, Mr. Walpole argued the Neceſſity of a Prorogation, and Mr. Lechmere that there was no Neceſſity, but nothing was done in this Affair.

We hear ſome of the greateſt Lawyers are of Opinion, that Miſt's Caſe amounts to High Treaſon.

We are aſſured that the Report from the Secret Committee, formerly mentioned, will certainly be made on Monday next, and in all likelihood it will be very Extraordinary, there is the greateſt Expectation imaginable to hear the Contents of it, and what will enſue thereon.

This Day the Committee of the Houſe of Commons allowed Mr. Sawbridge 5000 l. Mr. Tillard 15000 l. Mr. Turner 8000 l. which was the whole of his Account, except 96 l. Mr. Surmon 5000 l. And Mr. Grigsby is deferred to Monday.

Some Letters from Paris mention, That Sir Robert Sutton has procured the releaſe of the Proteſtants who are Galley Slaves for Religion.

FOREIGN AFFAIRS.

Conſtantinople, May 9. The youngeſt Son of the Sultan is dead. The Head of Ali Paſcia, late Governor of Egypt, is brought hither from Grand Cairo, and is laid before the Seraglio. And that the Boſtangi-Baſha, prime Favourite of the Sultan, who eſpous'd his Daughter, is fallen into Diſgrace, and will be ſtript of his Employments, and it is thought will be ſtrangled,

Geneva

News from Far and Near

FROM THE PRIMEVAL DAYS of drum-thumpings and smoke signals in the jungle to twentieth-century electronic devices on and above the earth, man has had a lively interest in the getting and sending of bulletins about his neighbors; and it appears that the Englishman's desire for "intelligence" has been more vehement than that of any other human being.

> The Love of NEWS is ne'er to be supprest,
> With great and small, it reigns in ev'ry Breast.

So reads a couplet—one of twenty-six—in a set of verses "On the Pleasure of reading News" printed in *Ayscough's Nottingham Courant*, number 239 (7 June 1760). "There is no Humour in my Countrymen," wrote Addison in the *Spectator*, number 452 (8 August 1712), "which I am more inclined to wonder at than their general Thirst after News." With his usual touch of light satire Addison suggested that it did not matter much to his compatriots

FIG. 6.—The written newsletters regularly received from London were widely used as sources of information about House of Common affairs. (By permission of the Trustees of the British Museum.)

whether the reports they read so eagerly were good or bad, trivial or tremendous: "A Victory or a Defeat is equally agreeable to them." Addison was enjoying himself by laughing at his contemporaries' eagerness to hear "the latest," but it was this same eagerness that led to the establishing of newspapers all over the country, and no matter what these papers were called—*Journal, Gazette, Mercury, Courant,* and so forth—their substance was chiefly what many a subtitle announced as freshest advices, foreign and domestic.

"Great must be the Curiosity of the Kingdom, which can support such a Cloud of News-Writers, who live chearfully upon the publick Thirst of Information." So wrote "Historianus" in his letter to "Criton" in the *British Journal* on 14 December 1723. His point and his method were very much like Addison's eleven years earlier, but he emphasized more sharply the failure of news writers and news readers alike to distinguish between the significant and the trivial.

> . . . a Story of a Prince, and a Story of a Drayman, are told in the same Style, and with the same Decorations, and with such thorough Information, that neither can a Prince strain his Ankle, nor a Drayman put his Knee out, but presently their Disasters, with the sending for Surgeons, and the Hopes of Cure, are committed with Care to divers faithful Three-Halfpenny Records itinerant.

Continuing the banter, "Historianus" complained that the printers of news usually separated foreign dispatches from the accounts of happenings at home, and suggested that it would be more agreeable if the two sorts of news were mingled. Then came examples of the proposed arrangement, for the guidance of "that Curious and Communicative Society, who daily and weekly instruct the World in what the World is doing":

> *Hamburgh; October 19.* Letters from *Petersburgh* relate, That the *Persian* Ambassador hath concluded a Treaty

of Alliance between his Czarish Majesty and the young *Sophi*. Hereupon the Ambassador entertain'd the Court at a sumptuous Banquet.

From *York* they write, That *Barnaby Thunder* and *Anthony Hotspur* Esquires, of that County, have put an End at last to their long Family Quarrel about the Boundaries of a Brick-Kiln; and, by the Mediation of the Curate, have consolidated their Fox-Hounds, intending for the future, as a sincere Mark of Reconciliation, to hunt together. Upon which, as a Seal of Peace and Friendship, they drank two Days and two Nights Hand to Fist.

"Historianus" supplied other illuminating examples, and concluded with advertisements in the same vein.

These essays in the *Spectator* and the *British Journal*, like *Tatler* papers number 18, 155, and 178, and Goldsmith's observations on the same theme in the fourth and fifth *Chinese Letters*, were written in fun. A more serious tone is detected in a letter from "Ned Friendly" to "Caleb D'Anvers" of the *Craftsman*, in number 546 (18 December 1736), on the subject of news writers and their blunders and artifices. The men who write news, says Ned, will doubtless allege in defense of their fictitious reports the plain fact that human beings are naturally eager for news of any kind, and as the newsmen have to publish *something* regularly, they might as well give up their papers if they cannot feel free to make up the stories they print. Besides, he adds, the printers of newspapers have found that their readers are as much pleased with false news as true; and if real news is scarce, they think there can be no harm in concocting acceptable imitations of the real thing. Coffee-house politicians have always been eager to read and—like Politic in Fielding's *Rape upon Rape* or Squeezum in Bernard Miles's *Lock up Your Daughters* —to believe whatever they see in print.

Scarcity of genuine news must in all ages be the newsman's nightmare, for the gaping columns have to be filled. "Not one Article of News in this Day's Gazette," said Robert Goadby in his *Sherborne Mercury* on 5 January

1756; and this was a complaint not infrequently made by others. "We hope, in the present Scarcity of News, the following Poems will not be unacceptable to our Readers," said Raikes and Dicey in the *Gloucester Journal* of 4 January 1725, and in other issues they made a point of promising that "in the Dearth of News" they would keep their *Journal* pleasant as well as profitable to readers by inserting "something New and Entertaining."[1] "I desire you to erase out my Name from among the Number of your Subscribers," wrote a correspondent in the *British Spy* early in December, 1728, "unless in your next you give me a just Reason of the Barrenness of your Intelligence"; and in number 79 (5 December 1728) S. Hodgkinson protested that it was hard to give his readers in Derby and vicinity the full measure which they expected every week:

> When the Mails fail us, and the People are unactive at home, when great Folks are so ill-natur'd as neither to marry nor die, nor beget Children, we are upon the Search for that scarce commodity call'd Wit, which, 'tis well known, is in these our Days as hard to come at in any Week (especially in *Derby,)* as Intelligence.

Indeed everybody recognized that there would inevitably be times when advices from home and abroad would be sparse and that other matters must on occasion serve in their place.

But news was the staple, and it was a rash proprietor who allowed other things to crowd out the news.[2] Samuel Johnson, who was not easily pleased by news writers, spoke for thousands of Englishmen when he declared in the first issue of the *London Chronicle* (1 January 1757), "The first Demand made by the Reader of a Journal is, that he should find an accurate Account of foreign Transactions and domestick Incidents." If some proprietors were willing to run the risk of losing readers by printing revenue-producing advertisements in place of news, there were many who let it be known that letters and contributed pieces would never be allowed to crowd out the news. Isaac Thompson, author of the very successful *Newcastle Journal,* made a clear statement to this effect at the top of his first column in number 15 (14 July 1739):

> We hope our Correspondents will not take it amiss that we do not immediately give their Letters a Place in this Paper; whenever the publick Intelligence will admit of it, we shall be sure to oblige every one in this Respect, as far as possible: But we have not Room this Week for any Essay; and perhaps (considering what Affairs at present seem to promise) this may often be the Case, which we believe our Readers will not only excuse, but expect.

The following issues of the *Newcastle Journal* even sacrifice Thompson's own treatise for the sake of news, as is explained in number 16 (21 July 1739): "The Quantity of News at present obliges us to publish our Geography by very short and abrupt Pieces."

News, then, was the *sine qua non* of the provincial weeklies, and not fictitious news either. It was the constant demand of the proprietors—as it really was of their readers—that the news should be true. Veracity, said the energetic John Jackson of the *York Gazetteer* (number 14, 15 December 1741), was "the only Substantial Qualification for one in our Business." Honest efforts were made to print only what was trustworthy, and several newspapers particularly requested correspondents to send in only well-attested reports. John Newbery and Charles Micklewright perhaps intended to impress readers as much as voluntary reporters when they placed this notice at the head of their *Reading Mercury* in 1742 and later years:

> ☞ As the Proprietors of this Paper are desirous to have it correct, and, as near as they can, to insert nothing but Facts, they hope their Correspondents in all Parts will take care to transmit no Accounts but what they know to be

true; and all Intelligence that is genuine will be thankfully receiv'd.

A notice with precisely the same wording was placed at the head of the *Doncaster Flying-Post; or, Hull and Sheffield Weekly Advertiser* in 1755, and the printers of several other papers made a similar request.

Such pleas for veracity were undoubtedly necessary, for many inaccurate reports were sent in and printed in good faith. "We are assured from Shrewsbury," wrote Thomas Aris in his *Birmingham Gazette,* number 391 (8 May 1749), "that the Account sent from thence last Week, and inserted in this Paper, in relation to the Fireworks there, was an entire Falsehood." Newspaper men may on occasion, like Daniel Defoe, invent news rather than wait for the mails to bring interesting stories,[3] but they hesitate to print accounts invented by others, unless, like Robert Whitworth of the *Manchester Magazine,* they place suspicious items under the heading "Rumours."

Printers of newspapers in Derby were notably reluctant to print details not well authenticated. S. Hodgkinson of the *British Spy: or, Derby Post Man* may have felt it wise to be especially circumspect because of an attack by a local clergyman, but he showed admirable editorial caution in number 14 (13 July 1727) in describing the effects of "an astonishing Sort of a Whirlwind, followed by a violent Tempest of Wind." The storm killed Jermain Harrison, a malt miller, and the lightning melted the coins in his pocket. "I hear of other Effects likewise of this Storm; but not being thoroughly inform'd of the Particulars, must omit the Insertion." In number 22 of his *British Spy* Hodgkinson protected himself from a possible charge of prevarication by naming the voluntary reporter and implied a degree of skepticism about a six-year-old girl's visions by the use of "he says":

Derby, Sept. 14. One Thomas Bostock of Buzlum near Newcastle under Lime, gives us the following Narrative, viz. He says that a noted Farmer living at Wiln-House, near Foukam-Moor, about a Mile beyond Leak in Staffordshire, having a Daughter about five or six Years old, the Girl has for as many Weeks past, seen, and still continues to see, some Daemon, Spectre, or Airy-Composure . . . assuming human Shape, but of little Magnitude, and imperceptible to all but his Child. . . .

When Sam Drewry, printer of the *Derby Mercury*, read a report of Commodore Anson's successes at sea in 1742, he could have been pardoned for being slightly skeptical about the statement that Anson's prizes included five millions of pieces of eight, but he nevertheless printed the account, for it had been sent in "a private Letter to a Gentleman in this Town," and was, he said, "thought to be authentick."

It is one of the hazards of journalism that a piece of "intelligence" may prove to be ill-founded; and if there is no time to verify a report before press time, the editor has to decide which of two risks to take: should he miss the opportunity of printing a good story or suffer the embarrassment of having later to correct a false one? The *Weekly Worcester Journal,* number 856 (19 November 1725), printed an exciting story about the finding of a body. The detail about the exact depth of the soil and the precise description of the clothing seem convincing:

Worcester, Nov. 18. Last Week as some Workmen were digging in the Yard in the Foregate-Street, commonly call'd *The Pound,* where now a handsome House is building, they found buried within 8 inches of the Surface, a Man having on a Calimanco Wastcoat, Holland Shirt, Jersey Stockins, and Boots; but as soon as his Apparel or Flesh was touch'd it fell to Dust. His Corps was taken thence and buried in St. Oswel's Hospital-Burying-Place.

But the next issue contained a note which shows how easy it must have been to accept as genuine a circumstantial report that came in just before press time:

In the *Worcester* Paragraph of our last Paper, our Readers are desired to take Notice, that it was a false Report brought us last Thursday a little before the News was compleated, of the Corpse of a Man found buried in his Cloaths; whereas upon examining the Workmen, do find it appear to be no more than some dry human Bones and a Skull, which they put in a Kipe and buried in the Hospital Burying-place close adjoyning. The Person that brought the Account nam'd the Person that buried the said Corpse, which proves as false as its having on Cloaths, or Flesh, on the Bones. . . .

The printer had not yet learned that reports brought in by excited onlookers needed confirmation before they were set up in type.

A more exciting piece of news reached the editor of the *Bath Advertiser*, who used italics for a heading and enclosed in quotation marks a special report, printed as the last item of news in number 46 (28 August 1756):

> *Extract of a letter from Portsmouth, Aug. 26.*
> "This Evening were brought in here, five French ships,
> "one of 60 Guns, one of 50, and three frigates, taken by
> "Admiral Boscawen, Part of a Convoy; more are expec-
> "ted, as a very great Firing has been heard for many Hours
> "in the Channel."

The report aroused the greatest excitement in the South of England; but a week later, Stephen Martin, printer of the *Bath Advertiser*, set as his first item of news under the heading "Bath, September 4" a second announcement to the effect that "the wish'd-for good News, after the strictest Enquiry" had proved to be false. It was not five enemy ships that had appeared in the Channel but a Dutch man-of-war, with a convoy, "brought to by the Admiral to be examined for contraband Goods." Strange flags and the firing of salutes had occasioned the reporter's mistake; and "a Desire of giving the earliest Intelligence to our Readers" had been responsible for the premature insertion of the paragraph.

It would be easier to condemn a provincial editor for fumbling credulousness if it were not for his readiness to correct the error, which was often not his fault. Again and again a report taken from a London "print" or from one of the well-established written newsletters proved to be erroneous. A typical example is the account "From Wye's Letter, October 7" copied verbatim in the *Gloucester Journal*, number 288 (10 October 1727):

> They write from Bristol, that the Colliers of Kingswood, who, assembled in great Bodies to pull down the Turnpikes, are now busy in mending the Highways, particularly the sandy Lane which lies between them and that City, which they are making a very good Road; they chuse to do this themselves rather than pay a Toll which they may never know the end of, but whether they will be excused or no on this Account, a little Time will shew, for the Commissioners are going to set up eleven Turnpikes in the Room of those pull'd down.

In the following issue of the *Gloucester Journal* was a very different statement of what the Kingswood colliers were doing:

> Gloucester, Oct. 14. The Account from Bristol, by the way of London, incerted in our last, relating to the Colliers repairing the Roads, proves a Mistake, and the Truth is as follows. That by a former Order of the Quarter Sessions at Gloucester, 6d. in the Pound hath lately been rais'd on the Land Holders in the Parish of St. Philip and Jacob, for repairing of their Highways; Sir Abraham Elton, Bart. and another of his Majesty's Justices, being appointed Expenditors for the said Purpose; the Colliers being not at all concern'd in it, except any of them that are hired for Day Labourers.

This correcting of a false report redeems Raikes from the charge of gullibility, but his best defence was the fact that he indicated where he had found the story.

Where did the news printed in these country papers come from? It can be said at once that most of it was taken directly from what were often described as "the most reputable Prints and Letters," by which were meant the printed newspapers and the written newsletters, mainly from London. All the accounts of what was going on in London, most foreign news, and even much of the matter under the caption "Country News" came to local printers from the *London Gazette,* from the other London papers—daily, thrice-weekly, twice-weekly, and weekly— or from the written newsletters of Stanley, Wye, and fifty others.[4] For news of shipping there was *Lloyd's List,* which apparently was available as early as 1726.[5]

A few printers of provincial newspapers gave no hint whatever of the sources of their news, merely indicating the days on which the several posts brought the usual selection of London papers. The *Norwich Post,* for instance, had a standard phrase in the heading of each of the three batches of news: "This Day's Post brought the following Advices." No indication of the source of news is given in *Pilborough's Colchester Journal.* In its earlier years John White's *Newcastle Courant* excluded all reference to the papers from which news had been abstracted; though in number 95 (8 March 1712), White disclosed that he customarily drew upon several sources; refuting the *Newcastle Gazette's* charge of "stuffing his Paper with Notorious Falcities," White admitted that some errors might occasionally be found "amongst so great variety of Intelligence from so many different Persons and Places."

Some printers—Stephen Bryan, of Worcester, for example—gave vague and non-committal hints that the news they printed was "From the London Prints," "From one of the London News Papers," "From Dyer's Letter and other Intelligence," "From Wye's Letter, St. James's—, the London-Evening-Post, and other Prints." Until the *Plymouth Weekly Journal* had been appearing for five years, its printer gave no hint of the papers from which news was usually transcribed; it was only in 1724 that E. Kent began to put at the end of groups of paragraphs such acknowledgments as "(So far *St. James's Eve. Post*)" or "(*Dormer's Letter*)."

Most printers throughout the period 1700-1760 indicated quite definitely in one way or another the several papers from which they regularly took their pieces of news. In 1757, *Whitworth's Manchester Advertiser* had under its date line the forthright assertion, "This Paper contains more News than any other sold in these Parts; and is collected from the *London Gazette*, all the *Evening Posts, Daily Papers, Lloyd's List*, and sometimes private *London Letters*." More precise evidence concerning London papers regularly taken by a local printer is the notice in *F. Farley's Bristol Journal*, number 98 (11 April 1746):

> *.* Any Merchant that may want to oblige a foreign Correspondent with the London Gazette, London and General Evening Posts, as also the Daily and General Advertisers that come on a Friday, may be supply'd therewith at an easy Rate, by applying to the Printer hereof.——Loose London Papers for several Months back may now be had.

Robert Walker and William Jackson assured readers of their *Oxford Flying Weekly Journal* that the twopence which they paid for a copy of the paper brought them the equivalent of an arm-load of daily and weekly newspapers from all over the kingdom and from Western Europe:

> The Advices inserted in this Journal are collected from the following Papers, viz. Amsterdam, Utrecht, Hague, Brussels, Paris and London Gazettes; the Paris Ala-Main; London, General, St. James's and Whitehall Evening Posts; London Courant; Daily Advertiser; General Advertiser; Daily Gazetteer; Craftsman; Westminster Journal; Dublin and Edinburgh News-Papers; Wye's, Fox's and other written Letters, and from all Country News-Papers, and Private Intelligence.

An almost identical list was placed at the head of the first column in the *Cambridge Journal*, printed by Walker and

Thomas James; and a similar list stood at the top of the first column of the paper which J. Keating printed in Stratford.

There were some—among them the *Northampton Mercury,* the *Reading Journal,* and *Schofield's Middlewich Journal*—which assured their readers that the news was authoritative by printing at the top of the first page a list of papers usually quoted, with a key to the abbreviations attached to the several articles or groups of articles in the columns below. Others omitted the list but attached to the individual items of news abbreviated acknowledgments like "Gen. Ev." or "Lond. Ev. Post." Where this was done it is possible to take almost the whole paper apart and uncombine the components, tracing them with the utmost ease to the exact columns in particular newspapers from which the "author's" scissors-and-paste method had taken them as he compiled each issue.

Nowhere is this synthetic process more obvious than in the *North Country Journal,* printed in Newcastle by various members of the Umphreville family from 1734 to 1739. The clues are listed in a note at the top of the first column, with the heading, "To the Reader":

> This News-Paper being Collected from the following London Prints, &c. the Letters at the end of each Paragraph shew from which the same is taken, viz.

G. E.	General Evening	L. E.	London Evening
P.	Postboy	S. J. E.	St. James's Ev.
Cr.	Craftsman	D. A.	Daily Advertiser
L. J.	London Journal	F. J.	Fog's Journal
W. M.	Weekly Miscellany	D. C.	Daily Courant
D. J.	Daily Journal	W. L.	Wye's Letter
C. J.	Corn Cutter's Jo.	D. P.	Daily Post

It is a very simple exercise to "unstick" all the items in any one issue of the *North Country Journal* and find the exact spot from which each was taken out of one contemporary London newspaper or another. It is a question whether anyone found this acknowledgment particularly reassuring; but the device had at least the merit of complete frankness, and the compiler could feel exonerated from any charge of having invented news; he honestly admitted that it was all stolen.

One important ingredient in the hotchpotch—material taken from written newsletters—is less easily traced to the original publication than are the excerpts from London or other "prints"; but that is so only because few of the written newsletters have survived. The General Post Office Letter and the bulletins supplied regularly by Stanley, Wye, Fox, Jackson, Le Bourdery, King, Godwin, Fountain, Calcroft, Tompkins, and many others throughout the period were widely quoted in country newspapers, especially for political news, the acknowledgment being either an abbreviation of the title appended to a quoted passage or a special caption preceding it, such as "From Green's News-Letter, October 9." Stanley and Wye were especially useful as sources of news from elsewhere in the provinces.

One provincial newspaper deserves special mention for its exceptional treatment of news from foreign journals. Ordinarily such news came to London printers in French or Dutch or Spanish newspapers and reached the provincial printers only after having been translated and printed in the London papers.[6] This took time; and as not all printers had translators on their staffs, the first translation to appear in print was unblushingly copied by any printers who desired to use it.[7] The provincial printers as a rule simply accepted whatever translations or summaries reached them. Among the items which *Adams's Weekly Courant,* number 885 (Tuesday, 28 March 1750), reprinted as having reached Chester in Saturday's post was "From the Paris A-la-main, March 27: An Arret of the Council of State is issued for suppressing a certain immoral Work, intituled, *The History of* TOM JONES, translated from the English." In *Adams's Weekly Cour-ant*, as in other papers, foreign news invariably stood at the head of every batch of news. But Andrew Hooke of Bristol and a "Society" of associates responsible for the publication of the *Oracle: Or, Bristol Weekly Miscellany* made a special feature of taking in the continental news-papers themselves and of translating selected articles for their readers. The gain in time was considerable.

The plan was explained in an announcement standing at the head of early issues of the *Oracle*—for example number 3 (Saturday, 17 April 1742): " . . . our Intelli-gences are directly transmitted to us from abroad; . . . all our Foreign News is translated by our selves from original Authorities, and, most commonly, composed for the Press before it comes from London in the English Papers." The issue of 8 May 1742 frankly stated that the latest news to come by that day's post had already been set up in type in the *Oracle* office: "it came to hand in the Original Papers Thursday, was translated here, and composed for the Press yesterday." Within a few weeks the proprietors of the *Oracle* were doing what must have seemed marvelously modern and efficient: they were post-ing their latest foreign news in a public place many hours before their rivals could exhibit their freshest advices. Hooke's headquarters were at the St. Michael's coffee house "in Maudlin-Lane, near St. James's Church-Yard." There, as one sees by a prominent notice under the date line of number 20 (14 August 1742) and subsequent issues, "the original foreign Gazettes from which our Intelligence is taken, with their English Translations, may be seen, generally a Day, and many times two Days, before it comes to any other Coffee-House." This notable effort by the proprietors of a provincial newspaper to provide their readers with the latest foreign dispatches is most praiseworthy, for the service could not have been more direct.

It remains a fact that much of what filled the columns

of news in the provincial papers did not originate locally; but it would be quite wrong to suppose that *every* item of news in country newspapers had already been published elsewhere. Examples quoted above and others to follow serve to show that, in addition to foreign and domestic advices copied from London newspapers, from papers printed in Edinburgh, Glasgow, Dublin, or Belfast, from the weekly newsletters, from Continental or colonial newspapers received by the local printer, and from other country newspapers, there was no lack of news derived from local and regional sources or sent in by correspondents at a distance. The news which is most entertaining and most illuminating to read now, indeed, is the news, *not* taken from printed newspapers and written newsletters, but either secured by the personal efforts of the local editor and his engaged reporters or sent in to him by friendly readers; the reports of local observers, the dispatches of special correspondents, and communications of traveling townsmen make a body of quite delightful reading, no matter what the subject.

Not every item of news introduced by such words as "They write from Eye in Suffolk" or "We hear from Trowbridge in Wilts" is necessarily a first-hand account, for these are formulas frequently used by Stanley and other writers of newsletters, and the passages so headed may have come by way of London. Sometimes the date of the account in relation to the date of the newspaper in which it occurs is sufficient to prove that the incident was reported directly, if the interval of time is too short for the story to have been copied from another publication. It is obvious that a report dated at Shields on 9 July 1717 announcing that "Yesternight came in here the Friendship of Boston in New-England, Mr. Rich. Mayhair Commander from Virginia . . . " was sent direct from Shields to Newcastle, for it appeared in small type as the final item of news in the *Newcastle Courant,* number 930 (10 July 1717). It can be assumed that the report of an incident in the *Gloucester Journal,* number 237 (18 October 1726), did not come from a London newspaper, for it begins, "Gloucester, Oct. 15. They write from Wooton Underedge, in this county. . . . " Similarly an account dated at Exmouth on 18 December and printed in the *Sherborne Mercury,* number 408 (20 December 1756), cannot have been taken from another newspaper; and a long letter dated at Liverpool on 13 April 1759 and printed in the *Union Journal* (Halifax) on 17 April cannot have reached the *Union Journal* office via a London paper.

Best evidence of originality is to be detected in specific references to "Our Correspondent in Oxford" or to the writer of particular accounts. "We thank our Correspondent at East Knoyle for his Occurrences," wrote Robert Raikes in the *Gloucester Journal,* number 231 (6 September 1726), "but his Letters not coming to hand till the 31st of August, we could not insert them till this Week." In this and subsequent issues are printed several items of news sent in by the anonymous reader at East Knoyle. A special letter from Yarmouth addressed to William Chase, the printer of the *Norwich Mercury,* reported "the Case of Elizabeth Thompson, who was executed here Yesterday." The *Newcastle Courant* had in its issue of 19 January 1734 a report "sent us from one of our Correspondents" concerning a charge laid against a Durham customs officer for assaulting John Armstrong, the Sutherland carrier, on the road. The *Salisbury Journal* reported that the previous week the western post had been stopped by three footpads near Coker Hill, about three miles below Yeovil, and that a later communication told of a second attack: "Last Night about 8 o'clock in the Evening, an Express came here from Sherburn in Dorsetshire, with an Account that the Western Post Boy was robb'd early in the Morning by three Foot-Pads near the same Place, and suppos'd to be the same Persons that robb'd it on Tuesday last as above mentioned. . . . "

News could be even fresher if it was brought in person by a witness rather than sent by a messenger. The *Gloucester Journal,* number 499 (2 November 1731), gave the first exciting account of a fatal duel, fought in a nearby city, which at that time had no newspaper of its own. The report, a single breathless sentence, was printed in italics:

> *Early this Morning a Man pass'd thro' this City for Herefordshire, by whom we have an Account, that one Mr. Price, a young Gentleman, whose Father lives in that County, was shot dead on the Spot Yesterday in the Afternoon at Bath, in an Engagement between him and an Irish Gamester, who is a very lusty Man, and has absconded.*

Later issues of the *Gloucester Journal* gave more details, including an advertisement inserted by the father of the victim and a letter sent to the printer from the Hague by Charles Jones relating "the Particulars of the Duel fought between him and the unfortunate Mr. Prise at Bath the 31st ult. . . . "

It is perfectly clear that the printers of the *Salisbury Journal,* the *Gloucester Journal,* and numerous other country newspapers often set up news from manuscript copy received from local or regional sources rather than from London "prints" and newsletters; but that is not all: there were several country papers which had special correspondents in London itself, whose reports supplemented those in the regular London paper. Caesar Ward provided readers of his *York Courant* in 1742 with special reports on affairs of state sent to him by "R.F.," whom Ward referred to as "our Correspondent at London." Thomas Aris, as was pointed out in Chapter II above, gave special prominence to reports sent to him by his London correspondent, and there is point in the subtitle of his *Birmingham Gazette: or, the General Correspondent.*

It is not clear how long and on what terms these London correspondents served, and there is the same uncertainty about correspondents in America. One paper, *F. Farley's Bristol Journal,* made a special feature of direct communication from across the Atlantic, in much the same way as Andrew Hooke five years earlier had boasted about his prompt translating of foreign newspapers for readers of his *Oracle.* On 14 November 1747, *F. Farley's Bristol Journal,* number 1589, printed items of news dated at New York and Boston and received "From our Correspondent at Boston in New England, by the Greyhound, Capt. Adlam." Farley then added a note implying that these rapid-transit dispatches—they were only about seven weeks old—were an exclusive feature in his *Journal:*

> N.B. The above Boston Correspondent (as also the Printer at Philadelphia) has engaged to supply us with the most early Intelligence from their Parts of the World, by all Opportunities.——Such Advantages cannot but render this Paper of still greater Amusement to its Readers—— who increase in such a manner, as to oblige us to make several *extra* Impressions almost every Saturday, whilst the *Interlopers* in the Opposition die away with the *utmost Contempt.*

Farley apparently expected that news would be brought to him direct from the American colonies by ships putting in at Bristol. This really was giving his readers special service; for ordinarily, like readers of other provincial papers, they could expect to hear of events that had taken place across the Atlantic only after the reports had been printed in London papers and copied in the local paper. There was plenty of American news, especially after the '45 had ceased to swell the columns; but only papers printed in or near seaports could ever offer American dispatches before they were seen by London readers.[8]

Some of the most interesting reports reached the provincial printers and their readers because alert observers took the trouble to write unsolicited accounts of occurrences witnessed by them. "As I imagine a particular

Narrative, from an Actor in it, will prove more satisfactory, than what the London Papers collect; I therefore send you the following, which please to receive as the first Offering of an Indian Correspondent; who intends (with your leave) occasionally transmitting what further occurs, in this Part of the Eastern World, . . . and what he can safely assert to you as authentic." So wrote Samuel Beaven from on board the "Revenge," Captain William Dick, "in Gariah Harbour (the late Capital Fort of Angria) in Lat. 16. 33 N. about 30 Leagues to the Northward of Goa." The communication, addressed to Benjamin Collins, author of the *Salisbury Journal,* was dated 18 March 1756, but would undoubtedly be read with interest by Collins' subscribers in the issue dated 29 November 1756. In number 78 (23 December 1755) of his *Leedes Intelligencer,* Griffith Wright offered readers an "Extract of a private Letter from a Gentleman at Lisbon, to a Merchant in this Town, dated Nov. 20." It gave a vivid account of the effects of the devastating earthquake in Lisbon at the beginning of November.

A piece of unsolicited reporting worth noticing appeared in the *Norwich Mercury* on Saturday, 16 September 1727, in the form of "A Copy of a Letter sent from Mr. Percival at Barton-Mills, to Justice Mott in Norwich." It is an account of a disaster at Burwell in Cambridgeshire on Friday evening of the previous week. One hundred and nineteen men, women, and children, who had assembled in a barn to enjoy a puppet show, lost their lives within four minutes when the barn caught fire from a "lanthorn" left lying in an adjoining hayloft by a man and a boy while they tried to see the show through a hole in the wall. Eleven other persons were severely burned, one of whom died soon after. Percival had not seen the blaze but got his information from Robert Kedal, one of the thirty-two survivors, and from one other person who, wrote Percival, "This Minute . . . acquainted me, That he saw two Cart-Loads of Dead Bodies put into the Ground, some with Arms and Legs burnt off, and others with their Heads miserably burnt, and one quite off." The report gave figures: ninety-three Burwell people died in the flames; and of the twenty-six others, four were from Lanward, eight from Reach, one from Upware, two from Great Swaffam, four from Soham, two from Exning, one from London, and four were the "Show People." [9]

It is beyond question, then, that the columns of news in English country papers two centuries ago contained reports of occurrences in many places and that the separate reports came from many sources, some printed, some written, some by word of mouth. The "editing" of a country newspaper may in some offices have been not much more than a physical process, a wielding of scissors, and journalism in such places was only a crude dissemination of secondhand bits and pieces; but in other offices—most of them, in fact—there was a commendable attempt to *gather* news and to prepare it for a special community of readers. Evidence that the country editor did not simply mark with an *X* the paragraphs to be set up in type by his obedient compositor but took the trouble to *handle* the news himself is to be seen in the newspapers published in Northampton and Gloucester by Robert Raikes and William Dicey. In the *Northampton Mercury* of 22 January 1722, one is given the impression that an editor has carefully gone over the printed and written newsletters from London, selecting items, rewriting some of them. Here are chatty editorial notes that almost make the bulletin read like a direct and personal communication: "Notwithstanding the Account we gave you in our last, Page 451, taken from the St. James's Evening Post, of the Pope's having granted to the Emperor the Investiture of the Kingdom of Naples, we find by the Holland Mail in this Post. . . . " "This is the Bulk of the foreign and domestick News in the London Gazette and Evening Post. . . . " "Having given our Readers all the Material Occurrences in the St. James's Post, we will now see what

the Whitehall Evening Post will afford. . . . " "And thus
we have gone thro' all the News in the Printed Papers
with Observation; and will now proceed to the Occurrences in the written Letters. . . . " "In Wye's Letter
there is the following Comment. . . . " "And now having
given our Readers the very best Occurrences by Tuesday's
Post . . . we will proceed to Thursday's News in the
same manner." This painstaking process is revealed in the
Gloucester Journal, too, number 13 (2 July 1722), for
example. Other newspapers usually reveal less patently
their authors' personal supervision in the preparation
of copy.

To "chuse, fashion, and dispose these Materials so as
to merit the general Approbation" would require, according to James Keating, of Stratford, "the Skill and Industry
of an ingenious Artist":

> Art, Application, and Care are capable of converting
> Things, which at first sight appear rude and unprofitable,
> to very useful Purposes, and it must be own'd, that among
> the Exuberance of daily, weekly, and other Papers, there
> are some valuable Materials out of which an elegant Com-
> position may be made. . . .[10]

The question now to be considered is this: what sort of
art, application, and care were exercised by Keating and
the hundred and eighty others who chose, fashioned, and
disposed the materials which went into the country papers
here examined?

As to "art," there seems at first glance little to commend
in the treatment of news extracted from other bulletins,
printed or written; for most editors were content to transcribe verbatim whatever they selected for their readers;
or if they altered the matter at all, it was to reduce its
bulk by striking out unnecessary details. Yet the eliminat-
ing of nonessentials is the true journalist's most enviable
talent, for newspapermen know that in writing as in other

arts the part is often greater than the whole, in spite of what the mathematicians say.

This refashioning is most clearly seen in the treatment of local or regional news sent in by correspondents. Robert Raikes of the *Gloucester Journal* did what most other country editors did when such communications were sent to the newspaper office, sometimes inserting them with or without comment, sometimes summarizing them, sometimes omitting them entirely. In the issue of 26 March 1738, for instance, he printed this notice: "N.B. The Letter from Tiverton, and that from Tetbury, are come to Hand, and will be incerted in our next"; but in the following week's issue, although he gave nearly two columns to the Tetbury letter, he reduced the other one to a single sentence: "They write from Tiverton, that one Will. Rice passing thro' the Lock there, slipt from off the side of the Boat into the Water, and was drowned." Raikes could put into twenty or thirty words what an untrained correspondent took ten times as many words to say. Clearly a man was at work *editing* the material for his paper, wielding a pen, not a pair of scissors.

Local journalists sometimes added comments of their own. These remarks were usually attached to news which did not come from London papers. Thus Francis Howgrave in his new *Stamford Mercury*, number 9 (10 August 1732), reported that "On Friday last the Assizes began and ended at *Oakham* in the County of *Rutland*, where neither Prisoner nor Cause was try'd." Then he added his own compliments: " . . . which shows the good Management the Administration of Justice is under in that County, as well as the honest and peaceable Disposition of the Inhabitants. Perhaps not to the Joy of the Council and Officers of the Court, tho' much to their Ease." An ampler comment on the findings of the local assizes is in *Williamson's Liverpool Advertiser*, number 137 (5 January 1759). Williamson gave special emphasis to his views on local crime by having the passage set up in italics:

We are very sorry to observe that the many hitherto un-heard of acts of cruelty which have happened in this town of late, loudly call for a punishment justly due to delin-quents who openly defy the laws of God and man; and what may we not expect if a stop is not immediately put to them. It is with pleasure we assure the public that our magistrates are endeavouring to detect all such offenders, and are determined to put the laws strictly in execution.

Comments such as these were neither infrequent nor insignificant.

Nevertheless the early provincial editors clearly saw their main business to be that of printing supposed facts, not expressing views about the implications of those facts. This is not to argue that there was no need for editorial opinions; it is a question of whether it was not better— as it has long since been found better—to have the news-paper's views set forth in a separate department as "edi-torials" or as contributed critical essays and letters to the editor. In most provincial newspapers it was the selecting of news rather than the writing of original observations upon the events reported that gave the local editor his opportunity to exercise his "art"—as Keating, of Strat-ford, used the word. Notable exceptions will be mentioned in the next chapter, in which the expression of opinion as distinguished from the reporting of news will be considered more fully.

Meanwhile it is expedient to note that there were readers who saw the local paper as a medium for directly influencing people both by the selecting of news and by the treatment of it. One of the "Constant Readers" of the *Salisbury Journal* wrote a vigorous letter to the "author" on 19 June 1738 expressing delight at the increase in the number of local presses and provincial newspapers but strongly recommending that unsavory news should be omitted, or if inserted "should be guarded with some proper Animadversions." He referred specific-ally to "the Slips and Failings of the Fair-Sex," declaring that elopements and similar goings-on "are often related in such a humorous and comical Manner, as . . . rather tends to encrease than diminish the Number of such Adventures."

> A virtuous, a generous or benevolent Action may be trusted in a News-Paper, without any Comment or Animadversion annex'd . . .: But in the Case of vile and criminal Actions, I conceive it to be not only needful, but even a Duty to caution the Readers against the Danger of receiving evil impressions.

Here is one man's view in a matter which has been debated for centuries and is not yet settled to the satisfaction of all.

Unfortunately this "Constant Reader" gave a specimen of the sort of editorial comments which he felt desirable, but his 650 words of censure degenerated into tiresome rant, much less readable and certainly much less effective as a deterrent than the forthright account of a deplorable act reported in the *Salisbury Journal* two weeks later without the benefit of "proper Animadversions."

> *Crewkerne, July 2.* About four o'clock on Tuesday Morning last, at Wayford, two Miles from this Place, a horrid Murder was committed by one Richard Elswood of Clapton in this Parish, on the Body of Farmer Norris his Uncle, in the following Manner: Elswood's Wife usually absenting herself from her Husband several Days together, on Friday last according to Custom, she went away while her Husband was at work, and as it now appears, went to this Mr. Norris's, who for some Time had a criminal Conversation with her: The Husband having some Information of it, got up early on Tuesday Morning last, and took out one of Norris's Windows, got into the House, went immediately up Stairs into his Chamber, found his Wife in Bed with his Uncle Norris, and in a Fury took up the Bar of the Door and gave the old Fellow such a Blow on his Head, that made the Blood fly all over the Cieling of the Chamber, and following his Blows, killed him on the Spot. He likewise beat his Wife so very cruelly that he left her for dead, but she is now in a fair way of Recovery, altho'

she is blind and much bruised: Then he went into the
Streets, and told the Neighbors the Story, and likewise
advis'd them to go into the House, to see how he had killed
his Uncle, saying he was resolv'd that the old Man shou'd
never commit Adultery more. He did not attempt to go
off, but was taken before a Justice of the Peace and committed to Ivelchester Goal.

It is to the credit of William Collins, the printer of the
Salisbury Journal, that he published the "Constant Reader's" letter; it is more to his credit that he refrained from
adopting the ill-advised suggestion to write a paragraph
of reproof and warning about such stories as the one
quoted above.

The principle by which Collins and his contemporaries
decided what to print and what to omit was indubitably
less restraining than the code of the most dignified English
newspapers of the twentieth century, but its basic implications were the same. The implication in the report of
a murder is that homicide, like other kinds of criminal
violence, is abnormal, an offence against the whole community. That is why it is reported. If homicide were as
common as mowing the lawn, it would never get into the
papers. There are always people who drool over stories
of lust and brutality, but no English provincial newspaper
of two centuries ago pandered to that kind of imbecility.
The violence that was reported was sometimes described
with surprising realism, but that was good reporting
rather than reprehensible indifference to public morals.
The principle was the same as that enunciated forcefully
by Milton in *Aeropagitica* a century earlier: a mature
person can claim to have virtue only if he has looked on
the bad as well as on the good and has preferred the good.
At any rate, the eighteenth-century country editors knew
which was which, and did not suppose the reporting of
a vicious act implied their approval of it. Besides, Collins
referred to Elswood's beating the life out of his uncle as
a "horrid" murder; was further animadversion needed?

Editorial discrimination had to be exercised no matter
what news came in and no matter where it came from.
The country editor knew that he had to fill out his four,
eight, or twelve columns with articles selected from a
mass of material occupying hundreds of column-inches
in the London papers regularly received, plus whatever
usable matter came in to his office from other sources.
Obviously, in the attempt to decide which items to use
and which to omit, the editor's sense of the relative significance of each dispatch would provide some sort of guide;
and yet, unless the editor allowed political bias to settle
the matter for him, it cannot always have been easy to
choose which of four or five accounts of the same event
he should use. It is amusing to find one editor, William
Craighton of the *Ipswich Journal,* doggedly printing in
parallel *half*-columns (in number 143, 7 November 1741)
both versions of a "private Letter from the Hague" which
he had found in that week's London papers. He did not
choose; he said nothing about the difficulty of choosing;
he let his readers see the conflicting views concerning
expected political developments abroad. Such offering of
a choice to readers was most unusual, of course.[11] Ordinarily Craighton, like other provincial editors, made up
his mind which of several accounts he would use and
ignored the rest.

From our point of view in the third quarter of the
twentieth century, much of what the early Georgian readers found in their newspapers seems at first glance remote
and unimportant indeed; though on second thought one
realizes that the proportion of permanently significant
news is not really less than in our own papers. It turns
out that almost every issue of an eighteenth-century
newpaper has something to catch the eye of a modern
reader. That is true partly because overleaping the gap
of two centuries—a romantic and exciting experience—
is so easily brought about by the simple act of holding
in one's hand the very paper which, "full charg'd with

news" and damp from the press, was so long ago held in the hand of its first reader, partly also because of one's natural curiosity to see what sort of news got into the papers read by our ancestors in the days of Swift, Fielding, and Johnson. What reports reached West Country readers concerning Marlborough's victory at Blenheim and Admiral Vernon's triumphs at Porto Bello? In what papers can one find references to music, hospitals, education, labor disputes, attacks on Methodist meetinghouses, the building of the new assembly rooms at York, the return of Halley's Comet, the Porteous riots in Edinburgh? What space was given to the escapes of John Sheppard in 1724, to the coronation of George II in 1727, to the capture of Dick Turpin in 1739, to the execution of Lord Lovat in 1746, to the trial of Mary Blandy in 1752? Did provincial readers see reports of Parliament's proceedings, in spite of rigid regulations prohibiting the publication thereof?

The only satisfactory way of getting answers to these questions is to examine the newspapers themselves. Because these original papers are scarce, it is expedient to quote examples, if only to show how wide was the area covered, how extensive the range of theme, and what degree of journalistic skill was achieved. For every item quoted there are ten thousand buried in the columns of the original papers, for the period here covered is very large—over three thousand weeks.

It is easiest to begin with reports from the most remote places—India, China, and the Near East. Such reports were comparatively few in number, brief, and—unless written by eyewitnesses like Samuel Beaven of the "Revenge"—lacking in interesting details. In the late summer of 1741, there were reports that Commodore Anson had rounded Cape Horn; and on 20 August of that year, the *Nottingham Post* repeated, as did other country papers, the undated announcement in London papers, "There is Advice from the East-Indies, that

Ponti-Cherry and Madras are both attacked by the Indians; the former (a French Settlement) by an Army of one hundred and fifty Thousand Men, Foot and Horse, and the latter by one hundred Thousand Men." Ship arrivals from various Eastern ports were occasionally announced. "The Royal George Indiaman, Capt. Beamish, is arrived at Portsmouth from Bengal. General Clive is come home in her." So began a forty-seven-line report of affairs in India included under the heading "Sunday's Post" in the *Union Journal: or, Halifax Advertiser,* number 76 (15 July 1760).

Naturally the news reaching England from across the Channel was much more abundant. As is still true, some of the reports from Continental cities were merely gossip about royal or noble personages. The Nottingham *Weekly Courant* of 14 January 1727 reprinted from Wye's letter the news that "The King of Poland has had one of his Toes, which began to mortifie, cut off by his Physicians." In the *Salisbury Journal* it was solemnly reported from Paris, under date 5 July 1730, that on the third the King had "review'd . . . the Gensdarmes and the Light Horse of his Household, and the next Day his Majesty took Physick by Way of Precaution." Most of the news from the Continent was, of course, serious and of direct concern to English readers, partly because their sovereign was also Elector of Hanover, partly because England's "standing" army seldom stood still. It is a memorable fact that in Rupert Brooke's sense of the words there was many a corner in a foreign field that during the first sixty years of the eighteenth century became forever a part of England, for thousands of English sons, brothers, husbands, fathers—like their ancestors at Crecy and Agincourt—fought and died and left their dust to merge with the soil on many a bloody battlefield of Continental Europe.

To transcribe even the most exciting war dispatches that were read all over England in this period would fill a dozen books. With what a strong sense of getting "freshest advices" (right from the horse's back) one comes upon this report in the earliest surviving issue of an eighteenth-century provincial newspaper, the *Bristol Post Boy*, number 91 (Saturday, 12 August 1704):

> Whitehall, August 10. This afternoon arrived an Express with a Letter from his Grace the Duke of Marlborough to my Lady Duchess written on Horseback with a Lead Pencil. A copy whereof follows.
>
> August 13 N.S.
>
> I have not Time to say more than to beg of you to present my Humble Duty to the Queen, and to let Her Majesty know, that Her Army has had a glorious Victory: Monsieur Tallard and two other Generals are in my Coach, and I am following the rest. The Bearer my Aid-de-Camp, Colonel Parkes, will give her Majesty an Account of what has passed. I shall do it in a day or two by another more at la[r]ge.
>
> Marlborough.
>
> * The Gentleman who brought this Express is gone to Windsor, to give her Majesty an Account of the Particulars, which will be published at his Return.

Here is history staring us in the face.

Wars and rumors of wars were naturally exciting to Englishmen at home, since so many Englishmen away from home were engaged in military or naval activities. There was a direct correlation between war and news, and therefore between the expansion or even the founding of a newspaper and the extra abundance of news which war or the threat of war provided.[12] There was no "iron curtain" in those days, and news came over the water in vast quantities. Nottingham readers of Thomas Collyer's *Post* in the summer of 1741 had in their hands all sorts of "intelligence" from both St. Petersburg and Stockholm concerning the growing tension between Russia and Sweden; then, in the issue of 20 August, they saw the full text of "The Motives at large which have induc'd the King of Sweden to declare War against Russia." [13] The *Nottingham Post* is typical of forty contemporary provincial newspapers. The issue of 20 August 1741 had 85 out of 129 column-inches devoted to war news from the Continent. In these reports there was no evidence of censorship,[14] though undoubtedly there was much official silence, and occasionally the only statement that could be printed in the newspapers was that "This Day one of the King's Messengers arrived with Dispatches of great Importance from Hanover." Since this was the last item of news in the *Nottingham Post*, number 608 (20 August 1741), perhaps it would whet the appetites of readers for the next week's issue. There was enough war news in that issue to last for a whole week, surely.

If the great mass of news from the Continent was read with a consuming interest week after week by people all over England, the same can be said about the growing body of news which reached them from the colonies in North America. There is in all the provincial newspapers before George III came to the throne a perceptible eagerness, a lively, well-disposed interest in what was going on in the lands across the sea. Knowing of this popular and increasing thirst for information about life in the New World, the editors of newspapers gladly printed not only the American news which they found in London papers but letters sent to local townsmen from English soldiers in Nova Scotia and English merchants at Kingston, Jamaica. Essays on the economic importance of Cape Breton were copied from other newspapers; numerous advertisements invited English families to settle in Maryland or Pennsylvania; reports of ship arrivals from New York and Boston were frequent; and there were often detailed lists of cargoes brought back in those ships— everything from rum to rhubarb, from mahogany logs to supplies of Seneca snakeroot for the cure of fevers. Reports from Boston in New England and (after 1749)

Halifax in Nova Scotia were more often in the papers than accounts of what was happening in Boston in Lincolnshire and Halifax in Yorkshire; Charlestown in South Carolina was mentioned in English papers more often than Coventry. It was natural, perhaps, that Bristol people should be interested in news that came from the lands to which the Cabots had so long before sailed from a Bristol quay, and Newcastle whalers would undoubtedly have some feeling for or against the English-speaking colonials whom they encountered in their long cruises in northern waters.[15]

Transatlantic traffic in goods and people is a study in itself, and there is abundant evidence in the Bristol, Plymouth, Liverpool, and Newcastle papers alone to show that the "Plantations" had a strong attraction for the more venturesome; at the same time many negro slaves and "transported" malefactors were taken there against their will. So much was going on that was different from the settled ways at home that there were (as there have always been in Britain) many whose sturdy spirit made them look with eagerness toward the New World, undismayed by the strange stories of Indian massacres, of tempestuous storms, of hardships on the "frontier."

Most readers of newspapers do not know personally the men and women or boys and girls whose fortunes and misfortunes are reported, but news would never be read so eagerly if the names were omitted. Even a dead body is more interesting (except to a mortician) if it has a name. The "Extract of a Letter from an Officer at Fort Cumberland, in Nova Scotia," printed in *Eyres's Weekly Journal* at Warrington on 13 July 1756, has the twofold merit of being written in the first person by an eyewitness and of naming one of the victims of an Indian raid:

As for news I have only to let you know, that on Monday last a number of Indians (supposed to be large) advanced towards fort Monckton, garrisoned by Capt. Hill, with 70 regulars, and killed nine; and the next day paid us a visit, and had the Impudence to send some of their number to this side Tantamar creek early in the morning, and killed one of the regulars, and took or killed one Noah Williams of Taunton, a young lad of our troops, belonging to captain Gilbert's company. I am fearful he is killed, as we have found the body of the regular stript naked, and scalped, and the lad's coat; this has set us in an alarm, and we are preparing to send a large body to Gaspereau to-morrow.

It was this kind of direct report which, even though it was not printed until ten weeks after it had been written, established a link of communication between the homeland and faraway Fort Cumberland that must have been all the more appreciated because of the remoteness in time and distance.

Dispatches, rumors, reports, and letters from America were naturally more numerous and more exciting at times when growing animosities broke into open hostilities, as they did along the coast of North and South America in 1740, after many months of what might be called guerilla warfare at sea between English and Spanish ships. There had been countless incidents of the sort which infuriated rather than terrified the skippers sailing under the British flag, and many of the encounters took place in American waters. Under the front-page caption "New England," the *Nottingham Post*, number 499 (3 August 1738), gathered from the London papers six paragraphs dated at Boston on 12 June, two of them reporting Spanish interference with American vessels bound from Jamaica to Boston. The same paper reported the Admiralty's commissioning of fourteen men-of-war on 28 July, and referred to the general jubilation of Londoners at the strengthening hopes of a war with the Spaniards, "to avenge the Robberies, Murders, and Insults committed on the British Subjects for Years past." Anti-Spanish feeling grew to a high pitch, especially when rumors circulated about the cutting-off of Charles Jenkins's ear.

During the next year or two, there was no news more eagerly looked for in the papers than reports of Admiral Vernon's operations against Spanish ships and fortifications. The *Leeds Mercury,* number 739 (8 April 1740), had on the front page a detailed account of the battle of Porto Bello, together with a two-column picture and a letter written on board the "Burford" by William Richardson giving "a more particular Account of Admiral Vernon's glorious Atchievements" in the Porto Bello engagement. Before long there were further reports of a victory across the water. Some of the reports and letters proved to be inaccurate, but there was no lack of well-attested dispatches, and each success was observed with tumultuous rejoicing in English towns and villages.

The event most eagerly awaited was the capture of Carthagena, Spain's most strategic stronghold in America. Finally the word came. On Monday, 18 May 1741, the *London Gazette* printed the official announcement that on the previous day letters dated from the harbor of Carthagena had been brought to His Grace the Duke of Newcastle by Captain Laws, commander of the "Spence," a sloop. The twenty-five-hundred-word statement was shortly afterward followed by a supplementary account prepared by William Richardson, the same eyewitness as had earlier described the engagement at Porto Bello. Both reports were widely reprinted in the country newspapers, several of which later published an "Exact Plan of the Town of Carthagena." There was wild excitement everywhere. At Nottingham, according to the *Post,* the welcome news "seem'd to give new Life to our Inhabitants, and diffus'd an universal Joy throughout the Town." At Leeds, as the *Mercury* recorded on 26 May, the agreeable news of Admiral Vernon's success at Cathagena arrived on the twenty-second, and again the town went wild:

. . . the Bells in our three Churches rang all Day. In the Evening the Gentlemen of the Corporation, with several

others met at the King's Arms, where Healths of his
Majesty, the Royal Family, the Admirals Vernon and
Ogle, and Brigadier Wentworth, with their further Suc-
cess, went merrily round, whilst the Dragoons quartered
here fired several Vollies. About Nine, the whole Town
was illuminated in the most splendid Manner, which with
Fireworks, Bonefires, and loud Acclamations from the
Populace, concluded one of the most pleasing Scenes of
Joy, that ever was known in this Place.

The newspapers of other towns told the same story; the
rejoicing was nation-wide. And there were more formal expressions of the nation's gratitude to the intrepid British
commanders. All the newspapers mentioned Vernon's election to Parliament, but they gave equal space to another
distinction: on London's day of rejoicing for the conquest
at Carthagena two lion cubs were whelped at the Tower
of London, and they were immediately named Vernon
and Ogle. As Humpty Dumpty said later, "There's glory
for you!"

Meanwhile, and for long afterward, the newspapers
carried accounts of other acts of aggression at sea, in
which English mariners were often victims of one of the
most indefensible yet most picturesque kinds of aggression
—privateering. Whole books could be written about this
very extensive mode of licensed marauding, in which
Spaniards, Frenchmen, Englishmen, and Americans all
engaged; and no one who has ever seen English or
American newspapers of the 1740's and later can forget
the exciting reports of privateering which they carried
in almost every issue. St. Sebastian was the most notorious
lurking place for the Spanish privateers, and the name
became a byword for ruthless and often successful attacks
on English merchant ships. To sink or capture a French
or Spanish privateer was to do a national service. When
Captain Gwynn blew up one of the Spanish privateers
early in 1741, the London insurance men, merchants, and
others concerned in trade collected a purse of guineas as
an expression of their gratitude. The *Nottingham Post*,

number 586 (19 March 1741), reported one circumstance in Captain Gwynn's exploit that had not previously been made public. At the time when his men sighted the Spaniard, the Captain was confined to his cabin by the gout. On that account, the report continued, he might have been excused from "exposing himself to the Shot of a much superior Vessel";

> but as soon as he was inform'd that they made a Ship, and suspected her to be an Enemy, he ordered his Men to carry him up, and place him on his Couch upon Deck, to animate his People, and give the necessary Orders himself for fighting the Ship, which answer'd so successfully, and in all Probability preserved many of our Merchants Ships and Mariners from visiting St. Sebastians, and wearing Spanish Shackles.

Dread of those shackles must have darkened the thoughts of many an English sailor, but none of them stayed ashore on that account.

An adventure with a privateer is reported in succinct and homely prose in the *Hull Courant*, number 107 (13 September 1757), which tells of the ordeal suffered by William Lawson, mate of the "Mills," after a French privateer had captured his ship off Nantucket nearly a year before. It is easy to imagine how Lawson and the others felt when, early in September, he brought the masterless ship back into its home port.

> On Sunday last arrived here, the Mills, burthen about 300 Tons. M'Cloude, late Master of Hull, from Virginia, who was taken by a French Privateer from Louisbourgh off of Nantucket Shoals in October last. The Frenchman took out the Master and most of the Crew, leaving the Mate William Lawson, second Mate, Carpenter, and two or three more Englishmen on board, along with 32 Frenchmen, with an intent to send her to Louisbourg. By distress of Weather they were beat off the Coast, having exhausted all the Provisions, even till they were obliged to eat the Cat and Dog, a Shark's Tail that was nailed on the Vessel Stern, a Horse's Hide, designed to preserve the rigging

when gauled, and Fowls Dung fry'd in Oil, they resigned
in December the Ship to the Hands of the English, who
carried her into Placentia Harbour in Newfoundland, having then little or no Water left, and in the utmost distress
for all the necessaries of Life. . . . As soon as they got
in (notwithstanding the Frenchmen had resigned the Ship
to Mr Lawson, none of them being capable to keep an
Account of the Ship's Way) . . . the Frenchmen . . .
pretended to be in Possession of her . . .; however Mr.
Lawson would not quit his right, wintered with them, and
left Placentia Harbour in June last, and then proceeded
for Hull.

There is hint enough in this short newspaper report for
a full-length novel or an exciting film.

London and country newspapers also had reports of
full-dress naval conquests over the enemies of England on
the broad Atlantic. One of these "epics of the sea" was
described in a communication from the chaplain of the
"Oxford," man-of-war, to the rector of Eyam in Derbyshire. The rector, the Rev. Thomas Seward,[16] sent the
account to James Lister, printer of the *Leeds Mercury,*
along with a letter in which he asserted that most of the
newspaper reports of the taking of the "Princessa," a
Spanish man-of-war of sixty-eight guns, by Lord Augustus
Fitz Roy, Commodore Mayne, and Captain Durell were
"not only exceedingly false, but wrote with a scandalous
Design of taking all the Honour from the brave and noble
Youth to whom the greatest part of it belongs, and ev'n
of casting the detestable Slur of Cowardice upon him."
By inserting a genuine and authentic account of the
action, said the rector of Eyam, the printer would oblige
many constant readers in Derbyshire and at the same
time vindicate the character of the young man. Lister
printed the Rector's letter and the Rev. Mr. Woodward's
statement in the *Leeds Mercury,* number 746 (27 May
1740).

News from abroad aroused much interest in English
towns and set many a bonfire alight; but there were many

purely domestic occasions for celebration, too—the birth of a prince, a royal wedding, the annual commemoration of a victory or a coronation, the result of an election—so many, in fact, that as one reads through the newspapers the number of bonfires per annum seems high. But life was lived with much gusto in those days, and bonfires did no harm—except that doubtless they consumed copies of local newspapers which we should now like to have. Besides, most of the "domestick Advices" did not stir up anything but conversation in the public houses and other places where people met for a chat. That the news in the local paper was talked about is not to be doubted, whether the events reported took place in Charlestown, Coventry, or Cardiff.

News from Wales did not often appear, which is the less surprising if one remembers that there was no newspaper in Wales, in either Welsh or English, until later in the century.[17] News from Ireland was printed as often in the provincial papers as in the London ones, and in some papers the news taken from Dublin or Cork or Belfast newspapers[18] (via London) was set apart under a special caption, "Ireland." Irish news concerned with shipping was fairly common, but otherwise there was little to interest readers in England. Too often there are only such statements as that in the *Nottingham Post,* number 616 (15 October 1741), that according to letters reaching London from several parts of Ireland many of the people had been successful in counteracting the recent outbreaks of fever "by eating Apples, and drinking Apple-Water."

News from Scotland, similarly set under a special caption, was much more abundant, both during the uprisings in 1715 and 1745 and at other times. It was reported in the Halifax *Union Journal* on 8 May 1759 under the caption "Scotland" that a group of Highlanders, who had been discharged and pensioned after being disabled at Ticonderoga and other places in America, had arrived in Edinburgh "in their way to their native country." The wounded men declared that on their way through England they had been "extremely well used. . . . " Echoes of their talk seem to have been caught up in what follows:

> They say the Indians are so fond of the Highlanders, that they would rush into the thickest of the enemy's fire to rescue them, and that they would frequently carry them on their backs for several miles, when they happened to be either sick or wounded. In short, we may attribute the success of the last campaign, and the present flourishing condition of our colonies, in a great measure to the Highlanders, as they are agreeable to the natives, and terrible to the French: they are hardy and enterprising, inured to fatigue, and capable of supporting all the vicissitudes of heat and cold, hunger and thirst, and there is so much enthusiasm in their love for their officers and chiefs, that under their conduct, they will surmount the greatest obstacles, and atchieve the most dangerous adventures.

These words of cordial tribute were penned in Edinburgh; they were printed and read in England, only thirteen years after Culloden.

The whole body of news about happenings outside of England was, from the first, much larger in bulk than the reports concerning events within the borders of England, but there was nevertheless a good deal of what is now called "national" news—reports of events in London or elsewhere in England of interest to everyone in the country. Some of this "national" news consisted of the London bills of mortality and lists of bankrupts, of newly elected members of Parliament, of the dates and presiding justices in the several circuits of the quarterly assizes, of state and ecclesiastical preferments. Not all these items are to be found in every issue of every provincial newspaper, but almost every newspaper provides examples of news of the sort which papers of our time would doubtless print, and in much the same language. In the *Kendal Weekly Mercury*, number 13 (Saturday, 3 May 1735), for instance, is the *London Journal's* report of a fire:

On Thursday Morning between Twelve and One, a
Fire broke out in the Dwelling House of Mr. Stocking,
a Baker in Swallow-street near Piccadilly, which entirely
consumed the same, and damaged some others.

His Royal Highness the Prince of Wales, his Grace the
Duke of Marlborough, Lord Delware, and several other
Noblemen, were there in Presence, animating the Firemen
and others, in extinguishing the Fire.

William Gurney, a Fireman belonging to the Sun Fire
Office, was so much hurt, that he lies in the utmost Danger.
It is said His Royal Highness and the Noblemen gave him
some Guineas and sent him home in a Chair.

One unforgettable report, in the *Hull Journal*, number 183
(Tuesday, 20 March 1759), tells of the execution at
London of Joseph Halsey, the twenty-three-year-old
Boston-born mate of a merchant ship, convicted of beating to death Daniel Davidson on the high seas and
condemned to be hanged "and afterwards his Body to
be anatomiz'd."

A fair sampling of the London news to be found in a
single issue of a provincial paper is given in the *Sherborne
Mercury*, number 16 (Tuesday, 7 June 1737). Half a
dozen articles selected from the twelve columns of this
paper will serve to show the sort of news from London
which the printers thought their readers would be glad
to see.

On Sunday the Rev. Dr. Gilbert, Dean of Exeter, and
Sub-Almoner to his Majesty, preached before their Majesties, the Prince and Princess of Wales, and the Princesses
Amelia and Caroline, at the Chapel Royal at St. James's.
His Majesty, according to Custom, offer'd Gold, Myrrh,
and Frankincense; and it being Collar-Day, the Knights
of the Garter, Thistle, and Bath appeared in the Collars of
their respective Orders. Their Majesties afterwards din'd
in Publick.

Yesterday Morning early a Fire broke out at the House
of Mrs. Cooper in Denmark-street near St. Giles's Church,
which entirely consumed the same, and Goods to the
Value of 200 £.

The same Day the Bill relating to common Players of Interludes pass'd the Hon. House of Commons.

On Sunday last the Wife of Mr. Martin of Ratcliff was deliver'd of four Children at a Birth, viz. three Boys and a Girl, by Mr. Cole of Brookstreet near Ratcliff-cross, and is in a hopeful way of doing well.

Mr. Ryley, the Maltster at Kingston, who was last Week robbed on Putney Heath, received such a Wound in his Arm by the Villains, that he has been obliged to have it cut off; and continues so dangerously ill, that his Life is despair'd of.

The Lords in a Committee went thro' the Oyster Bill. Read a 2d time the Bill for settling a Jointure of 50,000 £ per Ann. on her Royal Highness the Princess of Wales; and in a grand Committee went thro' the Bill for restraining the Liberty of the Stage, and order'd it to be read a 3d time on Monday, and all the Lords to be summoned. 'Tis remark'd, that the Excess of Theatrical Entertainments fill both Town and Country with Idleness and Debauchery, and, from being under no Restraint, exhibit to the Publick Encomiums on Vice, and laugh away the sober Principles of Modesty and Virtue; and that our Italian Opera's soften and enervate the Minds of the People, and also carry great Sums of Money out of the Kingdom.

These pieces comprise only about one-quarter of the London news in this particular issue of the *Sherborne Mercury*.

None of these reports—not even the one about quadruplets—can be said to have any enduring interest; but it is worth noticing that the *Sherborne Mercury* did not hesitate to reprint reports of what was going on in Parliament. This was in direct contravention of the wishes of the kingdom's legislators, though the printers of news had long defied both houses and continued to do so, not always with impunity. As early as 1640, there were London news books which reported Parliamentary votes and proceedings. From time to time official reports were permitted, but immediately after the Restoration and frequently thereafter there was strict prohibition against the reporting of Parliamentary matters in newspapers. For some years John Dyer was audacious enough to include accounts of Parliamentary proceedings in the newsletters which bore his name, and on several occasions he found himself in trouble on that account.[19] For many years Abel Boyer's monthly paper, the *Political State of Great Britain*, offered straightforward summaries of Parliamentary debates; but unlike Dyer he was seldom in difficulties with the authorities, perhaps because he reported the doings of Parliament only after the session had ended. So Elizabeth Adams of Chester in her *Weekly Courant* boldly printed "The Proceedings of the last Sessions of Parliament."

It was clear to Dyer, to Boyer, to Elizabeth Adams, to Edward Cave of the *Gentleman's Magazine*, to the proprietors of the *London Magazine*, and to the authors of newspapers in town and country that their readers were eager to read about the deliberations of both houses of Parliament and to examine the texts of the sovereign's addresses to Parliament; it was also clear that if they were determined to include Parliamentary news in their columns they must either disguise their reports or run the risk of prosecution for violating the privilege claimed by both houses. The written newsletters of Wye, Stanley, and others often had a good deal of Parliamentary news, and it was in these written newsletters that the country news printers found the accounts of Parliament which their readers were eager to see. In the *Ipswich Journal* of 1721, lengthy passages transcribed from *Stanley's News-Letter* can be read; speakers are named and portions of their speeches are quoted. John Bagnall quite openly declared his policy in number 29 (4 March 1721): "We having Weekly given an Account of the Proceedings of both Houses of Parliament (as transmitted to us by a discerning Hand) and particularly that Part relating to the late South-Sea Directors, . . . the following Debates of the Lords and Commons, . . . will (we hope) be an acceptable Amusement to our more Curious Readers."

Most country printers of newspapers avoided direct naming of the members by printing "the D. of M------h"
instead of "the Duke of Marlborough," "the C-----r of
the E-----r" instead of "the Chancellor of the Exchequer,"
and "Mr. At-----ey Gen---l" instead of "Mr. Attorney
General." Some, like Cave in the *Gentleman's Magazine,*
James Lister in the *Leeds Mercury,* and Andrew Hooke in
the *Bristol Oracle,* went to more trouble and printed
thinly disguised reports described as "the Debates of a
certain Society."

Country printers sometimes found themselves in difficulties for infringing the regulations; distance gave them
no protection or immunity if official inquiries were made.
Instances of punishment for mentioning decisions and
discussions in either house were not numerous in provincial towns, except in the West, where there seem to have
been both exceptional audacity on the part of printers
and special vigilance on the part of government agents.
One of the early printers of newspapers in that area,
Joseph Bliss, apparently had no fear that he might suffer
for reprinting Parliamentary debates, for on 25 January
1717 he announced in his *Protestant Mercury* that he was
about to resume twice-a-week publication, hoping to give
satisfaction by inserting in the paper "such Things as are
most material, especially during the Sitting of Parliament." On 28 November 1718, as *The Journal of the
House of Commons* shows,[20] all three of the Exeter newspapers printed accounts of the proceedings of Parliament,
and the three authors, Andrew Brice, George Bishop, and
Joseph Bliss, were all ordered to present themselves before
the House of Commons. Two of them dutifully obeyed;
Bliss evaded the messenger. By the middle of January,
1719, all three had admitted their guilt—Bliss by letter—
and were discharged after being reprimanded. Brice and
Bishop said the Parliamentary reports which they had
printed had been taken "from News-Letters sent to
Coffee-Houses at Exeter."

The Journal of the House of Commons recorded many complaints that the writers of newsletters and the printers of newspapers had been so bold as to give accounts therein of the proceedings of the House; and at each complaint the members reaffirmed their conviction that the less said about their deliberations the better. On 13 April 1738, for example, it was formally resolved,

> That it is an high Indignity to, and a notorious Breach of the Privilege of, this House, for any News Writer, in Letters, or other Papers (as Minutes, or under any other Denomination), or for any Printer or Publisher of any printed News Paper, of any Denomination, to presume to insert in the said Letters or Papers, or to give therein any Account of the Debates, or other Proceedings, of this House, or any Committee thereof, as well during the Recess as the Sitting of Parliament; and that this House will proceed with the utmost Severity against such Offenders.

This policy had many times before been spread on the pages of *The Journal of the House of Commons,* but it was a losing battle.

The whole story of that struggle need not be told here; it is enough to pick up the threads at 23 January 1723. On that day the House, hearing complaints that the debates and proceedings were frequently "misrepresented" in written and printed newsletters and papers, formulated two resolutions intended to cope with the nuisance: first, that "no News Writers do presume in their Letters or other Papers . . . to intermeddle with the Debates, or any other Proceedings, of this House"; second, that "no Printer, or Publisher, of any printed News Papers, do presume to insert in any such Papers any Debates, or any other Proceedings, of this House, or any Committee thereof."

Five years later—on 30 March 1728—that double resolution was read from the pages of the *Journal* to refresh the memories of the members, for a flagrant case involving both written newsletters and a printed newspaper had been brought to the attention of the House. The offending paper was the *Gloucester Journal,* number 310 (Tuesday, 12 March 1728), in which Robert Raikes had copied from Wye's letter a report beginning, "Yesterday the House of Commons. . . . " It was a report that the House had resolved itself into a "Grand Committee to consider of the State of the Nation in relation to the National Debt." When the division was taken, the report continued, there were 97 yeas and 256 noes; "so the main Question was resolved in the Affirmative." In the copy of the *Gloucester Journal* now at the Gloucester Public Library is a manuscript note identifying this as "The woful Paragraph" and stating that "this Paragraph cost R R 40£." Raikes and his Bristol agent, John Wilson, bookseller, of Horse Street, were ordered to attend the House on March 28 to be questioned. On the appointed day the two men were present, Raikes admitting that he had printed the issue of the *Gloucester Journal* complained of, explaining that Wilson had nothing to do with the printing of the paper, and declaring that he had received the paragraph in question from Edward Cave of the post office. Wilson was discharged, Raikes was taken into the custody of the sergeant-at-arms, and Cave was ordered to present himself at the House on the following Saturday morning. When Cave came, according to this command, he said that he had sent to Raikes *several* written newsletters which contained intelligence relating to the proceedings of the House, and he brought with him as samples copies of newsletters written by William Wye, John Stanley, John Willys, and Elias Delpeuch, all of them containing references to the debates and decisions of the House of Commons. Cave was adjudged guilty of a breach of the privilege of the House and was ordered into custody; the four news writers were required to attend on the following Tuesday morning. There were delays, but on 3 April it was ordered that Wye, Stanley, and Delpeuch should be taken into custody.

The news of what had happened to the Gloucester printer and to the men who had furnished him with prohibited news reached other parts of the country; "The Publick cannot expect to have an Account of the Proceedings of the Hon. House of Commons in this or other News Papers," wrote Thomas Gent in his *Original Mercury, York Journal: or, Weekly Courant,* number 138 (2 April 1728), "since the Printer of Gloucester is taken into Custody of the Serjeant at Arms for inserting the same; nay, even those who write, and transmit such Accounts, it seems are not excusable, four of whom being ordered to attend the Hon. House of Commons on that Account also."

In the issue of the *Gloucester Journal* bearing that same date, 2 April 1728, it was frankly stated that the printer of the paper had been "order'd into Custody of a Messenger, for Printing the Votes of the House from a written News-Letter or Letters," and that Wilson had been discharged; but a protest (in italics for emphasis) was registered against a false inference from the facts:

☞ *Since the Printer hereof hath been under the Displeasure of the House, it hath been industriously and maliciously insinuated, that it is for Printing against the Government; which is a false and scandalous Aspersion.*

Readers of the *Gloucester Journal* were no doubt pleased to find in the paper two weeks later an announcement that "On Monday last the Printer of this Paper was discharged out of the Custody of the Serjeant at Arms, on paying his Fees." Raikes had sent to the House of Commons on 5 April a petition in which he expressed his sorrow for the offence and humbly begged pardon, praying, "in regard he has a Wife and Family in the Country, to provide for, and his Affairs will suffer very much by his Absence," that he might be discharged. On 8 April, he was brought to the Bar of the House; there, upon his knees, he received a reprimand from the Speaker, and was ordered to be discharged out of custody. A day or two later Cave, Wye, Stanley, and Delpeuch, all of whom had sent petitions, were released on similar terms. This is precisely what had happened to Andrew Brice and George Bishop ten years before; but this time the suppliers of news, not just the printers, were taken into custody.

Much to the annoyance of the members of the House of Commons, and presumably to the annoyance of Raikes as well, a repetition of the offence took place early the following year, for the *Gloucester Journal* had in one of its columns on 11 February 1729 a passage of news about the proceedings of the House, and one of the messengers of the sergeant-at-arms served Raikes with an order to attend the House on 4 March. This time Raikes was—or said he was—so ill with a fever that he was unable to travel to London. His petition to be excused was read to the House on 26 February and was granted. His message, as recorded in *The Journal of the House of Commons*, contained the direct assertion that the offending paragraph had come from a newsletter "sent by Mr. Gyttens, Clerk of the Bristol Road, or his Assistant, to the King's Head in Gloucester." Once again this reference to a coffee house shows how Raikes was accustomed to get his copies of the written newsletters. But it is surprising to find as well an assertion which suggests that, in spite of his unhappy experience the year before, Raikes was in the habit of letting his compositor or some other workman in the printing office decide what should be copied from Wye's and Stanley's letters. He said that before the opening of the current session of Parliament he "gave Orders to his Servant not to insert in his Journal any of the Votes or Resolutions of [the] House"; the paragraph complained of was taken, he said he had been informed, from the newsletter sent by Gyttens, and had been inserted without Raikes's knowledge. Perhaps the Gloucester printer was simply driven by illness and desperation to wriggle out of the full editorial responsibility which he would normally have faced manfully; or perhaps he could not bear the thought of humbly kneeling once again before the House.[21]

There were equally stringent regulations concerning the publication of references to the deliberations of the House of Lords and to individual members of that House, yet one does not have to look very long in the provincial newspapers to find brief accounts of matters discussed in the upper house; and sometimes the reports were long, as when the *Leeds Mercury,* number 747 (3 June 1740), in response to popular demand, gave the full text—nearly five columns of small print—of the speech delivered in the House of Lords by "the Duke of A-----" on the taking of Portobello by Admiral Vernon. Printers of newspapers soon discovered that they need not even observe the letter of the law, provided there was nothing libelous or derogatory in the published observation.

Certainly no official objections were raised [22] when, after his defeat in the rebellion of 1745, Lord Lovat was named with vituperation in practically all the public prints in England. His flight, his capture, his progress to London, his trial, and his execution were all set forth in vivid detail week by week in the London and provincial papers alike. Here, if ever, the printers of eighteenth-century newspapers should have discovered the usefulness of headlines. What screaming types would have appeared if the twentieth-century style had been anticipated: "Rebel Chief Vanishes"; "Lovat found in Hollow Tree"; "Peer on Trial at Westminster"; "Axe Faces Condemned Lord"; "Grand-stand Collapses at Lovat Beheading"; "Jacobite's Head Shown to Crowd." All of the incidents suggested by these imaginary captions were described in newspapers then being published in the provincial towns.

Throughout the months of rebellion, most of the provincial newspapers eagerly copied from the London papers the reports of the movements of the Stuart forces and of the King's troops under General Wade, General Cope,

General Ligonier, and later the Duke of Cumberland. Many of the reports were only rumors and had subsequently to be corrected. For that reason one cannot safely base a history of the rebellion on the contemporary newspapers, though as R. C. Jarvis has pointed out [23] these paragraphs have a special interest because they were written when no one knew what the next week's news would be or what places in the line of march would be thrown into disorder. When Sam. Drewry in his *Derby Mercury* of 20 September 1745 prefaced his paragraphs of northern news with the words, "The Trouble in Scotland being now the principal Subject of Enquiry . . . , " he did not know that before long his paper would regularly have a section headed "By the North Mail to Derby, on Tuesday Night," and that by early December the marching columns of Stuart supporters would fill the streets of Derby, only to make in that very town their momentous decision to turn back instead of going on to the expected triumphs in London.

As was true of other national news, much of what the local papers printed about the progress of the 1745 rebellion came through the *London Gazette* or the *London Gazette Extraordinary* or another of the London papers and was necessarily long out of date by the time it was reprinted in provincial papers. By the time one week's "Advices from the North" reached London and were then reprinted in such places as Norwich and Gloucester, the rebellion had moved into another phase altogether. The exciting news of the Duke of Cumberland's victory at Culloden on 16 April 1746 reached London only after seven days, and even in northern towns the news was slow to arrive. The *Preston Journal* of 25 April 1746 had excerpts from private letters written in Glasgow reporting the three-hour battle and the defeat of the rebels by the Duke of Cumberland; readers of the *Manchester Magazine* and of the *York Journal* did not see the report until 29 April, thirteen days after the blood of English and Scots had congealed in the sod of Straghallen Moor.

Although much of the news of the '45 in local news-papers was anything but fresh and often consisted of rumors and speculations rather than known facts, the excitement grew rapidly and the reports became bulkier. So keen were Englishmen to know what was happening in the North—particularly after the rebels had begun to move West and South across the border—that gradually foreign news yielded place to what in August and early September had been labeled "Scottish Affairs" but soon appeared under a caption less suggestive of remoteness; and new papers—the *Eton Journal* early in October, 1745, and the *York Journal* on 26 November 1745—were founded expressly to carry the war news to impatient and anxious readers. "This Paper was first published on the breaking out of the Rebellion in the North," wrote the printer of the Eton newspaper in his number 61 (8 May 1746), "and for the more ready Intelligence, published twice a Week." [24]

A point to be made here is that the number of news reports and letters *first* printed in several of these local papers was considerable. They do not all yield original matter. Except for reports of spontaneous celebrations whenever good news arrived and announcements of regional "associations" organized for marshaling men and money in defense of the realm, there was in the papers of the South and the East[25] little purely local news con-cerning the excitement evoked by the rebellion. But as one examines the files of papers printed in Midland and Northern towns—Newcastle, York, Preston, Manchester, Derby, Stamford, Birmingham, Worcester, Northampton, Cambridge, and even Gloucester—one comes upon many direct communications much fresher than those reprinted from the London papers. There was, of course, no paper in either Liverpool or Carlisle. Of the *Leeds Mercury* only one issue from those critical months—number 1072 (25 February 1746)—appears to be extant; no issue of the *Kendal Weekly Journal* for the period of the rebellion is extant; no Hull paper printed earlier than 19 August 1746 has survived; there are now no copies of the Nottingham *Weekly Courant* for 1745 and 1746; and all issues of *Adams's Weekly Courant* (Chester) between July, 1741, and December, 1746, have disappeared, though many articles from those missing issues and some later ones were brought together by Elizabeth Adams in *The Chester Miscellany. Being a Collection Of Several Pieces, both in Prose and Verse, Which were in the Chester Courant from January 1745, to May 1750* (Chester: Elizabeth Adams, 1750).[26]

Communication must certainly have been difficult, but remarkably energetic efforts were made to gather and spread news. Newcastle-upon-Tyne was one of the centers from which, in one form or another, war news reached other places. On 26 October 1745, the *Cambridge Journal* and other papers reprinted a dispatch dated at Newcastle ten days earlier reporting the anxiety felt there for "one of the Persons imployed in getting Intelligence of the Motions of the Rebels," since it was rumored that he had been captured and hanged; but the Newcastle news-gatherer demonstrated the falsity of the rumor by returning safely. One reads of a professional carrier of news who reached Newcastle on Friday night, 15 November, delivered a letter to Marshal Wade, rode most of Saturday night to Kendal, and from that place at eight o'clock Sunday night sent an "express" which reached Manchester about five o'clock Monday evening, concluding that particular report—it is in the *Manchester Magazine* dated Tuesday, 19 November 1745—by saying, "I think to stay a few Days longer, and shall continue to give you as good Accounts as possible." In the *Scots Magazine* of February, 1746, is "*A particular account of the surrender of the town of Stirling. Published in the* Newcastle Journal, *and afterwards in the London papers.*" Four months earlier, Robert Whitworth's *Manchester Magazine,* number 455 (15 October 1745), had a "Copy of a Letter from Newcastle, to a Gentleman in Manchester, dated Oct. 11,

1745," and the following week's issue had similar communications from Newcastle and from York to recipients in Manchester.

One naturally turns to the Preston and Manchester and Derby newspapers in the hope of finding accounts of the incidents which occurred as the rebel forces moved through Lancashire into Cheshire and Derbyshire. The hope is justified. By good fortune a file of the *Preston Journal* for the months between September, 1745, and March, 1746, has recently come into the hands of a private collector in London, and three issues of the rival Preston paper, the *True British Courant,* also survive, one each for September, October, and November, 1745. The whole mass of report and speculation in these two newspapers cannot be described here, but it can be said that one no longer has to be satisfied with guessing what news may have reached local readers as the rebels moved in and about Preston. The reports range from a Preston tradesman's account of the defenses of Newcastle (in the *Preston Journal* of 18 October) to dispatches from Penrith (25 October), excited but uncertain communications from Dumfries (8 November), and two columns of fairly up-to-the-minute news from Kendal, Penrith, Newcastle, Carlisle, and Whitehaven (in the *Preston Journal* of 15 November). The dispatch from Whitehaven is a vivid firsthand description of what had been seen at the rebels' camp just outside Carlisle by a gentleman "disguised Countryman-like." The next issue of the *Preston Journal,* number 269 (22 November 1745), is missing; number 270 covers the gap from 22 November to 20 December and reports in some detail the retreat of the rebel forces through the town, for Friday the thirteenth saw the departure of the last of the Pretender's marching troops and the arrival of some of the King's forces.

In the November issues of the *Manchester Magazine,* Robert Whitworth printed many direct communications from the areas through which the rebels had passed or were expected to pass. Then, as in Preston, came silence; there was no *Manchester Magazine* on 3 December or 10 December, just as there was no *Derby Mercury* on 6 December. Manchester was occupied by the rebels at the end of November, and Whitworth did not attempt to bring out his paper; [27] Derby saw the rebel forces turn back toward Scotland less than forty-eight hours after they had entered the town, but in the confusion the *Mercury* could not be prepared. We are not left in doubt about the feelings of disgust for the invaders in either place. When Whitworth resumed publication on 17 December, he let his language reveal his animosity:

> In general it may with Truth be affirm'd, that such a Parcel of shabby, lousy, shitten Scoundrels were never seen in England before. The Majority of them deserve no better Character, and the whole of them have every where done enough to convince all who are not stupify'd with Notions of Hereditary Right . . . that nothing that is just or good can be expected of them.

The only known copy of the following week's issue of the *Manchester Magazine* is defective, but four full columns of its two surviving pages give in successive, dated paragraphs "An Account of the *Rebels* from their first Coming to *MANCHESTER,* to the last Time they left it."

After its silence, the *Derby Mercury* [28] also offered a long account of what had been going on in the two weeks before number 38 appeared on 13 December. [29] An eyewitness told of the rebels' bedraggled state when they entered the town on Wednesday afternoon, 4 December, "dress'd in dirty Plaids and Shirts, without Breeches, their Stockings not halfway up their Legs, some without Shoes, or next to none, and generally so fatigued with their long March, as to demand our Pity more than Fear"; and a letter written by a Derby gentleman described the insolent conduct of six rebel officers and forty men who had taken up quarters in his house. "Most of these Men," he wrote, "looked like so many Fiends turn'd out of Hell to ravage the Kingdom."

As historical documents, these and other newspaper accounts of the second attempt to place a Stuart on the throne of England by force of arms may be of dubious significance; as eyewitness reports, they are realistic and immediate enough to stir one's imagination long after the events described.

If it appears that less had been made in local papers about the earlier rising of the Jacobites, it is simply because there were few newspapers in 1715. Of special interest would be accounts in newspapers published close to the actual fighting; but there was no newspaper at Preston, or Kendal, or Leeds, or Halifax, or York. At Newcastle there was John White's *Courant;* and although no copies printed in 1715 have survived, there are numerous brief reports and references to the uprising in the issues of January and February, 1716. Number 695 (9 January 1716), for example, has a long list of "the most Considerable Chiefs in Scotland, and the Number of Men they can Raise"; number 704 (30 January 1716) has the text of the declaration of loyalty to the King presented on behalf of the people of Newcastle; and number 707 (6 February 1716) has communications from Edinburgh and from London, dated alike on 2 February, the former including a statement that, according to the Duke of Argyle's aide-de-camp, the rebels had retired from Perth at two o'clock in the morning the previous Monday (30 January), and two other encouraging reports, also from Edinburgh direct: "We hear General Cadogan is marched towards Dundee with a strong Body of Horse and Foot, to take Possession of that Place, and that Campbell of Glenlyon with some Highlanders, have been taken in the Castle of Tullibardine by some of his Majesty's Forces in their Way to Perth." The *Stamford Mercury* printed long extracts from the *Evening Post* and from the written newsletters of Miller and Fox relaying reports from Stirling and from Oxford, where Jacobite sympathizers had been seized for having "encouraged the Scholars to drink the Pretender's Health."

Papers published far away in the South of England gave the uprising the attention one would expect in view of the fact that there were threats of local risings in that region of Britain. In Exeter, Joseph Bliss offered readers of his *Protestant Mercury* a good deal of news about the excitement, both in reports that came from London and in others sent directly to him from other places. In his number 10 (28 October 1715), for example, is a report dated at Taunton two days before:

> There are already come into this Town about 500 Dragoons, well arm'd, and a Regiment is expected to morrow, besides a great Number of Foot Soldiers. A great many Arms (some say a Ship Load) are seized at Pool; and the Rebels design'd to rise this Week in several Towns in Dorset and Somerset. Yesterday several Persons were apprehended in Sherborne, and committed to Dorchester Goal. Great Hurry of Expresses passes to and fro.

During the following weeks, Bliss provided plenty of news about the rebellion, and on 2 December inserted another note from Taunton, this one reporting that "A great Quantity of Swords, Pistols, Carbines, &c. being Arms that were seized at the Bath, and mentioned lately in this Weekly Paper, are now brought to this Town in a Waggon for his Majesty's Service." On 9 December the *Protestant Mercury* carried a report that at Oxford on 30 November a shipment of "12 Dozen of Swords and Bayonnets," directed to one Mrs. Greenaway, had been seized in a barge that had come from London; and in the same issue a local instrument maker advertised that gentlemen and others who had occasion for kettle drums and other drums for the militia could be supplied at reasonable rates by George Light, living near the East Gate in Exeter.

Swords and bayonets seized in Oxford and Somerset and drums on sale in Exeter—they must have made the Devonshire people fully aware of the actuality of the Jacobite rising, but it was to Scotland, naturally, that the people looked for the most startling news, though the reports invariably came in a roundabout way. Bishop's *Exeter Mercury* on 28 October 1715 had reports about the rebellion from Edinburgh, Dumfries, and Berwick, copied out of the *Post Man,* the *Flying Post, St. James's Evening Post,* the *Gazetteer,* and Dormer's letter. Four weeks later, Bishop reported that a message reaching London by way of Edinburgh told of the great rejoicings at Manchester upon news of the rebels' defeat at Preston, and added that "one Tho. Syddall, who was a principal actor in pulling down the Meetinghouses in those Parts, and committed to Lancaster Goal for the same, was releas'd by the Rebels, and retaken by the King's Forces at Preston, and afterwards hanged." This issue of the *Exeter Mercury* also had an account of the Preston engagement; it was dated at London on 19 November and had been taken from "Private Letters by Yesterday's Post from Preston."

Norwich, in the East, doubtless had its reports of the Jacobite rising in 1715, but no copies of Henry Crossgrove's *Gazette* or of William Chase's *Weekly Mercury* issued in that year have survived; and there are no copies of the other local paper of the time, the *Norwich Courant: or, Weekly Packet.*

Worcester people did not wait for formal confirmation from London when letters from the North brought news of victory. They were in the mood to celebrate anyway, for on the last Sunday of October, 1715, they had observed the Prince of Wales's birthday by ringing bells and by "such other innocent Rejoycings, as the Sabbath would justly permit"; later they indulged in more demonstrative hilarity, for on Monday night "the Soldiers burnt the Effigies of the Earl of Mar, Pretender, Pope, and Devil in

a Bonfire made for that Purpose," and "Plenty of Liquor
. . . was given among the Soldiers." Then, on Wednesday,
16 November, word came of the decisive action at Preston,
and the town was elated. The *Worcester Post Man,*
number 334 (18 November 1715), recorded under the
date of Thursday, 17 November:

> Great Rejoycings were made here yesterday all the
> Day, upon Advice that some Persons receiv'd by Letters
> from their Friends towards Lancashire, of an entire Vic-
> tory obtain'd by the King's Troops over the Rebels at
> Preston, on Sunday and Monday last, killing, and taking
> most, if not all, Prisoners, after a desperate Fight, wherein
> many were kill'd on both Sides. The Particulars of which
> Action, you may expect at large, in our next, by way of
> London.

The following issue of the *Worcester Post Man* was filled
with accounts from Whitehall, Edinburgh, Stockport, and
other points.

Apart from these two periods of special stress within
the nation, there were many minor crises to be reported,
and a multitude of the everyday events which constituted
normal life. It is startling to see how swiftly the excitement over "the '45" gave way to a general anxiety about
the incidence of a disease affecting horned cattle. There
was a good deal of tittle-tattle about giant radishes,
strange lights seen in the sky, the trying out of a new
fire engine at Godmanchester, the death of a one-hundred-
and-four-year-old parrot at Exeter, and such things.

One of the best ways of studying the country-wide
treatment of "home" news is to see how quickly the papers
in various regions picked up the accounts of a notorious
murder and the ensuing trial of the alleged murderer. Of
the many such affairs which the eighteenth century witnessed, there were few to equal the Blandy case, if one
is to judge by the attention paid to it in the provincial
newspapers. It is not in the least surprising that the
thirty-three country newspapers which were being printed

at that time—1751-52—gave far more space to Mary Blandy's poisoning of her father than they gave a few months later to the change in the calendar or indeed to anything else that happened in England that year. Her name was on everybody's lips. This was not a London "case"; it originated in Oxfordshire. There was no newspaper in Oxford then; the nearest were at Reading, Gloucester, Stratford-upon-Avon, Northampton, and Worcester, but all the reports appeared first in London papers. The affair must at the beginning have seemed to be only one more death in the provinces—regrettable, of course, but nothing to fuss about, since these things happened so often. But it soon appeared from the inquest, held on 15 August 1751, that this particular homicide had all the concomitants that newsmongers gloat over— foul play suspected; daughter (fortunately quite lovely to look upon and to read about) believed implicated; daughter's lover also involved; startling disclosures by many witnesses at the inquest and at the trial; Miss Blandy—people began to call her Molly—incarcerated in Oxford Castle to await trial; a report—false—that Mary had escaped; a report that Oxford refused to permit the trial to be held in the theater, but would allow the Divinity School to be used; the trial itself, in March; the verdict—"guilty"; the sentence—death; the execution on 6 April.

So far as the newspapers and the public were concerned, the story did not end when the unhappy girl from Henley breathed her last; detailed accounts of the trial and of Mary's lover continued to fill many columns. As late as 16 May 1753, *Felix Farley's Bristol Journal* printed "An Elegy [by 'Draco'] for Miss Blandy, Who was executed at Oxford, Monday April 6, 1752, for poisoning her Father." Altogether the "Female Parricide" [30] can be held accountable for news reports, letters, verses, transcripts of various hearings spread over half a year, and advertisements [31] in newspapers from one end of England to the other. The *Cambridge Journal,* number 392 (21 March 1752), managed to find room for both the Blandy trial and an article on the proposed change in the calendar, but other papers gave priority to Mary. Joseph Harrop's new *Manchester Mercury* gave front-page space to "Miss Blandy's Own Narrative" and put on an inside page the eagerly awaited account of the execution of John Swann and Elizabeth Jeffries. Neither the escapes of John Sheppard nor the execution of Jonathan Wild had made such a stir in the counties of England as the *cause célèbre* of Mary Blandy and her conspiring lover, Cranstoun. Only the trial of James Annesley in November, 1743, produced anything like as much public interest.

There was no lack of intimations of immorality from all parts of the country. Two illustrations picked out of hundreds will serve to show how such matters were treated in country newspapers. The final paragraph of news in the *Sherborne Mercury,* number 16 (7 June 1737), reached the editor through his London correspondent, who, on June 4, communicated to him a two-hundred-and-eighty-word report dated at Canterbury on June 1. It told of the arrest and confession of Margaret Wickes, a single woman about twenty-two years of age, who had been "committed to his Majesty's Gaol of St. Dunstan's," near Canterbury, on suspicion of having murdered Lydia Fagg, eighteen-month-old daughter of her employer, a gentleman of Dover.

> This Maid Servant got up from the Bed where she lay with the Infant, at her Master's House in Dover, about four of the Clock on Saturday Morning last, and before she went out of the House, as she now says, she went up and kiss'd the Child three several Times, and at last took the Child from the Bed, and carry'd her asleep to the Seaside; when a great Wave wash'd the Child out of her Arms; that she saw the Child struggle several Times, and went into the Sea after it to save it, but could not. But 'tis confidently reported by strong Circumstances, that she flung the Child into the Sea, to be reveng'd of her Mistress.

> She can give no Reason for carrying the Child so early in
> the Morning to the Sea-side. This hard hearted Creature
> afterwards, instead of going Home, rambled about three
> Miles to St. Margaret's, where she was found, conceal'd
> in one of the Cliffs about ten o'clock the same Morning;
> and the Child about the same time was taken up in one of
> the Fishermens Nets.

A twentieth-century reader of this account, finding himself thinking of a folk ballad or of an incident in a Hardy
or a George Eliot novel, is moved to wonder what distress
of mind prompted Margaret Wickes to her strange action.

The other episode chosen here to represent stories of
violence reported in country newspapers is much too
bloody to suggest either Hardy or George Eliot. Bryan
Connell's motive for attacking a butcher at "Lousey
Weedon" appears to have been robbery, but why did he
give his victim fourteen or fifteen blows and then cut off
his head "so that it hung only by some Sinews"? At the
Northampton assizes in March, 1741, Connell was convicted, largely on the strength of testimony presented by
Elizabeth Watson. According to the report in the *Nottingham Post*, number 586 (19 March 1741), and in other
papers shortly afterward, she "gave so exact an Account
of every Circumstance attending that cruel Murder, that
the Judge and all the Hearers were perfectly satisfied."

> Amongst other Things, there was an extraordinary Piece
> of Evidence given by Elizabeth Watson, That walking some
> Time after the Murder, just upon the Spot of Ground
> where it was committed, with Bryan Connell, and one or
> two more of that Gang, he saw a Robin Red Breast in a
> Bush, and threw the Stick he had in his Hand at it and
> knock'd it down, and bringing it to Elizabeth Watson said,
> this is not the first Thing kill'd here, this is the Place where
> we murder'd the Butcher.

The report concluded with the statement that Bryan
Connell was to be hanged in chains on the spot where the
murder was committed.

It is pleasant to turn from this gruesome matter to consider briefly a few examples of more varied and more diverting provincial news taken from London papers and set up in type at country printing houses. One reads in the *Norwich Post,* number 594 (5 July 1712), that the workmen engaged in building "Blenheim," the Kingdom's gift to the Duke of Marlborough, were suing the Duke for £40,000 "owing to them for work done there." In the *Reading Mercury* on 8 July 1723 was a report from Chester that the Rev. Mr. Henchman had discovered and opened the coffin of Hugh Lupus, the first Earl of Chester, nephew to William the Conqueror, the most remarkable feature of the disinterment being that "the String which ty'd the Ancles together was whole and entire," although it was "more than 630 odd Years since the Interment of the Body." The *Derby Mercury* reported on 4 November 1743 the sad case of a Bristol cobbler bitten by a cat; the cat as well as the cobbler died from the effects. On 18 May 1745, the *Cambridge Journal* printed details of the attack on a Methodist meetinghouse by an unruly mob in Exeter earlier that month. On 24 October 1747, the *Ipswich Journal,* number 454, reported from Manchester a porter's successful demonstration that a cask supposed by some to contain snuff really was filled with gunpowder; in support of his contention he had dropped a live coal into it.

These and thousands of other delayed reports about provincial life are encountered in the country newspapers throughout the period; but each report can be read in a London paper dated a few days earlier. This is in some cases neither surprising nor disappointing, for it is perfectly natural that the news from Newcastle, Lancaster, and Kendal in the *Protestant Mercury: or, the Exeter Post Boy,* number 14 (11 November 1715), should have reached Joseph Bliss, the printer, by way of London. What strikes one as curious is that even news from nearby places sometimes reached local readers by way of

London. News of the collapse of a house in Taunton on November 22 did not reach readers of the *Sherborne Mercury* until two weeks later, the report being taken from a London paper, though Taunton is not much more than thirty miles from Sherborne.

As was observed earlier, whatever value the provincial newspapers have as contemporary records of events is to be found in the news that came from near-by places but not by way of London. Even here the lapse of time was sometimes great. St. Ives in Huntingdonshire is not fifteen miles from Cambridge, but it took more than a fortnight for a strange piece of news to be brought before the readers of Robert Raikes's new *St. Ives Post-Boy*, number 3, on Monday, the last day of June, 1718.

St. Ives, June 28

> We hear from Cambridge, That on Sunday was sen-night in the Afternoon, the Vice Chancellor turn'd all the People out of Great St. Mary's-Church; but for what Reason is not yet known.

During the following week a corrected account came in, and Raikes said in the fourth issue of his paper that the story from Cambridge had proved to be a mistake. "My Correspondent there," he said, "has given me the Right of it. . . . It being Commencement Time, . . . some Persons had got into a Place, call'd the Pit, which Place is only Appropriated to Masters of Arts, which some intruders got into, and therefore were deservedly turn'd out."

Raikes and his partner Dicey were much more prompt in reporting current events after they moved to Gloucester. A paragraph in the *Gloucester Journal* of 20 August 1722, presumably taken from the current issue (no longer extant) of the *Worcester Post Man*, gave an account of the execution of four persons condemned at the Worcester assizes. An act of intended mercy made the spectacle extraordinarily interesting:

Soon after they were turn'd off, some Person, who had been desir'd by Blackwell to do so, pull'd him by the Legs with such Force, that he pull'd him down. When he was put into the Cart again, he was speechless, but coming to himself a little after, he spoke again to the People, and was turn'd off a 2d time.

Raikes and Dicey were prompt enough also in reporting fully the assizes held in the Booth Hall in Gloucester on the 9th, 11th, 12th, and 13th of the following March, for the first article in the *Gloucester Journal,* number 50 (18 March 1723), filled the available space on the front page and three quarters of the second page with details of the trials of persons charged with crimes that brought sentence of death to five—including John Powel for stealing a black horse valued at six pounds, and a woman who was to be burnt at the stake for giving her husband "one mortal Wound on the Navel with a Knife"—and transportation for seven years to five others—including John Cranham for stealing "one Sixpenny Loaf, a Pair of Nutcrackers, a Bottle of Geneva, to the Value of 1s., together with a coarse Towel."

If one ranges through the columns of the *Gloucester Journal* or any other country newspaper for a few decades, one sees that they frequently reported exciting events in nearby places; for besides the assizes and the executions that inevitably followed, there were fires, floods, riots, explosions, and local calamities of many kinds. Reference was made earlier in this chapter to a direct and detailed report of a fire at Burwell in the *Norwich Mercury* on 16 September 1727; and there were vivid accounts of fires in Dorsetshire in the *Sherborne Mercury,* number 274 (18 May 1742) and number 303 (7 December 1742). The violence and rioting over turnpikes at Ledbury were reported effectively in the *Weekly Worcester Journal,* numbers 1303 (14 June 1734) and 1370 (26 September 1735); the *Salisbury Journal,* number 46 (11 December 1738), gave an account of the rising of the weavers at

Trowbridge; the *Leeds Mercury*, number 743 (6 May 1740), reported the Dewsbury riots; and *Aris's Birmingham Gazette*, number 118 (13 February 1744), gave an ample account of the violence of a mob which moved about in the area of Wednesbury, Darlaston, Walsall, and West Bromwich attacking all whom they took to be followers of John and Charles Wesley. Heavy damage by flooding at Kendal and Milnthorpe was reported immediately in the *Newcastle Journal*, number 185, on 16 October 1742.

Many of these pieces of regional news can be read with much interest now because the events are in themselves quite out of the ordinary or because they were reported with a certain forthright simplicity, if not sprightliness, of style. There is something memorably matter-of-fact about the report in the *Reading Post* under the date 26 May 1735 that "On Monday last a poor Man was unfortunately kill'd, at Berrings Hill in the County of Oxon, by the Drag Chain breaking and throwing him down, whereby the Wheel went over his Body and squeezed his Guts out." One is tempted to quote in full the incredible post-mortem account of James Richards, of Milverton in Somerset, who, according to the obituary notice in *Norris's Taunton Journal* on 5 January 1728, died at three-score years and ten the day after Christmas. Knowing that the old man had experienced peculiar internal symptoms ever since he had some months before drunk water from a brook, a surgeon at Wellington performed an autopsy and discovered in the stomach of the deceased a small animal resembling a combination of prawn and caterpillar. There was "Life in it after it was taken out," the report said, but it soon died and "is since Buried at the request of the Deceased's Daughter." On a somewhat different level is the exciting account in the *Ipswich Journal*, number 421 (7 March 1747), of a French privateer stranded at Trimley, near the opening of the Orwell estuary.

Anyone in search of a plot for a disagreeable novel can find it in *Howgrave's Stamford Mercury*, number 12 (31 August 1732), which gave a full column to the strange story of William Alcock, the miller of Bourne, in Lincolnshire. Eighteen years before, Alcock had left his wife because she had palsy; but when a personal enemy revealed his whereabouts, he returned, paid fifty pounds to compensate the town authorities for keeping her during his absence, and then strangled her. The same issue of Howgrave's paper carried a long advertisement announcing that the town of Bourne would pay a substantial reward to any person who apprehended Alcock.

The amount of strictly *local* as distinct from *regional* news is equally impressive—reports in the Norwich papers of what was going on in Norwich, the Exeter news in Exeter papers, and so on—for as one looks at the whole corpus of purely domestic news-writing, one discovers that the amount, the variety, and the journalistic skill are quite deserving of attention. It is true that in the course of six months there may have been in some communities little to report but the assizes, or a heavy fall of snow, or a bonfire; during the week separating one issue of the town paper from another not much may have happened, for floods, murders, riots, assaults on the Methodists, and visits of the Bishop did not occur every week. Too few men bit dogs. Another point is that even if a violent wind did tear the roofs off a few houses, everybody in town knew what happened long before the weekly paper appeared. Nevertheless there was local news even in some of the first provincial papers to be established; and by the middle of the century, there were a good many papers that regularly had half a column or more of mixed local and regional news, in addition to all that had come from the London papers.

There is little to show that in the reign of Queen Anne the authors of country newspapers made a point of trying to procure local news; but in the course of the next two reigns, the authors were not satisfied merely to print what was sent to them. It is noteworthy that when proposals were drawn up in December, 1758, announcing the first newspaper in Halifax, the *Union Journal,* it was naturally said that the paper would be "collected from all the London Papers," but there were to be other merits, among them good coverage of happenings near at hand. "As every one is desirous to know the Occurrences of his own Neighbourhood, Care will be taken to publish every remarkable Event, in this and other adjoining Parishes, a number of Gentlemen having engag'd to supply the Printer with Intelligence of this Sort." [32] It appears that some printers were at first reluctant to insert local news, thrusting the short bits in just before the bankrupts or the advertisements and often in smaller type than was used for the London and foreign news. But at least the distinctively regional or local news had a place to itself; one soon becomes accustomed to looking for such pieces in the third column of the third page.

At this point a word of caution is necessary. In looking through files of country newspapers one frequently sees a passage of news dated at the place of publication of the paper, but it is soon perceived that the report really concerns a nearby place and is not "local" but "regional" in the sense in which these terms have been used here. The *St. Ives Post-Boy,* number 6 (21 July 1718), for instance, has at the end a separate date line, "St. Ives, July 21," but the paragraph below this heading tells of a fire at Over, a Cambridgeshire village four miles to the east. In the *Maidstone Mercury,* number 25 (27 May 1725), is a paragraph beginning "Maidstone, May 24," but it tells of a misshapen piglet at Cranbrook, some fifteen miles to the south.

It is inexpedient in the present work to compile an inventory or even a classification of local news in the one hundred and fifty English country papers which at one time or another during the reigns of Queen Anne and the first two Georges were in circulation; but if one examines representative papers from each of the three reigns, it is soon apparent that the country papers published before 1715 gave little space to firsthand accounts, and that in the reign of George I and particularly in that of George II both the new papers and the continuing ones gave more and more space to original as distinct from borrowed reports. "If we (as some Ignoramus's would have us) were to be silent in what happens in and about this City," said Thomas Gent of York in his *Original Mercury*, number 160 (3 September 1728), "yet we see other Papers will not be so"; and he cited the practice of the *London Evening Post*—"since Authorities must be quoted"—to show that it was quite the accepted thing for a newspaper, whether published in London or in the country, to print news about local people. To omit such accounts, Gent declared, would be inexcusable. By 1754, no one would be surprised to read in the first issue of the *Leedes Intelligencer* (12 July 1754) the declaration by the proprietor that he expected local news to be more acceptable than what came from the London papers.

> Accounts of Occurrences, &c. in the Neighbourhood, whether serious or jocose, of our rural Diversions, and the like would be more Entertaining to the Generality of Readers in the Country than any Thing we have yet heard of the Routs, Riots, Drums, and Hurricanes of the Town.

Nearly forty different newspapers were being printed in English provincial towns when these remarks appeared in the *Leedes Intelligencer;* copies which are extant yield passages of original local news by the hundreds.

If the reign of Queen Anne yields very little local news, it is partly because there were only twenty-one country newspapers in all, partly because most of the issues have disappeared. Seven of the Queen Anne provincial papers have left no trace, or have survived only in later issues. For evidence about the nature and amount of local news

in country journals published before the Queen died at
the beginning of August, 1714, one has only a few scattered issues of fourteen papers, four of them printed in
Norwich, two in Exeter, two in Newcastle, two in Stamford, two in Nottingham, and one each in Bristol and
Worcester. There is no Bristol news in the four extant
issues of the *Bristol Post-Boy*, and the surviving issues
of two early Exeter papers likewise yield nothing of
interest about Exeter apart from advertisements. The two
surviving issues of the *Nottingham Post*, dated 18 July
and 19 December 1711, have no Nottingham news of any
particular interest except an announcement of the prizes
to be run for at a horse race. There is no local news in
the two surviving issues of the *Stamford Post* (17 July
1712 and 31 July 1712).

Although only nine issues of the *Norwich Post* have
survived out of its twelve years of continuous publication,
those nine issues tell a good deal about the old Norfolk
city and the surrounding district; they regularly gave the
prices of wheat, barley, and oats on the local market,
indicated the numbers of Norwich persons baptized or
buried during the preceding week, and, in addition to
numerous and revealing advertisements, had such single-
sentence reports as these: "This week a Man Impress'd
for a Soldier, broke out of the Castle, and made his
Escape" (in number 348, 1 May 1708); "Last Saturday
came on the Election for the Mayor of this City, and
Alderman Havers was unanimously chosen for to serve
the ensuing Year" (in number 349, 8 May 1708); "Thursday last being the Day appointed for a General Thanks-
giving to return Thanks to Almighty God for the Glorious
Successes of the last campaign, it was observed in this
City with the usual Solemnity on such Occasions" (in
number 390, 19 February 1709). Elizabeth Burges, the
printer of the *Norwich Post*, apparently felt that the
inclusion of local news would increase the sale of her
paper in the region round about Norwich.

From the surviving issues of the other Queen Anne papers, one can glean a handful of local items; and in the following reign there were papers which occasionally had district news. The remark made by Mr. H. L. Evans about the lack of local news in the *Stamford Mercury* [33] is indubitably true of that paper: " . . . what now comes within the general category of 'local news', even if it existed, found no place in the journals of those days"; and that is true enough of the *Plymouth Weekly Journal.* In Nottingham the two newspapers published during the reign of George I—Ayscough's *Weekly Courant* and John Collyer's *Nottingham Mercury*—printed very little local news. York's first newspaper, the *York Mercury,* recorded no local happenings except the assizes, and its successor, Thomas Gent's *York Journal,* did not print local news until later. On the basis of the twenty-eight issues of the *Manchester News-Letter* which have survived, one surmises that the printer did not think his readers would be interested in anything happening in Manchester.

Papers which did not regularly have local news occasionally printed accounts of special events. The Exeter papers issued during the reign of George I ordinarily had no local news, but once in a while occurrences of special interest were reported, sometimes at considerable length. In Bliss's *Protestant Mercury,* number 18 (1 June 1716), nearly two columns were given over to an account, taunting and satirical in tone, of "Notorious Behaviour of some Mobbing Tories in the Parish of St. Thomas." In his paper of 26 April 1717, Bliss reported an event which presumably had come to his notice just too late to be inserted in the previous issue. Under the caption "EXON," he put a column and a half beginning with this well-packed sentence:

> On Friday the 19th of this Instant April, one John Hinston, a Taylor, of the Parish of Blackauton, lying between Totness and Dartmouth, was brought Prisoner to

High-Goal, for (as his Mittimus expresses) barbarously Beating and Wounding his poor Wife two Days before till she dy'd.

With an eye for the unusual detail, Bliss added that the alleged wife-beater weighed nearly four hundred pounds! In 1726, Andrew Brice proudly reported in considerable detail the jubilation of Exonians when a local boy revisited his native city, not as plain Peter King, but as the Lord High Chancellor of England; *Brice's Weekly Journal,* number 11 (26 August 1726), has an account five hundred and fifty words long followed by complimentary verses by the editor himself, "Not a Line being written 'till Yesterday," he said, "nor compos'd for the Press 'till 4 a-Clock this Morning. . . . "

Two provincial papers in which both local and regional news became notably abundant in the reign of George I were Stephen Bryan's *Worcester Post-Man* and the Raikes-Dicey *Gloucester Journal.* Both papers had lively and pointed accounts of all the usual events of the two places. In the Gloucester paper one finds accounts of such things as the suicide of an hostler at the Star Inn, the fining of a local constable, the action taken by the mayor to lower the price of corn, the announcement of Samuel Worrall's appointment as distributor of stamps for the county, and the ordaining of priests and deacons by the Lord Bishop—in other words, precisely the sort of local news now printed in provincial newspapers. Such items as those just mentioned, together with many pieces of news from nearby places, contributions of verse and prose by local authors, the "Gloucester Weekly Bill of Mortality," local prices, and an abundance of commercial advertisements and personal notices, give one a fair glimpse of life in that corner of England. Local items were few in number in the *Worcester Post-Man* in 1713 and 1714, but they increased in number and interest in the third decade of the century. By 1730, it was as natural to look for Worcester news in the Worcester newspaper as it is today.

The next thirty years saw a considerable expansion of this element in the country newspapers; and if some of them—*Howgrave's Stamford Mercury,* for example, and the *Sherborne Mercury*—continued to give very little space to reports of local events, there were many more papers in which almost every issue had something, and the total for any one year was remarkably extensive. To suggest that either the local or the national and foreign news in those papers was all significant would be ridiculous. News was not written for posterity, and its worth should be tested only by the perennially valid standards of journalism. Novelty is legitimate in a newspaper, if etymology means anything. Would a twentieth-century reader of the *Salisbury Journal* not be excited by a report that a trout "of a prodigious Size . . . 9 Pound 13 Ounces" had been caught within the town limits? Such a report must have been just as exciting on 19 June 1739. What resident of Ipswich would not be interested to read in his local paper next Friday that the man who had just been made bailiff had at the same time won £10,000 in a lottery? That twofold change of fortune was reported about a man named Thirkle in the *Ipswich Journal,* number 462 (19 December 1747). Yet novelty soon fades, and one looks for other virtues before declaring the lasting worth of news.

It would be easy to enumerate the seven cardinal virtues of journalism, but at the head of anyone's list must surely go these three: succinctness, clarity, humanity. A news story sixty words in length is ineffectual if its substance could have been set forth in thirty words; it is less than satisfactory if it leaves any significant element in doubt; it falls short of its potential impressiveness if the human aspect is neglected. Judged by this threefold standard, how does the local news in the country papers in the reign of George II compare with the reports in the best newspapers of our time? The question cannot be settled by the quoting of a few samples, but it is easy to find in the early provincial papers a thousand statements as admirably direct and economical of words as this announcement in the *Cambridge Journal* on 11 August 1750: "On Friday last the Rev. Dr. Paris, Master of Sidney-Sussex College in this University, was unanimously chosen Principal Librarian of this University, in the room of Dr. Middleton, deceas'd." Brevity is not everything. James Lister's full-column report of violence in the streets of Leeds makes good reading now, in spite of its eight hundred words, for the account—it is in the *Leeds Mercury* of 3 July 1753—gives enough detail to evoke a sense of being there:

> . . . When Night came on and Candles were brought in, the Shutters of the Windows of the Room the Magistrates were in being closed, the Mob grew more outrageous than ever, and with large Stones knocked down the Centinels, broke their Firelocks, drove the Window Shutters and Windows into the Room, and continuing to pour into the said Room large Stones dug out of the Pavement in the Streets, obliged the Magistrates for the Preservation of their Lives to leave that Part of the House. . . .

Lister wrote his report with an admirable blend of detachment and concern. It could have been a frenzied tirade; instead it is a controlled statement of fact, with just that kind of implication of basic principle on the side of law and order which one expects from a responsible journalist.

One of the best samples of reporting in the country papers of two centuries ago is John White's account, in his *York Courant*, number 286 (2 March 1731), of the ceremonies observed at the laying of the corner stone of the new assembly rooms—here called "the Theatre"—in Blake Street. There are three paragraphs, and (apart from the text of the Latin inscription, which is given in full) the account is completed in four compound sentences. It begins with the most important fact:

York, March 1. This Day the Rt. Hon. the Lord Mayor, and Aldermen, with the Gentlemen in Town, lay'd the Foundation-Stone of the Theatre which is to be erected on a Plan of the Right Honourable the Earl of Burlington's, our Lord Lieutenant and Governor.

Then came dimensions and details of the structure itself, which was "to be for all publick Diversions, such as Assemblies, Concerts of Musick, &c.":

> . . . the Building will be 92 Feet in the Front, (where there will be a magnificent Portico) and it will be 136 Feet in Depth, and will consist of Seven fine Rooms, amongst which will be a spacious Hall, after the Egyptian Manner, 112 Feet in Length, and 40 in Breadth, and the same in Heighth, which will have a Colonnade of 48 Corinthian Pillars, supporting the upper Part of the Building, which will be enrich'd by the same Number of Pilasters, to the Number of 44, for the Convenience of Air in the Race Week.

The human touch followed:

> . . . and for the Benefit of the Populace, in case a Crown'd Head should ever grace this Place, there will be a Gallery all round on the Out-side, where People may look in at the Windows, and see all that Passes in the Inside.

The ceremony proper was described in the simplest terms:

> At 12 a'Clock, Three Troops of General Churchill's Regiment march'd in Order to the Lord Mayor's, who, attended by the Gentlemen, went to the Ground, and perform'd the Ceremony of laying the Stone, which had the following Inscription fix'd to it in Brass, and several Pieces of our Coin of the Year 1730, lay'd under it.

The inscription named "Richardus, Comes de Burlington, Hujus Urbis Praeses, Saeculi MAECENAS" as the builder of the edifice, which was dedicated to various social purposes:

Quo Publici Exhibeantur Ludi,
Quo Proceres undique Confluant,
Quo Artes efflorescant Liberales,
Quo (dilatanta Negotio) Gloriam Pristina
    Novo EBORACI Splendore
    Obumbretur.

The account closed with a brief statement of the general jubilation which marked the occasion:

> During the Ceremony, the Troops gave several fine Vollies, the People huzzaing, *Long live King George and Queen Caroline;* and the Evening concluded with Joy, there being a fine Assembly, Drinking of Loyal Healths, Ringing of Bells, Bonefires, &c.

It gave the writer of this book a pleasant sense of "being there" when, ten minutes after reading this account in the *York Courant* of 1731, he joined a company of Yorkshire people and others at a formal gathering in that same "theatre"; there were no "fine vollies" and no "bonefires," but the colonnade of Corinthian pillars maintained the solid dignity of York's 1731 splendour, and the place was full of wonderful ghosts.

Beyond doubt, the news in the *York Courant* and the other country newspapers offering freshest advices foreign and domestic was stimulating and informative to our eighteenth-century ancestors. It is no disparagement to say that two centuries later much of its original freshness has gone. The wonder is that it can still entertain so delightfully and inform so amply.

---

1. For an account of such entertaining matter, see Chapter VII.

2. When Robert Dodsley, of London, tried to avoid raising the selling price of his *Public Register* in 1741 by omitting the news so that the *Register* could be printed on unstamped paper, he found that his readers, "particularly in the Country," were "very desirous" of having the news

included in the paper, and he was obliged, therefore, to resume the printing of news, using stamped paper for that part of his publication.

3. These lines in a set of stanzas printed in the *Churchman; or Loyalist's Weekly Journal,* number 27 (3 December 1720), show that Daniel Defoe was regarded as especially skilled in fabricating news:

> The Post ye call Daily
> If Mails shou'd e'er fail ye
> Has an Author can guess ev'ry Sentence
> And make out his Grub,
> A rare Tale of a Tub
> *Oh! Father thou grant him Repentance.*

A note at the foot of the page identifies the author as "Robinson Crusoe, alias De Foe."

4. Local papers printed in nearby towns *were* sometimes quoted by provincial editors, often without acknowledgment. W. Craighton of the *Ipswich Journal,* by way of exception, was careful to show where he had found the country news which he printed. In number 130 (8 August 1741), for example, several articles are marked "Colchester Journal," "Bury Post," "Norwich Gazette," "Norwich Mercury."

5. Newcastle papers often had direct news of ship arrivals and departures at Shields, a few miles down the Tyne. As early as 1712, John White requested readers of his *Newcastle Courant* to provide him with shipping news. The issue of 12 January 1712 has this invitation at the end of the fourth page: "Whereas many Persons, living in or near Newcastle upon Tine, receive Letters from their Friends or Relations, giving an Account of the Arrival of Ships in diverse Ports (and sometimes of other Occurrences that happen in their Voyage) the knowledge whereof would be very acceptable to others, who may have Concerns in the same Ships; The Printer therefore of this Courant gives Notice, that if any of his Acquaintance, or others, will be pleased to communicate such Intelligence, or a Copy of it, to him so that it may be inserted in this Paper for the Benefit of the Publick, They may be sure of a kind Reception, and Acknowledgment of their Favour, with a suitable Return and Gratification for it."

6. Some London newspapers enjoyed the services of a foreign correspondent. When George James, printer of the *Post Boy,* was questioned officially about the source of a paragraph dated "From the Hague, October 7, N.S." and printed in the *Post Boy* on 3 October 1727, he said he has received it "from a private Correspondent at ye Hague, who furnishes him with what he calls his Hague Letter, wch in ye said Post Boy is distinguished from ye other News by Commas. . . ."

7. In the course of an official examination Edward Berington, printer of the *Evening Post,* said that the paragraph dated at Madrid on 28 June and printed in number 3119 (17 July 1729) of his paper had been taken from the *Daily Post* of that same date (P.R.O., S.P. 36/13/104).

8. Stephen Martin may have been able to print a notably large amount of American news in his *Bath Advertiser* because his Bristol agent, Samuel Nayler, helped him to get hold of reports reaching Bristol by sea.

9. In the issue of the *Norwich Gazette* on the same date, 16 September 1727, Henry Cross-grove did not give a lengthy account of the fire, stating only, "We hear that in the dreadful fire at Burwell, one Mr. James Brinley (a Wholesale Turner) and his Wife, who had been marry'd but that Morning, perish'd in the Flames: As also one Mr. Rhodes an Excise-Man and his Wife, who went to the Show after they had put their 4 Children to Bed: And a Woman who rose out of Bed from her Husband, to see the Show." But Cross-grove had already printed by itself on a stamped half-sheet selling for three half-pence what was labelled *A True Copy of a Letter* . . . ostensibly written to Mr. Cross-grove on 9 September by an eyewitness, George Large by name. Cross-grove gave names where Chase in the Percival letter did not, but there are strong grounds for suspecting that the George Large letter is a concocted substitute for the genuine letter actually sent from Barton Hills to Justice Mott.

10. From the introductory address "To the Public" in the *Stratford, Shipston, and Aulcester Journal,* number 1 (5 February 1750).

11. Henry Fielding made much of conflicting newspaper reports in his *True Patriot* a few years later.

12. The *Bath Journal* of 13 July 1752 refers in its first column to "the great Dearth of News, and the little Expectations of a War, which is the Fund for News-Writers."

13. Collyer copied the text from the *St. James's Evening Post* of 18 August.

14. For example, the issue of the *Nottingham Post* just referred to has among the items of news from London under the date of 18 August the notice that "The Torrington Man of War, Capt. Purcel, is daily expected from Jamaica, with a large Fleet of Ships under Convoy." It was presumably supposed that foreign agents did not read English newspapers. Movements of ships and troops were reported freely and in detail.

15. It was reported in the first issue of the *Reading Mercury* (8 July 1723) that according to letters received in London on 2 July and dated at Rhode Island on 28 April, one of the Rhode Island sloops had caught a whale of a "prodigious Size, which was reckon'd worth 800 £ including the Blubber."

16. The present rector of Eyam, the Rev. E. M. Turner, has assured me that the initials "T.S.," with which the letter to Lister was signed, must be those of the Rev. Thomas Seward, who was rector of Eyam from 1739 to 1790, though Seward spent less time at that village than in the comforts of the Close at Lichfield, where he was canon residentiary and prebendary. As Boswell recorded, Thomas Seward was known to Samuel Johnson, and was the father of Anne, the "Swan of Lichfield."

17. *Trysorfa Gwybodaeth* was published at Carmarthen in 1770. For an earlier effort to establish a Welsh newspaper, see Chapter I, p. 17.

18. Most of Dublin's numerous papers are listed by Crane and Kaye. Before the end of 1760, Belfast had only the *Belfast News Letter* (from 1737 on) ; Cork had the *Cork News Letter* (1723-25), the *Cork Evening Post* (1754-96), and *George Swiney's Corke Journal* (1754-69) ; there was also for a short time a *Waterford Flying Post* (1729), printed by the Thomas Cotton who later printed the *Kendal Weekly Courant* and the *Whitehaven Weekly Courant*.

19. See F. S. Siebert, *Freedom of the Press in England 1476-1776* (Urbana, Ill.: University of Illinois Press, 1952), p. 286. For the most important aspects of the early history of Parliamentary reporting, see that same work, pp. 202-18, 279-88, and 346-63. For the whole matter, see also Laurence Hanson, *Government and the Press, 1695-1763* (London: Oxford University Press, 1936), *passim*.

20. XIX, 30, 42, 43, 44, 53, 54.

21. Gyttens (or Gythens, or Giddins; the name is spelled in all three ways in *The Journal of the House of Commons*) was ordered to appear, and identified the author of the letter as John Stanley. When Stanley presented himself and admitted that he had written the letter, he was ordered to be taken into custody. Subsequently he petitioned to be released from custody, and a few days later he was discharged, having piously promised that in future nothing would induce him "to offend in the least against any Order of the House, upon any Account whatsoever."

22. In April, 1747, the printers of the *Gentleman's Magazine* and the *London Magazine* were called to account before the House of Commons for printing the trial of Lord Lovat ; but scores of newspaper references to the distinguished leader in the Stuart cause went unchallenged.

23. See "The Rebellion of 1745: The Passage through Lancashire, from Contemporary News-sheets," *Transactions of the Lancashire and Cheshire Antiquarian Society*, LVI (1941-42), 123-51, and "The Rebellion of 1745: The Turmoil in Cheshire, from Contemporary News-sheets," *ibid.*, LVII (1943-44), 43-70.

24. From 8 May onward, Pote said, his *Windsor and Eton Journal* would be published only once a week, because "the late happy Defeat of the Rebels" had removed the necessity of printing news twice weekly.

25. No Exeter newspapers and no copy of the *Western Flying Post* published in the months of the rebellion have survived.

26. "Among these," wrote Mrs. Adams in the Preface, "are some *Journals,* whose Contents (having been carefully extracted from the *London,* and other News-papers) will give a Series of Accounts relating to the Insurrection of the Scots, A.D. 1745."

27. Hints of what was going on in Whitworth's office at this time are seen in later issues of his paper, particularly numbers 491 (22 July 1746) and 497 (2 September 1746). During July, August, and early September, 1746, the *Manchester Magazine* printed on its front page the details about the trials of several Manchester men who had been charged with having joined the rebel forces. One of these men, Thomas Deacon, was identified by Whitworth's apprentice, Thomas Bradbury, as the man

who "in the absence of his Master [i.e., Whitworth] . . . brought him a Paper which they call'd a Manifesto, and said that he must print 3000 of them against Morning."

28. A copy of the *Derby Mercury,* dated 13 December 1745, is described in the *Nottingham Journal* of 9 August 1946 as having in the margin a brief letter written by a man at Derby to his children, who were apparently in Norfolk. The note draws attention to the *Mercury's* vivid account of the turmoil caused by the presence of the rebels in Derby.

29. The account was copied in other newspapers, among them the *Newcastle Journal* of Saturday, 21 December 1745.

30. Charles Micklewright, of Reading, published a pamphlet with these words in the title on 24 February 1752 — that is, two weeks before Miss Blandy's trial. It was sold also by Benjamin Collins of Salisbury.

31. Early in April, the *Norwich Mercury* and the *Cambridge Journal* advertised that a work on Mary Blandy was about to be issued in weekly numbers. The *Salisbury Journal* — and likewise the local edition entitled the *Portsmouth and Gosport Gazette* — advertised in the issue of 2 March 1752 a "Curious Print of Miss Molly Blandy . . . Taken from the Life in Oxford Castle. Sold at the Printing Office in Salisbury." On 31 March, the printer of *Orion Adams's Weekly Journal* provided for his readers a free supplement on the Blandy business; in the *Manchester Mercury* on that same day his rival, Joseph Harrop, printed a "Letter from a Clergyman to Miss Blandy" and promised the detailed story in the next week's issue.

32. Manuscript notes in a copy of the *Union Journal* which is in the library of York Minster indicate that the author of the proposals was the Rev. John Watson, M.A., who not only contributed much prose and verse to the columns of this paper but "performed, when Curate of Ripponden, the Editorial Duties to the Newspaper."

33. H. L. Evans, "*Stamford Mercury* — Our Oldest Paper," *Lincolnshire Magazine,* II (1934-35), 326-31.

Chapter VI

Editorial Comments

F EW READERS in the present century would disagree with the notion that the editor of a newspaper, if he chooses to do so, may offer comments of his own on the facts reported, and may invite or permit others to use his columns for that purpose, too. Yet an editor may feel that he is serving the public best if he refrains from writing "animadversions." There were some early London papers whose authors announced emphatically that no editorial remarks would be added to the reports. The first issue of London's earliest daily newspaper, the *Daily Courant* (11 March 1702), had in its "Advertisement" the editor's declaration that he would not print any comments or conjectures of his own but would relate only matters of fact, "supposing other People to have Sense enough to make Reflections for themselves." In the *Evening Post,* number 10 (16 September 1709), the author made a particular point of promising that there would be "no Remarks or Reflections made for the Reader." Unlike the *Tatler,* which began earlier that same year, the *Evening Post* was not designed to tell its readers *what to think.*[1] This detachment may at first sight seem laudable; but an alert and influential editor has ideas and standards of his own and will not always be satisfied merely to repeat what he hears. In fact, all references to the "liberty of the press" would be pointless if editors were compelled to stifle their opinions and print only bare statements. A great journalist's reputation is based on the twofold foundation of veracity in reporting and courage in commenting.

It will be found that, although many an early provincial newspaper has not a single word of direct comment on items in the news, some of them have editorial opinions expressed quite frankly and vigorously. An instance of spirited reporting with strong opinions woven into the texture of the news and also added in a following comment may be seen in the *Leedes Intelligencer*'s account of the violence shown by the people of Holbeck, who in August and September, 1754, demonstrated their unwillingness to welcome their new curate. This is what readers found in the issue of 27 August 1754, the adjectives and indeed the very types carrying evidence of the editor's indignation:

On Sunday last the Rev. Mr. Fawcett, attended with near 1000 People from LEEDES, and all the Constables of the Burrough, 18 in Number, made a second Attempt to perform Divine Service at the *Chapel* of HOLBECK, to which he was deservedly nominated by the VICAR OF LEEDES, the legal Patron, and *duly* licenc'd by the Archbishop of York; but immediately upon his approaching the *Chapel,* he was opposed by a *furious, frantic, lawless Rabble* of HOLBECKERS, who assaulted him with *Dirt, Stones,* and *Brickbats,* and whatever Instrument of *Violence* their *Fury* cou'd *furnish.* Being treated in this *insolent,* unheard of *audacious Manner,* and finding that no Access cou'd be gained to the *Chapel,* but by his Attendants exerting Violence and repelling *Force* by *Force,* he thought proper (consistent with his truly Christian Disposition) to retire under the Conduct of those, who went there voluntarily to protect his Person.

When a *spotless, innocent* CHARACTER, ABILITIES equal to the *ablest* of his *Brethren,* and a FUNCTION that shou'd be held *Sacred* can claim *no Respect;* nay more cannot *protect* from *personal* Injuries amidst a Set of People who *call themselves Christians;* what may not be apprehended! Whose *Property* is *secure?* or whose *Life* is not in *Danger.*

No one would call this an impartial report, but for that very reason the Holbeck items in the *Leedes Intelligencer* during the last months of 1754 make entertaining reading now.

Griffith Wright could use vehement language no matter what he decided to condemn. His third piece of local news in the *Leedes Intelligencer,* number 16 (15 October 1754), had something of the uncompromising severity which Cowper later put into his condemnation of public houses in *The Task.* "Last Tuesday, and several Days preceding, even Sunday not excepted," wrote the Leeds editor, "many loose idle Fellows were observ'd playing at *Shake Cap* in Lands-Lane." Then followed editorial censure of the offenders, a hint that the paragraph represented the view of reputable members of the community, and an exhortation to the authorities to take some action:

> . . . this practice is frequently continued all Day, and when Night comes on the *Unfortunate* in Gaming retires Home greatly chagrin'd, often Penny-less, and vents his *ill Humours* on his Wife and poor Children; while *Fortune's Favourite* resorts to the Ale-house spends the *Pence he cannot deem his own* and ends the Night with Revelling and Drunkenness; These are not the worst Consequences arising from such Practices. . . . At the Request, therefore, of some well-disposed People, we make this *notorious,* that our Magistracy, agreeable to their wonted Vigilance, may bring the principal Offenders to *condign* Punishment, or take such Methods as will put a Stop to this infamous Practice.

Here is a journalist who clearly sees his function to be that of commentator, not just reporter.

A hundred other passages of vigorous editorial comment attached to items of news could be brought forward at this point to show that one does not have to turn to London papers to find fearless expression of views. One further example will have to serve. In number 334 of the *Colchester Journal* (18 August 1739), John Pilborough did what was unusual in those days, though he had occasionally done it in earlier issues of his own paper: he placed important Colchester news on the front page. That particular issue began with "Foreign Affairs," and then, under the caption, "COLCHESTER, Aug. 17," he gave a seventeen-line obituary notice of "one of the People call'd Quakers," eight lines on a drowning accident, and then a full account of the assizes held at Chelmsford the preceding week, "when several Prisoners were try'd, but none capitally convicted." After listing the convictions, Pilborough wrote seventeen lines about a case in which, after a trial of more than four hours, the verdict was given in favor of the defendant. It was an action brought against Edward Long, a tailor, who had refused to pay "a certain Fine demanded for his following his Employment, and keeping an open Shop in the Corporation aforesaid, not being a Freeman thereof, contrary to Custom." Here was a matter demanding comment by the editor. Pilborough's editorial ran to more than forty lines, his contention being that a tradesman wishing to carry on business in Colchester ought to be required to purchase his "freedom" at a reasonable rate or else be compelled to pay a substantial fine.

> The Decision of this Affair as above, having occasioned some Heat and Disorder in the contending Parties, I cannot forbear wishing, that Colchester was govern'd in like Manner to London, for soon after a Tradesman sets up in the said City, not being free, he is summoned before the Chamberlain, who commands him to purchase his Freedom on the next Court-Day, (once a Month Courts are held for making Freemen and binding Apprentices) and on his Neglect or Refusal so to do, is subject to a Penalty of 5£ every Time he is seen following his Employment within the City, by which Means, he is forced to comply, or quit his Undertaking, and thereby make Room for some body else, for the Freedom of London is refused to none who make Application for it, and will purchase the same. . . .

Pilborough added that he hoped his observation would not be displeasing to Colchester people, and he declared that his reason for setting forth his views was that he knew "many credible Inhabitants . . . would willingly purchase their Freedom at a reasonable Expence (tho' hitherto deny'd them)." Once again, this is a fearless and timely expression of opinion about a local matter.

Editors did not always attach their opinions to a paragraph of particular news. Occasionally paragraphs of editorial comment are found among items of local and regional news, though not attached to any one of these. The tone is sometimes explosive, particularly if a rebuke is being administered, but here and there one comes upon a dignified statement such as this in the *Gloucester Journal* number 1908 (19 December 1758):

Glocester, Dec. 16.

It is observed with Regret, by Persons who wish well to their Country, that many of the Inhabitants of the several Parishes in this County, who have been bred to Labour, desert their lawful Callings, and betake themselves to the idle Practice of Begging, under Pretence of Want of Work, &c. tho' it is well known that Employment enough may be had if they were disposed to undertake it—This is a Grievance which calls loudly for Redress; and it more particularly demands the Attention of those Persons whose Duty it is to examine into and remove such Causes of Complaint, as it is a growing Evil, and certainly productive of Consequences very pernicious to Society.

This remark was not used merely as a space filler, for in that particular issue seven paragraphs of local and regional news follow the statement.

Expressions of editorial opinion are seldom attached to contributed pieces, but there are a few examples. Robert Whitworth, of Manchester, was moved to write with some vigor when he printed in his *Manchester Magazine,* number 458 (5 November 1745), a colorful

description of a military life sent to him by a correspondent, for he added a hundred words of wartime
propaganda:

> The above Paragraph is inserted to rouse, if possible a
> Spirit which seems to languish more in this County than
> in most others in the Kingdom; a Spirit necessary to pre-
> serve all that is dear and valuable to us; a Spirit of
> Self-Defence. But can we *unarm'd, undisciplin'd,* defend
> ourselves against armed and disciplin'd Foes? Why not
> arm then? Many wait for an Example. Who then will have
> the Glory of being the first in this momentous, this highly-
> important Cause. A Soldier is, now more especially, the
> greatest, the most aimiable [*sic*] Character. O Liberty!
> O Virtue! O my Country! should be in the Heart as well
> as the Mouth of every Briton.

The style of this appeal is uneven, but the intention is
clear and commendable.

The remarks and observations in a newspaper need not
all come from the pen of the editor or his associates, and
it is obvious that in papers dedicated to the support of
a party or a cause of any sort one may expect to find
letters, contributed editorials, and selected essays that had
a bearing on matters of current interest. Essays on controversial matters reprinted from the *Craftsman* and other
London newspapers outnumbered the communications
written expressly for publication in provincial papers, but
correspondents sent in pieces on all sorts of local and
regional affairs.

Eighteenth-century editors were not always willing to
print unsolicited communications, and they had many
reasons for rejecting them. They were less insistent than
twentieth-century editors that the sender of a letter give
his name, but they demanded that the postage be paid
in advance, that the style be succinct, and that the tone
be inoffensive. Rejection was seldom stated with such
severity as was used by Caesar Ward in the *York Courant*,
number 860 (6 April 1742), when he printed in eye-

catching italic this blunt sentence: *"The Writer of a Letter, sign'd* S. D. [the Post-Mark on which is WAKE-FIELD] *may well be asham'd of his Name, since 'tis hard to determine whether his Ignorance, his Lies, or his ill Manners are the most conspicuous."* Robert Raikes, of Gloucester, was usually quite firm in rejecting communications which were wordy, whether the matter was news or opinion. In the *Gloucester Journal* of 9 January 1728, for instance, he gave this explanation for not accepting a contribution:

> The Letter from Wilts of December 21, is come to hand, which being too prolix for the Limits of our Paper, we are obliged to omit inserting: However, we cannot but acknowledge, that the Author's Remarks are very just, and that we shall always be willing to oblige that ingenious Gentleman or any other of our Correspondents, provided the Subject be concise, and free from Personal Reflection or Scandal.

While Raikes and Dicey were still partners in their other successful paper, the *Northampton Mercury,* a letter from "an Anonymous Gentleman at Lutterworth" was rejected on the ground that its subject matter might jeopardize the *Mercury*'s reputation: "as publick Reflections may bring an Odium upon the Paper, the Business of which is rather to amuse than reform, we beg the Gentleman's Pardon for not inserting it."

This caution was shared by other editors. Thomas Cotton, of Kendal, in the *Kendal Weekly Courant* on 12 February 1732, expressed hearty thanks to correspondents who had sent agreeable and instructive contributions, but he felt it necessary to state with some emphasis his editorial policy:

> . . . I must entreat my Correspondents, (especially one who dates his Labours from Lancaster) to forbear sending me any private or publick Scandal, or any Innuendo of either. I am determin'd not to Print the Letters or the

Versifications of any Person (let the Conceits of them be ever so Witty in the opinion of the Authors) which attack the Reputation of another: For I will not suffer my Paper to be a Conduit to convey Envy, Detraction, Picque or Prejudice.

Cotton's caution may have proceeded from a personal desire to keep the tone of his paper decent, or at any rate inoffensive, or he may simply have wished to avoid suits for libel.

Often, one may suppose, an unsolicited contribution was tossed aside without explanation. Certainly few editors took as much trouble to justify their rejection of a manuscript as Roger Adams of Chester did in his *Weekly Courant,* number 151 (15 October 1735). There were, he said, three good reasons why he could not print a letter which he had received from Preston. In the first place, the subject was not likely to have a general appeal to readers; in the second place, it was "too Copious for a News Paper" and would fill "many Sheets of Print"; in the third place, "It would take up too much of a Printers time to Read, consider, and reduce the Arguments to form. . . . " All these excuses were unanswerable, for the editor had the last word.

Nevertheless a bookful of "letters to the editor" could be compiled from the unsolicited communications in the columns of eighteenth-century country newspapers. There are letters on the Excise Bill, on the Broad Wheel Scheme, on the bad habit of high tipping, on the improvement of the roads, on lotteries, on the cruelty of throwing at cocks, on a plan for supporting the widows and orphans of clergymen, on the education of poor children, on efforts to reduce profanity, on the heartlessness of the wealthy— this last sent by "A Cornish Tinner" to the *Western Flying-Post* for the issue of 14 January 1751.

In these communications addressed specifically to the editor of the local paper, the tone is sometimes facetious, as in the letter dated at Manchester and printed in the

Chester Weekly Journal of 5 July 1732 on the subject of the Tithe Bill; the five ironical arguments, in the manner of Swift, begin with the declaration that the passing of this Bill "would greatly lessen the exorbitant Incomes of the rural Clergy," who were said to receive on the average so generous a stipend as ninety pounds a year; "whether this is not an extravagant Allowance for only getting up in the Pulpit once a week, and reading an old Sermon, let every understanding Englishman consider." More often the tone is serious, and the prose is not infrequently dull. There is dignity and strength in the unsigned letter "To the Author of the Stamford Mercury" on 13 April 1738 urging that the Ministry immediately declare war on Spain if by the middle of May the English merchants who had suffered from the Spanish depredations had not received "ample Satisfaction."

A representative letter addressed originally to the printer of a country newspaper is the unsigned plea which a stay-at-home reader at Beverley in Yorkshire sent "to the Publishers of the Newcastle Journal." The letter, printed in number 654 (19 October 1751), deplored the migrating of Yorkshiremen to Nova Scotia:

Gentlemen,   Beverly, Oct. 12.

I am informed by a private Letter from a Friend in the South, that several Families design for Nova Scotia in the Spring, and are actually disposing of their Effects, with a full Determination to settle in that Part of the World, where great Encouragement is given to all labouring Men, that embark from hence, who, in a few Years, may make a very opulent Fortune, as they have Land, in a Manner, for Cultivation: Here is daily great Numbers about leaving off Business, in order to go next Spring for Nova Scotia; this is a general Intention among the Husbandmen and Farmers in Several Counties of England; so that Two Hundred Farms and upwards have been given up in Yorkshire, and the like hath happened in some other Counties Southward. Those Proceedings well deserve the Consideration of the Legislature, to prevent such Numbers evacuating Great Britain, and leaving her destitute of her most valuable Hands; by which, in Length of Time, we shall be reduced to the same deplorable Condition with Charles XII. of Sweden, who depopulated his Kingdom so much by War, that his Nation became in a Manner desolate, and the Women were obliged to till the Ground.

Many letters dealing with aspects of national prosperity appeared in London papers and were copied in local newspapers, but this gloomy letter from Beverley is a fair sample of communications sent directly to provincial printers.

There were, of course, numerous letters on purely local concerns—on the establishing of a hospital in Norwich, on the viciousness of crimes committed in Gloucester, on a change in the postal routes near Halifax, on the leasing of the waterworks in Nottingham, on the instituting of a Chamber of Commerce in Liverpool, on the appointment of Dr. Osbaldiston as new Dean of York in 1728, and, on the front page of the *Leedes Mercury,* number 1072 (25 February 1746), "Serious Reflections on the Succession to the Vicarage of Leedes humbly address'd to the Candidates and Electors in Trust to the same."

A good example of these special messages to readers is the communication filling the front page of *Adams's Weekly Courant,* number 847 (4 July 1749). It is given extra prominence, for it has one of the few headlines to be found in an eighteenth-century newspaper: *"The* CASE *of Mr.* Samuel *Cocks, one of his Majesty's Messengers in Ordinary."* According to the account sent to Mrs. Adams, Cocks had given offence in high places by entering a sutler's tent with his hat on while he was on an official mission from the Duke of Newcastle's office to "his R----l H------ss the D--- of C-------d" in Flanders, and he had been put into prison. Appeals for release had been in vain. "He has now no other Resource, than to make this public Appeal to his Country, to throw himself under the Protection of the C----l Laws of England. . . . " Mrs. Adams

278

offered no comment, but she printed as introduction to the statement of Cocks's predicament the full text of the accompanying letter addressed to her by a reader in "Newcastle-under-line":

> . . . I herewith send you a fresh Instance of most tyrannical Usage, viz. that of murdering Folks by Piece-meal, by starving a poor innocent Family. This is the deplorable Situation of the distressed Household of my unhappy Kinsman: And be assured, that there is sufficient Evidence to warrant every Fact and Circumstance contained in the following extraordinary Account. . . .

It is disappointing that no editorial observations follow the letter and the statement, but Mrs. Adams wisely saw that the communication was strong enough to speak for itself.

Newspaper editors sometimes found that local happenings gave rise to controversy which filled the columns with disputatious observations by readers and required little or no editorial comment. In September and October, 1727, the *British Spy* of Derby and the *Weekly Courant* of Nottingham gave much space and small print to the disturbances caused by opponents of the Rev. Dr. Michael Hutchinson, minister of the parish church of All Saints in Derby, with but little comment from the Derby editor. During the winter months of 1751-52, the columns of the *Norwich Mercury* frequently contained letters strongly opposing or strongly supporting "Mr. Wheatley the Methodist," who was at that time addressing many gatherings in Norfolk. In the *Leedes Intelligencer* during August and September, 1755, there were several letters in which the authors jeered at each other for "throwing indigested Hints into a common Newspaper" and for "officious intermedling in other People's Business."

One of the most refreshing qualities of eighteenth-century prose is the vigor with which rebukes were administered, often in the public press. In the *Suffolk*

Mercury on 23 April 1733, a reader at Sudbury declared that his character had been "scandalously aspers'd by a Gentleman commonly known by the Name of Doctor Scarling," and he addressed a letter "To the Candid Reader" in the hope of shaming the offender into better manners. The tone of the letter makes one think of Samuel Johnson's letters of censure:

> Sir,
>
> To go into Inns, and other Publick Houses, and, amongst the Rabble in the Kitchen, to set up your self for a Great Man; to say you are the only Physician in Sudbury, and that I am but a Quack; slily to desire a Friend to enquire into my Character at the University, and to injure my Reputation in my Absence; are mean and scandalous Arts, that may perhaps catch the unthinking Vulgar, but amongst Men of Sense and Learning, will always be look'd upon as unworthy the Character of a Person who sets up for a Gentleman and a Physician. . . .

Mr. Taverner's friends in Sudbury must have chuckled to read in later sentences his references to physicians "degrading themselves into the Characters of tattling old Nurses" and "keeping Company with the Scum of the People."

There were occasions when an editor who printed such abusive or libelous or seditious matter in his columns had to apologize or even suffer penalties of great severity. When the rector of Padworth, in the *Reading Mercury* on 9 September 1723, charged Loftus Brightwell with misleading the churchwardens into swearing "what they knew nothing of" and publicly called on Brightwell to justify himself if he could, there was no response, but the editor of the paper three weeks later printed a special note in italics: *"We think ourselves oblig'd to ask Mr. Brightwell's Pardon, for the Injustice done him in one of our former Papers; and not having sufficient Room in this Mercury to vindicate ourselves, we beg to be excus'd till our next."* The following issue, unfortunately, is not extant, but it is likely that whatever the editor of the *Reading Mercury* wrote, he would be out of the rector's good graces for a time.

Elizabeth Adams, of Chester, also got into trouble with a churchman, or rather two churchmen. In *Adams's Weekly Courant,* number 814 (29 November 1748), she used large type to print her apology and that of her son:

> I Elizabeth Adams, Widow, Printer of the Paper, call'd *Adams's Weekly Courant;* and I John Adams, son of the said Elizabeth Adams, both of the City of Chester, do hereby publickly confess and declare, that we are guilty of printing and publishing a base and scandalous Libel in the said Courant, of Tuesday, August 2, 1748, against the Right Reverend the Lord Bishop of Chester; for which we humbly beg his Lordship's Pardon; and do hereby testify our Shame and Sorrow for such unjust and unprovok'd Usage of his Lordship's Character, and shall ever be thankful for his Acceptance of this our Submission, instead of that just and legal Punishment, which our Crime has deserv'd.
>
> We also hereby acknowledge, that in the same Paper, we did very unworthily treat the Character of the Reverend Doctor Powell, Dean of St. Asaph, for which we also humbly desire his Forgiveness. Witness our Hands this 14th Day of November, 1748.
>
> Elizabeth Adams.
John Adams.

Base and scandalous libels of individuals are always dangerous, and Elizabeth had good reason to feel relieved that the two churchmen accepted her apology.

On at least one occasion Charles Micklewright, of Reading, had to acknowledge an error. In his *Oxford Gazette and Reading Mercury* on 20 October 1752 and on 11 December of that same year, he had printed queries and a letter concerning the proposed new gaol in Reading. These had caused much annoyance to "those . . . entrusted with the Execution of the Laws and Administration of Justice," and in number 375 (15 January 1753)

Micklewright gave a prominent place on the third page to his lengthy expression of regret. His signed statement ended, "I do hereby most humbly ask Pardon in this Public Manner for the Offence I have given in publishing the said Queries and Letter." There were still limits to the liberty of the press.

But not all controversial matters ended in apologies by the printer. If the subject evoked extensive comment in other provincial papers, the editor of the original paper might enjoy the unusual satisfaction of having his journal quoted in London. That happened to the *Gloucester Journal*'s twenty-two-hundred-word "Essay on Riots; their Causes and Cure," which followed reports of the weavers' riots in Wiltshire in the last weeks of 1738. This essay was violently attacked in the columns of the *Salisbury Journal* in January, 1739, but it was reprinted in the *London Evening Post* on 23 December, and from there copied in the *Leeds Mercury*, number 673 (2 January 1739), filling the first four and a half columns. It is apparent that traffic between London and provincial newspapers did not all move in one direction; the *Gloucester Journal*—in fact all of the newspapers of the West Country—seem to have been watched with particular attentiveness in London.

It was noted in Chapter V that several provincial printers were called to account for printing reports of Parliamentary debates. Printers were more frequently prosecuted, and sometimes more severely punished, for printing direct reflections on the government or on the sovereign. In 1716, Philip Bishop, printer of the *Exeter Mercury*, was imprisoned for publishing a pamphlet called *Nero Secundus*, which was construed as disloyal, and he died in prison. Earlier in that same year, according to the *Nottingham Mercury* of 22 March 1716, William Ayscough, printer of the other Nottingham paper, the *Weekly Courant,* "was fined and obliged to give Security for his Behaviour, &c. for the False and Scandalous Reflections on the Government."[2] Two years later, Henry Cross-grove, printer of the *Norwich Gazette or the Loyal Packet,* found himself in difficulties for having "inadvertently" (he said) offended the government. As he recorded in his paper on 13 December 1718, two of His Majesty's messengers were sent down to take him into custody; but he was not in his shop when they arrived, and they left without him, taking some papers and letters which they found on his premises. A week later, his paper carried the announcement that Cross-grove had surrendered himself to the Secretary of State. By 27 December he was still in custody in London, but he sent a cheerful message to readers of the paper: " . . . he wishes all his Customers a merrier Christmas than he is likely to have, and [as] Happy a New Year as he would wish himself."

A summons to London came also to John White in Newcastle, as several papers reported—the *British Spy* of Derby, number 192 (4 February 1731), among them:

> A Printer of News at Newcastle upon Tyne is taken into Custody of one of his Majesty's Messengers, as we hear, for reprinting Part of the Craftsman of last Saturday was Se'nnight, and the Saturday before, and is bringing up to Town by the said Messenger.

John White and other country editors might have taken warning against copying matter from the *Craftsman* and other outspoken London papers, for the newspapers frequently reported the arrest of printers and venders. "Last Night several Messengers went to the Printer of the Craftsman and seiz'd the whole Impression of the Day." So stated a report taken from the *London Evening Post* of 10 December 1737 and reprinted in several country papers, among them the *Leeds Mercury,* number 618 (13 December 1737).

No provincial printer in the reign of George II got himself into more serious difficulty than Edward Farley, of Exeter, who rashly reprinted from *Mist's Weekly Jour-*

nal, number 175 (Saturday, 24 August 1728), a letter signed "Amos Dudge" which was said to be "a perfect Relation of the present state of Affairs in Persia." This was in no sense news; it was a thinly disguised allegorical hint that there was justice in the Pretender's claim to the throne. The uttering of such matter was in direct violation of the Statute of 6 Anne, c. 7, under which one Matthews had been convicted and executed in 1719 for high treason, the charge being that he had printed an affirmation of the Pretender's right to the Crown. In the "Amos Dudge" letter, King George was referred to as an usurper, "Esreff" by name, and the Young Pretender was described as "the unfortunate young Sophi." Uncomplimentary things were said about "Esreff" and his ministers:

> You will naturally be suprised [*sic*], that a Prince so unequal to Imperial Dignity [as Esreff is], directed in all his Counsels by a Minister who is as famed for Corruption as *Sejanus,* and for Cruelty as *Nero,* should be able to maintain the Possession of the Empire, in Opposition to a lawful Sophi, whose undoubted Right is supported by the affection and Duty of the Generality of the People, by whom hourly Prayers are offered up for his Restoration.

Small wonder that Wye's letter on 29 August reported that "The Town was never so shock'd at the Reading of any Thing, like that contain'd in Mist's Journal of Saturday last." Small wonder that all the country newspapers copied out paragraph after paragraph about the King's exasperation, about the search for Mist's printer, Wolfe, about the sixteen persons taken into custody because they were suspected of having had some part in the printing or the distributing of the offending paper, about the official refusal to let *Mist's Weekly Journal* be distributed through the post office.

It was small wonder, too, that in Exeter a few weeks later the Grand Jury at the General Quarter Sessions on

7 October took notice, "with greatest Detestation and Abhorrence," that *Farley's Exeter Journal,* number 276, had reprinted from *Mist's Weekly Journal* what the fifteen jurymen looked upon as "an infamous, scandalous, seditious Libel, calculated and published with no other view but to instil groundless Jealousies into the Minds of his Majesty's Subjects, to endanger our Religious and Civil Liberties, and to disturb the Peace of his most Sacred Majesty. . . . " The full text of this presentment and one drawn up in similar terms on 10 October 1728 by "the Grand Jury at a General Goal Delivery for the City and County of Exon" were printed in *Brice's Weekly Journal* on 18 October 1728. Brice had frequently assailed Farley in the columns of his *Weekly Journal,* and it has been stated[3] that Brice had actually challenged Farley to reprint the "Amos Dudge" piece.

For Mist and all who were connected with his printing and publishing of the notorious issue the consequences were most serious;[4] for Edward Farley the outcome was calamitous. Apparently the treasonous libel, reprinted in *Farley's Exeter Journal* on Friday, 30 August 1728, had been set up by Farley's compositor, Richard Stretchley.[5] It is not clear whether Farley deliberately selected the piece, knowing its intended meaning, or whether he was innocently careless. Many months later in his pathetic petition to the Queen[6] (the King being at the time in Hanover), Farley said that this particular issue of Mist's paper had reached him "by the General Post in the usual Manner as it had before been constantly Sent to him, and was not sought out by any evil contrivance," and that as soon as it came to his hands he "inadvertently Suffered the Same to be reprinted in his newspaper without reading or being acquainted with the contents thereof." These words seem clearly to exonerate Farley from knowingly printing matter that implied the Pretender's right to the Crown. But on the strength of statements by the two witnesses for the Crown it was asserted in an unsigned but official communication to Lord Townshend dated 24 November 1728[7] that Farley must have understood clearly the implications of the allegory about "Esreff" and the "Sophi" because he had added a paragraph of his own. The truth of this assertion about the adding of a paragraph could easily be checked if a copy of *Farley's Exeter Journal* for 30 August 1728 could be found; but most of the copies were destroyed by the troubled printer. As soon as it had been pointed out to him that he would probably be prosecuted for printing and publishing a libel "he immediately gave orders to his Servants that the s[d] papers should be burnt which was accordingly done before twenty of the said news papers were dispos'd of."[8]

One of the two witnesses called by the Crown was Farley's father-in-law, Richard Science, who must have felt that in his first statements he had been too explicit, for he later proved "so far from being a willing Witness," the Crown's solicitor reported, that nothing could be drawn from him but what was "forced by Questions."

> And he now recedes from the most material part of his Evidence . . . and pretends that Farley was not in the Printing Office when Mr. Score came there the 30th of August in the morning, and that Score expostulated wth Farley's wife, and not with Farley, for printing and dispersing the s.[d] Journal or Libel and that Farley did not understand the Paper or know the meaning of it.[9]

Farley's hasty burning of all but twenty of the printed copies, presumably after Mr. Score's visit, cannot be taken as evidence of his knowing beforehand that it would be dangerous to print the "Amos Dudge" letter; but there is no doubt that he immediately became terrified, spending three or four days in hiding at the house of the Rev. Richard Long, of Broad Clyst, a village five or six miles from Exeter.

Mr. Long was called to appear before Lord Townshend on 14 October because a letter which had been "taken out of ye Pocket of Mrs. Farley on Fryday September 20th 1728" and which began "Mr. Farley" was on the outside addressed "To the Reverend Mr. Richd Long, Broad Clyst, to be Sent from Mr. Thomas Tronnicks, Exeter." Mr. Long's quavering signature stands at the bottom of the record of his declaration that the letter "never came to his hands" but that Farley had stayed three nights at his house.[10] A contemporary note on the letter itself[11] indicates that the writer, William Kittoe, intended the letter for Farley but had directed it to Mr. Long "for ye more safe Conveyance." Obviously Kittoe wrote the letter to confirm Farley's suspicion that the offense was dreadfully serious and that his position was precarious. Dated Monday, 9 September 1728, the letter repeated the statement in Wye's letter of 5 September that because of the great demand which there had been for *Mist's Weekly Journal* of 24 August a "certaine Printer" had reprinted it and had been "taken into Custody, carried to Hampton Court, Examined, remanded into Custody, and ordered to be prosecuted by the Attorney Genl for Treason." That word and Kittoe's final sentence must have struck terror to Farley's heart: the grand jury of Middlesex had recommended that all the guilty printers and publishers should be "brought to Condign Punishm^t."

There is no doubt that Edward Farley paid heavily for his mistake. Having been indicted for treason at the Exeter assizes—after a postponement because the text of the indictment had a flaw in it—he languished in prison month after month, loaded with irons (as he said in his petition to the Queen), not just pending judgment but while the highest legal authorities in the land were trying to decide whether the copying of the letter from Mist's *Journal* should be declared a misdemeanor or an act of high treason. It was seen that in the absence of two strong witnesses Farley could not be convicted of high treason, and yet it was felt improper to let the offence be tried merely as a misdemeanor.[12] The question was carried from the assize court to the attorney-general, to the Council, and to the Lord Chancellor. In the end, Farley was granted a pardon. Perhaps Sarah Farley and her father were relieved when word of the royal mercy was brought to Exeter; it made no difference to Edward Farley, for he had died in prison.

It was not only offending the government that got editors into trouble; a bold statement assailing the local authorities could also stir up official resentment and lead to fines or imprisonment. William Chase, of Norwich, found this to be so when in April, 1729, he openly accused the Tories of having permitted deceptions to be practised at the common-council elections earlier that month. In his *Norwich Mercury* for Saturday, 19 April 1729, Chase incorporated his charges in his report of the election, naming several persons who had cast votes to which they were not entitled:

> On Monday last the Scrutineers for the late Election of Common-Council-Men met again, when the Managers for the Tory-Poll gave fresh Instances of their *fair* and *honest* way of Proceeding therein, as is evident by the following Examples. One Stephen Rant poll'd in the Name of William Fake, who dy'd in London near a Year ago; and tho' the WHIG Managers would have prov'd this be sufficient Evidence, yet they could not be permitted. . . .

"Such compendious, but irregular Methods of Scrutining [*sic*], were never known in this City before," added Chase, giving several other examples. But on the following Wednesday he was in jail. No charge, he said, had been mentioned in the warrant of commitment, but he assumed that his fault was in printing the paragraph about the scrutineers. The mayor, who had already been told about the irregularity before Chase's paper appeared, apparently decided to exercise his authority against the Whig journalist rather than against the Tory scrutineers, for the record of the Quarter Sessions held in the Guild-hall on 19 July 1729 shows that Chase was fined £40.[13]

One of the best examples of newspaper criticism of civic maladministration is to be seen in William Dicey's *Northampton Mercury* in 1734, when it was noticed that new names were being added to the list of voters. In the *Northampton Mercury* of 8 April 1734, Dicey pointedly observed that the corporation had lately "admitted a great Number of Honorary Freemen, in Order (as is conceived) to support the Interest of a certain Gentleman, whom they've invited and prevailed upon to stand as a Candidate at the ensuing Election for a Burgess of the said Town, to represent them in Parliament." This procedure, said Dicey with telling restraint, was "extraordinary in its Kind," never having been attempted before in Northampton except when John Willoughby was mayor in "the unhappy Reign of K. James II." Dicey's handling of the matter was clever, and it must have been effective: he inserted a list of the names of all who had been admitted honorary freemen "as well in the Mayoralty of the said Mr. Willoughby, as of the present Mayor." The lists were continued in following issues, with a cumulative force which left no doubt in anyone's mind that political trickery had been exposed. Nor was Dicey alone among provincial editors in boldly censuring a civic corporation for corrupt practices. Another audacious newspaperman— at a time when audacity was needed—was James Jopson, printer of *Jopson's Coventry Mercury,* who appears to have been undaunted in his attacks upon the disgraceful misuses of power which was concentrated in the hands of the Coventry Council. According to an entry in the Coventry Council Minutes[14] under date 23 October 1742, it was resolved by the council to prosecute Jopson for scandalous reflections on the corporation or on its members. Here again is a newspaperman threatened with official severity because, acting as a spokesman for the community, he presumed to denounce the improper use of power by the civic authorities.

The hazards of exposing iniquity in the columns of early newspapers are more strikingly illustrated in the struggle of Andrew Brice, of Exeter, to obtain fair treatment of prisoners in one of the local jails. Brice was a keen participant in any controversy and seemed to rejoice when others joined in, or even when two other parties used the columns of his *Weekly Journal* for exchanging their differing opinions. For example, in *Brice's Weekly Journal,* number 236 (22 August 1729), nearly the whole of the first page was occupied by "A Letter to Mr. John Vowler, Senior, by J. Hallet, jun.," the tone and theme being indicated by the Rev. Joseph Hallet's declaration, "You have studied to injure my Reputation in the tenderest Point, by endeavouring to persuade People, that I have declared Christians are under no Obligations to practice moral Virtue." The controversy continued in the next five issues. But it was one thing for correspondents to quarrel with each other in Brice's columns, quite another for him to have to defend himself in his own paper from attack by forces too strong for him to withstand. It is not often that a journalist in the right has to abscond.

The story of Brice's campaign to expose the keeper of a jail for alleged cruelty and slovenliness is told piecemeal by Brice himself in several issues of his *Weekly Journal,* by "T.B.," of Ottery, in a letter which gave "a just Account of honest Mr. Brice's Case" in the issue of 25 September 1730, in "The Author's Case" appended to Brice's *Freedom: A Poem, Written in Time of Recess from the rapacious Claws of Bailiffs, and devouring Fangs of Goalers* (1730), and in an article by T. N. Brushfield a hundred and fifty years later.[15] Brice had for some months been disturbed by reports of heartlessness and filth in some of the jails in Somerset and Devonshire; and in September, 1726, he had printed a twopenny pamphlet under the title *An Appeal for Justice, and the Impartial World,* with a subtitle indicating that this was "a true and faithful Narrative, and just Complaint, of the unparallel'd and unjustifiable Barbarity and hellish Cruelty exercis'd on L. Hill, Esq; a Prisoner in the County Goal of Somerset, at Ilchester, by the Keeper thereof and his Adherents." A year later he printed in the columns of his *Weekly Journal* the first piece of evidence sent to him by "some cruelly oppressed Prisoners" in the jail in the St. Thomas ward of Exeter. This he did not just as a matter of popular interest; Brice was waging a campaign, and he was ready to accept for publication the complaint of Charles Lanyon, a merchant of Newlyn, near Penzance, who had been unsuccessful in appealing to George Glanvill, the keeper of St. Thomas's prison. Lanyon had been in prison over a year by the time he managed to get word to Brice, and from 6 February 1727 had been "confined in the Dark house, . . . double-gyved with the largest Irons which could be got in Bridewell."

Alert journalist that he was, Brice seized the opportunity to emphasize Glanvill's severity by commending in number 72 (27 October 1727) the keeper of the Southgate prison, whose humanity and good nature were very different from the "Revenge, Savageness, Cruelty, and a long ET Cetera of abhorred Things" which made Glanvill notorious. Within a few days Glanvill had sued Brice for £500 damages. Brice pleaded his cause in the columns of his own newspaper, later (in number 260, 27 February 1730) complaining that the case had never come to fair hearing in court—"that is to say, never a single Word of my Side was heard." Yet penalties were apparently imposed, and Brice had either to pay a fine of £103 or go to jail. He absconded. During the many months he remained in hiding, Brice suffered in many ways: his mother and his wife died, his business was left to others to conduct, his health was impaired; but he deserves to be remembered as a journalist who audaciously exposed a public scandal, insisting that a prisoner might as effectually be prevented from escaping by "Stone Walls, and Pondorous Chains, and Iron Grates . . . above Ground, in comfortable Light and wholesome Air, as by his being buried alive, to rot, and perhaps engender a Pestilence, to the Destruction of the Nation." This editor of an Exeter newspaper in 1727 showed admirable courage and alertness to appalling conditions which most of his fellow countrymen had long continued to ignore. Brice's courageous and self-sacrificing attempt to turn the public eye upon the unspeakable horrors of English jails and prisons should be remembered along with the effort of the "generous band"[16] appointed a year or two later to investigate prison conditions, and along with the better-known efforts of John Howard half a century later.

Nevertheless the reader looking for a great body of distinguished journalistic writing in the early provincial newspapers will be disappointed, for, with the exception of Andrew Brice and a few editors in Manchester, Chester, York, Coventry, Bristol, and Norwich, the fearless crusading journalists came into prominence only after the discreetly anonymous "Junius" had shown the way to audacious criticism in print and John Wilkes had campaigned with equally memorable boldness for the right of Englishmen to speak their minds about their government or anything else of public moment. On political matters most country newspapers printed before 1760 declared their intention to remain strictly neutral. Sam Farley announced on the title page of his *Bristol Post Man* in 1715 that the paper would be "free from all Party Cause, or Personal Reflections," and the first statement in the proposals of the *Newcastle Journal* in 1739 began with these words: "We declare we have no Design to enter into the Service of a Party. . . . " A few years earlier Francis Howgrave had said in the first issue of his *Stamford Mercury* that he would be "proud of any Assistance" from readers of the paper, provided their contributions were "neither Political, Personal, nor Obscene."

There were many kinds of political matter in which strict neutrality was possible. At suitable times formal declarations of loyalty to the sovereign were drawn up by the mayor and the others in the corporation of a town, and those addresses were reprinted in the local paper and copied into others. A printer can hardly be charged with political bias if after an election he reports without comment how many votes each candidate has polled, or if he prints a complete list of the members of Parliament, or announces (as the *Gloucester Journal* did on 5 September 1727) that the annual meeting of the Three Choirs Festival is postponed because of the elections. An unbiased editor may be only concerned to keep his readers in touch with current political thought when he reprints political essays from London papers, and perhaps no leaning toward one party or another can be detected in an article on the necessity of improving roads or the desirability of migrating to Nova Scotia.

Freedom from prejudice is a merit in newspapers as in men; but the rigid observance of neutrality in the press does not win elections and may lose readers who prefer fighting words to dispassionate exposition of principles. It is a clever proprietor who can please Whigs and Tories at the same time. Even editors who professed to be free from party allegiance or control had to decide which London papers to quote, and that choice involved some recognition of party, since there is abundant evidence that several London papers were heavily subsidized as political organs of this party or that. When a city or a country editor proclaimed his intention to remain severely nonpartisan and in the same paragraph declared his entire satisfaction with "the present Happy Establishment," it is apparent that he was more "neutral" to one side than to the other! And it is difficult to detect impartiality in the language of "A Chester Plumper," who addressed a letter to the editor of *Whitworth's Manchester Magazine*, number 3154 (28 October 1755), commending his political writing:

> . . . You have uniformly and constantly endeavour'd to promote a Love for the present happy Constitution, for

293

Liberty Civil and Religious, and to prevent the terrible Effects of the treasonable, enthusiastic Stuff, so long circulated in that Sink of Scandal and Nonsense, the *London Evening Post*, and in some *Country News-Papers.* . . .

From our twentieth-century point of view, the prejudices of 1755 are neither absurd nor deplorable; they are merely amusing.

In the long view, accounts of partisan ranting are more entertaining to read than sober declarations of principle, and it is not at all displeasing to find that there was plenty of what a correspondent in *Adams's Weekly Courant*, number 765 (22 December 1747), called the "Hurry and Brangle of political Dispute." Probably there is no activity of civilized man so productive of controversial letters to the press as campaigning for election to Parliament. Some of these communications are written by accomplished arguers, but most political observations soon lose their flavor and sparkle, unless one turns over the files of old newspapers in order to trace the progress of a particular struggle. For such purposes one might well begin with *Jackson's Oxford Journal*, which was started in 1753 primarily as a political paper.[17] *Schofield's Middlewich Journal*, even in its short lifetime, had on many a front page a political letter addressed "To the Printer of the Middlewich Journal"; and several other papers, among them the Chester and Manchester newspapers, had original contributions which were usually anything but neutral.

Some of the liveliest political writing published outside of the London papers, indeed, is to be found in *Adams's Weekly Courant*. Between this paper and Robert Whitworth's paper in Manchester raged a vigorous and incessant controversy which must have stimulated the sale of both newspapers all over that corner of England. The most notable participant was John Byrom, and front-page space was often given to more or less witty pieces in prose and verse by "Will. Whiglove," "Roderick Roast-Rump,"

"John English," and "H. Hotspur." In 1749, Elizabeth Adams published *Manchester Vindicated* . . . , a little volume intended to preserve for posterity the controversial pieces printed in her paper and in Whitworth's during the period 21 October 1746 to 26 January 1748.

That such fervid exchanges were taken seriously in their own time is to be seen in a letter addressed to the Duke of Newcastle by Bishop Samuel Peploe, of Chester, on 11 November 1740.[18] The Bishop was much concerned over "the unwearied industry of some to poison the common people with ill thoughts of the administration, with fair pretences of great respect to the King."

> This Poison is . . . chiefly conveyed by a couple of newspapers dispersed all over these and the neighbouring parts. We have a printing-press here at Chester, another at Manchester, another at Leeds and other places, all under the direction of seditious and disloyal men, scattering their papers all over the country at low prices. If any means could be thought of to stop them or make the reading of them dearer than it is, it would be happy. The authors pick their news out of the London prints, and give by halves, or with some sneer, whatever is favorable towards it.

Nothing was done to make the reading of newspapers "dearer" until a halfpenny was added to the Stamp Tax seventeen years later; and that tax had no lasting effect on the dissemination of political writings.

A glance at the *Gloucester Journal*, the *Sherborne Mercury*, and many other papers of wide circulation in 1740 and 1741 shows that months before and after Bishop Peploe's letter the papers were filled with letters and formal announcements concerning the candidates for the general election and certain by-elections. In London and all over the nation particular attention was directed toward the vigorous contest between George Fox and Cholmley Turner in the York by-election late in 1741. As the *Nottingham Post*, number 616 (15 October 1741), reported, the general expectation in Yorkshire was that the struggle for election as knight of the shire in "the Room of the late Lord Morpeth" would be as strong as was ever known in that county, for the two men were "making the utmost Application possible on this Occasion."

What that special effort meant in terms of newspapers was (a) the printing of duplicate issues—differing considerably—of Caesar Ward's *York Courant*,[19] (b) the establishing of the *York Gazetteer*, with fiery John Jackson as printer and publisher, and (c) the printing of numerous letters and formal notices in the York papers, in the *Leeds Mercury*, and even in the *Daily Gazetteer* of London. In the contentious months following the death of Viscount Morpeth early in August, 1741, strong support for Turner, the Whig candidate, came from the pen of a young parson living at Sutton-in-the-Forest, later to be celebrated as the author of *The Life and Opinions of Tristram Shandy*. Laurence Sterne's share in the controversy has been ably discussed by Mr. C. Collyer,[20] who shows that Sterne, as the author of several letters in the *York Courant* and the *York Gazetteer*, wrote largely under the direction of his influential uncle, Dr. Jaques Sterne.

The columns of the *York Courant* in 1741 and 1742 exhibit the usual eighteenth-century pattern of political campaigning: the calling of general meetings of the gentlemen, clergy, and freeholders (a Tory set and a Whig set) to nominate a proper person to represent the county in Parliament; public announcements of the candidates' names; formal thanks for the nomination, requests for votes, and promises of dedicated service by the chosen men; sneering and panegyric flung about in print by pseudonymous gentlemen, clergymen, and freeholders moved by a sense of duty to cast aspersions or to ask embarrassing questions; a "progress" through the constituency, with bonfires, feastings, drinking of healths, and reports to the effect that one or other of the candidates would be elected by a great majority.

The other York newspaper caught up in the excitement of the Turner versus Fox campaign—indeed, causing much of the excitement—was the *York Gazetteer*. In the earliest surviving issue, which appeared only a month before the York by-election, the printer asserted in his imprint that the paper had been started partly "to correct the Weekly Poison of the York Courant." Jackson, the author, said he hoped the "Well-wishers to the Cause of Liberty and Protestantism" would give it encouragement, and he drew attention to the inclusion at least every other week of a political essay which would be in no other newspaper in Great Britain. This spirited and outspoken journal is most delightfully one-sided in its views: whatever Mr. Turner said or did was presented in the most laudatory terms; nothing Mr. Fox did was right. In the issue of 15 December 1741, for instance, two political entertainments at Pontefract were reported, one all black and gloomy, the other beaming with happy assurance:

> We hear from Pontefract that on Tuesday last Sir John Bland's Steward, attended by one or two Gentlemen, came to this Town to treat the Freeholders in Favour of Mr. Fox. For this Purpose a grand Entertainment was provided at the Sign of the Bull and Boar; but, not being able to prevail upon any more than five Persons who have Votes to come to them (tho' there are above ninety in Pontefract) vex'd at their Disappointment they made their Stay here too short to create any great Profit to their Landlord.
> And Yesterday Sir Rowland Winn, and several other Gentlemen, accompanied by the Corporation, made an Entertainment at the Star for the Friends of Mr. Turner, to which the Freeholders came almost to a Man, where they expressed the highest Satisfaction upon the Occasion; and amongst many loyal and honest Healths that were then toasted, they drank to Mr. Turner's good Success, Prosperity to the County of York and to the Trade thereof, and

that we may never want a HOME BORN BAIRN to represent the one and protect the other.

That affectionate reference to a "home born bairn" was probably not what won the election for Cholmley Turner; but it was undoubtedly very tempting to Turner's supporters to insist that Fox was a "stranger."

Jane Austen said somewhere that in her opinion nothing was quite so amusing as the sight of a man in a fit of temper; to a twentieth-century reader the fervor and vehemence of political writing in the newspapers of 1741 seem equally ridiculous. But opinions were expressed; well before the middle of the century provincial journalism had begun to fulfil its second basic function, that of making comment on the events of the day.

1. "Isaac Bickerstaff" did not expect this remark in *Tatler,* number 1, to be taken literally; but in number 178 (30 May 1710), he may well have been serious when, in commenting on extravagant passages in the newsletters, he said, "These reflections, in the writers of the transactions of the times, seize the noddles of such as were not born to have thoughts of their own, and consequently lay a weight upon every thing which they read in print."

2. The passage is quoted in W. J. Clarke, *Early Nottingham Printers and Printing* (Nottingham: Forman, 1942); but Mr. Clarke did not recognize that the issue of the *Nottingham Mercury* dated 22 March 1715 belongs to 1716. In the same volume is quoted (p. 14) an entry in the *Records of the Borough of Nottingham* showing that on 19 July 1728, William Ayscough's widow, Anne, was charged at the Quarter Sessions with having printed "several scandalous and indecent expressions in a paper entitled the *Weekly Courant* Dated Thursday 11 July, 1728, tending to bring the King's Ministers of State into contempt."

3. *Notes and Queries,* Ser. 12, VII (28 August 1920), 166-67.

4. In the Public Record Office are many documents relating to the incident. Among them is a list (S.P. 36/8/64) of twenty-two persons charged with having been implicated. These include not only Mist's workmen, apprentices, devils, but even his housekeeper and seventy-year-old Elizabeth Nutt, who, with her daughter Alice and her agent, Anne Nevill, and three other "mercuries" had offered the offending paper for sale. Notes on this "List of Prisoners" show that among those arrested

was Mist's nephew, Robert Coombstock, "a little Boy," who was to be discharged and sent to Mist's house. One of Mist's devils, James Ford, was to be discharged "as below punishment"; Thomas Randal, Mist's other devil, was described as "a good one who gave us ye clue to printing and publishing" — that is, presumably young Randal had given the investigators the names of all persons concerned. Nor was Mist's printing office the only one visited on this occasion by His Majesty's messengers. William Burton, a neighboring and neighborly printer, had allowed Mist's men to use one of *his* presses for the printing of the paper containing the libel, and Burton himself was arrested, together with three of his employees.

5. Stretchley was named as one of the two witnesses in the case against Farley. He was thus described in the statement of William Gill, "Solicitor for the Crown below": "The s^d Stretchley was born in the City of Exon, and his Parents left him a handsome fortune, wch he has profusely and extravagantly spent, and he, having had some university Learning, became Farley's Composer of his Press for Bread."

6. Public Record Office, S. P. 36/16/268-269.

7. Public Record Office, S. P. 36/9/60.

8. Public Record Office, S. P. 36/16/268-269.

9. Public Record Office, S. P. 36/9/157.

10. Public Record Office, S. P. 36/8/225.

11. Public Record Office, S. P. 36/8/112.

12. The arguments against bringing Farley to trial for high treason and against prosecuting him for a misdemeanor are set forth with perfect clarity in a letter written on 14 July 1729 by P. Yorke to the Lord Chancellor, recommending a pardon (Public Record Office S. P. 36/13/69). As Yorke said, Farley had lain in prison almost a year, "which is some punishment, tho^h by no means adequate to so heinous a crime."

13. Norwich Quarter Sessions Minute Book, 1722-1732, now in the Norfolk and Norwich Record Office. The entry is on page 61.

14. A 14g, p. 67. 1742, Oct. 23. I am indebted to Miss Joan C. Lancaster, of the Institute of Historical Research, University of London, for this reference. The issues of *Jopson's Coventry Mercury* for 1742 are not extant.

15. "Andrew Brice, and the Early Exeter Newspaper Press," *Reports and Transactions of the Devonshire Association for the Advancement of Science, Literature, and Art,* XX (1888), 163-214.

16. See James Thomson, *Winter,* ll. 359-88.

17. The first regular issue of this paper, on 5 May 1753, had above the title the words, "News Boys! Election News"; and two experimental issues were entitled *News, Boys, News! or the Electioneering Journal* (11 April 1753) and *News, Boys, News! More and more News! Or, The Electioneering Journal with Improvements* (25 April 1753).

18. The text of the letter is reproduced in the *Manchester Guardian* of 22 January 1890.

19. Fifteen issues from number 829 (1 September 1741) to 846 (29 December 1741) in the file of the *York Courant* at the York Public Library are in two forms, in one of which the second and third pages are considerably different from the inner pages of the other in arrangement of items and in actual substance. The first and fourth pages in one set are the same as those in the other set.

20. "Laurence Sterne and Yorkshire Politics: Some New Evidence," *Proceedings of the Leeds Philosophical and Literary Society,* VII (1952), Part 1, 83-87. See also Lewis P. Curtis, *The Politics of Laurence Sterne* (London: Oxford University Press, 1929).

Chapter VII

Literary Features and Fillers

As EARLIER CHAPTERS HAVE SHOWN, eighteenth-century provincial newspapers contained reports of happenings at home and abroad, comments on current events, and advertisements, but there were few of the incidental features which are found in most newspapers of today. Some early papers offered mathematical problems for their readers to solve, but there were no crossword puzzles, no horoscopes, no weather forecasts, no announcements of radio and television programs, no comic strips, and no syndicated articles giving advice on love, lawns, lumbago. Nevertheless there was a wide variety of "literary" matter, some of it trivial, some of it dull, some of it still worth reading, for it is absurd to suppose that the readers of country newspapers were capable of nothing but inexplicable dumb shows and noise; they read the verses of Swift and the *Rambler* essays as eagerly as their city cousins did, and they sometimes wrote good things of their own.

Not all of this "literary" matter was printed in response to popular demand. Beyond question the printers sometimes found themselves with less news and fewer advertisements than normally came in and they had to fill gaps with whatever "fillers" were on hand. It was "for want of News this Post" that the author of the *Protestant*

Mercury in Exeter presented his readers on 9 December 1715 with nine roaring stanzas called "The Traytors Knell. Or, the Rebellious Jacobites Downfall." Near the end of December, 1722, "It being Christmas time, and there not being a mighty Glut of News," the *Gloucester Journal* had some holiday reading in the form of a narrative in verse—"The Fisherman"—and also an enigma (with solution two weeks later). The *Western Flying-Post*, number 516 (15 January 1759), had a column and a half on the front page filled with "Some remarkable Passages in the Life and Death of the celebrated Dr. Boerhaave," contributed by a reader, who reminded the editor that it was "a Season of the Year of little or no interesting News (as you observe in your last Journal)."

In the earliest country newspapers there was not much that can be called either "filler" or belles-lettres, for all available space was used either for news or for paid notices; but there were a few exceptions. The first two newspapers printed in Stamford had, in their earliest years, subtitles which indicated or implied that their contents would not be limited to news. Early issues of the *Stamford-Post, Or an Account of the most Material News, Foreign and Domestick, to which is added the Weekly Miscellany* are not extant, but by April, 1712, the printers made it clear that the paper would thereafter have half of its columns filled with a miscellany of useful and diverting subjects.[1] When the *Stamford Mercury* was established a few months later, it was described in its subtitle as comprising "Historical and Political Observations on the Transactions of Europe. Together with Remarks on Trade. The Whole being a Miscellany of Various Subjects, Prose and Verse." This principle of including extra reading was also part of the editorial plan of Thomas Goddard of Norwich, for the only surviving copy of the paper bearing the title *Transactions of the Universe* (17 July 1714) has on four of its twelve pages an essay on the delights of spring, introduced by

a phrase from Virgil: " . . . *Nunc formosissimus Annus.*"
The piece begins in leisurely fashion:

> Men of my Age receive a greater Pleasure from fine
> Weather, than from any other sensual Enjoyments. In
> spite of the Auxiliary Bottle, or any Artificial Heat, we are
> apt to droop under a gloomy Sky; and taste no Luxury,
> like a Blue Firmament and Sun shine.

At the end are verses transcribed from a manuscript poem
on hunting.

Some years earlier the man who emerged as Goddard's
strongest rival, Henry Cross-grove, had as a special
feature of his *Norwich Gazette* a department made up
of questions sent in by readers and Cross-grove's own
answers—something like John Dunton's *Athenian Mercury* in London. This feature became so popular that by
number 14 (5 March 1707), Cross-grove decided to
publish his paper twice a week instead of on Saturdays
only. Publication twice a week proved to be inexpedient,
but the questions kept coming in, and the answers were
long delayed. In number 150 (20 August 1709) the day's
question was this:

> Lynn, May 18. 1709.
>
> Mr. Cross-grove,
>
> Did the Apostles use Notes when they preached? I have
> sent You this Query twice before, and if I do not find it
> answered in your next Paper, I shall conclude You either
> cannot or durst not answer it.
>
> Yours Unknown, &c.

Cross-grove's answer to this persistent inquirer is typical
of hundreds which he printed in his newspaper during
1707, 1708, and 1709.

> Sir,
>
> I have a Bushel of Letters by me that came all to the same
> Tune with this of yours, *viz. You cannot or durst not An-*

swer it; but sometimes they see I dare do it, tho' I neglect other Letters more pertinent through want of Room. I have sometimes a Dozen Letters come in a Week, all in Post-haste for an Answer, and seldom Room to insert above One at a time, so that many must of Necessity lye by. But now for your dreadful puzzling Question, *Did the Apostles use Notes, &c.* To this I answer positively No; nor Bibles neither to hide their Notes in, take Notice of that; nor had they Pulpits to stand in as ever I heard of, and we may observe from their Sermons that they took no Texts: And what then? What would you infer from all this? The Apostles also never studied their Sermons, for they had an Extraordinary Gift of Preaching as well as of Speaking. But I shall say no more to your designing Question than this, That those Divines which read their Sermons, know how to improve their Time much better than in getting them like School-boys by Heart; and that a good Polite Discourse well read, is more worthy the Hearing than a Bundle of what comes uppermost tumbbl'd out Head and Heels. Yours, &c. H. C.

In April, 1708, Cross-grove decided to publish a little twopenny volume of these questions and answers under the title *Apollinaria,* and three months later he brought out a second collection under the same title.[2]

From about 1720 onward, many country papers, like those published in London, contained essays, poems, ficti-tious letters (as well as genuine ones), serialized fiction, geography, history, criminal biography, and other matter intended to divert or enlighten. That such pieces *were* intended to give pleasure seems clear enough if one looks at the papers themselves. In 1738, the *Salisbury Journal* placed at its head the phrase *"prodesse et delectare"* (along with the more famous phrase *"e pluribus unum"*), which suggests that readers could expect to be enter-tained as well as informed. Under the date line of Joseph Pote's *Windsor and Eton Journal,* number 147 (19 March 1747), is this statement: "Besides the news from the Gazette, and other early Intelligence, In this Paper will be frequently inserted Pieces of Poetry and Prose not in any other Newspaper. . . . " At the end of that year a "constant Reader" of the *Bath Journal* sent to the author of that paper a set of ten heroic couplets "On his Variety of Entertainments, besides his Collection of News," and he expressed his views with some emphasis:

> Whilst many Bards in You shall find a Place,
> 'Twill always make your *Journals* sell apace;
> Let those *ingenious Poems* still have Room,
> Which You, from Time to Time, receive from FROOM:
> 'Twill please your *Readers* more than *Foreign News,*
> Of *sordid* DUTCHMEN, and what *Towns they lose:*
> Tell us no more the Loss of BERG-OP-ZOOM,
> Of RUSSIAN TROOPS *which ne'er intend to come.* . . .

A footnote attached to the word "FROOM" suggests that contributions sent in from other places were equally welcome. In 1748, when Hervey Berrow took over the *Worcester Journal* from Stephen Bryan, he promised that his subscribers would find "miscellaneous Pieces, &c." in the paper under the new management. Many other editors made similar promises, and some of them even invited contributions.

The editorial desire to please by combining news and "literary" matter is well indicated in the *Gloucester Journal.* Raikes and Dicey were willing to publish "an enigmatical Copy of Verses by *Matilda Merry Lass,* at the Sign of the *Light Heart* at Littleworth," but they declared in advance (in number 9, 2 June 1722) that no material news would be omitted "for any thing of this Nature." The issues dated 15 and 22 April 1723 had fragments of poetry "collected from the best English Poets"; and there were more of these "Rhapsodical Pieces of Poetry" in number 57 (6 May 1723, improperly dated 29 April), "this Post affording little News." Sometimes Raikes and Dicey justified their printing of verses on rather better grounds. In number 34 (26 November 1722), the thirty lines of the Prologue to Steele's comedy, *The Conscious Lovers,* were printed with an introductory note telling that the play continued to charm London theater-goers, "and since (on Friday last) when Her Royal Highness went to see it acted, she seem'd extremely well satisfied with, and not a little moved by this excellent Play; the Prologue to so noble a Performance must certainly be an agreeable Entertainment to our Ingenious Readers." On 25 February 1723, Raikes and Dicey printed a column of heroic couplets by "S. J." in praise of a single life, and this led to replies by other local versifiers who preferred married life.

Raikes's and Dicey's expressed desire to make their *Journal* "the compleatest as well as the most diverting News-paper in the Country" led them to print a great amount of miscellaneous entertaining matter as the years went on. That such pieces were accepted by readers, not as mere fillers but as desirable features, is suggested by a letter in number 80 (14 October 1723) accompanying an enigma in blank verse:

To the Author of the Gloucester Journal

Sir,

As I have had frequent opportunity of conversing with various of your Readers, so I think it not improper to acquaint you that they are very desirous of seeing more frequently inserted in your Paper some pleasant Amusements in Prose or Verse. They are big with expectations weekly of seeing something of this kind, because they have been indulg'd thus far in time past. And as we are very desirous of what is here premis'd, so we cannot but think that your compliance with us would be attended with many advantages; for we have many witty Blades in Gloucestershire (as well as in other Counties) that may furnish you with something that may be entertaining to your Readers.

Your Friend
And Reader,
A——s.

The enigma which accompanied this letter, incidentally, seems to represent a newspaper bearing the name "Journal"; certainly that interpretation suits such passages as these:

> There's few can trace my ancient Pedigree,
> Or shew the fruitful Parent to the World,
> That Birth and Being on me first bestow'd.
> But tho' a Stranger to the World I seem'd,
> I am thro' England now familiar grown,
> And serviceable to the last degree
> Unto the present race . . .
> A Parent truly generous we had,
> Productive, of a numerous Family;
> We're more than ten that bear one common name. . . .

Whatever the right interpretation, Raikes and Dicey did not hesitate to print both the letter and the thirty-one lines of the puzzle; and their readers, whether big with expectations or not, found in most future issues of the *Gloucester Journal* a contributed essay or a letter or some verses, occasionally in Latin [3]—enough to fill a book which no one would now be interested in reading.

By way of exception, it is delightful to read in the *Gloucester Journal,* number 132 (12 October 1724), the seventy lines of Swift's sprightly verses on William Wood beginning

When Foes are o'er come, we preserve them from Slaughter,
To be Hewers of Wood, and Drawers of Water. . . .

It is pleasant also to come upon Swift's "Prometheus" in number 147 (25 January 1725), and no one could take exception to the reprinting of "The Wish, to a Young Lady on her Birthday" in number 138 (23 November 1724). It is worth noticing, too, that the verses printed in the *Gloucester Journal* included translations of Horace by "E.L." and "J.C.," and in number 217 (10 May 1726) there was a translation of Anacreon. In number 222 (5 July 1726), one finds an addition to Swift's *Cadenus and Vanessa.* Number 276 (18 July 1727) had "A Lilliputian Ode on the Accession of King George II to the Crown." This thin perpendicular string of dissyllabic lines has one or two bright passages. It begins

> Smile, Smile,
> Blest Isle. . . .

and there follow such passages as

> New King,
> Bells ring.
> New Queen,
> Blest Scene. . . .

and

> Trade's brisk,
> All frisk:
> Fear flies,
> Stocks rise.
> Wealth flows,
> Art grows;
> Bards write
> Things bright.

In the next issue was a Latin translation of the same piece.

More important than a long list of items in the *Gloucester Journal* is the printers' declaration in the issue of 12 April 1725 that when the paper changed its form two weeks later because of the enforcement of the Stamp Act, they would not omit anything of the kind usually printed in the paper "for the Entertainment of . . .

Readers." Even with restricted space the paper would have belles-lettres; and these were certainly not just odd scraps kept in the shop to fill spaces left vacant by a shortage of news. As was proper, news continued to come first; but, Raikes and Dicey told their readers in number 160 (24 April 1725), "we shall always endeavour (in the Dearth of News) to oblige them with something New and Entertaining."

In the *Gloucester Journal* and other papers most of the verses, and generally the best of them, were taken from books or papers already in print. If the labored verses of Stephen Duck are found, so is Pope's *Messiah,* and so is Christopher Smart's *Solemn Dirge.* The range of theme, as of mood and quality, is remarkable. The hundreds of pieces included such things as John Byrom's rattling pastoral, "My Time, O ye Muses, was happily spent," in the *Gloucester Journal,* number 146 (18 January 1725); Swift's "Furniture of a Woman's Mind" (in the *Weekly Worcester Journal,* number 1340, 28 February 1735); twenty-four lines commemorating Gray's friend, Richard West (in the *Leeds Mercury,* number 855, 22 June 1742); some more or less Swiftian verses (in several papers in August and September, 1747) on "The Grand Question . . . Whether a young Gentleman should be sent to a University or to Travel"; and a set of deliriously sottish verses called "Strip-Me-Naked, or Royal Gin for ever" (in the *Salisbury Journal,* number 688, 18 March 1751).

Verses written expressly for the newspapers in which they are now to be seen included some absurd ones, among them a Worcester poetaster's lines "On Surgery," commending the achievements of a local surgeon. They were sent to *Aris's Birmingham Gazette,* where they appear in number 33 (28 June 1742). Following the old pattern of *"felix qui . . . ,"* the piece begins well enough, but it soon betrays the hand of an amateurish versifier:

> Happy the Man, to whom kind bount'ous Heav'n
> Has in the healing Art much Knowledge giv'n.

The clinical bluntness of the next two lines makes one think of young John Dryden's ghastly verses on Lord Hastings:

> He huge phlegmatic Wens, can safely move,
> And the sharp, violent Pains of vicious Love.

No anthology would be the better for the inclusion of "On Surgery."

One paper notable for contributions of "original" verses by local poetasters is the *Cirencester Flying Post,* an attractive journal, well printed on good paper. Number 67 (29 March 1742), for instance, has "A Condolement for the Death of that Artist in Musick, and beloved Acquaintance, James Webb, of Broomham." Here there is a faint echo of a better poem by Dryden, the Anne Killigrew ode:

> 'Twas some kind Angel from his blissful Seat,
> Call'd him to make their Heav'nly Choir compleat.
> Too well they knew his Excellence and Voice,
> We mourn our Loss, but must commend their Choice.

These occasional verses are bad enough; less bearable are the efforts of local poets to evoke an imagined atmosphere, as when the proprietor of the *Cirencester Flying Post* printed in number 75 (24 May 1742) a specimen of the poetical works of Mr. Edward Stephens, a Cirencester bard whose volume was soon to be published by subscription. The sample selected as an inducement to subscribers was "The Dying Heathen." The unhappy expiring one began, "Thee, Death to Contemplate, how dread the Thought!" From there to the last lines of the piece the mood and the language become more and more "dread," the sinking savage finding himself decidedly uncomfortable at the end:

A cold, damp Sweat runs trickling o'er my Limbs;
Now am I launching on some foamy Sea;
Ye Gods, direct me to some blissful Port.

One must thrust out of one's head the momentary notion that the poor man just wanted a drink.

But there was better verse than that of Mr. Stephens. In Stamford, "Eusebius" felt moved to write verses on the occasion of giving the name "Georgia" to part of the territory formerly called Carolina, explaining in *Howgrave's Stamford Mercury,* number 37 (22 February 1733), that although he was unacquainted with the trustees of the scheme for the planting of Georgia he had great admiration for their "universal Benevolence," since they were "breaking up the World's uncultivated Wilderness, sowing the Seeds of future Nations, and giving Root to a wider Establishment of Christianity, Learning, and Virtue." Similar strong feeling moved a writer to send to Thomas Aris, of Birmingham, a full column of lines on liberty, printed in *Aris's Birmingham Gazette,* number 419 (20 November 1749). Better than these were the forty-two lines of heroic verse sent to the *Sherborne Mercury,* number 154 (29 January 1740), in praise of Pope's translation of Homer. They were headed "To Mr. Pope," and were the work of "Mr. Price, late of Christ-Church, Oxon.; Now a Land-waiter in the Port of Poole." The treatment is obvious enough—Homer was badly translated by Pope's predecessors,

a servile train
Of groveling pedants whose unhallow'd rage
Perplex'd and darken'd ev'ry shining page.

"But now at length," Mr. Price continued, through Pope's "officious cares," the "genuine Greek appears."

Pope was usually spoken of with admiration in the

country newspapers, but one correspondent in Thomas Cotton's *Kendal Weekly Courant,* number 43 (21 October 1732), rebuked him for his remarks on the death of Patroclus, in the sixteenth book (Volume IV) of his translation of the *Iliad.* Pope had praised Homer for having more of wisdom, learning, and all good qualities than other mortals, but had felt that at this particular point Homer had shown something less than perfect sanity, something of the madness of Don Quixote. It is a great fault in a commentator, said "M.N.," when amongst ten thousand acknowledged perfections he condemns a single incident, "the Necessity whereof (Ten thousand to One) he understands not." Here was a North Country critic using Pope's own principles to reprove the author of *An Essay on Criticism.* Let Pope compare himself to Sancho Panza if he will, he said; but Homer, the master, must not be likened to Don Quixote:

> To pair with Sancho is a modest strain,
> But to match Knight & Poet is profane.
> And for the sake of sacred Truth be't said,
> That Pope engages with unequal Head,
> That he's mistaken, not his Master mad.

Little bards must not presume to censure so great a song as Homer's; if they do, the gods will punish them. So it happened to Pope, said "M.N." rather spitefully:

> The Gods forsee our actions and dispence
> Sometimes, the Punishment before th'Offence:
> They saw thy foul Reproach, & for the same
> Prolepticaly doom'd thy jumbl'd Frame.

The reproach would be more memorable if the couplets were as good as Pope's own.

Pope was incidentally censured, not as translator of

Homer, but as writer of pastorals, in a communication addressed to the author of the *Leeds Mercury* and printed in number 771 (11 November 1740) of that paper:

Sir,

I have been always of Opinion that the Scotch manner of Pastoral Dialogue is preferable to the English, and comes much nearer to Nature. A correct Stile and Turns of Wit are both methinks exceedingly preposterous in the Mouth of a Shepherd; and, if I mistake not, some of the best Criticks have found Fault with Virgil himself upon that Account. Extremes are always to be avoided; too low as well as too high a Stile, may be faulty; amongst the English Writers Phillips seems to be guilty of the former, and Mr. Pope of the latter. Insomuch that the judicious Mr. Addison says that Mr. Pope's Pastorals are by no means Pastorals but something better. Allan Ramsay in my Opinion has steer'd a middle Course, and such as are Judges sufficient of the Scotch Language, I believe, will without Hesitation prefer his Manner to any Modern Pastoral Writer whatever. The following Pastoral is partly in Imitation of Allan's Method, which if you think proper to insert in your Paper, you will thereby oblige,

Sir, your humble Servant,

Scot Britannis.

The contributed piece fills a column and is not without merit. It bears the title "Samuel and Cuddy, a Pastoral on the Death of their Sheep," and it has a brief glossary explaining such words as *yamp* ("bark"), *Tod Lowrie* ("a fox"), and *cairn* ("a small House, or Cottage, built of Sod, and cover'd with Rushes, to shelter the Shepherds in bad Weather").

After a pointed inquiry about Cuddy's flock, Samuel announces that his "fleecy Vassals" have all died, and his two sheep dogs miss their charges:

Ranter and *Ringie* now may Yamp in Vain,
Who kept my Strayers on the verdant Plain,
And scar'd Tod Lowrie when he wad them slain.

Caddy has his troubles, too, for "that sad Traik"—Samuel calls it "plaguey Rot"—has also taken most of his flock. Their woe is emphasized by their accounts of life before disaster struck. Cuddy took particular delight in his morning duties:

> When the sweet Dawn blink't West the saffron Skye,
> I us'd to wrap my Plaid, Syne *Coaly* crye,
> First op'd the pleasant Fald wi' tenty Care,
> And hou'd my Sheep, out to their grassy Fare,
> The Skye serene, the pleasant Fields I scour'd,
> If not, the Cairn did Skug me when it shower'd.
> That little Structure, rais'd by rural Art,
> Did keep me frae the Wind's and Weather's Smart.
> Now every Nook wi 'Nettles is o'ergrown,
> And Pleasure fraw the Plain, Alas! is flown;
> To eat the Grass, I've scarce ae Bleater left,
> O Pan! ye gloom o'er fair, of au I'm reft.

The regret of these two pastoral bards has not sprung exclusively from dwindling flocks of sheep. Samuel recalls with yearning the happy noontide meals when "to the Cairn the Lasses came." He thinks of the music in which the lasses used to join; and he remembers there were other sweet mitigations of labor:

> Each on the Bosom of his Fair did lean,
> While we employ'd our Plaids, our Loves to Screen,
> And as we ta'k'd the Kiss did intervene.

Cuddy's strongest recollection is of returning at evening to the "bucht," defined in a footnote as "a Place made to confine Sheep while they are Milking." There the sight of Jane made both Cuddy's heart and Cuddy himself leap in ecstasy:

O when her gently Fingers tug'd the Pap,
I cou'd na thole but o'er the Flake [a wooden palisade] I lap,
I prest her to my Breast, whilst saftest Words
And Kisses sweet exchanged. . . .

These joys, says Cuddy, have departed. Yet Cuddy is not utterly disconsolate: "The Storm may last a while, but canna' lang," he rather abruptly exclaims. Samuel is less hopeful; with the badness of the Season, "and Leap-Year," there is in his view little to expect by way of improvement.

Like true pagans, Cuddy and Samuel agree that their best plan is to "bear wi' Patience" what the gods have sent to them:

'Tis not for naething that their Hands we feel;
As we deserve e'en so they turn the Wheel:
Let us, dear Sam! Aboon send our Address;
They soon can gi' us mair, we ne'er had less.

The reliance on "higher Powers" is commendable; even more so is their readiness to admit their own negligence. But it does not occur to them that they might have had a lower death rate in the flock if they had spent more time attending to their animal husbandry and less time sporting with the lasses in the bucht—perhaps also less time in fashioning heroic couplets and triplets for a pastoral dialogue.

"Samuel and Cuddy" would be a better poem if no reference had been made to Pan; but there are enough "homely" references to collies, cairns, and buchts to make inapplicable Crabbe's words about "tinsel trappings of poetic pride." It is one of the least tedious pieces of local versifying in a country newspaper.

Altogether too many of the local papers automatically reprinted from London papers the uninspired New Year odes of the poet laureate, and it is refreshing to come across evidence that Colley Cibber's verses sometimes

stuck in the gorge of country readers. In the issue of the
Newcastle Courant on 8 January 1732, John White filled
the third column of his second page with the words of
Cibber's latest "Song for New Year's Day," as it had been
performed at Court in the presence of their Majesties and
the whole of the royal family by Mr. Gates, Mr. Rowe—
Mr. Hughes being indisposed—and the children of His
Majesty's chapel. It is the one beginning

> Awake with joyous Songs the Day
> > That heads the op'ning Year.
> The Year advancing to prolong
> Augustus's Sway demands our Song,
> > And calls for universal Cheer.

In the following issue of the *Newcastle Courant*, White
was pleased to print a clever and thoroughly enjoyable
parody by a Newcastle wit calling himself "Tim. Bays."
"I have endeavour'd in the following Lines to be as much
like him as possible," wrote the Tyneside mocker of
banalities. His opening recitative makes nothing of the
whistling sibilance of Cibber's fourth line, but neatly
exposes the emptiness of the original:

> Acclaim with joyous Laughs the Day,
> > That leads the Laureat's Muse!
> His Muse advancing to prolong
> A gentle and unmeaning Song,
> All void of Flatt'ry and Abuse.

Cibber would not be pleased to find his carefully worked
out encomiums turned against himself, here and there
with more ease than he could command.

Cibber's first air somewhat feebly stretches a small idea
into the dimensions of an eight-line stanza:

> Your antient Annals, Britons, read,
>> And Mark the Reign you most admire;
> The present shall the past exceed,
>> And yield Enjoyment to Desire.
> Or if you find the coming Year
>> In Blessings should transcend the last,
> The Diff'rence only will declare
>> The present sweeter than the past.

The Newcastle mimic filled the eight lines of *his* first air rather more pointedly:

> Your ancient Poets, Britons, read,
>> And mark the dullest of the Choir;
> The present shall the past exceed
>> In want of Sense and want of Fire.
> Or if you think that Colley's Lays
>> Shall sink from whence they first begun
> You'll find the Diff'rence only says
>> His own Out-doings are outdone.

The second recitative is not particularly bright in either ode, but Cibber's image of the wakeful eagle in the second air gives the impudent local poet an opportunity to bring in quite tellingly a less noble bird:

> . . . and all he sings,
> Is Cuckoo—Cuckoo—once a Year.

Cibber's final air must surely have seemed a trifle befuddled when warbled to the assembled court; it is hard to make sense of it when one sees it on the printed page:

> Your annual Aids, when he desires,
> Less the King than Land requires;
> All the Dues from him that flow,
> Are but Royal Wants to you.
> So the Seasons lent the Earth
> Their kindly Rains to raise her Birth:
> And well the mutual Labours suit;
> His the Glory, yours the Fruit.

There is good satiric stuff in the answering stanza by Tim. Bays:

> When to his annual Song he falls,
> His Pension, not his Genius calls;
> All the Numbers of his Lyre,
> Flow by Duty, and from Hire:
> So Balaam's Ass by dint of Stroke,
> In Presence of an Angel spoke;
> Thus Cibber sings to Royal Ears,
> The Noise is his, th' Influence theirs.

Occasionally this sort of thing brightened the pages of early provincial newspapers; but "Tim. Bays" wrote far too seldom.

More numerous and of course much bulkier than verse are the prose pieces to be found in the columns of practically every country newspaper in the eighteenth century. The themes ranged from immortality to whistling, from Freemasonry to the proper use of the word "esquire." Anyone who takes up Cooke's *Chester Weekly Journal,* or *Adams's Weekly Courant,* or the *Kendal Weekly Courant* will find on the front page of almost every issue an essay or article selected by the editor from printed sources, or sent to him, or written by him. Any single year's fifty-two issues of the *Salisbury Journal* or of *Whitworth's Manchester Magazine* will yield several pieces of prose. The same is true of most other papers; there were articles copied from the *Universal Spectator*, extracts from the *Champion*, instalments of popular novels, and essays from the *Student*, the *Rambler*,[4] the *Adventurer*, the *World*, the *Connoisseur*, the "Idler," and even the old *Hermit* (1711-12) and *Guardian* (1713). The Bristol *Oracle* had a department headed "The Entertainment," which offered short stories, articles on taste, on custom, on love and marriage, and (in number 7, 15 May 1742) a good-natured satirical essay on critics. On 22 June 1744, the *Preston Weekly Journal* printed the text of Alexander Pope's will. Number 627 (3 April 1751) of the *Newcastle Journal* had a long article on the art of embalming. The *Worcester Journal*, number 2087 (20 July 1749), had a whole page—copied from the Chester *Weekly Courant*—giving full details of the massacre at Glencoe in 1692, and in the same paper, number 2095 (14 September 1749), was a most interesting "Letter from one of the Settlers in Nova Scotia to his Friend in London, dated at Chibucto Harbour, July 28, 1749." The Worcester paper alone, indeed, could furnish a fat volume of prose pieces, and among them might well be the pleasant discussion in number 2034 (14 July 1748) "On the State of Marriage in South Britain," the tone of which is indicated in the opening sentence: "If you see a Man and Woman, with little or no Occasion, often finding Fault and correcting one another in Company, you may be sure they are Man and Wife." [5]

There were many original prose pieces, both by contributors and by the editors themselves. Twenty-two successive issues of the *Kentish Post* in 1738 and 1739 had original essays contributed in a series headed "The Kentish Spectator" by "R.," "N.N.," "T.H.," and others. The editor of the *Union Journal* of Halifax, the Rev. John Watson, M.A., not only prepared the prospectus promising wit, humor, and occasional letters but contributed to his paper's columns several poems, a notably intelligent suggestion (in number 20, 19 June 1759) for improving the roads and the postal services in the area, and two communications (in number 11, 17 April 1759, and number 13) offering objections to the churchman's practice of turning to the east at certain places in the service. Some verses of his had already appeared in the *Sheffield Weekly Journal* before he wrote for the Halifax paper.[6]

In other papers it is usually difficult, but not always important, to assign the pieces to their authors. The real point is that the printers of newspapers asked for contributions and often got them. "If any Gentleman has a mind to communicate any choice Piece to the World, he shall be accommodated with a Place in this Paper"; so wrote Robert Raikes in his *St. Ives Post-Boy* in July, 1718, though just two weeks before—on 23 June—he had rejected a letter "From the Pope to the Pretender" by "T.L." with the excuse that it was "early Days" in his newspaper work in that town and he had therefore to be circumspect. "I can't tell whether it might not give Disgust to some of my Readers, for as I have declar'd my Self to be of no Party, I shall be very cautious how I give Distaste to either Party." During the next forty years, Raikes in Gloucester, Brice in Exeter, Collins in Salisbury, Bryan and Berrow in Worcester, and most other local editors extended a cordial invitation to potential contributors. The invitation was often accepted, though one must distinguish between the aggressive political tirades in so partisan a paper as the *York Gazetter* and the less polemical writings in more moderate or neutral papers.

Among these latter are the two Liverpool papers, *Williamson's Liverpool Advertiser* and the *Liverpool Chronicle*. Williamson's was the earlier of the two to be established. In the first issue (28 May 1756) there was a special invitation to men of letters and "those of vacant Hours" to contribute their favors, the proprietors having no doubt that "sprightliness of Wit and Humour, Purity of Morals, and Soundness of good Sense" would occasionally enrich and embellish the paper. The other Liverpool newspaper began (on 6 May 1757) with an excerpt from an essay on the utility of newspapers, the relevant passage being the one which emphasized that people who looked at news might be led involuntarily to read more substantial matter as well, if that more substantial matter were printed in the same paper: " . . . the articles of news seem to be a natural decoy to draw great numbers to the reading these short dissertations, who, perhaps, scarce read any thing else; and . . . numbers are induced, over their coffee, to throw their eyes for a few minutes on a short essay wrote with art and vivacity, who scarce read any thing else in a twelvemonth."

Of the quantity of contributed prose in the country newspapers there is no question whatever; of the enduring worth of these pieces no extravagant claim should be made, but a hundred of them can now be read with pleasure, and a handful deserve more than passing attention, either for the soundness of their substance or for the liveliness of their style. There is a certain success in sustaining the mood of a piece in the *Western Flying-Post; or, Sherborne and Yeovil Mercury*, number 26 (24 July 1749). Here, without unkindness, the language and modes of thought of a country Quaker were parodied in Obadiah Prim's letter to a watchmaker with a request that a better adjustment was required: "I find by the Index of his Tongue he is a Lyar, . . . which makes me believe he is not right in the Inward Man . . . I will board him with thee a few Days. . . . " Better writing is found in the jovial, satiric essay on scandal-mongering in the *Bristol, Bath and Somersetshire Journal*, number 56 (4 June 1743): the ninth commandment, said the writer, if rightly enforced would "effectually shut up all the pretty prattling Mouths in Great Britain, and entail Dumbness on the most voluble Part of the Creation, as well as the most musical." But there was wisdom in ignoring the commandment which forbids the bearing of false witness, he went on, "since the prudent fine Creatures know from Experience, that to stop their Mouths would be to stop their Breath, and that therefore the Ninth Commandment would be the Death of the whole Species. I cannot well blame them for preferring the Law of Self-preservation to the Law of Moses."

Of all these original pieces perhaps the ones most cordially accepted by local readers were those inserted in the front-page columns of Thomas Cotton's *Kendal Weekly Courant*. Among these were several letters written by a cultured gentleman who had recently retired to the country a few miles from Kendal. The first of these letters, in the *Kendal Weekly Courant*, number 3 (15 January 1732), was sent in by "C. D.," who reminded Cotton of his promise in the paper's first issue to instruct or divert his readers by occasionally inserting "some useful, entertaining Speculation or piece of History." More letters would be sent, he said, if the critics were not too severe and discouraging. Although that first letter was given over largely to praising the sedate virtues of moderation and frugality, the serious theme and tone proved acceptable, and there were more letters from the same hand. Number 7 (12 February 1732) had one on the folly of country people in spending so much time in reading newspapers that they neglect their own concerns. Another letter is less notable for its originality than for doing what few letters written to a newspaper editor do even now: it offered for local readers a passage of thirty-four consecutive lines from one of Shakespeare's plays— the whole of Duke Vincentio's speech on life and death in the third act of *Measure for Measure*. The speech had particular relevance at the time because of "the severe and untimely Breaches, undistinguishing Death had lately made upon some Families in Kendal."

Because of these letters and many other pieces of prose and verse in its front-page columns, the *Kendal Weekly Courant* is one of the most interesting local papers printed in the eighteenth century. Certainly its most notable feature was the encouragement it gave to local writers. In the issue of 15 April 1732, an enthusiastic letter from J. Markinstone, of Wensleydale, paid particular tribute to Cotton for including "the ingenious Labours of some of our Countrymen."

> I always thought this Northern Climate was capable of producing as fine Wits as any in the World; for methinks we breath an Air as free and unpolluted as any County under the Sun. . . . Nothing has been awanting to set our Wits to work but proper Incentives and Encouragements. But now, since we have the advantage of appearing in your *Papers,* bless me! how our Brains begin to Ferment!

Cotton printed the five quite respectable stanzas sent in by Markinstone; and other authors in the region invariably found Cotton's columns open to them if their subjects were inoffensive.

That readers were ready to accept pieces of literature along with news—and in fact demanded them—is perhaps best seen in the columns of an Exeter paper. Both in *Brice's Weekly Journal,* which began in 1725, and in the same man's earlier Exeter paper, the *Post-Master; or, the Loyal Mercury,* the author made a feature of including in almost every issue some entertaining piece of prose or verse, either reprinted from a London paper, or copied from a new book, or sent in by a correspondent, or written by himself. Most notable in size and significance was Defoe's *Captain Singleton,* reprinted in the *Post-Master* during 1720 and 1721. That this lively work, which had been published in London only a few weeks before Brice began to reprint it, was not regarded as column stuffing is apparent: each instalment began and ended with complete sentences instead of being chopped off when the space available was filled, the instalments were of considerable and nearly uniform length, occupying the first two of the six pages in the *Post-Master,* and at one point

Brice "thought proper to pass over a few Paragraphs of the Original . . . , nothing very material occurring therein" and took the trouble to prepare a summary of two hundred and twenty-five words with which to begin the instalment in number 55 (11 August 1721).

In following issues of the *Post-Master,* Brice gave his readers a wide variety of pieces, asserting in number 72 (8 December 1721) that "something besides News" was now expected from him in every paper. Among these pieces were an essay on the causes of the extensive vocabulary in the English language, some of the letters of "Cato" in the *London Journal*—"in Compliance with the Request of several Gentlemen, my good Friends"—a report of the notorious Layer trial, and a number of moral discourses, such as that running through eight issues on "The Wickedness of a Disregard to Oaths; and the pernicious Consequences of it to Religion and Government." From "a small Book, call'd *Occasional Devotions,*" Brice copied an account of the great London plague of 1665, and, in number 73 (wrongly numbered 72, 15 December 1721), began a series of short accounts of similar calamities; these, he supposed, would not be unpleasing, at least to the more unlearned of his readers, "which 'tis likely are by much the greatest Number."

There is evidence that what a correspondent described as Brice's "Introductory what d'ye call'ums" were well received, and that readers asked for more. Brice, too, asked for more. He repeatedly requested "Men of good Genius" to send in contributions.

> I cannot but with some Regret admire that I have yet received so little of that Assistance from 'em which (at my first setting out) I craved & expected. My Design seemed to have met with universal Approbation; and seeing how many of my Customers were Clergymen, Physicians, Lawyers, &c. and those of each Class of some Eminence, I were [thus] encouraged to hope for a much better Correspondence with them.

As the months went on, Brice's eminent customers occasionally proved obliging. "Sir," wrote one of them in a letter printed in number 108 (24 August 1722), "I highly approve of the Method you have taken, in prefixing either a diverting or an instructive Lecture to your Weekly News." Brice was probably disappointed that no original composition came with this letter, but he nevertheless printed in five consecutive issues of the *Post-Master* the portions of Robinson Crusoe's *Serious Reflections* which the man sent as an indication of his desire to assist.

It is to Brice's credit that he wrote many of the prose pieces himself. He was an aggressive man—on one occasion, when his readers objected to excerpts from "the well-digested and seasonable Writings of Philanthropus Oxonienses," he said bluntly in print that it was a pity that pearls should be cast before swine—yet he was modest enough about his own abilities as an author, declaring in number 74 (22 December 1721) that the essays he reprinted from books and other newspapers were probably as recreative and not so tedious as weekly articles from his own pen would be. That he often printed original pieces of his own composing is revealed in an introductory paragraph printed in 1730 with his *Freedom: A Poem, Written in Time of Recess from the rapacious Claws of Bailiffs and devouring Fangs of Goalers*:[7]

> Partly to amuse myself and partly to divert, and now and then it may be to inform, some of the Perusers of my Weekly Paper of Intelligence (*there being Readers suited to the meanest Writer*), in Default of better Supplies from Correspondents, I have (too presumptuously, perhaps) us'd to insert little Occasional Essays of my own scribbling.

Later, caught up in an editorial campaign which ultimately forced him to abscond, Brice's prose was notably vigorous; his little occasional essays were persuasive and never perfunctory.

Brice continued to print essays and excerpts from books

even after the renewal of the Stamp Tax caused him, in April, 1725, to alter the format of his paper from a small sheet and a half (six pages) to a large half-sheet (four pages); "nor shall I," he said to his readers, "deviate from my method of entertaining them with something or other which may be diverting, &c." He felt that, through the assistance of correspondents, he had sometimes succeeded in giving pleasure to most readers, "however great the Difference or Contrariety of their Tastes might be."

It is important for a newspaper editor to be aware of that diversity of tastes in his readers, and Brice quite clearly recognized it. In introducing the first instalment of *The History of the Pyrates* in his *Weekly Journal*, number 23 (15 October 1725), he said he knew it would be difficult to please all at the same time. "As I have not a few for my stated Customers who are Gentlemen distinguished for Learning, Judgment, and a polite Taste; so, no doubt, I have more of a different Species. Whereby it cannot but happen, generally, that what is grateful to the one is contemn'd by or unacceptable to the other." It is not surprising that this continued to be a difficulty, for no journalist in any century has succeeded in pleasing all his readers all the time. What deserves notice is that whenever Brice for one reason or another omitted the belles-lettres, his readers complained. "Many of our Customers," he observed in number 200 (7 February 1729), "have express'd some Uneasiness at the so long Discontinuance of the Entertainment wont to fill the Frontispiece of our Paper, for the sake of which principally they took it in." The printing of these articles was resumed, but until more issues of Brice's paper come to light it will not be possible to say how many issues published between 1730 and 1758 [8] contained this sort of entertainment.

From the hundreds of pieces in prose and verse to be found in the surviving issues of Brice's newspaper, it would be easy to select a dozen that would be typical. Among these would be the thousand-word yarn sent in

by a correspondent (in number 199, 13 November 1724)
about a half-strangled criminal taken down from the
gibbet by a compassionate countryman and his son and
hanged again by them after he had repaid their kindness
by stealing a suit of clothes, to the subsequent astonish-
ment of the villagers, who noticed the changed attire of
the suspended corpse. One should mention the poem in
six cantos called "The Petticoat," [9] on the front page of
six consecutive issues in July and August, 1725, and the
long letter in number 6 (22 July 1725) in which "E.H."
described in lively fashion the conduct and conversation
of some gossipy women. There was in number 32 (20
January 1727) a five-column essay on the responsibilities
of teaching school. The list could go on and on; but surely
the piece most deserving to be examined in the twentieth
century is a dialogue between two sisters, Wilmot and
Thomasin Moreman, who spoke with picturesque vehemence in their local Exmoor dialect while sitting at their
spinning wheels. This "Exmoor Scolding Dialogue," as
Brice called it—and he may very well have been its
author—so caught the interest of the eighteenth century
that it was frequently reprinted. A portion of this extraordinary conversation was printed in *Brice's Weekly
Journal,* number 51 (2 June 1727), and it must have
aroused favorable comment, for the second part appeared
twelve weeks later, in number 63 (25 August 1727).

The "Exmoor Scolding" is now more interesting linguis-
tically than otherwise, though the transcribing is inexact.
The following excerpts from the second part show how
the author of the piece went about the phonetic representation of a West Country dialect. Wilmot has been
heaping up reproaches against her sister for slovenliness
in her performance of family chores:

> Nif tha beest a zend to Vield wey the Drenking, or ort, to
> tha Voaken, where they be shooling oh Beat, or hand-beat-
> ing, or angle-bowing, nif tha comst athert *Rager Hosegood,*
> tha wut lackee an over while avore tha comst I; and may

be net trapsee hum avore tha Disk of tha Eavling, ya blow-maunger Barge Oll vor palching about to hire Lees to vine-dra Voaks. Whan tha goest to tha melking oh the Kee in the Nuzzey-park, that wut come I oll a dugged, and thy Shoes oll mux, and thy Whittle oll besh—Tha wut let tha Cream shorn be oll horry, and let tha Melk be buckard in buldering Weather.

But sister Thomasin has plenty to say about Wilmot's deficiencies:

And nif tha dest pick Prates upon me, and tell Veather oh, chell tell a zweet rabble-rote upon thee, locks zee. Vor whan tha shudst be about thy Eavling's Chuers, tha wut spudlee our tha Yewmors, and screedle over men: And more en zo, tha wut roily eart upon won, and cart upon another, zet Voak to bate, lick a gurt Baarge as tha art; and than Getfer *Rager Sherwell* he must qualify 't agen. Whan tha art zet agog tha desnt caree who tha scullest. 'Twos ollweys thy Uze. And chem agest tha wet vore and aen. Tha hast tha very Daps of thy old muxy Ont *Sybly Moreman* uppazet.

They go on calling each other "ya mulligrub Gurgin," "A gottering hawchamouth Theng," "a brocking Mungrel, a skulking Meazle," "ya gurt Lillipot," and "ya gurt kick-hammer Baggage," until Wilmot pulls her sister's "poll" and Thomasin screams, "Oh! Mo-ather! Mo-ather! — Murder! Oh! Mo-ather!"

When old Julian Moreman enters, she attempts to separate the struggling young females: "Labbe, labbe, Soze, labbe. —Gee o'er, gee o'er, Tamzen." But Julian ends by contributing to the uproar:

And thee be olwey wother agging or veaking, ge awing or sherking, blazing or racing, keerping or speaking cutted, chittering or droing vore oh Spalls, purting or chowering, yerring or chounting, taking owl oh won Theng or a pip oh tether, chockling or pooching, ripping up or round-shaving won tether, stivvering or grizzeling, tacking or busking, a prill'd or a muggard, blogging or glumping,

> rearing or snapping, vrom Candle-douting to Candle-tecning in tha Eaveling,—gurt hap else.

Julian's thumping recapitulation of Thomasin's deplorable habits looks queer on a printed page, but the rebuke would be wondrously impressive if one heard it delivered in a full-flavored mixture of West Country vowels and consonants.

Brice took his supererogatory matter very seriously and felt that his newspaper should divert and instruct as well as inform. He obviously agreed with the author—if, indeed, he was not himself the author—of an essay on the usefulness of fables, in number 18 (14 October 1726):

> 'Tis true, it ought to be the Aim of every (at least pub-lick) Pen to instruct rather than divert, and inculcate the solid Rules of Piety and Good Manners, than titulate light and airy Fancies by ludicrous Vanities and sportive Trifles.

But, as Samuel Johnson said later, that book is good in vain which the reader throws from him.

> What *Profit* [the piece continued] will those whom 'tis presum'd he designs to *profit* gather from all his Lucubrations and solemn Lectures, tho' ever so reasonable and effi-cacious in convincing in themselves, unless he can also contrive a Method to make such People *read* 'em, and that too with some sort of Pleasure?

Brice followed this principle in his newspapers. What he tried to do was to provide in them a pleasing variety so that both his learned readers and his "merrily-dispos'd Friends" would read them with some sort of pleasure.

Like Brice's Exeter papers, most country newspapers of the period carried "literary" matter as a regular feature.[10] If one were to assemble in bound volumes— perish the thought!—all the works of one kind or another which were inserted in the columns of provincial news-papers or attached to them as supplements, one could fill a very large bookcase; for in addition to thousands of verses, essays, and letters, there were many long works which appeared in instalments. A list of these continued pieces may one day distend the appendix of more than one doctoral thesis. It is naturally tempting to assume that most of these pieces printed serially were only space fillers, or that it was only immediate topical interest that jusified their regular place in a weekly newspaper. It is easy to see that Thomas Gent's reason for printing in his *York Journal* instalments of "The Life and Actions of John Sheppard; written by himself during his Confinement" was that, as his paper reported in the issue of 23 November 1724, Sheppard had been executed only the week before and the corpse taken under heavy guard to the Church of St. Martin in the Fields for burial. It was also popular interest in the subject rather than literary splendor that justified such things as the series of reports on the Annesley trial in the *Sherborne Mercury* in 1744, and instalments of the "Memoirs of Dr. Archibald Cameron, Brother to the famous Donald Cameron of Lochiel, now under Sentence of Death" in the *Cambridge Journal* in 1753. Some lingering interest in the Jacobite rebellion of 1745, together with a desire to elicit public attention to a work which he was then (1746-47) publishing in weekly numbers, led David Henry to print in his *Reading Journal* portions of Samuel Boyse's *Historical Review of the Transactions of Europe from the Commencement of the War in Spain in 1739, to the Insurrection in Scotland in 1745*. Political allegory may make its way in the world if its point is obvious enough; though as one remembers the uproar over a similar piece in *Mist's Weekly Journal* in 1728,[11] it is surprising that authorities raised no objections to "The Persian Cromwel; or, The Life and Actions of Meriweys, Great Duke of Candabar, and Protector of the Persian Empire" in the *Worcester Post* early in 1725. Such pieces would not have been regarded as padding.

It is true, and not in the least surprising, that before

the reduction in size of newspapers from a sheet and a half to a half-sheet in 1725, some printers regularly had room for an instalment of a work in considerable length, though that is no reason why one should assume that instalments were without interest to readers. Reference has already been made to Andrew Brice's reprinting of Defoe's *Captain Singleton* in his *Post-Master*. The *Gloucester Journal* printed serialized fiction—for example, the story of Shalum and Hilpa in numbers 106 (13 April 1724) and following issues, the history of Captain Avery and other pirates (number 115, 15 June 1724, and later issues), and "Bath Intrigues; In Four Letters to a Friend in London" in number 135 (2 November 1724) and following issues. Other examples are easy to find, and among these are pieces that look suspiciously like space fillers. It is understandable that J. Watson might suppose readers of his *Maidstone Mercury* in the early weeks of 1725 would be interested in a serial description of Kent which filled the front page of several issues, and it is to be noted that in number 6 (22 March 1725) he said that those wishing to have earlier numbers to complete the set could obtain them, extra copies having been printed. But for what particular reason did Stephen Bryan fill the last page of his *Worcester Post* in 1723 with instalments of a history of England?

Undoubtedly some printers were hopeful that these continued pieces would serve the same purpose as the detachable supplements issued with eight or ten of the provincial papers, namely to extend the circulation.[12] Certainly, as has been shown elsewhere,[13] these serialized works were numerous after 1725 and were obviously not then used as space fillers to avoid the newspaper tax; they were included because readers liked them. Early in 1738, William Chase placed on the front page of his *Norwich Mercury* instalments of what he announced on 14 January as "an Essay towards the Character of her late Majesty Queen Caroline," and he said he was printing this work "At the earnest Desire" of his customers as well as to oblige others. In the summer of 1746, the proprietors of the *Sussex Weekly Advertiser* offered in their proposals to print instalments of "Directions for Gardening," but the subscribers emphatically declared their preference for instalments of a romantic novel, a sample of which nearly fills the front page of number 5 (7 July 1746); and it is unlikely that the front page of the *Sussex Weekly Advertiser* for nearly two years from the latter part of 1749 had most of its front-page space in every issue taken up with instalments of Smollett's *Roderick Random* only because there was nothing else to go there.[14]

Fiction was probably more acceptable in serial form than any other kind of prose. The *Leedes Intelligencer* had instalments of Voltaire's *Zadig* in a dozen issues in 1754; and in 1759, *Jopson's Coventry Mercury* reprinted portions of *The History of the Countess of Dellwyn*, "Written by the Author of David Symple," Henry Fielding's sister Sarah. The *Cambridge Journal* entertained its readers—were Cambridge students and dons among them? —with such narratives as "Narzenes: or, the Injur'd Statesman" (September to December, 1749), "The History of Polydore and Emilia"[15] (June and July, 1752), "Female Revenge; or, the Happy Exchange" (November and December, 1752), followed by "The Distress'd Beauty; or, Love at a Venture" and "Good out of Evil, or The Double Deceit." To some readers these insipid romances were not so dull as most of the news was; and when the passage of fiction had to be omitted for some reason, the printers took the trouble to apologize.

Whatever the intention, the men who from week to week prepared and printed the country newspapers of England used an astonishing variety of serialized matter, and it is quite possible that country readers who had no libraries of their own might actually have looked forward with some eagerness to the successive portions of "The genuine History of the Good Devil of Woodstock" in

Orion Adams's Weekly Journal (1752), or to extracts of "the Rev'd and ingenious Mr. Hervey's Contemplations on the Starry Heavens" in *Felix Farley's Bristol Journal* (1752). Who knows? Perhaps readers of Robert Whitworth's *Manchester Magazine* really did enjoy the instalments of "The Chronicles of the Kings of England, written in the Manner of the Ancient Jewish Historians, by Nathan Bensadde" (1742). Can it have been lack of news that, in 1739, led the printer of the *Lancashire Journal* to fill the first page of half a year's issues with "The Life of Mr. Cleveland, natural Son of Oliver Cromwell, Written by Himself"? Perhaps the serialized descriptions of Virginia, Pennsylvania, and New Jersey in Isaac Thompson's *Newcastle Journal* in 1742 started some North-of-England people thinking about migrating to the American colonies. Stay-at-home readers of the *Newcastle Gazette* doubtless liked to read the two or three columns of Ned Ward's "characters" on the fourth page of each issue for many weeks in 1748. There can be no convincing proof that *anyone* actually read those continued pieces in the columns of country newspapers in those days; but the fiction, history, and biography so released piecemeal to many thousands of readers may have induced some of them to cast their eyes on something other than news, as the author of the *Liverpool Chronicle* said might happen.

It is not part of the plan of this book to discuss the "literary" periodicals produced in the country before 1761, but a few of these may be mentioned because they came from the same presses as those on which the local newspapers were printed. One such periodical, the *Agreeable Miscellany; or Something to please every Man's Taste,* published fortnightly in 1749-50 by Thomas Ashburner, printer of the *Kendal Weekly Mercury,* was designed to provide the varied literary matter for which he did not think he had room in the columns of his newspaper. It had advertisements, but no news, and is properly classed as a literary periodical. Of precisely the same nature, if one may judge by the announcements in the *Leeds Mercury*, number 698 (26 June 1739) and later, was James Lister's proposed *North Country Magazine*. It was not to have news, but was to contain "curious Letters, Exercises of Wit, and remarkable Occurrences, appearing from Time to Time in the London Journals, and other Publick Papers, which in the Compass of a News Paper cannot possibly be communicated to the Publick." No copy of the *North Country Magazine* has survived. Perhaps it failed to appeal to readers of the *Leeds Mercury* because they did not like Lister's plan to issue this "monthly" magazine at the rate of one sheet every week for three halfpence, with a title page and table of contents added to every fourth sheet. Five years earlier, Lister had attempted to establish a similar magazine, apparently with indifferent success. The two issues of the *Monthly Miscellany* which have survived—those of January and February, 1734—show that his object was to reprint moral and political essays from ten or a dozen of the London newspapers. Other "literary" periodicals published in this period by the proprietors of provincial newspapers were the *Northampton Miscellany*, published by Robert Raikes and William Dicey in 1721; the quarterly *Miscellaneæ Curiosæ; or Entertainments for the Ingenious of Both Sexes*, printed in York by Thomas Gent in 1734 and 1735; the very successful *Newcastle General Magazine*, published monthly by Isaac Thompson from 1747 to 1760; the *Humourist: or, Magazine of Magazines. Calculated for the Improvement and Entertainment of the People of Lancashire, Cheshire, &c.*, published fortnightly by Orion Adams, of Manchester; the same man's *Plymouth Magazine: or, the Universal Intelligencer* (1758); and the *Northern Light by Lucifer*, announced in February, 1757, by Griffith Wright, printer of the *Leeds Intelligencer*.[16]

If, with the exception of the *Newcastle General Magazine*, these fortnightly and monthly magazines never became very firmly established, the cause may well have been that the newspapers themselves provided all the "Exercises of Wit" demanded by most country readers. In the tenth *Spectator* paper (12 March 1711), Joseph Addison declared that it was the purpose of that periodical to bring philosophy out of the closets and libraries and into the clubs and coffee houses; the belles-lettres in the country newspapers included little enough of philosophy, but there was a great deal of practically everything else which the term belles-lettres can possibly mean. Who can complain if the verses range from translations of Propertius to "Strip-me-Naked, or Royal Gin for ever" and the prose includes such diverse morsels as the "Exmoor Scolding" and an essay on embalming?

1. See the note in item 134 of the Register at the end of this book.

2. Later in the century, other printers of country newspapers did much the same thing, either publishing separately the pieces for which they had not room in the newspaper or else bringing out in a separate volume a selection of pieces which had already appeared in the newspaper columns. Because many "constant Readers" of the *Northampton Mercury* preferred to have the complete works of Stephen Duck rather than to read them piecemeal in the columns of that paper, the proprietors announced in the issue of 26 October 1730 that they had "alter'd the Design" of inserting them in the *Mercury* and proposed to publish at sixpence the seventh edition of *Genuine Poems on several Subjects,* "Written by Stephen Duck." In November, 1745, David Henry, of Reading, published a *Seasonable Miscellany* at threepence and a month later brought out a second collection under the same title. In his *Reading Journal,* number 161 (17 November 1746), Henry advertised *Twenty Discourses on the Most Important Subjects* as available at two shillings stitched up in blue covers and at half a crown bound in boards. These were his own compositions. Reference was made in Chapter V, above, to *The Chester Miscellany,* a volume of prose and verse culled from the columns of Elizabeth Adams's *Weekly Courant* between January, 1745, and May, 1750.

3. Number 111 (18 May 1724) has thirty-eight lines of Latin verse in vindication of a sermon on the divine right of kings recently printed by Raikes and Dicey.

4. It will interest students of Johnson to learn that the first of the *Rambler* essays, dated Tuesday, 20 March 1750, was set up in type again

before the end of that same week and appeared in the *Bristol Weekly Intelligencer,* number 27 (Saturday, 24 March 1750). *Rambler* essays were also reprinted in the *Bath Journal,* the *Leeds Mercury, Aris's Birmingham Gazette, Whitworth's Manchester Magazine,* the *Western Flying-Post,* the *Salisbury Journal,* and its "twin" the *Portsmouth and Gosport Gazette.*

5. The bantering tone is carried forward delightfully into the statistical account of "the present State of Matrimony," setting forth that, out of 872,564 married pairs in England and Wales, there were 191,023 living in open war under the same roof, 162,320 living in a state of inward hatred for each other (though it was concealed from the world), 1,102 reputed happy in the esteem of the world, 135 comparatively happy, and 9 couples absolutely and entirely happy.

6. "An occasional Epilogue, wrote by the Rev. Mr. Watson, of Ripponden, Yorkshire, and spoken in Halifax, March 1, 1756, by Mr. John Hargrave, in the character of Cato."

7. Brice's verses written "in Absconsion" are pathetically bad; his uncompleted education for the Church gave him some knowledge of books, but he too easily conformed to the contemporary fashion in "poetic" diction, writing "æm'lous Vespertines" and then having to explain in a footnote that he meant "Evening-Posts, of which are various Rivals."

8. The single surviving issue of *Andrew Brice's Old Exeter Journal; or, the Weekly Advertiser,* marked "No. 53 [Or above 2000; this Paper being in the 42d Year of its Age]" (7 July 1758), has only news, prices, shipping news from Exmouth, and advertisements.

9. Attributed by Halkett and Laing to John Durant de Breval, by *C. B. E. L.* to Francis Chute.

10. Surviving issues of the *Plymouth Weekly Journal* and of *Pilborough's Colchester Journal* give no indication that any effort was made by the authors of these two papers to provide "literary" matter.

11. See above, pp. 283-84, 285, and 298 n. 4.

12. See Chapter III, above.

13. R. M. Wiles, *Serial Publication in England before 1750* (London: Cambridge University Press, 1957), pp. 26-52.

14. In the issue of 25 March 1751, a correspondent's letter on the offense of poaching was, at his suggestion, used in place of the instalment of *Roderick Random.*

15. This was a reprinting of a popular short novel by Mrs. Mary Hearne, first published in London in 1718 under the title *The Lover's Week.*

16. The *Student: or, the Oxford Monthly Miscellany* was not published by the printer of an Oxford newspaper.

Chapter VIII

At COVENTRY,

On Tuefday *and* Wednefday *the* 16th *and* 17th of
September *next, will be performed,*

The ORATORIOS of
Samfon *and the* Meffiah,

For, and under the Direction of, Mr. BOND.

The VOCAL PART by Mifs *Thomas,* Meffrs. *Wafs, Price, Mence, Brown, Saville,* and the principal Voices from the Choirs of *Worcefter, Glocefter,* &c. And the INSTRUMENTAL PART by Mr, *Pinto,* Meffrs. *Vincents, Millar, Adcock,* and other capital Performers.

After each ORATORIO will be A BALL as ufual.

Tickets, at 5 s. each, to be had at Mrs. Jopfon's, Printer; Meff. Ratten and Parker's; and of Mr. Bond.

At BIRMINGHAM,
THE
Sacred ORATORIO of MESSIAH,
AND THE
ORATORIOS of SAMSON and
JUDAS MACCABÆUS,

Will be performed at the NEW THEATRE, on *Tuefday, Wednefday,* and *Thurfday,* the 16th, 17th, and 18th of *September* next, by a Band of the moft eminent Performers, Vocal and Inftrumental, from LONDON, &c.

The Whole will be conducted by Mr. HOBBS,
Who will perform Pieces on the ORGAN.

After the PERFORMANCES will be BALLS,
To which none but thofe who have Pitt Tickets will be admitted.

The Band will be lead by Signior PASSERINI, who will play Solos between the Acts; and will confift of the following principal Mafters, who will alfo perform Pieces on their refpective Inftruments, Sig. *Scolu, Antoniotti,* Meff. *Simpfon, Abington, Miller, Baumgurton, Zucker,* and others.

The principal Vocal Performers are, Signiora *Pafferini,* Mifs *Young,* Meff. *Beard, Champnefs, Waltz, Bailden,* &c. with a numerous Chorus.

The kind Indulgence which Mr. HOBBS received from the Public, in his firft Attempt, towards the Performance of Oratorios in this Town, has induced him to fpare no Trouble or Expence, in procuring the firft Performers that are to be had in London, both Vocal and Inftrumental, as he would by no Means think of exhibiting the above Oratorios (efpecially thofe of SAMSON and JUDAS MACCABÆUS) without engaging thofe particular Perfons whofe Talents enable them to fill the Characters of the Drama with Dignity and Propriety; and as Mr. HOBBS's Expence will amount to 300l. and upwards, he hopes that he fhall meet with fuitable Encouragement thereto, his great Aim being that of highly pleafing and entertaining.

The Boxes and Pitt will be laid together, at 7 s. each Ticket, and the Tickets for the Gallery will be 3 s. 6 d. each.

The Books for each Oratorio will be publifh'd by the Middle of next Week, for the Perufal of thofe who are defirous of entering into the thorough Enjoyment of thefe Performances, and are to be had of Mr. Hobbs, Mr. Aris, and all the Inns in Town, at 8 d. each Book.

The Performers are defired to meet on Monday the 15th, by Nine o'Clock in the Morning, to proceed to Rehearfal.

Disclosures

THERE ARE TWO SENSES in which, without straining the term, newspapers can be regarded as "primary sources." In the first place a newspaper is itself a "fact," an indispensable document in the history of journalism. For that specific chapter in the story of man's enterprises, there is no other body of direct evidence so basic and so abundant; only by examining the surviving issues can one answer the obvious questions concerning the size, the shape, the price, the contents, and the distribution of early papers. The other sense in which newspapers—early ones in particular—are "source" material is this: they comprise a record, not only of what people used to read, but of what they did and of what they were. The press has its own peculiar power to control public opinion and to influence decisions of government, but it also stands as the amplest continuing record of everyday life. One learns much about life in England two or two-and-a-half centuries ago from the diary of Celia Fiennes, from the notebooks of Caroline (Girle) Powys, from John Macky's *Journey Through England* (1724), from Daniel Defoe's *Tour thro' the Whole Island of Great Britain* (1724-26),

---

FIG. 7.—Music in the provinces, announced in *Jopson's Coventry Mercury* on 18 August 1760. (By permission of the Coventry City Libraries.)

and from the observations of such visitors as Henri Misson and Cesar de Saussure; much that is both realistic and authentic is to be found in the novels of Fielding and Smollett and Graves, as also in the verses of George Crabbe. But the newspapers, written to be looked at immediately and to be thrown away after a week, caught something of the off-guard actuality of people and things as they were. Surviving copies of the 150 newspapers published in sixty English towns before George III came to the throne throw a revealing, if never dazzling, light on many aspects of social life during a particularly absorbing period in England's history. To know a man who lived in former times, one must see his portrait and read his letters; to know a community as it was two centuries ago, one should read its local newspaper of that time.

This is not the place for gathering together an assortment of oddities from those Queen Anne and early Georgian columns of print, nor is it expedient to set forth here the great mass of contemporary detail upon which a new and somewhat different social history of England could be written. But it is reasonable to insist that unless the social historian consults the columns of the *Norwich Gazette*, the *Northampton Mercury*, the *York Courant*, the *Leedes Intelligencer*, and the other papers distributed weekly to thousands of readers, he is largely uninformed, not only about the eighteenth-century provincial press as a cultural influence, but about music, the theater, public health, education, inland and seaport trade, politics, the weather, transportation, and practically every activity of those multitudes of English folk who preferred not to live in London. Scattered among those newspapers, there is information on road building, on the erecting of hospitals and infirmaries, on industrial working conditions, on privately owned schools, on teachers' salaries, on markets and fairs, on steps taken to control distemper in horned cattle, on local bills of mortality,[1] on the services of dentists and other practitioners, on the shocking incidence of crime, and on the equally shocking modes of punishment.

The sheer variety of these multitudinous details is astonishing. One can read of body snatchers at work in Chester in 1725, of a child won in a game of cards at Chester le Street in 1735, of turnpike riots in Herefordshire, of hooligans who smashed lamps and stole brass doorknockers in Manchester in 1752, of nine vagrants— five of them women—publicly whipped at Reading in 1753. There is also a good deal of news concerning the preaching of Wesley and Whitefield, and about the violence of mobs against the Methodists. A big book could be written about the music that was composed, rehearsed, played, sung, and enjoyed by listeners in country towns; about the concerts and formal balls planned for assize week and during the races; about the plays that were performed at local theaters and schools; about the public lectures that were delivered to paying audiences; about the books that were bought or were borrowed from the circulating libraries in St. Ives, in Leeds, in Nottingham, and in Liverpool.

Without attempting to anticipate that big book, one ought perhaps to give here a few specific examples of the kind of "revelations" which the newspaper reports of events and the newspaper advertisements provide concerning the life of English people in the days of Fielding, Johnson, and many another man who grew up in a provincial environment. What people ate and drank, what they enjoyed looking at, both indoors and out of doors, what they wore, how they traveled, what they read, what they taught their children, what they did to public offenders, what efforts they made to make life easier, what they died of—these are all revealed on the thousands of pages which, though neglected for twenty decades, can now be read with new interest. That interest sometimes springs from quite unlikely matters.

A closer look at a few details will show what sort of light they throw upon the daily life of those days. Even the London and local bills of mortality are fascinating, not only for their figures showing the incidence of smallpox in various parts of the kingdom, but for the list of afflictions which snuffed out the lives of people of all ages. The London weekly bill of mortality must have interested provincial readers then as much as it catches the attention of a modern reader who sees the lists in a local newspaper of 1725 or 1730. If eleven infants were stillborn in a week and one was taken with worms, there might be two or three with "Horshoe-head" or "Head-mouldshot," and a few cut off by "Loosness," "Hooping Cough," or "Evil." A hundred and thirty or forty others of all ages would die of convulsions in a week, and forty or fifty from "Teeth"; the fatal ailment might be "Imposthume," "Chin Cough," "Rising of the Lights," "Tissick," "Twisting of the Guts," "Thrush," "Tympany," "Grief"; or the end might just be reported as having come "Suddenly."

Sudden death did not always come from natural causes, for the provincial papers all reported the local assizes, at which the death sentence was pronounced almost as often as the less final punishments of transportation, whipping, or burning the hand. Executions were looked upon as exciting spectacles, and great crowds attended. A notice in the *Sherborne Mercury,* number 218 (21 April 1741), requested the officers of the sheriff of Somerset to meet one week later at Robert Fry's house in Chard by nine o'clock in the morning in order that they might attend the sheriff at the execution of William Hawkins, who was to be hanged in chains on Chard Common that day. Such an announcement was practically a public invitation, issued a week in advance, for all interested persons to witness the killing of a man.

No community, however small or remote, was immune to violence, either malicious or official, and no account of

English life two centuries ago would be either accurate
or complete without some of the eyewitness reports which
found their way into the newspapers. One public execution
which drew "a prodigious Concourse of People" took place
at Cure Green, near Wells in Somerset, on Monday, 3
September 1753. At least a dozen papers reported how
death came to Susannah Bruford, a nineteen-year-old wife,
who had been convicted of poisoning her husband, a
farmer at Mounton, near Taunton. The account in the
Salisbury Journal, number 812 (17 September 1753), is
detailed enough to take one in imagination to the very
place of Susannah's last moments:

> . . . She was had out of the Star-Inn in Wells about Four
> o'Clock in the Afternoon, dress'd in Black, with a Black
> Hood over her Face, and drawn on a Sledge, with a Hurdle
> and Pitch Barrel thereon, to the Place of Execution; where
> a Clergyman attended, with whom she spent about Half an
> Hour very devoutly in Prayer: She was then had to the
> Stake, and put on a Stool, with the Halter about her Neck;
> where after standing a few Minutes, earnestly begging for
> Mercy, she dropt a black Handkerchief which she had in
> her Hand, as a Signal to the Executioner, who thereupon
> instantly strangled her with the Halter; and having fas-
> tened the Body to the Stake, by two Iron Hoops, to sup-
> port it, the Faggots were placed round, with a Pitch Barrel
> in the Middle, and Fire set thereto, which burnt furiously
> near an Hour: In which Time the Body was almost con-
> sumed, and the small Remains were put in a Coffin, and
> carried away to be interred.

What of the attorney's clerk who had alienated the young
farm wife's affections? Did he watch the burning on that
September afternoon?

Watching public executions was only one of many
outdoor pastimes two centuries ago, and the papers have
much to tell of less gruesome diversions—horse racing,
cock fighting, wrestling, cricket, throwing at cocks, and
bull-baiting. There were those who did not approve of
games in which living creatures suffered, and occasionally

one comes upon letters from objectors such as "Clemens," who in February, 1756, addressed a letter to the printer of the *Reading Mercury* beginning, "As the Season for throwing at Cocks in now approaching, I beg leave, by means of your Paper, to discourage (so far as I am able) that barbarous Custom, which I think reflects great Dishonour upon our Nation." There were less tender opinions about these "barbarous Customs," and for every letter against them there were ten advertisements inviting gentlemen "and others" to witness and enjoy the spectacle. Representative of these announcements is one in the *Gloucester Journal* of 30 September 1729:

> This is to give Notice,
>
> To all Gentlemen, that are lovers of Bull-Baiting, that on Friday the 10th of October next, there will be the finest BULL in the World baited on Clacton-Down, near Bath, he being superior in that Game to any of his Species; therefore all being desirous of seeing this noble Beast once match'd (if possible) for Encouragement there will be a very good Dinner dress'd after the best Manner, and a Quart of excellent good Ale for each Man that brings a Dog. . . .

There were not yet enough men in England who felt as Kester Woodseaves did in *Precious Bane*.

Several entertaining essays could be written on other diversions in which English people indulged two centuries ago, none perhaps so pleasant to write or to read as an account of a distinctively English exercise of skill—the ringing of church bells. Societies of bell-ringers were—and still are—to be found in scores of towns and villages in every corner of England, and the newspapers frequently reported extraordinary performances or published challenges. References to bell-ringing were particularly numerous in the Norwich papers. In the *Norwich Gazette*, number 1070 (8 April 1727), for instance, it was reported that on the preceding Saturday "was rung by 8 Men,

346

at the Church of St. Michael Coslaney in this City, the Quarter Peal of Treble Bob Royal, (call'd by some in England Union Bob) containing 10080 Changes, which they rung in 6 Hours 28 Minutes, with not a Bell out of Course, or any thing amiss." Invitations to ring in competition were frequently issued in the columns of local newspapers. On the last Saturday of May, 1739, it was announced in the *Ipswich Journal* that on Monday, 4 June, six pairs of gloves, the gift of Mr. George Cooper at the Crown, would be rung for at Godenham, "and that Company that Rings the Peals of Grandsire and Old-Doubles best, according to the opinion of such Judges as shall be appointed, shall have the Prize." The selecting of unprejudiced judges must have been difficult. In the *Oxford Gazette: and Reading Mercury* of 6 July 1747 notice was given to all gentlemen ringers that on the last day of September six good hats would be rung for at Shinfield, where three local men were to serve as umpires to all the peals and the fair thing would be done "if possible."

The fair thing may have been done in bell-ringing; what of "fair" trading in business? Much has been written on economic aspects of English life, but many precise details still lie buried in local newspapers. It is worth noting that ten of the newspapers considered in this book have the words "Together with an Account of Trade" in the subtitle. Obviously the best source of information about the shopkeepers and the wares they sold is the thousands of tradesmen's announcements in the local papers. Hatters, booksellers, grocers, mercers, sadlers—these and other dealers in all imaginable commodities reminded readers of the papers that new goods were arriving weekly and that satisfaction was assured. Simon Young, a confectioner in the Northgate Street, Chester, announced in the *Manchester Weekly Journal* on 24 September 1724 that he sold "Wet and Dry Sweetmeats, true Barley Sugar Comfits, . . . Oyles, Powder and Wash

Balls, Snuff and Sugar, . . . Christning Cakes and Sugar Biscakes for Burials, either wholesale or retail, at reasonable Rates." John Mingay, of Stratford, in Suffolk, advertised in *Pilborough's Colchester Journal* on 24 February 1739 that he made "Coaches, Chariots, Chaises, and Chairs, of all sorts, to go either in the Ruts, or upon the Quarter," adding that these might be altered from one to the other with very little trouble. In *Jopson's Coventry Mercury* in 1759, "T.F." recommended Mr. Dubourg's life-preserver, designed to make sea bathing safe: "even the most timorous and delicate young lady might boldly venture, with one of these Waistcoats, into a rough Sea." Gamaliel Holden, peruke maker of Hadleigh in Suffolk, announced in the *Ipswich Journal* of 7 April 1739 that every two or three weeks he would do business on market days at certain inns in Colchester, Ipswich, and Sudbury, guaranteeing that his prices were lower than those of any other wig maker and offering to remake or take back any wig that proved unsatisfactory to the wearer. His best wigs, "Beautiful Grey, or White, of Human Hair, neatly wrought of any form, or length," cost thirty shillings; the three grades of "Gristle Human Hair" could be had for one guinea, twenty-five shillings, or twenty-seven shillings; twelve shillings would buy wigs of "Fine White Horse Hair" or "Fine Gristled Horse mixed with Human"— though Holden "ingenuously" suggested that horse-hair wigs were "rather for Sight than Service" but with "Oyling, Buckling, &c." would "wear genteely one Year, for Dressing, and for Riding, another Year." His prices for making "Pale and Brown Wiggs, intirely neat and without Mixture, of any Form, Mode, or Length" ranged from eight to sixteen shillings; and he charged five shillings for making a wig from the customer's own hair.

In the advertisements of commodities and services, the prices were seldom given, except for books and medicines, but several papers regularly gave the local and regional prices of grain, butter, and other farm products. Current prices on local markets were given in Norwich, St. Ives, Reading, Stratford-upon-Avon, Manchester, Sherborne, Gloucester, Doncaster, and Warrington papers; most other papers gave only the London figures.

One other valuable kind of information is the lists of ship arrivals and their cargoes. These are a regular feature of the Bristol, Hull, Kendal, Liverpool, Manchester, and Newcastle papers. The papers of some inland towns also regularly had lists of imports at nearby ports and at London. The *Doncaster Flying-Post; or, Hull and Sheffield Weekly Advertiser*, number 37 (7 January 1755), lists the "Hull Imports," naming the ships and indicating their main cargo: "Republic, Wm Masterman, from Amsterdam, with wainscot boards, old iron and madder"; "Charlotte and Ann, Abraham Thompson, From Seville, with lemons and olives"; "York, Thomas Foulkes, from Jamaica, with sugar, fustic, ginger, cotton, wine, elephants teeth, and rum."

Reminders that in many ways the eighteenth century was not yet quite "modern" are to be seen in numerous papers. On 2 November 1732, the *Gloucester Journal* reported that barbers would be fined for shaving customers on Sunday; and on 28 June 1735, the *Norwich Mercury* carried official notices forbidding the sale of fruit and the crying of milk on Sunday. The *Gloucester Journal* a few years earlier—on 22 March 1726—warned its readers that no material but English wool could legally be used for making burial shrouds, and in other issues of that paper are official notices and unofficial proposals which now seem severely restrictive: it was solemnly announced on 11 December 1739 that persons burning lamps instead of candles in their houses would be fined forty shillings for each offence; on 15 February 1757, a "Well-wisher to the Community" proposed to the author of the *Gloucester Journal* that, under an old statute still in effect, churchwardens should levy a fine of one shilling upon everyone who neglected to "resort duly to Church, or to some Place of Publick Worship, upon all Sundays, and there to continue the whole Time of Divine Service." The same correspondent proposed that anyone (except a traveler) found tippling in an ale house on Sunday should be taken by the constable or the tythingman before a justice of the peace, who might fine the offender three shillings and fourpence and the ale seller ten shillings.

To a twentieth-century reader the most diverting of these restrictions, perhaps, is the official statement, in three successive issue of the *Gloucester Journal* in July and early August, 1746, that the act just passed by Parliament "more effectually to prevent profane Cursing and Swearing" was to be rigidly enforced in the county of Gloucester. The penalty was not to depend on the violence of the bad language but on the social status of the offender. Upon conviction for using offensive language, a day laborer, a soldier, a sailor, or a seaman must pay a shilling; for a more offensive outburst, other persons "under the Degree of Gentleman" paid two shillings; gentlemen and those of higher social rank, perhaps because it was assumed that they had access to a more extensive vocabulary, had to pay five shillings for each profane utterance. One thinks of Swift's remark in the introduction to his *Complete Collection of Genteel and Ingenious Conversation* (1738) that only a man "of superior Parts, of good Memory, a diligent Observer, one who hath a skilful Ear, some Knowledge in Musick, and an exact Taste" could use profanity with maximum effectiveness. "A Footman can swear," said Simon Wagstaff, "but he cannot swear like a Lord. He can swear as often: But can he swear with equal Delicacy, Propriety, and Judgment?" The statute of 1746 imposed double fines for a second offence, treble after that; and if the fines were not paid, the offender had to suffer the stocks for an hour or ten days of hard labor in the house of correction, according to his social class. High social rank may have brought enviable privileges to a gentleman or a man of title, but his cursing cost him more.

Compulsory church attendance, restrictions on "free" speech, fines for using a new kind of lighting, and the prohibiting of imported fabrics for wrapping corpses suggest lingering medievalism, but there were innovations, too. The *Gloucester Journal* on 7 December 1725 gave details of the new machine erected at Derby by Messrs. Thomas and John Lombe for "working Italian Organize Silks." With this remarkable labor-saving mechanism, which contained 26,586 wheels, a girl of eleven years could do the work of thirty-three persons. Working conditions and the rewards of labor were very different from those of our time, but there is something that suggests a modern "union" meeting in this announcement in *Aris's Birmingham Gazette*, number 236 (19 May 1746):

> The Filers of Gun-Barrels are desired to meet and consult about keeping up the Price and Goodness of their Work, and to let their Masters and the Buyers of Gun-Barrels know, that if their Prices are lower'd, the Barrels will be as much worse.

The struggle between employers and employed for an equitable scale of wages had doubtless begun many centuries earlier, and it is a dispute which is perpetually renewed, though the figures change from century to century. There is nothing of the mid-twentieth century in the scales of wages paid to workmen two centuries ago. On 2 July 1756, readers of *Williamson's Liverpool Advertiser* saw advertisements concerning wages paid to journeyman shoemakers and journeyman tailors. The latter group made this announcement:

> Whereas the Master Taylors have reported, That we, the Journeymen Taylors, have refused working unless they would pay us 10s. per Week; this is to assure the Gentlemen of this Town, that we are willing to work for 9s. per Week; and if any Master refuses taking in their Customers Work, it is not our Faults.

A difference of one shilling in a week's pay now seems a small matter to quarrel over, but that was the century in which a head ploughman, waggoner, or seedsman could be hired for eight pounds a year, and farm laborers got fourteen pence a day.[2]

Stipends for professional people were also pitifully small. The provincial papers had numerous advertisements for school teachers, and it is clear that schoolmasters, no matter how much their heads could carry, had no hope of being paid as much as parsons. No forty pounds a year for them. On 13 March 1750, a group of school trustees advertised in the *Manchester Magazine* that a "School Master, properly qualified to teach English"—nothing else was mentioned—was required at Rochdale, the salary for teaching twenty "petty" scholars being six pounds per annum, though that was "like to be improv'd." The successful applicant would enjoy a house and school rent-free, and he would be at liberty to take in additional pupils for his own benefit. But salaries were not so low at some other places. The *Leeds Mercury,* number 778 (30 December 1740), had a notice that a schoolmaster was needed at Rawcliffe, in the parish of Snaith, Yorkshire, to teach the children to read and write "true" English and arithmetic; there was an endowment of £11 or £12 a year for teaching fourteen children and "attending on the Chappel as Clerk." In May, 1758, the trustees of the Free School at Haworth advertised in the *Leedes Intelligencer* that a graduate of Oxford or Cambridge would be engaged to teach grammar, English, writing, and arithmetic "in the best Method," but only if the applicant was "sufficiently recommended for his good Conversation." The last line of the invitation to apply began with a pointing hand and proudly read, "The Salary is Eighteen Pounds a Year."

One wonders how good the teaching can have been. Richard Steele had said some harsh things in the *Spectator* about "the ignorance and undiscerning of the generality of schoolmasters" (number 157), and Oliver Goldsmith voiced the same complaint in his *Bee,* number 6 (10 November 1759), declaring that men unsuccessful in other professions became schoolmasters, though Goldsmith later wrote with admiration and affection about the schoolmaster in sweet Auburn. Those masters probably earned more than they got, and the conditions in which they worked must often have been quite distracting. There is a Dickensian touch about a circumstance that must have made attendance at Henry Whitaker's school a hazardous experience for children. This particular school was conducted in the former Wheat-Sheaf Inn, Deansgate, Manchester, and the boys to whom Whitaker attempted to teach English, Latin, writing, arithmetic, and "Merchants Accompts" had to pass through a courtyard which, as he regretfully admitted in *Orion Adams's Manchester Journal* on 12 May 1752, was "crouded three Days every Week with Carriers Horses." Whitaker's advertisement reassured the parents that the horses had now been removed to another place and would no longer be a menace to their children.

Whatever the Nicholas Nicklebys may have thought about their difficult working conditions and slender incomes, it was not they but the skilled laborers who complained loudly enough to be noticed in the press. Most frequently reported are the discontents of the weavers and the framework knitters in various parts of England. The years 1726 and 1727 saw much agitation among the weavers in the West Country. They complained of low wages and unfair practices by their employers. Acts of violence were committed in protest, and a formal paper of grievances was drawn up. A report dated at Bristol on 13 August 1726 was printed in the *Gloucester Journal* three days later:

> We hear that the Journeymen Weavers without Lawford's Gate, in the Suburbs of this City, have risen, and for these two days past committed great Outrages, occasioned (they say) by their Masters making their Chains longer, and their Price shorter; upon which Account many of them will not work themselves, nor suffer others to do

353

so, but do in a riotous and tumultuous Manner break into the Houses where they know any to be at work at that Rate, and cut the Work out of their Looms, tearing and burning of it, and the Harness and Slays wherewith they work it.

Such demonstrations by the weavers continued, as the newspaper accounts indicate, but it is clear from letters and statements in the press that honest efforts were made by both weavers and clothiers to deal with the basic problems, one of which was a certain laxity in the appointing of apprentices. The author of a cool-headed statement in the *Gloucester Journal* on 11 April 1727 said he was convinced that the laws already made were adequate for the settling of disputes between the clothiers and the weavers who worked for them.

A statute of the realm may prove ineffectual unless public attention is drawn to violations, and it is one of the functions of the newspaper press to do that. The *Nottingham Weekly Courant* of 15 June 1749 carried an advertisement, dated the day before, giving notice that framework knitters who hired runaway apprentices would be prosecuted. Two such runaway youths, Richard Rowbottom and George Hodgkinson, were named and a warning against them issued. Three weeks later, a framework knitter in Beeston, in the County of Nottingham, admitted in a signed statement that he had been guilty of employing Rowbottom, and declared that he had made full satisfaction to Abraham Broadbent, to whom Rowbottom had been apprenticed. Another industrial complaint illustrated by the newspaper reports was that some employers insisted on paying their workers in cloth instead of in money, a practice prohibited by law. In 1727, the clothiers of Gloucestershire made a point of announcing in the *Gloucester Journal*, number 289 (24 October), that they were ready to take action against violators:

Whereas for many Years past Great Abuses have been practised by some Clothiers, by using Ends and Thrums in working up their Cloth, and also by paying their Work-people with Goods of several Sorts, forcing them to take such Goods at their exorbitant Prices; by which illegal Practices the Poor are starved, the fair Trader injured, and a Disreputation brought upon the Woollen Manufacture both at Home and Abroad. And whereas our Legislators in their great Wisdom have lately passed an Act of Parliament to prevent such evil Practices for the future; in order to put the said Act in Execution, we whose Names are hereunto subscribed, being Clothiers in this County, do promise, that whosoever shall make Information of such Practices used by any Clothier living in this County, shall immediately upon Conviction receive of us the Reward given by the Act for so doing, and we do engage to be at the whole Expence, which shall be caused by such Convictions.

Fifty-one Gloucestershire clothiers appended their names to this advertisement.

Some of the labor disputes reported in the provincial press were merely local quarrels, less significant than the weavers' revolts and the troubles among the framework knitters, but no less indicative of a sturdy determination to establish or invoke reasonable principles. One such dispute arose in Derby, over who should enjoy a monopoly in the sale of biscuits for funerals. A notice in the *Derby Mercury* on 22 July 1748 reminded readers that it had for some time been the custom in Derby and surrounding villages for mourners to procure biscuits for funerals from the apothecaries, a practice not followed in other places. It was argued that the article in question ought to be supplied by the bakers, not the apothecaries.

This is therefore to inform the Gentry, and Others, who may have Occasion, that they may be supply'd at any Time with the best and cheapest Biscuits for Funerals, by any of the Bakers of the said Place, upon giving their Orders.

With bakers ready to provide funeral biscuits for the bereaved and weavers authorized to prepare woolen shrouds for the deceased, the end of life could be solemnized with due attention to the needs of the lamented and the lamenting.

Moved by concern for the hereafter, readers in 1712 must have turned with considerable eagerness to the advertisement in the *Newcastle Courant,* number 142 (25 June 1712), describing a means of obtaining "Perpetual Security"; but it is soon apparent that this security was "perpetual" only during one's mortal lifetime; no financial scheme could relieve one's anxiety concerning the life everlasting. To "Industrious House-Keepers, Handicraft Tradesmen, Day Labourers, Keel-men, Pitt-men, and all other Diligent Persons," Edward Slaters offered "present Sums of Money, according to their Necessities, when disabled from Working, either by Sickness, loss of Limbs, Strength, Senses, or any other Accident whatsoever." All it cost a subscriber was one penny a week, collected every six weeks; and a threepenny pamphlet describing the scheme was obtainable at the office next door to the Crown Tavern on the "Key." Whether Edward Slaters or anyone else found the scheme financially advantageous is perhaps doubtful; but there is something engagingly optimistic about the offer.

Other kinds of financial assistance were available in the country towns. According to notices in the *Leeds Mercury* in 1738 and following years, Benjamin Worsdale's "Office of Intelligence" in Crosby Court, Upper Headrow, near the Cross, served as a clearinghouse for all sorts of financial transactions: the sale and mortgaging of properties, the lending of money on good security, the purchase (for a client) of the advowson of a living "situate within twenty-five Miles of Leeds, of the Yearly Value of £150 or upwards, and the Incumbent advanced in Years." Similar financial transactions were performed at "the Universal Register Office of Intelligence near the Sign of the Griffin" in Conisford, Norwich, in 1753, and likewise by Thomas Watson, who advertised in *Keating's Stratford and Warwick Mercury* on 9 April 1753 that he might be consulted any market day at Warwick, at the White Lion in Stratford, at the Talbot in Henley, and at the Peycock in Coventry.

Another service available to readers of country newspapers was the labor exchange, for London was not the only center in which employment offices were set up in the eighteenth century. *Creswell's Nottingham Journal,* number 47 (27 November 1756), had a notice in which Sarah Wood, who sold tea, sugar, candles, tobacco, and cheese, announced that she was ready to help servants to obtain places and householders to hire servants:

> This is to inform the Public, that Sarah Wood, the late Mistress of St. Mary's Workhouse, is by the Advice of her Friends determined to open such an Office, at her House opposite the Sun in Bridlesmithgate; where Servants may hear of Places suitable to their Qualifications, and Mistresses of Servants, by enquiring of the said Sarah Wood, and registering their Names at One Shilling each.

Sarah's varied experience while in charge of the workhouse doubtless gave her exceptional shrewdness both as tradeswoman in groceries and as the proprietress of an employment bureau.

Patient searching brings to light innumerable references to every aspect of trade and industry, none perhaps more revealing than those concerned with the transporting of goods and persons from one part of England to another. Reference was made in Chapter III of this book to the corps of newsmen who distributed local newspapers and also carried such commodities as the printers wished them to sell en route. Many of these newsmen were willing at small charge to deliver parcels or messages in their respective territories. Reference was also made in that chapter to the numerous regular carriers whose routes crisscrossed the whole face of England, and whose saddlebags and wagons in the course of a year must have transported goods of considerable weight and bulk. When the time

357

comes for someone to write the complete story of coaching
services, goods carriers, freight barges, and coastal shipping, the local newspapers will prove invaluable as a
source of information. For instance, one sees by advertisements in *Aris's Birmingham Gazette* in June and July,
1742, that the "Litchfield and Birmingham Stage Coaches"
set out every Friday, one from the Bell Inn in Wood
Street, London, the other from the Swan in Lichfield—
and from Mr. Francis Cox's at the Angel and Hen and
Chickens in the High Street, Birmingham—arriving at the
other end of the run the following day, though an extra
day was required in winter. The fare was twenty-five
shillings, with a luggage allowance of fourteen pounds, the
excess payable at three half-pence per pound. Parcels
were carried, and the service was performed "if God
permit" by A. Jackson. This is the standard form of
notice, and there were scores like it.

Sometimes these advertisements gave much greater
detail as to routes and times. An earlier announcement
of the Birmingham to London service listed the fares to
points between the Coach and Horses in New Bolton
Street, Broad St. Giles's, London, and either the Angel
and Hen and Chickens in Birmingham or the Swan Inn in
Lichfield. These are the rates specified by the proprietors,
John Sharpless of Lichfield, William Boome of London,
"and Company," in the *Lancashire Journal* of 20 July
1738:

	£	s.	d.
From London to Dunstable	0	6	0
To Fenny Stratford	0	8	0
To Stony Stratford	0	10	0
To Towcester	0	12	0
To Daventry	0	15	0
To Coventry	1	1	0
To Birmingham	1	5	0
To Litchfield	1	5	0

It was pointed out in this advertisement that whereas several ladies and gentlemen had been "disappointed by the Undertakers from Warwick, by their not having a due Attendance in the Winter, as well as in the most seasonable Part of the Year," this service would "with God's Permission" be faithfully performed throughout the year.

By 1758, it was possible to cover a journey of ninety-five or a hundred miles in a single day—but what a day! According to advertisements in *Jopson's Coventry Mercury* in May of that year, the Coventry Flying Stage Machine set out from Thomas Dullison's at Bishop-Gate in Coventry every Monday, Wednesday, and Friday morning at *three* o'clock and reached the Castle and Faulcon, Aldersgate Street, London, that same evening. The return journey, on Tuesdays, Thursdays, and Saturdays, likewise began at three A.M. Dullison and his associate, Gyles Tattingham, said they had been making the one-way journey in sixteen hours, but the luggage allowance was only eight pounds, and the rates for this breakneck speed were somewhat higher than had been charged by the Sharpless-Boome Company twenty years earlier.

Some services were for the carriage of goods only, and the charges varied with the weight and distance. The *Leicester and Nottingham Journal,* number 313 (28 April 1759) and following issues, printed the full text of an official notice setting forth the maximum charges, established four days earlier by the General Quarter Sessions of the Peace in Leicester, for the carriage of goods from London to Leicester, Market Harborough, Lutterworth, Mountsorrel, Loughborough, Hinckley, Ashby-de-la-Zouch, Market Bosworth, and Melton Mowbray. The reason for this official action was that "divers Waggoners and other Carriers by combination amongst themselves" had been charging excessive prices for the carriage of goods from London to points in Leicestershire, "to the great prejudice and obstruction of Trade." Parcels weighing less than fourteen pounds were now to be carried to any of the places named for one shilling at any time of the year. For heavier pieces the charges were specified in two schedules, one for the fair-weather season (from 25 March to 29 September), the other for the more difficult six months. In summer the charge for transporting one hundredweight from London to Leicester was to be no more than five shillings, in winter, 5/6; to Ashby-de-la-Zouch the rates were to be 5/6 and 6/6. "And so after the same Rates respectively for every greater or lesser quantity, . . . (Parcels under the weight of fourteen pounds only excepted)."

Such services for the carriage of goods were numerous, both local and long distance. They included traffic by river and by sea as well as by the road; and although the journey by water was slow, it was dependable. Lawrence Price and Richard Powell gave notice in the *Gloucester Journal*, number 904 (28 August 1759), that every Saturday at three or four o'clock in the afternoon there set out from the Star on Worcester Key "a good Barge for Gloucester," discharging her loading every Monday morning at Price's cheese shop and wine house. The utmost care was taken to forward goods as directed, and there was "no Housage, only Porteridge."

Regularity of service was also a strong point in the announcement in *Pilborough's Colchester Journal* on 24 February 1739 that beginning on 28 February the two united Colchester packets, the "Dove," Edward Tibball, master, and the "Concord," Thomas Hopkins, master, would sail between the New Hithe in Colchester and Custom-House Key, London, clearing every Tuesday afternoon, the "Dove" from one port, the "Concord" from the other, "Goods or no Goods." But the two masters ran into difficulties. Just one week later *Pilborough's Colchester Journal* printed this advertisement of a competitor:

Whereas great Complaint hath been made against the Masters of the COLCHESTER Packets, Mess. TIB-BALL and HOPKINS, for not sailing in due Time, to the great Disappointment of Trade:
This is to give Notice,
That, at the Desire of several eminent Merchants, and Trades, will sail from the Crane at the New Hithe, Colchester, on Tuesday next, March 6th, for LONDON, and continue to do so every Tuesday Fortnight,
The CERES, *George Perry,* Master
And will sail from Sommer's-Key, near Billingsgate, LONDON, on Tuesday, March 13th, and continue to do so every Tuesday Fortnight throughout the year. . . .

The story does not end there: on 10 March the local newspaper carried the announcement of Edward Tibball's death at sea.

There were competing services on some of the land routes, too. Advertisements in the *York Courant* show that in March, 1740, two competitors were running stage coaches between York and Hull, and four months later competing services between York and Scarborough were announced. Other regions also had rival operators of coaches.

Notices such as those given above, taken at random from scores of transportation advertisements, indicate the sort of information just waiting to be collected if anyone wishes to investigate the means and costs of moving about in eighteenth-century England; and the same abundance of material can be found in early country newspapers to throw light on every other aspect of life in a swiftly developing nation. The author of the *Connoisseur,* number 45 (5 December 1754), stated that he looked upon the "common intelligence" and the advertisements of newspapers as "the best account of the present domestic state of England that can possibly be compiled." In his view there was nothing which could give posterity so clear an idea of the taste and morals of his age as a bundle

of newspapers. The justice of this observation can be
tested by considering not only the few examples of provincial activities and interests used in illustration of this
brief final chapter on "disclosures" but the very nature
of the newspapers themselves, for in them one sees what
political and economic questions were of chief concern to
their thousands of readers, what incidents in the normal
day-by-day life of people were thought to be worth
reporting, what kinds of prose and verse the local papers
disseminated throughout England's fifty thousand square
miles, and what efforts were made by printers to keep
the public informed about events in other parts of the
nation and of the world.

Spreading news is still the primary purpose of newspapers, and those published several generations ago can
be judged by the same criteria as one applies to this
morning's paper. Differences in outward appearance—in
arrangement of matter, in size and number of pages, in
design of types, in texture of paper—do not alone justify
the writing of a book about early newspapers. To us they
may seem quaint; but to the readers for whom they were
printed, they were not curiosities; they were read for their
substance, and it is for their substance that they still
deserve to be examined.

If it is true that no account of English journalism in
its apprentice days could be either complete or accurate if
the papers listed in the attached Register were ignored, it
is no less true that what those papers tell of their times
is as important as what they tell of themselves. A book
about early newspapers may very well be dull, whether
its emphasis is upon format or upon contents; but the
newspapers themselves were not—and are not—dull.
Compared with the stately official papers in the nation's
archives, each of the ephemeral and hastily produced
weekly bulletins of news discussed in the preceding chapters may seem pathetically unimportant as historical docu-

ments; yet their numerous details of fact and speculation disclose, perhaps more strikingly than any other body of evidence, the ethos of early Georgian provincial England.

1. Most papers reprinted the London weekly bills of mortality, but in a few places—Ipswich from 1721 onward, for instance, Reading in 1723, Gloucester in 1726—the local bills of mortality were published, particularly during periods when cases of smallpox became numerous.

2. These figures were reported in the *Chester Weekly Journal* of 10 May 1732 as the rates fixed by the justices presiding at the General Quarter Sessions held at Canterbury on 26 April after taking into consideration "the many illegal Practices used by Servants in Husbandry, in order to extort excessive Wages. . . ."

Appendixes

The *Gloucester Journal:*
Area of Distribution in 1725

THE IMPRINTS AND COLOPHONS of several eighteenth-century newspapers enumerated large numbers of agents from whom, with a minimum of delay, the papers could be obtained and through whom advertisements could be sent to the printer. Some of these lists of places and agents are given in Chapter III and in the Register (Appendix C); but nowhere else is the plan of distribution so clearly and so amply set forth as in the *Gloucester Journal,* number 160 (24 April 1725). In that issue, the proprietors, hoping to impress readers and especially advertisers with the extent of the paper's circulation, stated that the territory in which the *Gloucester Journal* was distributed had been divided into thirteen divisions, each with its own chief distributor. The list of places shows that the Raikes and Dicey men took the paper to towns and villages in a region embracing twelve English and Welsh counties, with a total area of over eleven thousand square miles, the most distant places being Llandaff in Glamorganshire, Ludlow in Shropshire, Wantage in Berkshire, and Trowbridge in Wiltshire. The names are given here as they stand in the *Gloucester Journal.* The routes in each division can be traced with ease on a map showing local roads and paths as well as the main highways.

First Division.

John Chapman, Distributor to
the City of Gloucester.

Second Division.

John Wilson, Bookseller in
Horse-street, Bristol, and
his Agents, Distributers to
the City of Bristol.

Third Division.

John Butler, Distributer.
Stroudwater, Gloucestershire
Tedbury, ditto
Malmsbury, Wilts
Chippenham, ditto
Caln, ditto
Devizes, ditto
Roud, ditto
Brumham, ditto
Stanton, ditto

Fourth Division.

John Young, Distributer.
Marshfield, Gloucestershire
Bath, Somersetshire
Bradford, Wiltshire
Trowbridge, ditto
   And several Villages.

Fifth Division.

Walter Nelms, Distributer.
Frampton, Gloucestershire
Cambridge-Inn, ditto
Estlington, ditto
Froster, ditto
Cowley, ditto
Camm, ditto
Dursley, ditto
Stinchcomb, ditto
Newport, ditto

North Nibley, ditto
Wootton-under-edge, ditto
Kingswood, Wiltshire
Charvil, Gloucestershire
Wickwar, ditto
Chippen Sudbury, ditto
Yeat, ditto
Nibley, ditto
Earn, ditto
Acton, ditto
Lutteridge, ditto
Thonrbury, ditto
Oldbury, ditto
Hill, ditto
Bartley, ditto
  and other Towns and Villages.

Sixth Division.

John Wood, Distributer.
Newnham, Gloucestershire
Lidney, ditto
Chepstow, Monmouthshire
Carlton, ditto
Newport, ditto
Cardiff, Glamorganshire
Landaff, ditto
  besides Villages.

Seventh Division.

Rice Price, Distributer.
Little Dean, Gloucestershire
Speech House, ditto
Coleford, ditto
High Meadow, ditto
Newland, ditto
Redbrook, ditto
Monmouth, ditto

Rockfield, Monmouthshire
Tavernback, ditto
[   ], ditto
Llandillo, ditto
Llanabley, ditto
Llanddwirhyddch, ditto
Abergavenny, ditto
Llanellen, ditto
Llanover, ditto
Pont a Poole, ditto
Usk, ditto
Rhaglan, ditto
Treglagg, ditto
Abbey Winton, ditto
    besides Villages.

Eighth Division.
James Powell, Distributer.
Huntley, Gloucestershire
Mitchel Dean, ditto
Ross, Herefordshire
Llangarren, ditto
Gutheridge, ditto
Hereford
Weobley, ditto
Heay, Brecknockshire
    besides Villages.

Ninth Division.
John Winslow, Distributer.
Newent, Gloucestershire
Ledbury, Herefordshire
Bromyard, Worcestershire
Tenbury, ditto
Leominster, Herefordshire
Ludlow, Shropshire
    and several Villages.

370

Tenth Division.

William Kirby, Distributor.
Tewksbury, Gloucestershire
Upton upon Severn, Worcestershire
Evesham alias Easom, ditto
Parshore, ditto
Worcester
Droitwich, ditto
Bromsgrove, ditto
        besides Villages.

Eleventh Division.

James Whithorne, Distributer.
Cheltenham, Gloucestershire
Presbury, ditto
Charlton Kings, ditto
Upper Dowdeswel, ditto
Lower Dowdeswel, ditto
Winchcomb, ditto
Stanway, ditto
Stanton, ditto
Broadway, ditto
Campden, ditto
Mickleton, ditto
Stratford upon Avon, Warwickshire
Preston upon Stower, ditto
Alderminster, Worcestershire
        besides Villages.

Twelfth Division.

James Warwick, Distributer.
Burlip, Gloucestershire
Withington, ditto
Northleach, ditto
Sherborne, ditto
Burford, Oxfordshire
Bampton o' th' Bush, ditto

Clanfield, ditto
Farringdon, Berkshire
Stanford, ditto
Wantage, ditto
Lambourn, ditto
Cricklade, Wilts
    besides Villages.

Thirteenth Division.
James Peloteris, Distributer.
Painswick, Gloucestershire
Bisley, ditto
Cirencester, ditto
Fairford, ditto
Lechlade, ditto
Highworth, ditto
Swinden, ditto
Marlborough, ditto.
Woottonbasset, ditto.

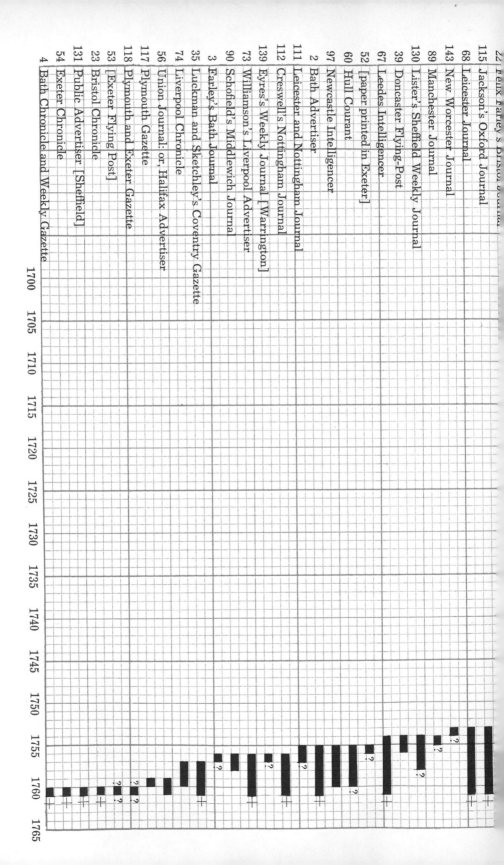

Chronological Chart

THE CHART THAT PRECEDES indicates the life span (to the end of the year 1760) of each provincial newspaper believed to have been published in England within the period 1701-60. Only the earliest known title of each paper is given; subsequent titles will be found in the appropriate entry in the Register (Appendix C). The numbers at the left are those assigned to the papers in the Register. A plus sign shows that the paper is known to have continued after December, 1760. A question mark before or after a band is used to suggest that the period of publication may have begun earlier or lasted longer than the band indicates, but that evidence is lacking or inconclusive. Thus the *Norwich Gazette* is shown as having begun in 1706 and as having been published to the end of 1749, but the question mark at the right end of the band points to the possibility that this paper continued beyond that year.

Register of English Provincial Newspapers, 1701–1760

TITLES are grouped by place of publication, the places being in alphabetical order and the titles in chronological order according to the known or conjectured dates of first issues. Direct references to particular titles may be found in the General Index. The chart in Appendix B shows the strictly chronological order of the whole set.

To each newspaper here identified as a separate publication a serial number has been assigned for ease of reference. Such identification will, in some cases, seem arbitrary and unjustified. Mere change of subtitle is not regarded as marking the termination of one newspaper and the beginning of another, nor is the changing of the main title, unless change of management or ownership is also known to have taken place; but indication is given wherever it is known or strongly suspected that one paper directly and immediately succeeded another. Changes in title are included as part of the entry for each paper, except when a change was preceded —or may have been preceded—by a gap of at least several weeks, in which case it is assumed that a new paper was started, and there is a separate entry at the appropriate place in the chronological sequence.

Many papers published prior to the inescapable application of the Stamp Tax in 1725 nominally came to an end with the last issue of April in that year and were succeeded by "new" papers, usually with completely different format and title. The separation of the papers published just before and just after 30 April 1725 has perhaps only slender warrant. It will also be easy to challenge the separate listing of *F. Farley's Bristol Journal* and *Farleys Bristol Advertiser,* which appeared on alternate Saturdays, with the same advertisements and for many weeks with interlocking serial numbering, number 45 of one being followed by number 46 of the other; but the relations of these two and the relations of both to earlier Bristol papers are clarified rather than obscured by the separation. On the other hand, Stephen Martin's *Bath Chronicle,* which began with new numbering on 16 October 1760, is here listed as a continuation of the same printer's *Bath Advertiser,* in number 261 of which (11 October 1760) the change of title was announced.

Certain papers which might appear to have been consecutive are here separated if they are now known to have overlapped—as is true of the earlier *Stamford Mercury* and *Howgrave's Stamford Mercury*—or if the gap was considerable. Such a gap separated the *Salisbury Journal* which Charles Hooton stopped printing in 1730 and the *Salisbury Journal* which began in 1736.

As was pointed out in the Note on the Dating of Early Newspapers at the beginning of this book, all dates are here given in the form "15 Oct 1740," though some space-conscious librarians would prefer a further reduction to "15 O 40." All dates have been silently adjusted to give a uniform year date for all papers published between 1 January and the following 31 December. An issue dated February 23, 1726-27, is here dated 23 Feb 1727, as is also a paper known to have been issued on that same day but dated February 23, 1726.

Other adjustments are these: volume numbers, where given, are here always in roman numerals; serial numbers of issues are here always in arabic numerals.

Conjectured serial numbers and dates are enclosed in square brackets, with an interrogation mark attached if there is uncertainty. The form "[no. 1 (9 Jun ? 1746)]" means that

375

the issue has not been seen and the date of it is conjectural. The form "[no. 1 (20 Jul 1741)]" implies that the date is well attested but that the issue has not been seen.

Unless a statement is made to the contrary, it is to be assumed that each paper had four pages and had three columns to the page.

The details assembled under each title are in this order:

1. subsequent titles of the same paper, with dates;

2. date, known or conjectured, of the first issue;

3. serial number and date of the earliest issue seen, if that was not number 1;

4. other known dates, if needed to establish continuity or to record change of serial numbering;

5. the terminal date of the paper, if known and if the paper came to an end before 31 December 1760 (a plus sign indicating that the paper is known to have continued after 31 December 1760);

6. the day of publication;

7. the number of pages *if not four;*

8. the number of columns to the page *if not three;*

9. the imprint or colophon of the earliest issue seen (other sources of information being clearly indicated if no issue has been seen);

10. significant subsequent variations of the imprint or the colophon;

11. in a few cases, notes concerning the history of the paper;

12. holdings of libraries in the United Kingdom, in order of proximity to the place of publication;

13. holdings in the United States and Canada.

In these entries a few abbreviations are used, most of them obvious; the five to be particularly noted are these:

con.: continued, or continuation

def.: defective, i.e., the copy is imperfect

fac.: facsimile

inc.: incomplete, i.e., some issues of the run are missing

rep.: reprint or reprinted

BATH

1. The Bath Journal. [By 29 Nov 1756 con. as]: Boddely's Bath Journal.

[vol. I, no. 1 (27 Feb ? 1744)]—vol. I, no. 2 (5 Mar 1744)—vol. XVII, no. 52 (29 Dec 1760), + .

Mon.

[Under title of early issues]: Printed and Publish'd by Thomas Boddely in Bath. [From 26 Mar 1750]: Printed at Bath by Tho⁵· Boddely, in King's-Mead-Street. [From 17 Dec 1750]: Printed at Bath by Tho⁵· Boddely at Pope's-Head, in King's-Mead-Street. [Under title in 1756-60]: Printed for John Keene, Brother-in-Law of Mr. Thomas Boddely Deceased, at the Printing-Office in King's-Mead-Street.

The death of Thomas Boddely on Wednesday morning, 9 Jun 1756, is announced in the *Bath Advertiser*, no. 35 (Sat, 12 Jun 1756).

Bath Municipal Library: vol. I, no. 11 (7 May 1744) to vol. XII, no. 52 (29 Dec 1755), nearly complete, many duplicates; vol. XIV, no. 5 (31 Jan 1757) to vol. XVII, no. 52 (29 Dec 1760), + , many duplicates.

Bristol Reference Library: vol. I, no. 2 (5 Mar 1744) to vol. XIV, no. 52 (26 Dec 1757), nearly complete; vol. XV, nos. 12 (20 Mar 1758) to 39 (25 Sep 1758).

Bodleian Library: vol. X, no. 39 (24 Sept 1753); vol. XIV, nos. 4 (24 Jan 1757) to 50 (12 Dec 1757).

British Museum: vol. I, nos. 7 (9 Apr 1744) to 54 (4 Mar 1745), fourteen issues only; vol. II, nos. 2 (1 Apr 1745) to 52 (17 Mar 1746), thirty-five issues only; vol. III, nos. 1 (24 Mar 1746) to 53 (23 Mar 1747), nearly complete; vol. X, no. 40 (1 Oct 1753); vol. XIII, no. 48 (29 Nov 1756); no. 51 (30 Dec 1756).

Private library of Sydney R. Turner, Esq., Cheam: vol. IV, nos. 5 (27 Apr 1747) to 48 (22 Feb 1748), nine issues only.

Yale University Library: vol. III, no. 1 (24 Mar 1746) to vol. IV, no. 52 (21 Mar 1748); vol. VI, no. 1 (27 Mar 1749) to vol. VIII, no. 52 (16 Mar 1752).

Historical Society of Pennsylvania: vol. III, no. 11 (2 Jun 1746).

Library of Congress: vol. II, no. 26 (16 Sep 1745) to vol. IV, no. 26 (21 Sep 1747); vol. VI, no. 26 (18 Sep 1749) to vol. IX, no. 9 (25 May 1752), lacking three issues.

University of Texas Library: vol. II, no. 1 (25 Mar 1745) to vol. III, no. 14 (23 Jun 1746); vol. III, no. 23 (25 Aug 1746) to vol. V, no. 52 (20 Mar 1749), lacking six issues.

2. The Bath Advertiser. [From 16 Oct 1760 con. as]: The Bath Chronicle: Or, Universal Register.

Vol. 1, no. 1 (18 Oct 1755)—vol. V, no. 261 (11 Oct 1760)—vol. I, no. 1 ["No. 262 since the commencement of the Bath Advertiser"] (16 Oct 1760)—vol. I, no. 11 (25 Dec 1760), + .

Sat; from 16 Oct 1760, Thu.

Bath: Printed by Stephen Martin, at the Printing-Office, just without West-Gate. . . . *.* This Paper will be published in Bristol every Saturday Morning, By Samuel Nayler, Printer, in Broad-Mead. . . . [Passage from *.* removed after 20 March 1756.]

[From 6 Nov 1760 this statement follows the imprint]: "This paper is served One Hundred and Twenty-six Miles in Length, from Reading in Berkshire, to the lower Parts of the County of Somerset; extending besides over most Parts of Wiltshire and Gloucestershire; the Cities of Wells, Bristol, &c. being also duly serv'd therewith. . . . "

Bath Municipal Library: vol. I, no. 1 (18 Oct 1755); no. 5 (15 Nov 1755); nos. 17 (7 Feb 1756) to 63 (25 Dec 1756), lacking four issues; vol. II, nos. 64 (1 Jan 1757) to 104 (8 Oct 1757), lacking four issues; vol. III, nos. 105 (15 Oct 1757) to 138 (27 May 1758); no. 155 (23 Sep 1758); vol. IV, nos. 186 (5 May 1759) to 242 (31 May 1760); vol. V, nos. 252 (9 Aug 1760) to 255 (30 Aug 1760), nos. 257 (13 Sep 1760) to 261 (11 Oct 1760); vol. I [of the *Bath Chronicle*], no. 1 (16 Oct 1760), no. 2 (23 Oct 1760), nos. 4 (6 Nov 1760) to 10 (18 Dec 1760).

Bristol Reference Library: vol. II, no. 64 (1 Jan 1757); vol. V, nos. 226 (9 Feb 1760) to 260 (4 Oct. 1760), lacking seven issues.

British Museum: vol. I, no. 1 (18 Oct 1755) to Vol. II, no. 64 (1 Jan 1757).

Press Club: vol. V, nos. 229 (1 Mar 1760) and 230 (8 Mar 1760).

Yale University Library: vol. II, nos. 54 (23 Oct 1756) to 85 (28 May 1757); nos. 87 (11 Jun 1757) to 104 (8 Oct 1757); vol. IV, no. 157 (7 Oct 1758); nos. 159 (21

Oct 1758) to 184 (22 Apr 1759); nos. 186 (5 May 1759) to 205 (15 Sep 1759), two def.; no. 207 (29 Sep 1759); no. 208 (6 Oct 1759), def.; vol I [of the *Bath Chronicle*], nos. 1 (16 Oct 1760) to 11 (25 Dec 1760), + .

3. Farley's Bath Journal.

[No. 1] [27 Sep 1756]—18 Oct 1756—?

Mon.

Bath: Printed by Samuel Farley, in the Market Place.

First issue advertised in *Felix Farley's Bristol Journal* on 18 Sep 1756 as to appear on Mon, 27 Sep.

Issue dated 11 Oct 1756 has this note:

> The kind Reception this Journal has met with, not only from the Citizens of Bath and Bristol, but the Inhabitants of other Places, calls for proper Acknowledgement. In this Manner I return my most grateful Thanks, and begging the Continuance of my Customers Favours, remain,
>
> Their oblig'd humble Servant,
> Samuel Farley.

British Museum: 11 Oct 1756; 18 Oct 1756.

4. The Bath Chronicle and Weekly Gazette.

Vol. I, no. 1 (16 Oct 1760) — vol. I, no. 11 (25 Dec 1760), + .

Thu; 4 cols.

[Under title]: Printed and publish'd by C. Pope, and Cᵒ· at the Printing-Office in Stall-Street. . . . The above C. Pope serv'd his Apprenticeship with the late Mr. Boddely, and has had the sole Management of the Bath Journal for these last five Years.

Bath Municipal Library: vol. I, no. 11 (25 Dec 1760), + .

Bristol Reference Library: vol. I, nos. 1 (16 Oct 1760) to 6 (20 Nov 1760).

BIRMINGHAM

5.   The Birmingham Journal.
    [No. 1 (9 Nov ? 1732)] — no. 28 (21 May 1733) — ?
    Thu; from 21 May 1733, Mon.
    Birmingham: Printed by T. Warren, . . .
    In no. 28 it is stated that, in response to requests, the day of publication has been changed from Thursday to Monday, and this is added: "we hope it will not be taken amiss that we postponed our last Thursday's Paper . . . . "
    Office of the *Birmingham Post*: no. 28 (21 May 1733).
    Birmingham Reference Library: no. 28 (21 May 1733), fac.

6.   The Warwick and Staffordshire Journal: with the Exposition on the Common-Prayer. [From 29 Oct 1737 con. as]: The Warwick and Staffordshire Journal: with the History of the Holy Bible. [From 25 Jun 1740 con. as]: The Warwick and Staffordshire Journal: with the History of the Life of Jesus Christ.
    [No. 1 (20 Aug ? 1737)]—no. 3 (3 Sep 1737)—Jun 1743.
    Sat; from Wed, 16 Nov and Thu, 17 Nov 1737, pub. in two series, one on Wed, the other on Thu.
    London, Printed by R. Walker, the Corner of Seacoal Lane, next Fleet Lane. [From 28 Dec 1738]: London, Printed by R. Walker in Fleet Lane.
    Though for several years printed in London, this paper was intended for circulation in Birmingham and other towns in that area. No. 69 (Thu, 7 Dec 1738) has this note: "Mr. Jolly, who serves Birmingham and other Towns adjacent with this and all other Books and

Papers printed by R. Walker, in London, is removed out of Edgbaston-Street, Birmingham, to Mr. Cox's, at the Angel and Hen and Chickens in the said Town." By late 1741, according to a statement in Thomas Aris's *Birmingham Gazette,* no. 1 (16 Nov 1741), Walker apparently printed the *Warwick and Staffordshire Journal* in Birmingham. See above, p. 143 n. 2.

Birmingham Public Library: nos. 3 (Sat, 3 Sep 1737) to 148 (Thu, 12 Jun 1740), with "supplements" of nos. 13 to 17 and of nos. 19, 40, 43, 97; nos. 61 (Wed, 19 Aug 1741) to 66 (Wed, 23 Sep 1741), and no. 68 (Wed, 7 Oct 1741), with "supplements," also "supplements" of nos. 80 to 95; nos. 97 (Wed, 20 Jun 1739) to 149 (Wed, 18 Jun 1740), with "supplements."

William Salt Library, Stafford: nos. 35 (Thu, 13 Apr 1738) to 147 (Thu, 5 Jun 1740), nearly complete.

7.   The Birmingham Gazette: or, the General Correspondent. [From 1 Mar 1742 con. as]: Aris's Birmingham Gazette: or, the General Correspondent.

No. 1 (16 Nov 1741)—end of 1760, + .

Mon.

Birmingham: Printed by T. Aris. . . . [From 11 Jul 1743]: Birmingham: Printed by T. Aris and Comp. . . . [By 12 May 1746]: Birmingham: Printed by T. Aris. . . .

A History of . . . Famous Pirates was issued in folio sheets as supplement to this paper in 1742.

Birmingham Public Library: no. 1 (16 Nov 1741) to end of 1760, + .

William Salt Library, Stafford: vol. III, no. 120 (27 Feb 1744) to end of 1760, + .

Bath Municipal Library: vol. V, no. 226 (10 Mar 1746).

British Museum: no. 1 (16 Nov 1741); no. 239 (9 Jun 1746)

Press Club: vol. IX, no. 469 (5 Nov 1750).

Private library of W. B. Morrell, Esq., London: vol. I, nos. 60 (3 Jan 1743) to 115 (23 Jan 1744), nearly complete; vol. III, nos. 116 (30 Jan 1744) to 130 (7 May 1744), nearly complete; vol. VI, nos. 276 (23 Feb 1747) to 308 (5 Oct 1747), nearly complete.

New York Public Library: vol. XIV, no. 735 (22 Dec 1755), def.

BRISTOL

8. The Bristol Post-Boy, Giving an Account of the most Material News both Foreign and Domestick.

    [No. 1 (Nov ? 1702]—no. 91 (12 Aug 1704)—no. 340 (26 Aug 1710)—?

    Sat; but no. 287 is dated Wed, 7 Sep to Sat, 10 Sep 1709; 2 pp.; 2 cols.

    Bristol, Printed and Sold by W. Bonny in Corn-street, 1704.

    Bristol Reference Library: no. 91 (12 Aug 1704); no. 281 (20 Mar 1708); no. 287 (10 Sep 1709); no. 340 (26 Aug 1710).

9. Sam. Farley's Bristol Post Man: or, Weekly Intelligence, From Holland, France, Spain, &c With General Occurrences, Foreign and Domestick.

    [No. 1 (21 Feb ? 1713)]—[no. 24 (25 Jul 1713), according to F. A. Hyett and William Bazeley, *The Bibliographer's Manual of Gloucestershire Literature* (3 vols.; Gloucester: Bellows, 1895-97), III, 287]—no. 29 (28 Jan 1716)—[May, 1722]—?

Sat; 12 pp.; single col.

Printed at my House in St. Nicholas-street, near the Church; Deliver'd to any publick or private House in this City for Three Half-pence a Paper; and seal'd and deliver'd for the Country at Two Pence.

Mentioned in the *Gloucester Journal*, no. 8 (28 May 1722). Perhaps con. as *Farley's Bristol News-Paper* (item 11 in this Register). Letter by Samuel Farley's niece in the *Bath Journal*, vol. X, no. 52 (24 Dec 1753), quoted in item 16 of this Register, suggests that *Sam. Farley's Bristol Post Man* was followed in unbroken succession by *Farley's Bristol News-Paper* (item 11 in this Register), *Farley's Bristol Journal* (*ibid.*), *F. Farley's Bristol Journal* (item 16 in this Register), and *Farleys Bristol Advertiser* (item 17 in this Register).

Bristol Reference Library: nos. 24 (24 Dec 1715) to 29 (28 Jan 1716).

10. The Bristol Weekly Mercury from Holland, France, Spain, &c. with Fresh Advices, Foreign and Domestick: Far Exceeding all other News Papers.

[No. 1 (5 or 8 Oct ? 1715)]—no. 61 (1 Dec 1716)—[no. [?] (7 May 1726)]—1727.

Sat; 12 pp.?; 2 cols.

Price Three Half-Pence, or Eighteen Pence Per Quarter in Town. Any Person may have this Paper, every Monday Morning, at Mr. John Palmer's Book-seller in Gloucester. Bristol: Printed by Henry Greep.

The *Gloucester Journal*, no. 217 (10 May 1726), has a report dated at Bristol May 7 beginning, "We hear there happen'd a terrible Fire at Bath Yesterday in the Afternoon, which Mr. Greep in a Paper, he printed this Day, acquaints us . . . began . . . in a publick Wash-house. . . ."

Below the subtitle of *Farley's Bristol News-Paper*, nos. 104 (29 Apr 1727) to 178 (28 Dec 1728), S. Farley printed this statement: "Note, After all Ignorant and Fruitless Attempts of Pretenders, No other News-Paper is Printed in this City; which Circulates above 50 Miles round."

Bristol Public Library: no. 61 (1 Dec 1716), fac., def.

Press Club: no. 61 (1 Dec 1716), fac., def.

11. Farley's Bristol News-Paper. Containing the most Genuine Occurrences, Foreign and Domestick. [From 27 Aug 1726 con. as]: Farley's Bristol News-Paper. Containing the most genuine Occurrences, Foreign and Domestick. Abstracted from all the Printed and Written News Papers Extant; and Publish'd every Saturday Morning soon after the London Post comes in . . . . [By 30 Mar 1734 con. as]: Sam. Farley's Bristol Newspaper. [By 29 Aug 1741 con. as]: Farley's Bristol Journal.

[No. 1 (8 May ? 1725)]—no. 20 (18 Sep 1725)—no. 16 (21 Nov 1730)—no. 552 (29 Aug 1741)—?

Sat (except no. 34, published Fri, 24 Dec 1725, and no. 35, published Fri, 31 Dec 1725); 2 cols.; by 12 Feb 1737, 3 cols.

Printed at my House in Wine-street, near Newgate. . . . [From 8 Jan 1726]: Printed at my House, below the Dolphin, in Wine-street. . . . [From 21 Aug 1731]: At S. Farley's Printing Office in Wine-street, Gentlemen may be supply'd with . . . .

May be a continuation of *Sam. Farley's Bristol Post Man* (item 9 in this Register). Probably con. as *F. Farley's Bristol Journal* (item 16 in this Register) and *Farleys Bristol Advertiser* (item 17 in this Register), published on alternate Saturdays from 3 Dec 1743.

Bristol Reference Library: nos. 20 (18 Sep 1725) to 190 (21 Dec 1728), lacking twelve issues; no. 213 (31 May

1729); no. 232 (11 Oct 1729); no. 257 (4 Apr 1730); no. 16 (21 Nov 1730); no. 17 (28 Nov 1730); no. 55 (21 Aug 1731); no. 130 (27 Jan 1733); no. 191 (30 Mar 1734); no. 200 (1 Jun 1734); no. 250 (17 May 1735); no. 309 (3 Jul 1736); no. 314 (7 Aug 1736); no. 340 (12 Feb 1737); no. 421 (26 Aug 1738), fac., 2 copies; no. 552 (29 Aug 1741).

12. The Oracle: Or, Bristol Weekly Miscellany. [From 17 Jul 1742]: The Oracle: Or, Bristol Weekly Miscellany. By Andrew Hooke, Esq.

Vol. I, no. 1 (3 Apr 1742)—vol. I, no. 40 (31 Dec 1742).

Sat (except vol. I, no. 40, published on Fri, 31 Dec 1742).

Bristol: Printed for the Society, By Benjamin Hickey in Nicholas-street, 1742. [No. 10 (5 Jun 1742) has]: Bristol: Printed for the Society, 1742. [No. 11 (12 Jun 1742) has]: Bristol: Printed by Benjamin Hickey, in Nicholas-street, for the Society, 1742. [No. 16 (17 Jul 1742) has]: Bristol: Printed by B. Hickey, for the Author, 1742. [No. 33 (13 Nov 1742) has]: Bristol: Printed by B. Hickey, in Nicholas-street, for the Author, 1742. [No. 40 (31 Dec 1742) has]: Bristol: Printed by J. Watts, in Shannon-Court, for the Author, 1742.

This paper was followed by (1) the *Bristol Oracle, and Country Intelligencer* (item 14 in this Register) and (2) the *Bristol Oracle, and Country Advertiser* (item 15 in this Register), published on alternate Saturdays, beginning in January, 1743.

Bristol Reference Library: vol. I, nos. 1 (3 Apr 1742) to 11 (12 Jun 1742); nos. 13 (26 Jun 1742) to 32 (6 Nov 1742); nos. 35 (27 Nov 1742) to 40 (31 Dec 1742).

British Museum: vol. I, no. 20 (14 Aug 1742) and no. 26 (25 Sep 1742).

Press Club: vol. I, no. 33 (13 Nov 1742).

13. The Bristol, Bath and Somersetshire Journal. By. R. Winpenny, and E. Collins.

[No. 1 (1 May ? 1742)]—no. [58?] (4 Jun 1743)—[no. 68 (13 Aug 1743)]—?

Sat.

Bristol: Printed by R. Winpenny and Company, at the Bible in Castle-Street. . . .

The serial number of the only copy seen is partly cut away and appears as LVI. The correct number may be either LVII or LVIII. The number [57] is given in R. T. Milford and D. M. Sutherland, *A Catalogue of English Newspapers and Periodicals in the Bodleian Library 1622-1800* (London: Oxford University Press, for the Oxford Bibliographical Society, 1936); but the number LVIII would fit into the sequence indicated by the only other issue reported. According to Hyett and Bazeley, *op.cit.* (see item 9 in this Register), III, 279, a heading with title and "No. LXVIII (Sat. Aug. 13, 1743)," cut from the rest of the copy, was once in a scrap book in the Bristol Museum and Library, but the fragment cannot be found either in the Bristol Museum or in the Bristol Reference Library.

Bodleian Library: no. [58?] (4 Jun 1743).

14. The Bristol Oracle, and Country Intelligencer. By Andrew Hooke, Esq.

Vol. I, no. 1 (8 Jan 1743)—vol. III, no. 60 (6 Apr 1745).

Alternate Sat.

Bristol: Printed by J. Watts, at the Sign of the Bible in Shannon-Court, Corn-Street. . . . [From 18 Aug 1744]: Printed for A. Hooke, at the Sign of the Bible in Shannon-Court, Corn-Street, . . .

This newspaper and the *Bristol Oracle, and Country Advertiser* (item 15 in this Register) were published on alternate Saturdays and were essentially the same paper, differing only in title and in having separate serial numbering. These two papers were followed by a similar pair, the *Bristol Oracle* (item 18 in this Register) and the *Country Advertiser* (item 19 in this Register), likewise published on alternate Saturdays.

Bristol Reference Library: vol. I, nos. 1 (8 Jan 1743) and 2 (22 Jan 1743); nos. 5 (5 Mar 1743) to 28 (21 Jan 1744), lacking seven issues; nos. 31 (3 Mar 1744) to 35 (28 Apr 1744); vol. II, no. 38 (9 Jun 1744) to vol. III, no. 60 (6 Apr 1745), lacking eight issues.

British Museum: vol. II, no. 34 (14 Apr 1744).

Press Club: vol. I, no. 4 (19 Feb 1743).

15.   The Bristol Oracle, and Country Advertiser.

Vol. I, no. 1 (15 Jan 1743)—vol. III, no. 60 (13 Apr 1745).

Alternate Sat (except vol. I, no. 22, published Fri, 4 Nov 1743).

Bristol: Printed by J. Watts, at the Sign of the Bible in Shannon-Court, Corn Street, . . . [From 13 Aug 1743]: Bristol: Printed for A. Hooke, at the Sign of the Bible in Shannon-Court, Corn-Street, . . . [From 25 Aug 1744]: Bristol: Printed by A. Hooke, at his Printing Office.

See note attached to item 14 in this Register.

Bristol Reference Library: vol. I, no. 2 (29 Jan 1743) to vol. II, no. 39 (30 Jun 1744), lacking three issues; vol. II, no. 43 [numbered 45] (25 Aug 1744) to vol. III, no. 60 (13 Apr. 1745), lacking three issues.

British Museum: vol. II, no. 44 (8 Sep 1744).

16. F. Farley's Bristol Journal. [From 16 Jan 1748 con. as]:
S. Farley's Bristol Journal. [From 30 Jan 1748 con. as]:
Farley's Bristol Journal. [From 26 Mar 1748 con. as]:
The Bristol Journal.

[No. 1 (3 Dec ? 1743)]—no. 17 (24 Mar 1744)—no.
2167 (20 Nov 1756)—end of 1760, + . Not published
28 Sep 1745, nor from 19 Apr to 24 May 1746.

Sat; fortnightly to 29 Mar 1746, from 7 Jun to 16 Aug
1746, and for a time early in 1748; weekly from 12 Apr
1746 to 24 May 1746, from 30 Aug 1746 to 26 Dec
1747, and from 30 Jan 1748.

Bristol: Printed by Felix Farley, at Shakespeare's-Head
in Castle-Green. [From 12 Aug 1749]: Printed by Samuel
and Felix Farley, at Shakespeare's Head in Castle
Green. [From 4 Sep 1746]: Printed by S. [i.e., Sarah]
Farley, in Castle-Green.

Probably con. from *Farley's Bristol Journal* (item 11 in
this Register). Serial numbering sometimes alternates
with that of *Farleys Bristol Advertiser*, sometimes is
independent of it.

This letter by Sarah Farley, dated at Bristol on 22 Dec
1753, is in the *Bath Journal*, vol. X, no. 52 (24 Dec
1753):

> Whereas it hath been industriously spread about
> this City, &c. on the Demise of Samuel Farley,
> Printer, in Castle-Green, that his Paper (upwards
> of Thirty Years Standing, always held in Esteem
> for the Accuracy and Adaption of its News) would
> be dropt, with his other Business; This is therefore
> to inform the Friends and Customers of the late
> Samuel Farley, that his said Business, in all its
> Branches, will be carried on by his Neice, with a
> proper Manager and Assistants, who have conducted
> the same, during the long Time of her Uncle's
> Illness. . . .

Certainly Felix Farley was the proprietor of *F. Farley's Bristol Journal*, as is clear not only from the title of the paper but from the fact that in number 1590 (21 Nov 1747) he signed his name to a notice as "the Proprietor of this Paper"; but the paper here listed must not be confused with *Felix Farley's Bristol Journal* (item 22 in this Register).

Bristol Reference Library: no. 17 (24 Mar 1744), def.; nos. 19 (21 Apr 1744) to 34 (25 Aug 1744); no. 38 (22 Sep 1744); nos. 42 (20 Oct 1744) to 46 (17 Nov 1744); no. 50 (15 Dec 1744); no. 64 (23 Mar 1745); no. 68 (20 Apr 1745); nos. 71 (18 May 1745) to 130 (10 Jan 1747); nos. 132 (24 Jan 1747) to 146 (25 Apr 1747); nos. 1561 [*sic*] (2 May 1747) to [1615] (14 May 1748), lacking ten issues; no. [1638] (22 Oct 1748); nos. 1649 (7 Jan 1749) to 1682 (6 Jan 1750), nineteen issues only; nos. [1684] (20 Jan 1750) to 1703 (9 Jun 1750), lacking seven issues; no. 1722 (27 Oct 1750); no. 1723 (3 Nov 1750); no. 1774 (26 Oct 1751); no. 2085 (19 Apr 1755); no. 2142 (29 May 1756); no. 2167 (20 Nov 1756); no. 2439 (3 Apr 1762), + .

Oxford University Press Ephemeral Collection: no. 88 (23 Nov 1745).

British Museum: no. 2156 (4 Sep 1756).

17.   Farleys Bristol Advertiser.

[No. 2 (10 Dec ? 1743)]—no. 18 (31 Mar 1744)—no. 111 (23 Aug 1746); no issue published between no. 97 (5 Apr 1746) and no. 100 (31 May 1746); after no. 111, con. as *F. Farley's Bristol Advertiser*, last two issues numbered 1597 (9 Jan 1748) and 1599 (23 Jan 1748).

Sat (fortnightly), alternating with *F. Farley's Bristol Journal* (item 16 in this Register) from beginning to 23 Aug 1746 and again for two issues, 9 and 23 Jan 1748.

Bristol: Printed by Felix Farley, and Comp. at Shakespeare's-Head in Castle-Green.

Probably con. from *Farley's Bristol Journal* (see item 11 in this Register).

Bristol Reference Library: nos. 18 (31 Mar 1744) to 51 (22 Dec 1744), lacking three issues; no. 59 (16 Feb 1745); no. 65 (30 Mar 1745); nos. 70 (11 May 1745) to 82 (14 Sep 1745); nos. 84 (5 Oct 1745) to 97 (5 Apr 1746); no. 100 (31 May 1746); nos. 104 (28 Jun 1746) to 111 (23 Aug 1746); no. 1597 (9 Jan 1748); no. 1599 (23 Jan 1748).

18.   The Bristol Oracle.

Vol. I, no. 1 (20 Apr 1745)—vol. III, no. 65 (16 Sep 1749).

Alternate Sat.

Printed by A. Hooke, at his Printing Office in Shannon-Court, Corn-street, . . . [From 17 Sep 1748]: Printed for Andrew Hooke in Bristol.

This newspaper and the *Country Advertiser* (item 19 in this Register) were essentially the same paper, published alternately and differing only in title and in having separate serial numbering. These two papers succeeded a similar pair, the *Bristol Oracle, and County Intelligencer* (item 14 in this Register) and the *Bristol Oracle, and Country Advertiser* (item 15 in this Register), likewise published on alternate Saturdays. It is presumably the end of the *Bristol Oracle* (together with the *Country Advertiser*) that is referred to in Edward Ward's *Bristol Weekly Intelligencer*, no. 1 (23 Sep 1749): "As a Fellow Citizen . . . has thought fit to decline the Publication of his Journal, and only one Publick News-Paper appears now to be exhibited. . . ."

Bristol Reference Library: vol. I, nos. 1 (20 Apr 1745) to 52 (21 Mar 1747), lacking three issues; vol. III [*sic*], nos. 2 (18 Apr 1747) to 18 (28 Nov 1747), lacking three issues; nos. 22 (23 Jan 1748) to 41 (15 Oct 1748), lacking six issues; no. 50 (18 Feb 1749); nos. 53 (1 Apr 1749) to 65 (16 Sep 1749), lacking one issue.

Press Club: vol. III, no. 7 (27 Jun 1747).

19. The Country Advertiser. [From 25 May 1745 con. as]: The Oracle Country Advertiser.

Vol. I, no. 1 (27 Apr 1745)—vol. III, no. 64 (9 Sep 1749).

Alternate Sat.

Printed by M. Nayler, in Bristol, . . . [From 13 Aug 1748]: Printed for Andrew Hooke, in Bristol.

See note attached to item 18 in this Register.

Bristol Reference Library: vol. I, nos. 1 (27 Apr 1745) to 51 (28 Mar 1747), lacking eight issues; vol. III [sic; II not used], nos. 1 (11 Apr 1747) to 39 (24 Sep 1747), lacking nine issues; nos. 50 (25 Feb 1749) to 64 (9 Sep 1749), lacking one issue.

20. The Bristol Mercury.

[By Apr 1746]—no. 24 (20 Oct 1748)—[Sep 1749?].

Thu; from 29 Oct 1748, Sat; 2 pp.

Printed by Edward Ward, in Castle-street, by whom all Manner of Printing is done reasonable . . . .

In *Farleys Bristol Advertiser,* no. 97 (5 Apr 1746), is this statement:

> Our Readers will observe that in this Paper they have generally on a Saturday News a Post sooner than can be found in either of the other Papers.

The implication seems to be that in addition to the *Bristol Oracle* and the *Oracle Country Advertiser,* published on alternate Saturdays and essentially one paper with alternating title, there was at that time another weekly newspaper in Bristol. There is in F. A. Hyett and William Bazeley, *The Bibliographer's Manual of Gloucestershire Literature* (Gloucester: Bellows, 1897), III, 280, a reference to a *Bristol Mercury* printed by Edward Ward from 1747 to 1749; and in *F. Farley's Bristol*

Journal, no. 1584 (10 Oct 1747), it is claimed that "Only *Two* of our People sell as many as are *printed* of the *Mercury* . . . ." The *Bristol Mercury* doubtless came to an end before Ward started his *Bristol Weekly Intelligencer* (item 21 in this Register) on 23 Sep 1749.

Bristol Reference Library: no. 24 (20 Oct 1748).

21. The Bristol Weekly Intelligencer.

No. 1 (23 Sep 1749)—no. 487 (3 Feb 1759)—?

Sat.

Printed by E. Ward, in Castle-street. . . . [From 24 Mar 1750]: Printed by E. Ward, in Broad-street. . . . [From 27 Jun 1752]: Printed by E. Ward, just Removed from Broad-street, to the Shop late Mr. Croft's, at the King's-Arms, on the Tolzey. . . . [From 3 Feb. 1759]: Printed by Edward Ward, opposite the Post Office. . . .

Bristol Reference Library: nos. 1 (23 Sep 1749) to 92 (29 Jun 1751), lacking five issues; nos. 96 (27 Jul 1751) to 169 (30 Dec 1752), lacking six issues; no. 177 (24 Feb 1753); no. 223 (12 Jan 1754), def.; no. 241 (18 May 1754); no. 275 (11 Jan 1755); no. 285 (22 Mar 1755); no. 296 (7 Jun 1755); no. 298 (21 Jun 1755); no. 311 (20 Sep 1755); no. 325 (27 Dec 1755); no. 346 (22 May 1756); no. 372 (20 Nov 1756); nos. 378 (1 Jan 1757) to 429 (24 Dec 1757), twenty-four issues only; nos. 434 (28 Jan 1758) to 449 (13 May 1758), nine issues only; no. 462 (12 Aug 1758), def.; no. 487 (3 Feb 1759).

Bodleian Library: nos. 27 (24 Mar 1750) to 52 (22 Sep 1750), lacking two issues; no. 57 (27 Oct 1750); no. 60 (17 Nov 1750); no. 61 (24 Nov 1750); no. 63 (8 Dec 1750); no. 66 (29 Dec 1750).

22. Felix Farley's Bristol Journal.

Vol. I [serial numbers were not used in this paper until the year 1774], issue dated 2 May 1752—vol. IX, issue dated 27 Dec 1760, +.

Sat.

Publish'd at his Printing-Office at Shakespeare's-Head in Small-Street, every Saturday Morning. [From 29 Aug 1752]; Publish'd at his Printing-Office at Shakespeare's-Head in Small-Street [removed from Castle-Green]. [From 5 May 1753]: Publish'd at the Printing-Office. . . .

In Edward Ward's *Bristol Weekly Intelligencer,* no. 131 (28 Mar 1752), is a notice addressed "To the Publick":

> Whereas Felix Farley, from discontinuing the Partnership with his Brother Samuel, is about to publish a New Paper in Opposition to the old Bristol Journal; as their Interest must be divided, it may be modestly presum'd, that each Paper will by these Means become less popular. . . .

In *Felix Farley's Bristol Journal,* dated 5 May 1753, is this announcement:

To the Publick:

> Whereas it hath pleased God to take to Himself the late Proprietor of this Journal: This is to give Notice, That the Same, with Printing in all its Branches, is continued, and carried on by his Widow and Son, at the Printing-Office in Small-Street . . . .

Bristol Reference Library: vol. I, issue dated 2 May 1752, to vol. IX, issue dated 27 Dec 1760, + .

Bath Municipal Library: vol. IX, issue dated 12 Jul 1760.

23. The Bristol Chronicle, Or, Universal Mercantile Register.

Vol. I, no. 1 (5 Jan 1760)—no. 52 (27 Dec 1760), + .

Sat; 8 pp. 2 cols.

Printed by John Grabham, in Narrow-Wine-Street, . . . [From 29 Mar 1760]: Printed by John Grabham and William Pine, in Narrow-Wine-Street.

Bristol Reference Library: vol. I, nos. 1 (5 Jan 1760) to 52 (27 Dec 1760), + .

BURY ST. EDMUNDS

24. The Suffolk Mercury: or, St. Edmund's-Bury Post. Being an Impartial Collection of the most Material Occurrences, Foreign and Domestick. Together with An Account of Trade. [By 20 Feb 1727 con. as]: The Suffolk Mercury: or, St. Edmund's Bury Post. Being An Impartial Collection of the most Material Occurrences, &c. [By 9 Apr 1733 con. as]: Suffolk Mercury: Or, Bury Post. [From 1742 to 1752 perhaps entitled]: Bury Journal.

[Vol. I, no. 1 (15 Apr ? 1717]—vol. [II], no. 43 (3 Feb 1718)—vol. XXVI, no. 26 (30 Jun 1740)—vol. [?], no. [?] (29 Jul 1752)—?

Mon; by 29 Jul 1752, perhaps Wed.; from 1725, 8 pp.; by 10 Aug 1730, 4 pp.; single col.; by 18 Mar 1723, 2 cols.; by 10 Aug 1730, 3 cols.

St. Edmund's-Bury: Printed by W. Thompson, and T. Baily, next Door to the Griffin, near the Market-Cross. [From 9 Jul 1722]: St. Edmund's-Bury: Printed by T. Baily and W. Thompson, in the Long-Breakland, near the Rose, . . . [From May 1723]: St. Edmund's-Bury: Printed by T. Baily and W. Thompson, at the Bible in the Long-Breakland, . . . [From 1725]: St. Edmund's-Bury: Printed by T. Baily and W. Thompson, in the Butter Market. [By 9 Apr 1733]: Bury St. Edmunds, Printed by T. Baily in the Butter-Market, . . .

The *Bury Post* is quoted in the *Ipswich Journal* of 16 Jan 1742; the title page of the *Gentleman's Magazine* lists a "Bury Journal" to the end of December, 1742; and the *Ipswich Journal* of 1 Aug 1752 quotes "From the Bury Journal" a local item of news dated "Bury St. Edmund's, July 29, 1752."

Bury St. Edmunds Public Library: vol. VI, no. 2 (11 Jan 1720) to vol. X, no. 17 (21 Oct 1723), inc.; vol. XVI, no. 3 (17 May 1725) to vol. XIX, no. 3 (3 Feb

1729), inc.; vol. XXIV, no. 67 (9 Apr 1733) to vol XXV, no. 38 (16 Apr 1739), inc.

Suffolk Institute of Archaeology, Bury St. Edmunds: no. 43 (3 Feb 1718), def.; vol. XVI, no. 52 (2 May 1726); another issue, perhaps dated 16 May 1726, pp. 3-6 only; vol. XXI, no. 32 (10 Aug 1730); vol. XXII, no. 40 (4 Oct 1731); vol. XXVI, no. 26 (30 Jun 1740.)

Press Club: vol. IV, nos. 12 (23 Mar 1719) and 13 (30 Mar 1719).

Yale University Library: vol. XVI, no. 28 (8 Nov 1725) to vol. XVIII, no. 14 (24 Apr 1727).

Private Library of R. M. Wiles, Hamilton, Canada: vol. XIX, no. 9 (17 Mar 1729).

CAMBRIDGE

25. The Cambridge Journal, and Weekly Flying Post. [From 14 Jul 1753 con. as]: The Cambridge Journal.

[Vol. I, no. 1 (22 Sep ? 1744]—vol. I, no. 26 (16 Mar 1745)—vol. XVI, no. 835 (27 Sep 1760)—end of 1760, + .

Sat; Fri, for a short time in Jun 1749.

Cambridge: Printed by R. Walker and T. James, next the Theatre Coffee-House, . . . [From 17 Nov 1750]: Cambridge: Printed by T. James, next the Theatre Coffee-House, . . . [From 4 Nov 1758]: Cambridge: Printed by S. James. [From 3 Mar 1759]: Cambridge: Printed by S. and J. James.

Issues in 1758 have under dateline: ". . . This Journal is dispers'd with the greatest Expedition through the following Countries, viz. Cambridgeshire, Huntingdon-shire, Bedfordshire, Hertfordshire; Northamptonshire,

Lincolnshire, Leicestershire, Rutlandshire, Nottingham-shire, Derbyshire, and some parts of Norfolk, Suffolk, and Essex."

Cambridge University Library: vol. I, no. 26 (16 Mar 1745) to vol. XI, no. 535 (28 Dec 1754), inc.; many duplicates.

British Museum: vol. II, no. 68 (4 Jan 1746) to vol. III, no. 114 (22 Nov 1746), inc.; vol. VII, no. 341 (30 Mar 1751) to vol. XVI, no. 835 (27 Sep 1760), inc.

Yale University Library: vol XIII, no. 637 (11 Dec 1756).

CANTERBURY

26. The Kentish Post: or the Canterbury News-Letter, Containing A Historical and Political Account of the most Remarkable Occurrences Foreign and Domestick. Together with the London Bill of Mortality. [From 24 Jun 1721 con. as]: The Kentish Post: or Canterbury News Letter. [From 15 Feb 1729 to 23 Dec 1730 entitled]: The Kentish Post, or the Canterbury News-Letter.

[No. 1 (16 Oct 1717)]—no. 4503 (31 Dec 1760), + .

Wed; by 24 Jun 1721, Wed and Sat; 12 pp.; from 1725, 4 pp.; single col.; from 1725, 2 cols.

Canterbury: Printed by Thomas Reeve, in Castle street, for the Proprietors, 1717. [From 5 Jan 1726]: Canterbury, Printed and Sold by J. Abree in St. Margaret's. [From 21 Jun 1727]: Canterbury, Printed and Sold by J. Abree and William Aylett in St. Margaret's. [From 20 Jun 1732]: Canterbury, Printed by J. Abree and A. Aylett, . . . [By 7 Dec 1737]: Canterbury: Printed and Sold by J. Abree in St. Margaret's. . . .

Public Library, Canterbury: no. 346 (24 Jun 1721); no. 530 (23 Mar 1723); no. 785 (1 Dec 1725); nos. 846 (2 Jul 1726) to 1371 (21 Jul 1731), inc.; no. 1650 (27 Apr 1734); no. 2095 (7 Dec 1737); nos. 2337 (2 Apr 1740) to 2937 (27 Nov 1745), inc.; no. 3097 (15 Jul 1747); no. 3528 (31 Aug 1751); nos. 3745 (10 Oct 1753) to 4023 (9 Jun 1756), inc.; no. 4102 (12 Mar 1757); no. 4277 (8 Nov 1758); no. 4331 (16 May 1759); no. 4376 (13 Oct 1759); no. 4469 (3 Sep 1760); no. 4494 (29 Nov 1760).

British Museum: no. 1 (16 Oct 1717), ink drawing of title page (mutilated); nos. 795 (5 Jan 1726) to 898 (31 Dec 1726); no. 910 (11 Feb 1727); nos. 1003 (3 Jan 1728) to 1616 (29 Dec 1733), lacking nine issues; nos. 1891 (24 Dec 1735) to 2728 (31 Dec 1743); no. 2789 (1 Aug 1744); nos. 2833 (2 Jan 1745) to 4503 (31 Dec 1760), + .

Press Club: no. 2427 (11 Feb 1741); no. 4059 (13 Oct 1756).

Oxford University Press Ephemeral Collection: no. 244 (12 May 1739).

Duke University Library, Durham, North Carolina: nos. 3251 (4 Jan 1749) to 3354 (30 Dec 1749); nos. 3665 (3 Jan 1753) to 3977 (31 Dec 1755); nos. 4082 (1 Jan 1757) to 4186 (31 Dec 1757); nos. 4293 (3 Jan 1759) to 4503 (31 Dec 1760), all very nearly complete.

Private library of R. M. Wiles, Hamilton, Canada: no. 2998 (2 Aug 1746).

CHESTER

27. The Chester Weekly Journal; Being a Collection of the Most Material News Both Forreign and Domestick. [From 10 Nov 1731 con. as]: The Chester Weekly Jour-

nal: With the most material Advices both Foreign and Domestick. [From 10 May 1732 con. as]: The Chester Weekly-Journal. With the freshest Advices both Foreign and Domestick.

[No. 1 (11 May ? 1721)]—no. 105 (9 May 1723)—vol. XXXVI, no. 8 (18 Jul 1733)—?

Thu; by 10 Nov 1731, Wed; 12 pp.; by 10 Nov 1731, 4 pp.; 2 cols.; by 10 Nov 1731, 3 cols.

[By 9 May 1723]: Chester: Printed by and for Wm. Cooke, and for H. Anyon, J. Munks and are to be Sold at their Houses in Liverpool. [By 21 May 1724]: Chester: Printed by Wm. Cooke, ...

Early issues have above imprint: Licens'd and Entr'd in the Stamp-Office. Vol. XXIX, no. 6 (24 Nov 1731), and issues from 12 Jul 1732 have this note under the date line:

> This establish'd Paper is carry'd through Nine Counties, and some Thousands are Sold Weekly; so People may consider the Advantage of Advertising in it.

Chester Public Library: no. 159 (21 May 1724); no. 167 (16 Jul 1724); nos. 202 (18 Mar 1725) to 204 (1 Apr 1725); vol. XXXVI, no. 8 (18 Jul 1733).

University College of South Wales and Monmouthshire Library: vol. XXIX, no. 4 (10 Nov 1731), to vol. XXXIII, no. 1 (20 Sep 1732).

Bodleian Library: vol. XXX, no. 4 (2 Feb 1732); vol. XXXVI, no. 1 (30 May 1733) and no. 5 (27 Jun 1733).

New York Public Library: no. 105 (9 May 1723), def.

28. Adams's Weekly Courant. With News both Foreign and Domestick.

[No. 1 (29 Nov ? 1732)]—no. 51 (14 Nov 1733)—no. 1263 (30 Dec 1760), + .

Wed; by Oct 1746, Tue.

Chester: Printed by Roger Adams . . . . [By 9 Jun 1742]: Chester: Printed by Elizabeth Adams . . . . [From 9 Dec 1746]: Chester: Printed by Eliz. Adams, by whom Advertisements are taken in; also taken in by Mr. Durston, Bookseller in Shrewsbury, where this News-Paper may constantly be had every Week. This Paper likewise may be had every Tuesday, at Mr. Ansdale's, Bookseller in Liverpoole; and every Wednesday, at Mrs. Jackson's, in the Old Coffee-House Entry, Manchester. . . .

Many articles from this newspaper were reprinted in *The Chester Miscellany. Being a Collection Of several Pieces, both in Prose and Verse, Which were in the Chester Courant From January 1741, to May 1750* (Chester: Elizabeth Adams, 1750), and in *Manchester Vindicated: being a compleat collection of the papers Lately published in defence of that town, in the CHESTER COURANT, Together with All those on the other Side of the Question, Printed in the MANCHESTER MAGAZINE or elsewhere, which are answered in the said CHESTER COURANT* (Chester: Eliz. Adams, 1749).

Chester Public Library: no. 51 (14 Nov 1733), fac.; no. 167 (4 Feb 1736); no. 168 (11 Feb 1736); no. 477 (9 Jun 1742); no. 756 (22 Dec 1747); no. 818 (27 Dec 1748); nos. 822 (24 Jan 1749) to 847 (4 Jul 1749), five issues only; nos. 964 (1 Oct 1751) to 1099 (14 May 1754), lacking many issues.

Office of the *Chester Courant:* no. 724 (10 Mar 1747); no. 759 (10 Nov 1747); no. 763 (22 Dec 1747); no. 766 (5 Jan 1748); nos. 861 (10 Nov 1749) to 1076 (2 Oct 1753); nos. 1145 (1 Apr 1755) to 1172 (14 Oct 1755); nos. 1263 (5 Jul 1757) to 1160 [*sic*] (26 Dec 1758); nos. 1211 (1 Jan 1760) to 1263 (30 Dec 1760), + .

Manchester Reference Library: no. 51 (14 Nov 1733), fac.; no. 279 (29 Mar 1738); no. 295 (19 Jul 1738); no. 711 (9 Dec 1746); no. 714 (30 Dec 1746); nos. 722 (24

Feb 1747) to 766 (5 Jan 1748), thirteen issues only; no.
775 (1 Mar 1748); no. 785 (10 May 1748); nos. 872 (26
Dec 1749) to 929 (29 Jan 1751), lacking seven issues;
nos. 931 (12 Feb 1751) to 980 (21 Jan 1752), lacking
eleven issues, with some duplicates; no. 987 (10 Mar
1752); no. 1008 (4 Aug 1752); nos. 1019 (31 Oct 1752)
to 1027 (26 Dec 1752), lacking two issues.

The Vicarage, Mottram in Longdendale, Cheshire: no.
143 (20 Aug 1735); no. 151 (15 Oct 1735); no. 158 (3
Dec 1735).

William Salt Library, Stafford: no. 431 (8 Jul 1741);
no. 910 (18 Sep 1750); no. 1009 (11 Aug 1752); no. 1014
(19 Sep 1752); no. 1080 (5 Feb 1754); nos. 1109 (16
Jul 1754) to 1160 (8 Jul 1755), seven issues only.

York Minster Library; nos. 297 (2 Aug 1738) to 299 (16
Aug 1738); no. 307 (11 Oct 1738); no. 312 (15 Nov
1738); no. 318 (27 Dec 1738); no. 321 (17 Jan 1739).

Bodleian Library: no. 994 (28 Apr 1752).

British Museum: nos. 322 (24 Jan 1739) to [339] (23
May 1739), seven issues only; nos. 724 (10 Mar 1747) to
814 (29 Nov 1748), sixteen issues only.

Press Club: no. 2340 [i.e. 240] (29 Jun 1737); no. 814
(29 Nov 1748).

New York Public Library: no. 728 (7 Apr 1747).

Yale University Library: no. 51 (14 Nov 1733), fac.

29. The Industrious Bee, or Weekly Entertainer. Containing
Something to hit every Man's Taste and Principles Being
more in Quantity than any Thing of the Kind Published
at the Price.

[No. 1 (1 Aug ? 1733)]—[no. 23 (9 Jan 1734)]—?

Wed.

Colophon not recorded.

For details, see Chapter III, page 108.

No copy found.

30. The Chester Weekly Tatler. Containing the Freshest Advices foreign and Domestick, with a New Voyage round the world.

[No. 1 (28 Aug ? 1734)]—[no. 4 (18 Sep 1734)]—?

Wed.

Colophon not recorded.

Evidence that at least four issues of this paper appeared in August and September, 1734, is to be found in a sworn statement dated 15 February 1734 (i.e., 1735) now in the Public Record Office [K. B. 11/32/4] recording the conviction of William Cooke for having published number 4 (18 Sep 1734) of the paper, unstamped, the informer being John Adams. Cooke had to pay the £40 fine to the Crown and twenty shillings in costs to Adams. See above, page 109.

No copy found.

CIRENCESTER

31. Cirencester-Post: or, Gloucestershire Mercury. Being an Impartial Collection of the most Material Occurrences, Foreign and Domestick. Together with an Account of Trade.

[No. 1 (17 Nov ? 1718)]—no. 18 (16 Mar 1719)—vol. VI, no. 5 (9 Dec 1723)—?

Mon; 12 pp.; single col.

Cirencester: Printed and sold by Thomas Hinton, in Pye Corner, . . .

Bingham Public Library, Cirencester: vol. II, no. 23 (18 Apr 1720) and the last four pages of other issues, including pp. 56-59 of vol. VI, no. 5 (9 Dec 1723).

British Museum: nos. 18 (16 Mar 1719) to 29 (1 Jun 1719); vol. II, no. 37 (25 Jul 1720).

32. The Cirencester Flying-Post, and Weekly Miscellany. [From 24 Oct 1743 con. as]: The Cirencester Flying-Post.

[No. 1 (15 Dec ? 1740)]—no. 42 (5 Oct 1741)—no. 313 (15 Dec 1746)—1750?

Mon.

Cirencester: Printed by G. Hill and Comp. [From 22 Mar 1742]: Cirencester: Printed by Tho. [later, Thomas] Hill and Comp. . . .

In the *Gloucester Journal,* no. 1321 (1 Sep 1747), a letter dated at North Cerney on 29 Aug 1747 refers to a piece "inserted in . . . the last *Cirencester Journal.*" In the *Stratford, Shipston, and Aulcester Journal,* no. 1 (5 Feb 1750), is a statement that that paper was "now Substituted in the Room of the OXFORD and CIRENCESTER FLYING POSTS . . . ."

Bingham Public Library, Cirencester: nos. 42 (5 Oct 1741) to 164 (6 Feb 1744).

Gloucester Public Library: no. 152 (5 Sep 1743); no. 172 (2 Apr 1744); nos. 180 (28 May 1744) to 251 (7 Oct 1745); nos. 253 (21 Oct 1745) to 313 (15 Dec 1746).

COLCHESTER

33. The Essex Mercury: Or, Colchester Weekly Journal. [By 3 Feb 1739 con. as]: Pilborough's Colchester Journal: Or, The Essex Mercury containing, The most remarkable Occurrences, Foreign and Domestick. [By 3 Mar 1739 con. as]: Pilborough's Colchester Journal Or, Essex

Weekly Mercury. [By 11 Aug 1739 con. as]: The Colchester Journal: Or, Essex Advertiser.

[No. 1 (17 Mar ? 1733)]—no. 151 (31 Jan 1736)—no. 340 (29 Sep 1739)—1751—?

Sat.

Colchester: Printed by J. Pilborough, over-against St. Nicholas Church . . . . [By 3 Feb 1739]: Colchester: Printed by J. Pilborough, over-against the Three Cups Inn. . . . [By 20 Apr 1739]: Colchester: Printed by J. Pilborough, at the Printing-Press over-against the Three Cups. 1739.

Passages from "the Colchester Journal" were quoted in the *Ipswich Journal* until late in 1746; and Dr. Cranfield has drawn attention to a reference to the "Colchester news printer" in the *Norwich Mercury* dated 12 January 1751.

Colchester Public Library: nos. [306] (3 Feb. [1739]) to 326 (23 Jun 1739), lacking four issues; nos. 333 (11 Aug 1739) to 336 (1 Sep 1739); nos. 338 (15 Sep 1739) to 340 (29 Sep 1739).

British Museum: no. 151 (31 Jan 1736); no. 173 (3 Jul 1736).

COVENTRY

34. Jopson's Coventry Mercury, or the Weekly Country Journal. [From 21 Feb 1743 con. as]: Jopson's Coventry and Northampton Mercury, or the Weekly Country Journal. [From 4 Jul 1743 con. as]: Jopson's Coventry Mercury, or the Weekly Country Journal.

[No. 1 (20 Jul 1741)]—no. 343 (14 Dec 1747)—no. 1017 (29 Dec 1760), + .

Mon.

Coventry: Printed by J. Jopson, in Hay Lane, where letters and advices (post paid) are taken in; also by the men who sell this paper, who constantly travel the following counties, viz. Warwickshire, Staffordshire, Derbyshire, Nottinghamshire, Leicestershire, Oxfordshire, Buckinghamshire, and Bedfordshire. . . . [From 28 Feb 1743]: Northampton: Printed by J. Jopson, in Gold Street. [From 11 Apr 1743]: Coventry: Printed by J. Jopson, over against the Black Bull Inn, in High-street. [By 14 Dec 1757]: Coventry: Printed by J. Jopson, and sold at his Shop, next Door to the White Bear Inn, in High-Street. . . . [From 12 Mar 1759]: Coventry: Printed by E. Jopson, in the High-street. . . .

Information about early titles and imprints is taken from Benjamin Poole, *Coventry: Its History and Antiquities* (London: Smith, 1870), pp. 393-94.

Coventry City Libraries: no. 343 (14 Dec 1747); no. 355 (7 Mar 1748); no. 390 (7 Nov 1748); no. 541 (4 Nov 1751), def.; no. 717 (5 May 1755); no. 728 (21 Jul 1755); nos. 914 (8 Jan 1759) to 1017 (29 Dec 1760), inc., + .

Bodleian Library: nos. 881 (22 May 1758) to 888 (10 Jul 1758); no. 909 (4 Dec 1758); nos. 912 (25 Dec 1758) to 916 (22 Jan 1759); nos. 921 (26 Feb 1759) to 929 (23 Apr 1759).

British Museum: no. 670 (10 Jun 1754), def.

35. Luckman and Sketchley's Coventry Gazette: or, the Weekly Country Magazine. [By 17 Sep 1761 con.

as]: Luckman and Sketchley's Coventry Gazette, and Birmingham Chronicle.

[No. 1 (31 Mar ? 1757)]—vol. V, no. 234 (17 Sep 1761)—?

Thu.

Printed by and for the Publishers, T. Luckman, Printer and Bookseller, near the Cross, Coventry, and J. Sketchley, at the Universal Register-Office in High-street, Birmingham . . . . [Under title]: Published every Thursday Morning by T. Luckman, in Coventry, and J. Sketchley, in Birmingham; and dispersed from thence, with the greatest Expedition, thro' Warwick-shire, Leicestershire, Derbyshire, Staffordshire, Shrop-shire, Worcestershire and Northamptonshire.

Advertisements from current issues of *Luckman and Sketchley's Coventry Gazette* are reprinted in the *Public Ledger* (London) from March, 1760, onward.

Birmingham Public Library: vol. V, no. 234 (17 Sep 1761).

DERBY

36. The Derby Post-Man, Or A Collection of the most material Occurrences, Foreign and Domestick; Together with An Account of Trade. To be continued Weekly.

[No. 1 (1 Dec ? 1720)]—no. 8 (19 Jan 1721)—no. 25 (18 May 1721)—?

Thu; 12 pp.; single col.

Derby: Printed by S. Hodgkinson near St. Warburg's Church; . . . [By 18 May 1721]: Derby: Printed and Sold by S. Hodgkinson at the Printing-Office near St.

Warburg's Church; and by Hen. Alestree, Bookseller in Derby, Wm. Holt in Wirksworth; and may be had at Burton, Litchfield, [at Shenston by Thomas Barfoot] Sutton, Birmingham, by Thomas Hide, and at Ashbourn, Uttoxetur [*sic*], Stafford and Stone by Thomas Hauworth, and will be left for any Gentlemen (by the Men who will come every Week to the above said places) at ls. 6d. the Quarter; at all which Places Advertisements are taken in at 2s. each. [Price Three-Half-Pence].

Derby Borough Library: no. 8 (19 Jan 1721); no. 10 (2 Feb 1721); no. 25 (18 May 1721).

37.   The British Spy: Or, Derby Post-Man.

No. 1 (6 Apr 1727)—no. 203 (22 Apr 1731)—?

Thu; 4 pp., except nos. 16 (27 Jul 1727) to 20 (24 Aug 1727), which have 8 pp.; 2 cols. to 24 Aug 1727; from 14 Sep 1727 to 12 Dec 1728, 3 cols.; from 2 Jan 1729, 2 cols.

Derby: Printed by S. Hodgkinson, in the Sadlergate, . . . 1727. [By 18 Jul 1728]: Derby: Printed and sold by S. Hodgkinson; and are likewise to be had of H. Allestree, Bookseller at the Market-Head; Jer. Roe, at the upper End of the Sadlergate, in Derby aforesaid; J. Collyer, Bookseller in Nottingham; . . . Sold also by W. Turner in Burton upon Trent, David Watson in Ashby-de-la-zouch, Richard Smith in Ashburn, William Holt at Wirksworth, and William Walker in Uttoxeter; . . . [By 28 May 1731]: Derby: Printed and sold by S. Hodgkinson in Irongate; . . .

Derby Borough Library: vol. I, no. 1 (6 Apr 1727); no. 9 (1 Jun 1727); nos. 14 (13 Jul 1727) to 42 (21 Mar 1728), thirteen issues only; no. 62 (8 Aug 1728); nos. 70 (3 Oct 1728) to 80 (12 Dec 1728), lacking two issues; no. 87 (30 Jan 1729); vol. II, no. 109 (3 Jul 1729); no. 124 (16 Oct 1729); no. 156 (28 May 1730); vol. III, no. 186 (24 Dec 1730); no. 202 (15 Apr 1731).

Nottingham Central Library: vol. I, no. 11 (15 Jun 1727); nos. 19 (17 Aug 1727) to 98 (17 Apr 1729), twenty-five issues only; vol. II, nos. 103 (22 May 1729) to 159 (18 Jun 1730), seventeen issues only; vol. III, nos. 176 (15 Oct 1730) to 203 (22 Apr 1731), ten issues only.

Newberry Library, Chicago: no. 16 (27 Jul 1727), pp. 3-6 only.

38. The Derby Mercury.

First issue, unnumbered (23 Mar 1732)—vol. I, no. 1 (30 Mar 1732)—vol. XXIX, no. 41 (26 Dec 1760), + .

Thu; from 28 Oct 1743, Fri; 2 cols.; from 12 Jun 1740, 3 cols.

Derby: Printed by Sam Drewry, in the Market-Place; and to be had of Mr. Henry Allestree [misprinted Alleseree], and Mr. Jer. Roe, Booksellers in Derby; also at Burton, Uttoxeter, Ashborne, Ashby-De-La-Zouch, and Wirksworth. [From 17 Aug 1732]: Derby: Printed and Sold by Sam. Drewry, in the Market-Place; also by Mr. Henry Allestree, and Mr. Jer. Roe, Booksellers in Derby; Mr. William Ward, Bookseller in Nottingham; Mr. Richard Smith, in Ashborne; Mr. Benjamin Astle in Burton; Mr. —— [later, William] Walker, in Uttoxeter; Mrs. Elizabeth Unwin, in Ashby-de-la-Zouch; Mr. J. Stanley in Wirksworth; Mr. J. Slater, Bookseller in Chesterfield; and Mr. J. Garnet, at Castlegreen Head in Sheffield. . . . [From 21 Jun 1733]: Derby: Printed and Sold by Sam. Drewry, in the Market-Place; . . .

Derby Borough Library: first issue (23 Mar 1732) to vol. XXIX, no. 41 (26 Dec 1760), + , practically complete.

Yale University Library: vol XII, nos. 1 (17 Mar 1743) to 52 (9 Mar 1744); vol. XVI, nos. 1 (25 Mar 1748) to 52 (17 Mar 1749).

DONCASTER

39. The Doncaster Flying-Post: or, Hull and Sheffield Weekly Advertiser.

[No. 1 (30 Apr ? 1754)]—no. 37 (7 Jan 1715)—Aug, 1755.

Tue.

Doncaster: Printed by R. Homfray and J. Rawson, at their Printing-Office, at the Blue Bell in New-Street. Subscriptions are taken in by the above Persons at their Shops in Sheffield and Hull; Mr. Simmons, Bookseller in Sheffield; Mr. Joseph Health, Bookseller, in Nottingham, and at his Shop in Mansfield, every Market-Day; Mr. William Wilson, Peruke-Maker, in Rotherham; Mr. Thomas B[l]attersby, at Anston, every Tuesday Night, and at Worksop, on Wednesday Morning; Mr. Saunderson, Bookseller in Bawtry; Mr. Saunderson, Bookseller in Pontefract; Mr. William Wingfield, Tallow Chandler, in Bakewell, and at the Boot and Shoe, in Tidswall; Mr. Joseph Smith, Bookseller in Barnesley; Mr. J. Rogers, the Sheffield Carrier at Chesterfield; the Printing-Office above, and the Persons who carry this News. [Under date line]: *⁎* This Paper is distributed in the following Towns, viz. Rotherham, Sheffield, Barnsley, Pontefract, Wakefield, Leeds, Bradford, Otley, Skipton, Halifax, Huthersfield, Thorn, Snaith, Selby, Rawcliff, Howden, Cave, Hull, Beverley, Preston, Hedon, Pattrington, Hornsea, Bridlington, and through all Holderness, Chesterfield, Bakewell, Hope, Castleton, Chapel le Frith, Buxton, Tiddeswall, Mansfield, Bawtry, Nottingham, Newark, Redford in the Clay, Worksop, Blythe, Tickhill, Lincoln, Isle of Haxholm, Gainsborough, Brigg, Caister, Louth, Barton, Barrow, Goxhill, Winterton, Winteringham, &c.

Under the title is this notice: "With this Paper is given Gratis, one half Sheet in Octavo, of a compleat History of the Lives and Exploits of the Most Remarkable High-waymen, Pirates, Street-Robbers, Murderers, &c. To make four Vols."

Dr. Cranfield gives the title as *Sheffield Register & Doncaster Flying Post.*

In August, 1755, this paper was amalgamated with *Lister's Sheffield Weekly Journal* (item 130 in this Register).

Library of Congress: no. 37 (7 Jan 1755).

DURHAM

40. The Durham Courant.

[No. 1 (?1733)]—1740—?

In the lists flanking the title of the *Gentleman's Magazine* between September, 1733, and December, 1740, Durham is named among the provincial towns having newspapers. Proposals dated at Durham on 12 August 1736 for printing by subscription *The Letters of Sir Robert Bowes, of Streatham Castle in the County Palatine of Durham* were printed in the *Gentleman's Magazine,* VI (August 1736), 49, with the information that subscriptions would be taken in "by Mess. Ward and Chandler, at their Shops in London and Scarborough, Mr. Hildyard at York, Mr. Alex. Symers at Edinborough, by the Booksellers of Newcastle; by Mrs. Waghorn Mr. Aisly, and I. Ross at Durham, and by the Carriers of the Durham Courant, in their several Roads." In John Sykes, *Local Records; or Historical Register of Remarkable Events . . . in Northumberland and Durham . . . ,* (2 vols.; Newcastle: Sykes, 1833), I, 152, is this statement: "It evidently appears that there was a 'Durham Courant' in existence at this time [1735], and perhaps in 1736 and 1737. Mr. Matthew Thompson, of Durham, upholsterer, . . . has an old book with extracts of various newspapers pasted in it, some of which prove this fact, by articles addressed to the Durham Courant. The publisher was Patrick Sanderson, bookseller, . . . " It cannot be doubted, therefore, that there was a paper bearing the title *Durham Courant*. The printer may have been J. Ross (the I. Ross named in the advertisement quoted above), who printed Dr. Christopher Hunter's *Durham Cathedral, As it was before the Dissolution of the Monastery*, with this imprint: Durham, Printed by J. Ross, for Mrs. Waghorn, 1733. One must recognize the slender possibility that "Durham Courant" was only a special title printed on the copies of John White's *Newcastle Courant* which were intended for readers living in and around Durham, in the same way as *Henry's Reading Journal, or Weekly Review* was, in 1746, also issued with the heading *Henry's Winchester Journal;* but the references given above strongly support the belief that the Durham paper had an independent existence.

No copy found.

ETON

41.   The Eton Journal or Early Intelligencer. [By 27 Jan 1746 con. as]: The Windsor and Eton Journal: containing the Earliest Intelligence both Foreign and Domestick. [By 8 May 1746 con. as]: The Windsor and Eton Journal.

[No. 1 (7 Oct ? 1745)]—[no. 14 (21 Nov 1745)]—no. 106 (19 Mar 1747)—[no. 170 (9 Jun 1748)]—?

Mon and Thu until 8 May 1746; thereafter Thu.

Eton: Printed for J. Pote Bookseller . . . .

A file of this paper, destroyed in the war of 1939-45, is described by the author of an anonymous article, "The Earliest Eton Journal" in *Etoniana,* No. 20 (12 Apr 1916), pp. 315-17. In this article the following note is quoted from the *Windsor and Eton Journal,* no. 61 (8 May 1746):

> This Paper was first published on the breaking out of the Rebellion in the North, and for the more ready Intelligence, published twice a Week: But on the present Situation of Publick Affairs, by the late happy Defeat of the Rebels, it may be sufficient to print a Weekly Journal only.—This News-Paper therefore, for the future, will be publish'd every Thursday morning, on a larger Paper than the former Journal, and be neatly Printed, at the Price of Two-pence each.
>
> As the Paper is now greatly enlarged, the Journal will constantly give a full and regular Account of the Publick Affairs, both Foreign and Domestick, as also the News of the Gazettes, and other Papers, besides many Entertaining Pieces in Poetry and Prose; and the Publick may be assured it will at all Times be our constant Care to give the best Account of the News, and to make this Journal as full and instructive as any published.

Private library of Mr. P. Manley, Windsor: no. 106 (19 Mar 1747).

Private library of R. M. Wiles, Hamilton: no. 106 (19 Mar 1747), photostat copy.

EXETER

42. Sam Farley's Exeter Post-Man: Or Weekly Intelligence, From Holland, France, Spain, Portugal, &c. With General Occurrences both Foreign and Domestick.

[No. 1 (? 1704)]—no. 556 (10 Aug 1711)—23 Sep 1715.

Fri; 2 pp.; 2 cols.

Printed at my House near the New-Inn.

A few days after Sam. Farley gave up his *Exeter Post-Man*, he started a paper of similar title though different in format, the *Salisbury Post Man: or, Packet of Intelligence, from France, Spain, Portugal, &c.* (item 127 in this Register); and it is worth noting that this new paper was issued thrice weekly. Yet one cannot draw the conclusion that *Sam. Farley's Exeter Post-Man* was probably also issued thrice a week, for another paper with exactly similar title, *Sam. Farley's Bristol Post-Man: or, Weekly Intelligence, From Holland, France, Spain, &c With General Occurrences, Foreign and Domestick* (item 9 in this Register), began to appear in 1713 and (according to its title page) was "constantly Publish'd every Saturday Morning." If the serial number of the only surviving issue is correct, and if the paper was issued regularly once a week from the beginning, then *Sam. Farley's Exeter Post-Man* first appeared in December, 1700, and is the earliest regular provincial newspaper; but Dr. Cranfield (in his *Hand-List*, p. 7) cites a statement in the *Boston News-Letter* of 9 April 1705 (quoted in W. G. Bleyer, *Main Currents in the History of American Journalism.* [Boston: Houghton Mifflin, *c.* 1927], p. 48) to the effect that the first Exeter newspaper was established "much about the same time that we began here." The *Boston News-Letter* began to appear in April, 1704. On the strength of this slender piece of contemporary evidence, the later date—1704 rather than 1700—is here accepted. Only the discovery of at least one issue earlier than number 556, or of some other contemporary reference, can settle the question of when the paper really started. *Sam. Farley's Exeter Post-Man* was superseded by the *Exeter Mercury* (item 44 in this Register), as it indicated by this announcement in vol. II, no. 2 (30 Sep 1715), of that paper:

This is to certify all my News-Customers, that I am come to an Agreement with Mr. Bishop, (to save double Charges) That he shall always Print the News; and you shall be as duly served with this as hitherto with Mine; and abstracted from the same Papers as Mine ever was: Not but that I continue on all other Business; and shall Print Advertisements single. If this be acceptable, 'twill be very obliging to

Your Humble Servant,

Sam. Farley.

Oxford University Press Ephemeral Collection: no. 556 (10 Aug 1711).

43. Jos. Bliss's Exeter Post-Boy containing An Impartial Collection of the most Material News both Foreign and Domestick.

[No. 1 (8 Apr ? 1709)]—no. 211 (4 May 1711)—no. 241 (17 Aug 1711)—?

[Tue?] and Fri; 2 pp.; 2 cols.

Exon: Printed by Joseph Bliss, at the Exchange-Coffee-House, in St. Peter's Church-Yard.

Possibly con. as the *Protestant Mercury: or, the Exeter Post-Boy* (item 45 in this Register).

Oxford University Press Ephemeral Collection: no. 241 (17 Aug 1711).

British Museum: no. 211 (4 May 1711).

44. The Exeter Mercury: or, Weekly Intelligence of News: Being A Faithful [by 28 Oct 1715, an Impartial] abstract of all the News Papers of Note. Containing the Material Occurrences Foreign and Domestick: With a Particular Account of what Books and Pamphlets are Publish'd in Great Britain, France, Holland, &c.

No. 1 (24 Sep 1714)—vol. III, no. 553 (23 Jan 1722)—?

Fri; by 28 Oct 1715, Tue and Fri; 6 pp.; 2 cols.

Exon: Printed by Philip Bishop at his Printing-Office in St. Peter's Church-yard, 1714 [etc.]. [By 28 Nov 1718, according to *The Journals of the House of Commons,* XIX, 30, the printer was George Bishop.]

Devon and Exeter Institution: vol. I, nos. 1 (24 Sep 1714) to 52 (16 Sep 1715); vol. II, no. 1 (23 Sep 1715); no. 2 (30 Sep 1715); no. 6 (14 Oct 1715); no. 33 (17 Jan 1716); no. 42 (17 Feb 1716); no. 70 (25 May 1716).

Bodleian Library: vol. II, no. 10 (28 Oct 1715); no. 12 (4 Nov 1715); nos. 18 (25 Nov 1715) to 20 (2 Dec 1715); no. 22 (9 Dec 1715); no. 23 (13 Dec 1715); no. 39 (7 Feb 1716); no. 40 (10 Feb 1716).

British Museum: vol. II, no. 58 (13 Apr 1716); no. 60 (20 Apr 1716), pp. 1-4 only; no. 62 (27 Apr 1716); vol. III, no. 553 (23 Jan 1722), def.

45. The Protestant Mercury: or, the Exeter Post-Boy with News Foreign and Domestick: being the most Remarkable Occurrences, impartially collected, as Occasion offers, from the Evening-Post, Gazette, Votes, Flying-Post, Weekly-Pacquet, Dormer's Letter, Postscript to the Post-Man, &c. So that no other can pretend to have a better Collection. [From 15 Mar 1717 con. as]: The Protestant Mercury: or, the Exeter Post-Boy with News Foreign and Domestick: containing every Friday the Whole Weeks Occurrences, viz. Saturday, Monday, and Thursday-Nights Post.

[No. 1 (27 Sep ? 1715)]—no. 4 (7 Oct 1715)—no. 13 (13 Sep 1717)—[no. [?] (28 Nov 1718), mentioned in *The Journals of the House of Commons* XIX, 30]—?

Tue and Fri; from 8 Jun 1716, Fri; 6 pp.; 2 cols.

Printed by Jos. Bliss, at his New Printing-House near the London-Inn, without East-Gate. [By 15 Mar 1717]: Printed by Jos. Bliss, . . .

While this paper was issued twice weekly, the news in the Tuesday issue was repeated in the Friday issue, which had additional news on the sixth page. From January, 1716, to 29 March 1717, Bliss printed some copies on fine paper at three halfpence and the others on coarse paper at one penny.

Exeter Public Library: no. 13 (13 Sep 1717).

Devon and Exeter Institution: [vol. I], nos. 4 (7 Oct 1715) to 28 [wrongly numbered 24] (30 Dec 1715) lacking all the Tue issues except no. 11 (1 Nov 1715); [vol. II], nos. 2 (6 Jan 1716) to 26 [wrongly numbered 25] (30 Mar 1716), lacking all Tue issues except no. 3 (10 Jan 1716); [vol. III], nos. 2 (6 Apr 1716) to 49 (28 Dec 1716), lacking all the Tue issues; [vol. IV], nos. 1 (4 Jan 1717) to 24 (14 Jun 1717); [vol. V], nos. 1 (21 Jun 1717) to 12 (6 Sep 1717).

Bodleian Library; [vol. I], no. 14 (11 Nov 1715); no. 18 (25 Nov 1715); no. 22 (9 Dec 1715); [vol. II], no. 12 (10 Feb 1716).

New York Public Library: [vol. II], no. 8 (27 Jan 1716), pages 1 to 4.

46. The Post-master; or The Loyal Mercury.

[No. 1 (Mar ? 1717)]—no. 6 (2 Sep 1720)—no. 223 (23 Apr 1725).

Fri; 6 pp.; 2 cols.

Exon, Printed by Andrew Brice, at the Head of the Serge-Market in Southgate-street. [From 17 May 1723]: At Exon, printed by Andrew Brice, at the Sign of the Printing-Press, over-against St. Stephen's Church, in the Highstreet.

Followed by *Brice's Weekly Journal* (item 48 in this Register). Although the serial number of the first surviving issue suggests that the *Post-master* began on 29 July 1720, there are indications that the paper may have started over three years earlier. Dr. Cranfield has noted that in the *Protestant Mercury* of 22 March 1717, Jos. Bliss, the printer, declared his satisfaction at having received "reiterated Assurances" of continuing support from several gentlemen, "notwithstanding that Villain Brice's Opposition." The passage seems to imply that Brice was printing a newspaper at that time. Clearer evidence is to be seen in the record of Brice's being summoned to answer a charge laid against him at the end of the year 1718 (*Journals of the House of Commons, XIX*, 43, 53, 54) for having "falsely represented and printed" the resolutions and proceedings of the House of Commons in the issue of his *Post-master* dated 28 Nov 1718. Furthermore, *Andrew Brice's Old Exeter Journal; or the Weekly Advertiser*, no. 53 (7 Jul 1758), has after its serial number "Or above 2000; this Paper being in the 42d Year of its Age." If the *Post-master, or the Loyal Mercury* had started in March, 1717, it would have completed forty-one years of publication in March, 1758, and would in July of that year be in the forty-second year of its age.

Devon and Exeter Institution: nos. 16 (11 Nov 1720) to 112 (14 Sep 1722); nos. 120 (17 May 1723) to 223 (23 Apr 1725), many issues def.

British Museum: nos. 6 (2 Sep 1720) to 220 (9 Apr 1725), inc.

47. Farley's Exeter Journal.

[No. 1 (24 May ? 1723)]—no. 104 (14 May 1725)— no. 286 (8 Nov 1728)—?

Fri; 2 cols.; by 20 May 1726, 3 cols.

Exon: Printed by S. Farley, over against the Guild-Hall. [By 20 May 1726]: Printed at Exon by Edward Farley, over-against the Guild-hall, . . . [By 18 Nov 1726]: Printed at Exon by E. Farley, at Shakespear's Head, over-against the Guild-Hall, . . . Persons in the Country, by Letter may be constantly supply'd, either by Post or Carrier, with this Paper. [By 18 Oct 1728]: no imprint.

The death of Edward Farley in the Exeter gaol was reported in various newspapers in May, 1729. See above, pp. 283-88.

Devon and Exeter Institution: nos. 104 (14 May 1725) to 107 (4 Jun 1725); nos. 156 (20 May 1726) to 159 (10 Jun 1726); no. 257 (19 Apr 1728).

British Museum: nos. 156 (20 May 1726) to 286 (8 Nov 1728), twelve issues only.

48. Brice's Weekly Journal.

No. 1 (30 Apr 1725)—no. 325 (4 Jun 1731)—?

Fri; 2 cols; from 30 Jul 1725, 3 cols.

At Exon printed by Andrew Brice, over-against St. Stephen's Church, in the High street. 1725. [Later]: Exon: Printed by Andrew Brice, at the Sign of the Printing-Press, in the High-street.

This paper superseded *The Post-master; or The Loyal Mercury* (item 46 in this Register). See also items 49 and 51 in this Register.

Exeter City Library: nos. 218 (20 Jun 1729) to 325 (4 Jun 1731).

Devon and Exeter Institution: no. 1 (30 Apr 1725); no. 2 (7 May 1725); nos. 5 [*sic*] (11 Jun 1725) to 53 (13 May 1726); nos. 1 (17 Jun 1726) to 129 (13 Dec 1728); nos. 193 [*sic*] (20 Dec 1728) to 216 (6 Jun 1729).

British Museum: nos. 1 (30 Apr 1725) to 257 (6 Feb 1730), inc.

49. Brice's Weekly Collection of Intelligence.

[No. 1 (21 May ? 1736)]—no. 134 (8 Dec 1738)—?

Fri.

No imprint.

Exeter City Library: no. 134 (8 Dec 1738).

50. Farley's Exeter Weekly Journal.

[No. 1 (1 May ? 1741)]—no. 33 (11 Dec 1741)—?

Fri.

Printed by Felix Farley, next Door to Kittoe's Coffee-House in St. Peter's Church-Yard.

Yale University Press: no. 33 (11 Dec 1741).

51. Andrew Brice's Old Exeter Journal; or the Weekly Advertiser.

[No. 1 (24 Jan ? 1746)]—no. 326 (17 Apr 1752)—no. 53 [Or above 2000; this Paper being in the 42d Year of its Age] (7 Jul 1758)—?

Fri.

Printed by Andrew Brice, at his Printing-Office in North-gate-street.

Exeter City Library: no. 326 (17 Apr 1752); no. 53 (7 Jul 1758).

Issue entitled the *Old Exeter Journal and Weekly Advertiser* and dated 12 Sep 1755 mentioned by Thomas N. Brushfield (see item 52 in this Register).

52. [A newspaper published by Andrew Brice's nephew Thomas Brice, mentioned in the *Old Exeter Journal and Weekly Advertiser*, dated 12 Sep 1755, according to Thomas N. Brushfield, *The Life and Bibliography of Andrew Brice, Author and Journalist* (privately printed, 1888), pp. 39 f. Andrew Brice's complaint was that his "pushing Nephew—(now again for the third Time—after having been twice forced to give it over) publishes a Paper . . . on unstamped Paper, Price a Halfpenny,

a day or two preceding the stated time of 'Andrew's'
for Publication."]

[No. [?] (12 Sep 1755)]—?

Wed or Thu.

No copy found.

53. [Exeter Flying Post]

?—1760—?

A newspaper bearing this title is listed (with abbreviation E. F. P.) among the papers cited in the *Public
Ledger* (London), number 1 (12 Jan 1760). In the next
issue of the *Public Ledger,* E. P. stands as the symbol
for *Edinburgh Flying Post;* but in the next four issues
E. P. is identified as the *Exeter Flying Post.* No advertisements from an *Exeter Flying Post* are actually cited
in the *Public Ledger* in 1760.

No copy found.

54. The Exeter Chronicle: or, Universal Register.

[No. 1 (15 Sep ? 1760)]—no. 32 (10 Apr 1761)—?

Fri; 8 pp.

[Under title]: Printed by J. Spencer, in Gandy's Lane;
  . . .

Press Club: no. 32 (10 Apr 1761).

GLOUCESTER

55. Gloucester Journal. With the most material Foreign
Advices, And the largest Account of Home News. [From
28 Jan 1723]: Gloucester Journal. With the most Material
News, Foreign and Domestic. [From 6 Apr 1724]:

The Gloucester Journal. With the most Material News Foreign and Domestic [from 7 Jun 1726 to 4 Jul 1727, . . . Domestick]. [From 14 Nov 1727]: The Gloucester Journal. With the most Material Occurrences Foreign and Domestic [from 3 Aug 1736, . . . Domestick]. [From 4 Sep 1739]: The Gloucester Journal. [From 16 Apr 1754]: The Glocester Journal.

No. 1 (9 Apr [1722])—vol. XXXIX, no. 2014 (30 Dec 1760), + .

Mon; from 30 Nov 1725, Tue; 6 pp.; from 3 May 1725, 4 pp.; 2 cols.; from 6 Sep 1725, 3 cols.

Gloucester: Printed by R. Raikes and W. Dicey, over-against the Swann-Inn; . . . [From 11 Feb 1723]: Gloucester: Printed by R. Raikes and W. Dicey, in the South-gate Street, . . . [From 17 Sep 1725]: Gloucester, Printed by R. Raikes, ... [From 16 Aug 1743]: Gloucester: Printed by R. Raikes, in the Black-Fryars. . . . [No. 1833 (12 Jul 1757]: Glocester: Printed by R. Raikes, Jun. in the Black-Fryars, . . . [From 19 Jul 1757]: Glocester: Printed by R. Raikes, in the Blackfryars, . . . [From 22 Aug 1758]: Glocester: Printed by R. Raikes, in the Southgate-Street, . . .

Gloucester Public Library: no. 1 (9 Apr [1722]) to vol. XXXIX, no. 2014 (30 Dec 1760), + .

Bristol Reference Library: vol. VI, no. 307 (20 Feb 1728) to vol. XVI, no. 820 (17 Jan 1738), inc.; vol. XVIII, no. 922 (1 Jan 1740) to vol. XIX, no. 947 (24 Jun 1740); vol. XXVI, no. 1334 (1 Dec 1747); vol. XXXV, no. 1768 (13 Apr 1756).

Bath Municipal Library: vol. XXXIV, no. 1763 (9 Mar 1756) to vol. XXXV, no. 1789 (7 Sep 1756), ten issues.

Bodleian Library: vol. II, no. 98 (17 Feb 1724).

British Museum: vol. IV, no. 195 (28 Dec 1725); vol. V, no. 228 (16 Aug 1726) to vol. XV, no. 735 (25 May 1736), inc.; vol. XXIII, nos. 1165 (28 Aug 1744) to 1194

(19 Mar 1745), four issues only; vol. XXVIII, no. 1420 (25 Jul 1749) to vol. XXX, no. 1502 (9 April 1751), inc.; vol. XXXI, nos. 1573 (18 Aug 1752) and 1593 (16 Jan 1753); vol. XXXV, no. 1772 (11 May 1756) to vol. XXXVII, no. 1895 (19 Sep 1758), inc.

Private library of W. B. Morrell, Esq., London: vol. XXVII, no. 1390 (27 Dec 1748).

Private library of Sydney R. Turner, Esq., Cheam: vol. XIII, no. 670 (25 Feb 1735); vol. XXXII, nos. 1617 (3 Jul 1753) to 1619 (17 Jul 1753) and 1626 (4 Sep 1753).

The Library Company of Philadelphia: vol. VII, nos. 331 (6 Aug 1728) to 335 (3 Sep 1728); vol. VIII, no. 410 (10 Feb 1730); vol. IX, nos. 449 (17 Nov 1730) to 462 (16 Feb 1731), six issues only; vol. X, no. 501 (16 Nov 1731) to vol. XI, no. 566 (20 Feb 1733), inc.

HALIFAX

56. The Union Journal: or, Halifax Advertiser.

No. 1 (6 Feb 1759)—vol. II, no. 84 (9 Sep 1760).

Tue.

Halifax: Printed by P. Darby, . . .

Manuscript note by Ja[me]s Cropley in a copy at York Minster Library indicates that the Rev. John Watson, M.A., "performed, when Curate of Ripponden, the Editorial Duties in relation to the Newspaper."

Halifax Public Library: prospectus; vol. I, nos. 11 (17 Apr 1759) and 14 (8 May 1759); vol. II, no. 76 (15 Jul 1760).

Bankfield Museum, Halifax: vol. I, nos. 2 (13 Feb 1759) to 5 (6 Mar 1759); nos. 7 (20 Mar 1759) to 44 (4 Dec

1759); no. 46 (19 Dec 1759); vol. II, nos. 49 (8 Jan 1760) to 73 (24 Jun 1760); no. 77 (23 Jul 1760); no. 78 (30 Jul 1760).

York Minster Library: vol. I, no. 1 (6 Feb 1759), to vol. II, no. 84 (9 Sep 1760), two sets.

HEREFORD

57. The Hereford Journal. With the History of the World given Gratis.

[No. 1 (26 June ? 1739)]—no. 12 (11 Sep 1739)—?

Tue.

Hereford: Printed by Willoughby Smith in By-Street, ...

Hereford City Library: vol. I, no. 12 (11 Sep 1739).

HULL

58. The Hull Courant.

[No. 1 (24 Nov 1739)]—no. 368 (19 Aug 1746)—no. 518 (11 Aug 1749)—1750.

Tue; by 22 Jan 1748, Fri.

Printed by J. Rawson, at the Star in Lowgate: . . .

Note in the *York Courant*, no. [1294] (31 Jul 1750), begins, "Such Persons as used to take in the HULL JOURNAL, or the HULL COURANT, both which are now no longer printed, . . . "

Kingston-upon-Hull Central Library: no. 368 (19 Aug 1746); no. 441 (22 Jan 1748); no. 442 (29 Jan 1748); no. 496 (17 Feb 1749); no. 502 (6 Apr [*sic*] 1749); no. 503 (14 Apr 1749); no. 510 (9 Jun 1749); no. 512 (23 Jun 1749); nos. 514 (7 Jul 1749) to 518 (11 Aug 1749).

Kingston-upon-Hull Museum: no. 508 (26 May 1749).

59. The Hull Journal.

?—1750.

Note in the *York Courant,* no. [1294] (31 Jul 1750), begins, "Such Persons as used to take in the HULL JOURNAL, or the HULL COURANT, both which are now no longer printed, . . . "

No copy found.

60. The Hull Courant.

[No. 1 (7 Oct ? 1755)]—no. 34 (25 May 1756)—no. 183 (20 Mar 1759)—?

Tue.

Hull, Printed by J. Rawson, in Lowgate, . . .

Kingston-upon-Hull Central Library: no. 34 (25 May 1756); no. 107 (13 Sep 1757); no. 119 (6 Dec 1757); no. 183 (20 Mar 1759).

Berrow's Newspapers, Ltd., Worcester: no. 34 (25 May 1756).

IPSWICH

61. The Ipswich-Journal, or, The Weekly Mercury. With the Freshest Advices Foreign and Domestick. [From 22 Apr 1721 con. as]: The Ipswich Journal, or, Weekly-Mercury:

With the Freshest Advices Foreign and Domestick. [By 27 Jan 1733 con. as]: The Ipswich Gazette.

[No. 1 (20 Aug ? 1720)]—no. 14 (19 Nov 1720)—no. 902 (26 Nov 1737)—?

Sat; from 24 Sep 1736, Fri; 6 pp.; by 10 June 1727, 4 pp.; 2 cols.; by 26 Nov 1737, 3 cols.

Ipswich: Printed by John Bagnall, in St. Mary-Elmes, 1720. [By Mar 1721]: Ipswich: Printed by John Bagnall, in St. Mary-Elmes. And Sold by Elizabeth Hewers, Bookseller in Colchester; . . . [From 23 Dec 1727]: Ipswich: Printed by John Bagnall in the Butter-Market, . . . [From 13 Jul 1728]: Ipswich: Printed by John Bagnall, in the Butter Market: And Sold by Mrs. Burnham, Bookseller, Daughter to the late Mrs. Hewers in Colchester, 1728. [By 27 Jan 1733]: Ipswich: Printed by John Bagnall, in St. Nicholas's Street, . . .

Ipswich Central Library: no. 19 (24 Dec 1720), def.; no. 20 (31 Dec 1720); no. 22 (14 Jan 1721); no. 24 (28 Jan 1721); no. 25 (4 Feb 1721), def.; no. 31 (18 Mar 1721); nos. 466 (19 Jul 1729) to 557 (17 Apr 1731), lacking one issue; vol. XV, no. 740 (19 Oct 1734) to vol. XVII, no. 855 (31 Dec 1736), lacking twelve issues; vol. XVII, no. 858 (21 Jan 1737); vol. XVIII, no. 902 (26 Nov 1737).

Norwich Public Library: no. 400 (13 Apr 1728).

Cambridge University Library: no. 504 (11 April 1730).

British Museum: nos. 14 (19 Nov 1720), def., to 52 (12 Aug 1721); nos. 356 (10 Jun 1727) to 454 (26 Apr 1729), lacking four issues; no. 504 (11 Apr 1730), fac.; vol. XIII, no. 650 (27 Jan 1733) to vol. XVI, no. 854 (24 Dec 1736), inc.

62.   The Ipswich Weekly Mercury.

[No. 1 (22 Feb 1735)]—?

Sat.

Date, imprint, and an advertisement were quoted by
G. R. Clarke, *The History and Description of the Town
and Borough of Ipswich* . . . (Ipswich: Piper; and
London: Hurst, Chance, [1830]), p. 215.

Ipswich: Printed by T. Norris, in the Cross Key Street,
near the Great White Horse Corner, . . .

No copy found.

63. The Ipswich Journal.

No. 1 (17 Feb 1739)—no. 1146 (27 Dec 1760), + .

Sat.

Ipswich: Printed for W. Craighton, Bookseller near the
Butter-Market; And Sold by Mr. Watson, Bookseller in
Bury; and Mr. Kendall, Bookseller in Colchester; . . .
[From 1 Jan 1743]: Ipswich: Printed for W. Craighton;
and Sold by S. Watson, Bookseller in Bury; J. Kendall,
Bookseller in Colchester; W. Eaton, Bookseller in Yar-
mouth; and J. Gleed, Bookseller in Norwich: . . . [From
12 Jan 1745]: Ipswich: Printed for W. Craighton.

Ipswich Central Library: nos. 1 (17 Feb 1739) to 1146
(27 Dec 1760), + .

Colchester Public Library: nos. 7 (31 Mar 1739) to 42
(1 Dec 1739), lacking five issues; nos. 569 (6 Jan 1750)
to 620 (29 Dec 1750), lacking one issue; nos. 724 (6
Jan 1753) to 778 (5 Jan 1754), lacking three issues; nos.
788 (16 Mar 1754) to 831 (11 Jan 1755); nos. 837 (22
Feb 1755) to Sep, 1760, many duplicates.

Cambridge University Library: no. 724 (6 Jan 1753); no.
944 (12 Feb 1757); no. 966 (16 Jul 1757); no. 968 (30
Jul 1757); no. 969 (6 Aug 1757).

British Museum: nos. 1 (17 Feb 1739) to 106 (21 Feb
1741); nos. 203 (1 Jan 1743) to 461 (12 Dec 1747),
lacking two issues; nos. 517 (7 Jan 1749) to 671 (21
Dec 1751); nos. 768 (27 Oct 1753) to 1146 (27 Dec
1760, inc., + .

Yale University Library: nos. 332 (22 Jun 1745) to 343 (1 Sep 1745); nos. 350 (26 Oct 1745) to 471 (20 Feb 1748), lacking eighteen issues; no. 479 (16 Apr 1748); nos. 482 (7 May 1748) to 593 (23 Jun 1750), lacking ten issues; nos. 1043 (6 Jan 1759) to 1146 (28 Dec 1760), lacking three issues.

Huntington Library: no. 705 (15 Aug 1752).

KENDAL

64. The Kendal Weekly Courant. Containing the most Material Advices, Both Foreign and Domestick.

[No. 1 (1 Jan ? 1732)]—no. 2 (8 Jan 1732)—no. 240 (14 Aug 1736)—Dec ? 1736.

Sat.

Kendal: Printed and Sold, by Thomas Cotton, . . .

Cotton began to print a newspaper in Whitehaven by mid-December, 1736.

Kendal Public Library: nos. 2 (8 Jan 1732) to 51 (16 Dec 1732).

Kendal Museum: no. 240 (14 Aug 1736).

65. The Kendal Weekly Mercury. Containing the most material Advices both Foreign and Domestick.

[No. 1 (8 Feb ? 1735)]—no. 13 (3 May 1735)—no. 429 (19 Mar 1743)—no. 90 [sic] (26 Sep. 1747)—?

Sat.

Printed by Thomas Ashburner, in the Fish Market in Kendal, . . . [By 5 Nov 1737]: Kendal, Printed by Thomas Ashburner, Book-Seller in the Fish-Market.

Kendal Public Library: no. 13 (3 May 1735), fac.; no. 149 (5 Nov 1737).

"Town End," (National Trust), Troutbeck, Windermere: no. 90 (26 Sep 1747).

British Museum: no. 13 (3 May 1735), fac.

Private library of J. S. Dearden, Esq., Greenways, Hillway, Bembridge, Isle of Wight: no. 429 (19 Mar 1743).

LEEDS

66. The Leeds Mercury Being The freshest Advices, Foreign and Domestick. Together with An Account of Trade. [From 27 Apr 1725 con. as]: The Leeds Mercury, containing the freshest Advices Foreign and Domestick. [From 14 Sep 1725 con. as]: Leeds Mercury; [sometimes] The Leeds Mercury; [sometimes] The Leedes Mercury.

[No. 1 (May ? 1718)]—vol. III, no. 50 (18 Apr 1721)— [no. 1816 (17 Jun 1755)].

Tue; 12 pp.; from 27 Apr 1725, 4 pp.; single col.; from 27 Apr 1725, 2 cols.; by 24 Oct 1732, 3 cols.

By 18 Apr 1721: Leeds, Printed and Sold by John Hirst, over against Kirkgate-end, Mr. Penrose and Mr. Swale, Booksellers in Leeds, Mr. Dyson Bookseller in Halifax, Mrs. Bartlett and Mr. Preston in Bradford, Mr. Darley in Ripley, Mr. Austin Bookseller in Rippon, and at his Shop in Richmond, Mr. Smirk Livery-lace-Weaver in Manchester, Mr. Joseph Lacock, Cutter in Wetherby, Mr. Hodgson Clockmaker in Skipton, Mr. Robert Barugh Grocer and Mercer in Otley, and Mr. Hepworth Post-Master, in Pontefract. . . . [Names added and changed in later issues.] [From 20 Feb 1733]: Leeds: Printed and Sold by the Executors of John Hirst, . . . [By 16 Aug 1737]: Leeds: Printed by James Lister in New-Street, . . . [By 10 Mar 1741]: Leeds: Printed by James Lister, at New-Street-End, . . . [By 1 Aug 1749]: Leedes: Printed by James Lister, for the Proprietor, at New-Street-End: . . .

Evidence for beginning is the statement in Sir Edward Baines, *The Life of Edward Baines, Late M. P. for the Borough of Leeds* (London: Longman, Brown, Green, and Longmans, 1851), p. [37]: "The *Leeds Mercury* was one of the oldest of the provincial newspapers, having been originally established in May, 1718, by John Hirst. The earliest numbers known to be in existence are from November 10, 1719, to November 1, 1720, in the possession of the author."

The death of John Hirst, "Master of the Printing Office in this Town," on 20 February 1733, was announced in the *Leeds Mercury,* no. 402 (27 Feb 1733). This statement followed:

> We have only further to add, that the Care of the *Leeds Mercury, &c.* (which has met with so kind a Reception from the World) is committed to skilful Hands; and will be continued, as usually, for the Benefit of his Children, who are all Minors, and Orphans of tender Age. This we are advised to represent to the Readers of the *Leeds Mercury,* hoping they will be pleased to take it in, as formerly; and thereby improve their Kindness shown to the Father, by their Continuance of it to his Children, into a Christian Vertue.

This announcement appeared in the *Leedes Intelligencer,* no. 52 (24 Jun 1755):

> Last Tuesday died, after a tedious Illness, The Leedes Mercury, aged 1816 Weeks. He has left the *Good-will* of his Circuit, which is *very considerable,* to the York Courant.

Extracts selected by G. D. Lumb from the *Leeds Mercury* in the period 1721-51 were printed in volumes XXII, XXIV, XXVI, XXVIII, and XXXIII of *Publications of the Thoresby Society: Miscellanea.*

Leeds Reference Library: vol. III, no. 50 (18 Apr 1721); vol. VI, no. 23 (8 Oct 1723); no. 46 (17 Mar 1724); no. 188 (3 Dec 1728); no. 384 (24 Oct 1732); no. 393 (26 Dec 1732); no. 395 (9 Jan 1733); nos. 401 (20 Feb 1733) to 403 (6 Mar 1733); no. 557 (7 Sep 1736); nos. 609 (16 Aug 1737) to 750 (24 Jun 1740), many duplicates; no. 777 (23 Dec 1740); nos. 804 (7 Jul 1741) to 1028 (25 Jun 1745), nearly complete; no. 1072 (25 Feb 1746); nos. 1264 (1 Aug 1749) to 1580 (11 Jun 1751); nos. 1518 [*sic*] (18 Jun 1751) to 1524 (30 Jul 1751); no. [?] (3 Jul 1753).

York Minster Library: vol. IV, no. 29 (21 Nov 1721) to vol. VI, no. 29 (19 Nov 1723); nos. 1 (27 Apr 1725) to 338 (7 Dec 1731); nos. 498 (7 Jan 1735) to 545 (8 Jun 1736); nos. 547 (22 Jun 1736) to 722 (11 Dec 1739), many duplicates; no. 729 (29 Jan 1740); nos. 743 (6 May 1740) to 788 (17 Mar 1741), fifteen issues only; nos. 858 (13 Jul 1742) to 884 (11 Jan 1743), lacking seven issues.

Cambridge University Library: no. 321 (10 Aug 1731); nos. 324 (31 Aug 1731) to 327 (21 Sep 1731); no. 331 (19 Oct 1731); no. 332 (26 Oct 1731).

Private library of Kenneth Monkman, Esq., London: nos. 724 (25 Dec 1739) to 726 (8 Jan 1740).

67. The Leedes Intelligencer.

No. 1 (2 Jul 1754)—no. 349 (30 Dec 1760), + .

Tue.

[Imprint, 2 Jul 1754]: Printed by Griffith Wright, in the Lower Head-Row. [Colophon, 2 Jul 1754]: This Paper may be had of Mr. Stringer, Bookseller in Wakefield; Mr. Scolfield, Bookseller in Rochdale; Mr. Edwards, Bookseller in Halifax; Mr. William Pullen, in Bradford; Mr. Hirstwood in Ripponden; Mr. Nathaniel Binns, Bookseller in Halifax, and at his Shops at Huddersfield and Eland; Mr. Robert Richardson, Grocer in Otley;

. . . They will be sent also by the York, Tadcaster, Knaresbro', Weatherby, Pontefract, Barnsley, Doncaster, and Skipton Carriers;—And delivered at any Place according to Directions. [From 21 Oct 1755]: Printed by Griffith Wright, at New-Street-End [colophon gives large number of distributors]; [From 6 Jun 1758]: . . . and the Paper may be had of the following Persons, viz. Mr. Scolfield, in Rochdale. Mr. Edwards and Mr. Binns, in Halifax. Mr. Horsfall, in Huddersfield. Mr. Wilkinson, in Elland. Mr. Hirstwood, in Ripponden. Mr. Pullan, in Bradford. Mr. William Spencer, in the Road to, and at Skipton. Mr. Barugh, in Otley. Mrs. Lord, Mr. Meggit, and Mr. Stringer, in Wakefield. Mr. Lund, in Pontefract. Mr. Bent, and Mr. Smith, in Barnsley. Mr. Ellis, in Rotherham. Mr. Welch, in Sheffield. Mr. Parker, in Keighley. Mr. King, the Coln-Carrier. Mr. Berry, in Manchester. Mr. Williams, at the C[h]apter Coffee-House, London. And of the News-Men.

Extracts selected by Charles S. Rooke from the first four volumes (1754-58) of the *Leedes Intelligencer* were printed in *Publications of the Thoresby Society: Miscellanea*, IV (1895), [226]-44.

Leeds Reference Library: no. 1 (2 Jul 1754); no. 49 (3 Jun 1755); vol. III, nos. 132 (4 Jan 1757) to 140 (1 Mar 1757); nos. 142 (15 Mar 1757) to 154 (7 Jun 1757); no. 155 (14 Jun 1757), pp. 1-2 only; nos. 156 (21 Jun 1757) to vol. VI, no. 296 (25 Dec 1759).

Brotherton Library, University of Leeds: nos. 2 (9 Jul 1754) to 79 (30 Dec 1755), lacking six issues; nos. 106 (6 Jul 1756) to 349 (30 Dec 1760), inc., some def., + .

Office of the Conservative Newspaper Company, Leeds: no. 59 (12 Aug 1755), def., to no. 101 (1 Jun 1756), lacking five issues and two pages of nine others; vol. VI, nos. 271 (3 Jul 1759) to 322 (24 Jun 1760).

British Museum: vol. IV, no. 183 (3 Jan 1758); vol. V, nos. 223 (10 Oct 1758) and 228 (14 Nov 1758).

LEICESTER

68.   Leicester Journal. [By 8 Nov 1755 con. as]: The Leicester and Nottingham Journal.

[No. 1 (5 May ? 1753)]—no. 132 (8 Nov 1755)—no. 399 (27 Dec 1760), + .

Sat.

Printed for J. Gregory, Bookseller, in Leicester; and S. Creswell, Bookseller, in Nottingham; . . . [By 7 Jan 1758]: Leicester: Printed by J. Gregory, in the Market-Place; . . .

It is stated by W. J. Clarke in *Early Nottingham Printers and Printing* (Nottingham: Forman, 1942), p. 23, that in Nottingham, on 1 September 1753, Samuel Creswell was "summoned to appear before the Magistrates for selling the *Leicester Journal*" but was "let off with a reprimand." For a contemporary account of the incident, see above, pages 58-59.

A notice in no. 132 (8 Nov 1755) begins thus:

> John Gregory of Leicester, and Samuel Creswell of Nottingham, Printers: Take this Method of acquainting the Public that by the Advice of their Friends, they have lately enter'd into Partnership in the Mystery of Printing, and that they are determined to publish this Weekly Paper early every Saturday Morning, at their respective Shops in Leicester and Nottingham . . . .

Office of the *Leicester Mercury:* microfilm of nos. 297 (6 Jan 1759) to 399 (27 Dec 1760), lacking six issues, + .

Nottingham Reference Library: no. 132 (8 Nov 1755).

University of Nottingham Library: nos. 246 (7 Jan 1758) to 284 (30 Sep 1758), lacking eleven issues; no. 303 [*sic*] (18 Nov 1758); no. 295 (23 Dec 1758); no. 393 (8 Nov 1760); no. 397 (6 Dec 1760), + .

Office of the *Nottingham Guardian-Journal:* no. 255 (11 Mar 1758); no. 386 (20 Sep 1760).

British Museum: microfilm of nos. 297 (6 Jan 1759) to 399 (27 Dec 1760), lacking six issues, + .

LEWES

69. The Sussex Weekly Advertiser, or Lewes Journal.

[No. 1 (9 June ? 1746)]—no. 5 (7 Jul 1746)—no. 757 (29 Dec 1760), + .

Mon.

Lewes: Printed by E. Verral and W. Lee, . . . [From 24 Feb 1752]: Lewes: Printed by W. Lee, . . . [with list of wares sold by E. Verral].

Sussex Archaeological Society: no. 5 (7 Jul 1746).

Private library of Rev. Douglas G. Matthews, Hailsham, Sussex: no. 515 (10 May 1756); no. 517 (24 May 1756); no. 520 (14 Jun 1756); nos. 523 (5 Jul 1756) to 535 (27 Sep 1756); nos. 537 (11 Oct 1756) to 757 (29 Dec 1760), + .

Brighton Public Library: no. 157 (19 Jun 1749); no. 172 (2 Oct 1749); no. 184 (25 Dec 1749); no. 249 (25 Mar 1751); no. 297 (24 Feb 1752); no. 308 (11 May 1752); no. 329 (16 Oct 1752); no. 336 (4 Dec 1752); nos. 625 (19 Jun 1758) to 755 (15 Dec 1760), thirty-five issues only, + .

London Library: no. 36 (16 Feb 1747); no. 37 (23 Feb 1747); no. 41 (23 Mar 1747); no. 44 (13 Apr 1747); no. 45 (20 Apr 1747); no. 284 (25 Nov 1751).

Yale University Library: no. 470 (30 Jun 1755).

LINCOLN

70.   The Lincoln Gazette, or Weekly-Intelligencer.

[No. 1 (12 Dec? 1728)]—[vol. I, no. 14 (9 Mar 1729)] —[vol. I, no. 45 (23 Oct 1729)]—?

Printed for William Wood, Bookseller, at his office in Lincoln; where Advertisements are taken in, and carefully inserted.

Thu; 8 pp.

Nos. 14, 44, and 45 are described in notes by C. L. Exley (Lincolnshire Archives Office, Exchequer Gate, Lincoln).

No copies found.

71.   Lincoln Journal.

[No. 1 (4 Aug ? 1744)]—?

Sat.

[Lincoln: Printed] by William Wood. Of whom may be had all Sorts of Blank Warrants, . . .

Listed in manuscript notes by John B. King (MS. U.P. 1844 in Lincoln Public Library).

Lincoln Public Library: fragment (3rd and 4th pages) of an issue which may be no. 16 (17 Nov 1744).

LIVERPOOL

72.   The Leverpoole Courant, being an Abstract of the London and other News.

[No. 1 (13 May ? 1712)]—[no. 18 (18 July 1712)]— [no. [?] (13 Nov 1712)]—?

Tue and Fri; by 13 Nov 1712, Thu; 2 pp.; 2 cols. [?]

Leverpoole: Printed by S. Terry, in Dale Street, where all persons willing to subscribe, by sending their Names and Places of Abode may be constantly served herewith every Tuesday and Friday morning.

No. 18 is described and quoted by (a) Henry Smithers, *Liverpool, its Commerce, Statistics, and Institutions, with a History of the Cotton Trade* (Liverpool: Thos. Kaye, 1825), p. 321; (b) the *Liverpool Mercury* (10 Feb 1837); (c) Richard Brooke, *Liverpool as it was during the last quarter of the eighteenth century, 1775 to 1800* (Liverpool: Mawdsley, 1853), p. 92; and (d) Arthur C. Wardle, "Some Glimpses of Liverpool during the First Half of the Eighteenth Century," *Transactions of the Historic Society of Lancashire and Cheshire*, XCVII (1945), 146. It has been stated by J. A. Picton, "Early Printing in Lancashire," *Notes and Queries*, 5th ser., III (20 Feb 1875), 147, that in *A True and Impartial Account of the Election of the Representatives in Parliament, for the Corporation and Borough of Leverpool, in the County Palatine of Lancaster, October the 16th, 1710* (published anonymously in London in 1710) there was a reference to "a Liverpool newspaper (name not given)"; but the only mention of a newspaper in that pamphlet is the statement, "The News Paper return'd them [candidates for election] thus . . . ." The reference was probably to a London newspaper; the passage cannot be taken as evidence that a local newspaper was being published in Liverpool as early as 1710.

No copy found.

73. Williamson's Liverpool Advertiser. And Mercantile Register. [From 7 Sep 1759 con. as]: Williamson's Liverpool Advertiser, and Mercantile Chronicle.

Vol. I, no. 1 (28 May 1756)—vol. V, no. 51 (26 Dec 1760), +.

Fri.

Liverpool: Printed by R. Williamson, Bookseller and Printer, near the Exchange, . . . [From 10 Sep 1756]: Liverpool: Printed by R. Williamson, Bookseller and Printer, at the Circulating Library, near the Exchange, . . .

Under the title in early issues: This Paper is circulated through London, Bristol, Edinburgh, Glasgow, Dublin, Cork, Hull, Scarborough, Whitehaven, Chester, Lancaster, Manchester, Warrington, Preston, Blackburn, Bolton, Kendal, Shrewsbury, Wrexham, Flint, Denbigh, Northwich, the adjacent Neighbourhood, and many other Capital Places in Great-Britain, Ireland, and the Isle of Man.

"Extraordinary" issues were published occasionally.

Liverpool Reference Library: vol. I, no. 1 (28 May 1756) to vol. V, no. 51 (26 Dec 1760), including six "extraordinary" issues, + .

York Public Library: vol. III, no. 119 (1 Sep 1758).

74. The Liverpool Chronicle: and Marine Gazetteer.

No. 1 (6 May 1757)—no. 121 (24 Aug 1759).

Fri.

Subscriptions and Advertisements are taken in by the Publishers, R. Fleetwood, Bookseller, near the Exchange; R. Robinson, Broker; G. Parker, at the Toy-shop in Castle-street; and J. Sadler, Printer, . . . [Note in no. 29 (18 Nov 1757)]: Mr. Sadler, being engaged in the Enamelling Tiles, &c, has declined the Printing this Paper, in favour of Mr. Owen, by whom it will be done for the future: But he will continue the Printing Business in all the Branches as heretofore, (except the News-Paper) and hopes a continuance of favours from his Friends. [Imprint of no. 30 (25 Nov 1757)]: Subscriptions and Advertisements are taken in by G. Parker, in Castle-street, and E. Owen, Printer in Moore-street.

Advertisements are also taken in by R. Fleetwood, Bookseller, near the Exchange. [By no. 36 (6 Jan 1758) the names in the imprint are G. Parker and J. Sadler, Printer, in Herrington-street.]

Under the date line of earliest issues: This Paper is circulated thro' Lancashire, Cheshire, Shropshire, great Part of Wales, the Isle of Man, &c. and sent Gratis to the principal Coffee-houses and Taverns in London, Bristol, Edinburgh, Glasgow, Dublin, Corke, Whitehaven, York, Leeds, Hull, Birmingham, and other capital Towns.

An "extraordinary" issue was published on Saturday, 17 [i.e. 16] June 1759.

Liverpool Reference Library: nos. 1 (6 May 1757) to 121 (24 Aug 1759), including "extraordinary" issue dated 17 June 1759, but lacking eleven issues.

LONDON

75. The Shropshire Journal, with the History of the Holy Bible.

[No. 1 (19 Dec 1737)]—[no. 73 (12 Feb 1739)]—?

Mon.

London: Printed by R. Walker, in Fleet Lane. Of whom, and of the Person who serves this Paper may be had the former Numbers to complete Sets [i.e. sets of the detachable supplement, *The History of the Holy Bible*].

Title and imprint of no. 73 from W. E. A. Axon, "Shropshire Newspaper Printed in London," *Notes and Queries,* ser. 11, II (1910), 26. The first seventy-two issues were described briefly by Charles Hulbert in the *Salopian Magazine,* I (1815), 452, note. Both these articles are cited by Llewelyn C. Lloyd in "The Book-Trade in Shropshire," *Transactions of the Shropshire Archaeological and Natural History Society,* XLVIII (1936), 91 f. Note Walker's other newspapers printed in London for distribution in Warwickshire and Staffordshire (item 6 in this Register), in Derbyshire (item 76), in Northamptonshire (item 78), in Lancashire (item 86), and in various provincial areas (item 77).

No copy found.

76. The Derbyshire Journal with the History of the Holy Bible.

[No. 1 (24 May ? 1738)]—no. 2 (31 May 1738)—?

Wed.

London: Printed by R. Walker, the Corner of Seacoal Lane, next Fleet Lane. . . .

No. 2 has ad. of Dr. Friend's Balsam, "sold . . . Mr. Unwin, Printer at Leicester; and Mr. Akers printer in Maidstone; They may also be had of . . . the Printer of this Paper in London; . . . They may likewise be had of the Persons who serve Reading, Newbury, Henly, Wallingford, Abingdon, Oxford, Warwick and Coventry with this Paper."

Derby Borough Library: no. 2 (31 May 1738).

77. The London and Country Journal: With the History of the Old and New Testament. [From 10 Nov 1741 con. as]: The London and Country Journal: with the Freshest News, Foreign and Domestick.

Although this newspaper was printed in London, it is included in this Register of provincial papers because it was obviously intended to circulate in various parts of the country, and in some cases (see items 6, 75, 76, 78, 86 in this Register) the title was altered to suit the particular areas of England to which the papers were sent. The issues entitled *The London and Country*

438

Journal, with or without subtitle, are here brought together as one item, but it is possible to distinguish several series, each with separate serial numbering, each differing slightly in substance from the others issued a day or two earlier or later. Some issues of the same date and serial number differ significantly in contents. There was a Tuesday series, which began in January, 1739; four months later, a Wednesday series began; and then or shortly afterwards, a Thursday series began. By August, 1740, there were two series of Wednesday issues and two series of Thursday issues. A notice in no. 19 (Thu, 27 Sep 1739) indicates that a Friday series was started at that time:

> These are to certify all the Customers to this Work, that these Books which have been used to be published on the Wednesday and Thursday, will for the future be publish'd on Thursday and Friday, on which Days our Customers may depend of [*sic*] having them carefully delivered as usual.

The reference to "these Books" is not to the newspaper as such but to the accompanying supplements. A new series of Friday issues appeared in 1742.

It appears that each series was intended to circulate in a different section of England. Notices printed in early issues of the first Wednesday series indicate that special efforts were made to distribute it in Bristol and Bath, in spite of opposition from Sam. Farley. No. 3 (Wed, 6 Jun 1739) and following issues have this announcement:

> Note. All Persons who are desirous to take in the London and Country Journal with the History of the Holy Bible, or the Reign of King Charles I. &c. are desired to apply to Jos. Collett, at the Sign of the Star and Stays on Phillips-Plain, Bristol, and they may depend upon having them carefully delivered at their own Houses, or where they shall think fit; I being settled in Bristol on purpose to serve this City and Bath.
>
> Jos. Collett.

No. 5 (20 Jun 1739) adds this statement by the London proprietor himself:

> Whereas the Printers of the Bristol Journal have industriously propagated many scandalous Falsities against the Performance of this Work, and to Me the Printer thereof, in order to prejudice the Sale in these Parts; only because it meets with a kind Encouragement suitable to its Worth and Usefulness; this is publish'd to satisfy all Persons who are my Subscribers, that this very valuable Work has been publish'd and finish'd in London, where it met with a good Reception, and likewise in several other Parts of this Kingdom, and I do promise to continue the same to the End, according to my printed Proposals, with the strictest Honour and Punctuality, notwithstanding what such envious Snarlers may say to the contrary; and the Publick may always depend on whatever Books I send into the Country, that I shall be always punctual in what I promise.
>
> R. Walker.

No copy of *Sam. Farley's Bristol Newspaper* of June, 1739, has survived, but the nature of the accusations brought therein against Walker may be judged from the declarations in the letter printed in the *London and Country Journal*, no. 7 (4 Jul 1739):

> There is lately come to my Hand a Paper published by the Bristol Printer, full of Lies and barefaced Impudence, which I shall take a proper Time to answer; and if he was a Man of any Worth, or Character, sue him for what he has falsely asserted, in saying such Things of Me, which is not in his Power, or any other Man, to prove against me. But I don't much wonder at such a Man's Impudence, who has had the Front to assert, that he will make, or cause to be made, Affidavit of my being in Bristol lately, and of what I said there, in relation to my Country Customers; which are notorious Falsities, for I never was at Bristol nor Bath in my Life; but will speedily be there; and answer whatever such an invidious Fellow will say to me. As to what he charges me with in calling my Customers Country

Flats, I absolutely declare it to be false; for I never heard of that Expression, till I had it from the Bristol Printer. And I do likewise assure the Publick, that I will speedily print a News Paper in Bristol, as large as that already published by Mr. Farley, and with the freshest Intelligence, at the Price of Three Half-pence, that the Country may see how they have been imposed on by such a Fellow, in giving Two-Pence for a Newspaper only, when it may very well be afforded for Three Half-pence; and take this Opportunity of returning Thanks to my Subscribers, hoping for a Continuation of their Custom, as I shall make it my constant Endeavour to please.

R. Walker

N.B. Next Week I will lay before the Publick the whole Affair; to shew the Design of Farley [printed Forley], and his Block-headed Agent Astley the Bookseller, the pretended fair Trader.

But the following week Walker was "obliged to go into the Country" because of "an unforeseen Accident" and he could not take time to answer Farley's "scurrilous Advertisement," nor did Walker's paper take up the quarrel again. Perhaps he let Jos. Collett carry on the dispute. In any case it is clear that the earlier Wednesday series of Walker's paper was intended for distribution in the Bristol area.

(*a*) The Tuesday series (titles as above):

[No. 1 (2 Jan ? 1739)]—no. 8 (20 Feb 1739)—no. 149 (3 Nov 1741)—no. 1 (10 Nov 1741)—no. 7 (22 Dec 1741)—?

London, Printed by R. Walker, in Fleet Lane.

British Museum: nos. 8 (20 Feb 1739) to 30 (24 Jul 1739); nos. 34 (21 Aug 1739) to 147 (20 Oct 1741); no. 149 (3 Nov 1741); nos. 1 (10 Nov 1741) to 7 (22 Dec 1741).

(*b*) The earlier Wednesday series:

[No. 1 (23 May ? 1739)]—no. 3 (6 June 1739)—no. 122 (16 Sep 1741)—?

London, Printed by R. Walker, in Fleet Lane.

British Museum: nos. 3 (6 Jun 1739) to 22 (10 Oct 1739), with several duplicates.

Library of Congress: nos. 18 (19 Sep 1739) to 33 (2 Jan 1740); nos. 35 (16 Jan 1740) to 122 (16 Sep 1741).

(c) The later Wednesday series:

[No. 1 (23 Jul ? 1740)]—no. 3 (6 Aug 1740)—no. 100 (16 Jun 1742)—?

London, Printed by R. Walker, in Fleet Lane.

Birmingham Public Library: no. 3 (6 Aug 1740).

Yale University: nos. 10 (24 Sep 1740) to 12 (8 Oct 1740); no. 27 (21 Jan 1741); no. 74 [sic, for 82] (10 Feb 1742); no. 100 (16 Jun 1742).

New York Public Library: no. 27 (21 Jan 1741); pages 3 and 4 of two other issues.

(d) The earlier Thursday series:

[No. 1 (24 May ? 1739)]—no. 3 (7 Jun 1739)—no. 142 (4 Feb 1742)—?

London, Printed by R. Walker, in Fleet Lane.

British Museum: nos. 3 (7 Jun 1739) to 47 (10 Apr 1740); nos. 49 (24 Apr 1740) to 67 (28 Aug 1740); nos. 69 (11 Sep 1740) to 142 (4 Feb 1742).

(e) The later Thursday series:

[No. 1 (24 Jul ? 1740)]—no. 15 (30 Oct 1740)—no. 138 (10 Mar 1743)—?

London, Printed by R. Walker in Fleet-Lane.

University of Reading: no. 18 (20 Nov 1740).

Bodleian Library: no. 15 (30 Oct 1740); no. 18 (20 Nov 1740); no. 22 (18 Dec 1740); no. 24 (1 Jan 1741); no. 28 (29 Jan 1741); no. 30 (12 Feb 1741); no. 35 (19 Mar 1741); no. 38 (9 Apr 1741); no. 62 (24 Sep 1741); no. 68 (5 Nov 1741); no. 72 (3 Dec 1741); no. 73 (10 Dec 1741); no. 76 (31 Dec. 1741); no. 83 (18 Feb 1742); no. 89 (1 Apr 1742).

Yale University: nos. 13 (16 Oct 1740) to 19 (27 Nov 1740); nos. 21 (11 Dec 1740) to 26 (15 Jan 1741); no. 29 (5 Feb 1741); nos. 34 (12 Mar 1741), def., to 49 (25 Jun 1741), def.; nos. 50 (2 Jul 1741) to 55 (6 Aug 1741), def.; nos. 56 (13 Aug 1741) to 58 (27 Aug 1741); nos. 60 (10 Sep 1741) to 81 (4 Feb 1742); nos. 83 (18 Feb 1742) to 91 (15 Apr 1742), def.; nos. 92 (22 Apr 1742) to 95 (13 May 1742); nos. 97 (27 May 1742) to 99 (10 Jun 1742); nos. 102 (1 Jul 1742) to 138 (10 Mar 1743), even-numbered issues only.

(*f*) The Friday series:

[No. 1 (13 Nov ? 1741)]—no. 32 (18 Jun 1742)—no. 33 (25 Jun 1742)—?

London Printed by R. Walker in Fleet Lane.

The notice quoted above from no. 19 (Thu, 27 Sep 1739) suggests that there was a Friday issue of the paper at that time.

British Museum: no. 32 (18 Jun 1742); no. 33 (25 Jun 1742).

78. The Northamptonshire Journal with the History of the Old and New Testament.

[No. 1 (?)]—no. [?] (19 Mar 1741)—?

Thu.

In the only issue found, dated 19 Mar 1741, at Northampton Public Library, the serial number and imprint have been trimmed off, but the letter press is identical with that of the *London and Country Journal: with the History of the Old and New Testament,* no. 116 (Tue, 17 Mar 1741), printed by Robert Walker of Fleet Lane, London, from the same setting of type. Only the top line of the title and the date line have been altered. Walker's Thursday edition of the *London and Country Journal* for that week is substantially the same, but there are changes in the news of the first column on the fourth page.

LUDLOW

79. The Ludlow Post-Man. or the Weekly Journal. Being a True and Impartial Collection of the most material Transactions, both at Home and Abroad.

No. 1 (9 Oct 1719)—no. 22 (4 Mar 1720)—?

Fri; 6 pp.; single col.

Ludlow: Printed by W. Parks [some issues have Parkes] . . . .

British Museum: no. 1 (9 Oct 1719); no. 2 (16 Oct 1719); no. 7 (20 Nov 1719); no. 12 (25 Dec 1719); nos. 14 (8 Jan 1720) to 17 (29 Jan 1720); nos. 20 (19 Feb 1720) to 22 (4 Mar 1720).

MAIDSTONE

80. The Maidstone Mercury With the freshest Advices Foreign and Domestick.

[No. 1 (4 Mar ? 1725)]—no. 6 (22 Mar 1725)—no. 25 (27 May 1725)—?

Mon and Thu; 6 pp.; by 27 May 1725, 4 pp.; 2 cols.

[Colophon of no. 6 missing; colophon of no. 25]: Maidstone: Printed by J. Watson in High-Street, near the Little Conduit, . . .

Maidstone Museum: no. 25 (27 May 1725).

Press Club: no. 6 (22 Mar 1725).

81. The Maidstone Journal.

[No. 1 (22 Sep ? 1737)]—no. 3 (6 Oct 1737)—?

Thu; 2 cols.

Maidstone: Printed by Jacob Ilive and John Akers, at the Printing-Office, at the Bible in East-lane, near the Fish-Cross, . . .

Maidstone Museum: no. 3 (6 Oct 1737).

MANCHESTER

82. Manchester News-Letter, Containing the Freshest Advices, Both Foreign and Domestick. [From 20 Aug 1724 con. as]: The Manchester Weekly Journal, Containing the Freshest Advices, Both Foreign and Domestick. To be continued Weekly.

[No. 1 (Jan ? 1719)]—no. 291 (6 Aug 1724)—no. 325 (25 Mar 1725)—?

Thu; 12 pp.; 2 cols.

Manchester: Printed and sold by Roger Adams, at the lower End of the Smiby-door [sic, for Smithy-door] . . . .

Manchester Reference Library: no. 325 (25 Mar 1725), pages 1 to 8 only.

Harris Public Library, Preston: no. 304 (29 Oct 1724); no. 305 (5 Nov 1724); no. 307 (19 Nov 1724); no. 308 (26 Nov 1724); no. 310 (10 Dec 1724); no. 311 (17 Dec 1724); nos. 315 (14 Jan 1725) to 317 (28 Jan 1725); no. 319 (11 Feb 1725); no. 320 (18 Feb 1725), pp. 9 to 12 only.

All Souls' Library, Oxford: nos. 291 (6 Aug 1724) to 313 (31 Dec 1724).

83. The Manchester Gazette. [By 20 Dec 1737 con. as]: The Manchester Magazine. [By 2 Jan 1739 con. as]: Whit-

445

worth's Manchester Magazine: with the History of The Holy Bible. [By 24 Jun 1740 con. as]: The Manchester Magazine. [By 26 Dec 1752 con. as]: Whitworth's Manchester Magazine. [From 29 Apr 1755 con. as]: Whitworth's Manchester Magazine, or, Universal Advertiser. [From 9 Dec 1755 con. as]: Whitworth's Manchester Magazine, and Weekly Advertiser. [From 20 Jul 1756 con. as]: Whitworth's Manchester Advertiser, and Weekly Magazine.

[No. 1 (22 Dec 1730)]—no. 27 (20 Dec 1737)—no. 3414 (25 Mar 1760).

Tue.

Manchester: Printed by R. Whitworth, Bookseller at the Three Bibles over against the Corner of the Exchange near the Cross. [Note in no. 287 (20 Dec 1748)]: The Printer hereof is removed to a Shop betwixt the Angel and Bull's Head Inns. [Imprint in 1752]: Manchester: Printed by R. Whitworth, Bookseller, next the Angel. [Imprint in 1757]: Manchester: Printed by R. Whitworth, Bookseller, next the Bull's Head.

In *The Annals of Manchester* (London and Manchester: Heywood, 1886), p. 80, W. E. A. Axon stated that the *Manchester Gazette,* published by Henry Whitworth, began on 22 December 1730.

This note is in no. 462 (17 Dec 1745): "We have not published any News for a Fortnight."

Manchester Reference Library: no. 27 (20 Dec 1737); no. 94 (17 Oct 1738); no. 105 (2 Jan 1739); no. 107 (16 Jan 1739); no. 108 (23 Jan 1739); no. 111 (13 Feb 1739); no. 182 (24 Jun 1740); no. 201 (6 Jan 1741), and many issues to no. 364 (27 Dec 1743); nos. 428 (2 Apr 1745) to 1088 (31 Dec 1751), inc.; no. 1096 (25 Feb 1752); no. 1097 (3 Mar 1752); no. 3002 (26 Dec 1752); nos. 3076 (5 Feb 1754) to 3414 (25 Mar 1760), inc.

Central Library, Salford: no 230 (2 Jun 1741); no. 496 (20 Aug 1746); no. 1014 (27 Nov 1750).

Press Club: no. 1058 (23 Jul 1751); no. 3175 (1 Nov 1757).

Private library of Sydney R. Turner, Esq., Cheam: no. 259 (29 Dec 1741); nos. 1023 (26 Feb 1751) to 1088 (31 Dec 1751), eleven issues only; nos. 3213 (11 Jan 1757) to 3170 [sic] (27 Sep 1757), ten issues only; nos. 3333 (20 Feb 1759) to 3383 (14 Aug 1759), seven issues only.

York Minster Library: nos. 3198 (24 Aug 1756) to 3183 [sic] (27 Dec 1757); nos. 3326 (2 Jan 1759) to 3413 (18 Mar 1760).

84. [Manchester Weekly Courant].

1732 ?—2 Jul 1733—?

Mon.

As Dr. Cranfield's *Hand-list* indicates, a *Manchester Weekly Courant,* dated 2 July 1733, was quoted in the *Daily Courant* (London), no. 5382 (7 Jul 1733). The following "Extract of a private Letter from Manchester, dated July 8, 1732," was printed in the *Chester Weekly Journal,* vol. XXXII, no. 3 (12 Jul 1732):

> Sir, We hear (at the Request of several Gentlemen and Tradesmen of this Town) that a Printing-Press, with New Letter, is coming hither from London, the Proprietor whereof proposes (after having Address'd the Inhabitants with a Laudable Essay on the Excellency of that Noble Art and Mystery) to do all Manner of Printing-Work after the neatest Manner and lowest Rates, and that to the entire Satisfaction of the Publick.

This announcement makes no reference to the starting of a newspaper; but if the unnamed printer published a paper in opposition to Whitworth's *Manchester Gazette* [item 83 in this Register], it may have been this *Manchester Weekly Courant.*

No copy found.

85. The Manchester Journal.

[No. 1 (30 Mar ? 1736)]—no. 22 (24 Aug 1736)—?

Tue.

Manchester: Printed by A. S. at his Printing-Office, at John Berry's near the Cross, and Sold in the following Towns, (viz.) Warrington, Ormskirk, Liverpool, Chester, Wigan, Bolton, Bury, Stockport, Macclesfield, Ashton, Preston, Knutsford, Blackburn, &c. . . .

Central Library, Salford: no. 22 (24 Aug 1736)

86. The Lancashire Journal: with the History of the Holy Bible. [From 30 Jul 1739 con. as]: The Lancashire Journal. [From 24 Mar 1740 con. as]: The Lancashire Journal. With a Description of the Spanish Territories in America not Publish'd in any other Paper sold in Lancashire. [From 22 Dec 1740 con. as]: The Lancashire Journal.

[No. 1 (6 Jul ? 1738)]—no. 3 (20 July 1738)—no. 142 (16 Mar 1741)—?

Thu; by 11 Sep 1738, Mon; from 2 Oct 1739, Tue; from 19 Nov 1739, Mon [but no. 81 was pub. on Sat, 12 Jan 1740].

London, Printed by R. Walker, the Corner of Seacoal Lane, next Fleet Lane. Subscriptions to this Work, and also to the Life of Queen Anne, are taken in by Mr. Richard Gough, at the Spread-Eagle in Castle-Lane, Chester; Mr. Sears, at the White Lyon in Liverpool; at the White Lyon in Bridge-Street, Warrington; and by Mr. Green, at the Reedmakers Arms in Stafford. [No. 11 (11 Sep 1738) has] Manchester: Printed by John Berry, at the Dial near the Cross, . . . [From no. 12 (18 Sep 1738)]: Manchester: Printed and Sold by John Berry, at the Dial near the Cross, and also Sold by Mr. Ozly at the White-Lyon in Warrington, Mr. Sears at the White-Lyon in Liverpool, Mr. Gough at the Spread-

Eagle in Chester, Mr. Maddock Bookseller in Nampt-wich, Mr. Green in Stockport, Mrs. Lord in Rochdale, Mr. Hodgson Bookseller in Hallifax, Mr. Rockett Bookseller in Bradford, Mr. Bradley Peruke-maker in Wakefield; . . .

Manchester Reference Library: nos. 15 (9 Oct 1738) to 142 (16 Mar 1741), inc.

The Vicarage, Mottram-in-Longdendale, Cheshire: no. 3 (20 Jul 1738).

York Minster Library: nos. 11 (11 Sep 1738) to 46 (14 May 1739); nos. 57 (30 Jul 1739) to 69 (23 Oct 1739).

87.   Orion Adams's Weekly Journal; or, The Manchester Advertiser. [From 31 Mar 1752 con. as]: Orion Adams's Manchester Journal; or, The Lancashire and Cheshire Advertiser.

[No. 1 (7 Jan ? 1752)]—no. 3 (31 Jan 1752)—no. 27 (7 Jul 1752)—?

Tue.

Manchester: Printed by O. Adams, and Sold at his Shop, the Upper-End of the Smithy-Door. [Added in no. 9 (3 Mar 1752)]: This Paper may be had every Tuesday at Mr. Higgenson's, Bookseller in Warrington, . . .

Manchester Reference Library: no. 3 (21 Jan 1752), def.; nos. 4 (28 Jan 1752) to 27 (4 Aug 1752).

88.   Harrop's Manchester Mercury. [From 28 Apr 1752 con. as]: Harrop's Manchester Mercury, And General Advertiser. [From 12 Jul 1757 con. as]: The Manchester Mercury and Harrop's General Advertiser.

No. 1 (3 Mar 1752)—no. 463 (30 Dec 1760), + .

Tue.

Manchester: Printed by Joseph Harrop, at the Sign of the Printing Press, opposite the Exchange, . . .

449

Manchester Reference Library: no. 2 (10 Mar 1752); no. 441 (29 Jul 1760); no. 452 (14 Oct 1760); no. 453 (21 Oct 1760); no. 460 (9 Dec 1760).

Chetham's Library, Manchester: nos. 1 (3 Mar 1752) to 463 (30 Dec 1760), some issues lacking two pages, +.

Private library of Kenneth Monkman, Esq., London: no. 49 (13 Feb 1753), first two pp. only; no. 73 (31 Jul 1753), first two pp. only; no. 81 (25 Sep 1753).

89. The Manchester Journal.

[No. 1 (2 Mar ? 1754)]—no. 2 (9 Mar 1754)—?

Sat.

Manchester: Printed by J. Schofield and M. Turnbull, Printers and Booksellers, at their Printing Office, down the Fountain Court, at the Back-Side of the Exchange, . . . [Under title:] Publish'd by J. Schofield and M. Turnbull.

Chetham's Library, Manchester: no. 2 (9 Mar 1754).

MIDDLEWICH

90. Schofield's Middlewich Journal: or, General Advertiser. [By 12 Oct 1756]: Schofield's Middlewich Journal: or, Cheshire Advertiser.

[No. 1 (13 Jul ? 1756)]—no. 5 (10 Aug 1756)—no. 46 (24 May 1757).

Tue.

Middlewich: Printed by James Schofield, . . . *.* Subscriptions and Advertisements for this Paper, are taken in at the following Places. Mr. Clarke, Bookseller in Manchester, Mr. Valans, Bookseller in Liverpool, Mr.

Parsons, Bookseller in Newcastle & Stafford, Mr. Leach, Bookseller in Knotsford, Mr. Rathbone, in Macclesfield, Mr. Purcell, in Congleton, Mr. Maltus, in Northwich, Mr. Church, in Namptwich, Mr. Ralph Hulse, and Mr. Skerrat, Attorney, in Sandbach, Mr. Vernon, at Holms-Chapel, And at the Printing Office in Middlewich.

End noted in *Whitworth's Manchester Advertiser,* no. 3153 (31 May 1757).

British Museum: vol. I, nos. 5 (10 Aug 1756) to 12 (28 Sep 1756); nos. 14 (12 Oct 1756) to 28 (18 Jan 1757); no. 30 (1 Feb 1757) to vol. II, no. 46 (24 May 1757).

NEWCASTLE

91. The New-castle Gazette: or the Northern Courant. Being an Impartial Account of Remarkable Transactions For-reign or Domestick. [By 1712 con. as]: The Newcastle Gazette: or the Northern Courant. Being an Impartial Account of Remarkable Transactions Forreign or Domestick.

[No. 1 (29 Jul ? 1710)]—no. 65 (25 Dec 1710)—no. 308 (14 Jul 1712)—?

Mon, Wed, and Sat; 2 pp.; by 19 Apr 1712, 4 pp.; 2 cols.

Gateside: Printed by J. Saywell for J. Button on the Bridge. [By 19 Apr 1712]: Printed and Sold by H. Law-rence (from the Queen's Printing-House in London) at his House in Pipewell-gate, Gateside.

A letter by Button to Daniel Defoe while he was in Edinburgh shows that the two men were on the most friendly terms. The letter is with the copy of no. 65 in the National Library of Scotland.

The three surviving issues of 1712 have the same heading blocks as were used in Ridpath's *Flying Post* (London).

Newcastle Reference Library: no 271 (19 Apr 1712); no. 304 (5 Jul 1712); no. 308 (14 Jul 1712).

National Library of Scotland: no. 65 (25 Dec 1710).

92.   The Newcastle Courant: with News Forreign and Domestick. [By 25 Sep 1714]: The Newcastle Courant, Giving an Account of the Most Material Occurrences, both Foreign and Domestick. With Such Remarks and Observations upon them as are to be found in the best New [*sic*] Pamphlets. [By 29 Jun 1717]: The Newcastle Courant, Giving an Account of the Most Material Occurrences, both Foreign and Domestick. [By 8 Oct 1720]: The Newcastle Weekly Courant: Or, A General View of the Most Material Occurrences, both Foreign and Domestick: But more particularly of Great-Britain: With Useful Observations on Trade. [By 11 Nov 1721]: The Newcastle Weekly Courant. [From 29 Feb 1724]: The Newcastle Courant.

[No. 1 (1 Aug ? 1711)]—no. 2 (4 Aug 1711)—no. 4396 (27 Dec 1760), + .

Mon, Wed, and Sat; by 8 Oct 1720, Sat; 4 pp.; from 1712 to 24 Apr 1725, 12 pp.; from 1 May 1725, 4 pp.; 2 cols.; from 1712 to 24 Apr 1725, single col.; from 9 Jan 1725, advertisements in 2 cols.; from 1 May 1725, 2 cols.; from 19 Oct 1728, 3 cols.

Newcastle, Printed and Sold by John White, at his House over against the Jevel-groop in the Close; . . . [From 7 Jan 1712]: Newcastle, Printed and Sold by John White, at his House in the Close; . . . [From 26 Nov 1712]: Newcastle upon Tine, Printed and Sold by John White, at his House on the Side. MDCCXII. [By 28 Jul 1716]: Newcastle upon Tine, Printed and Sold by John White, at his House at the Head of the Painter-Heugh. [On 8 Oct 1720]: Newcastle, Printed and Sold by J. White, Mr. Russel in Sunderland, Mrs. Freeman in Durham, Mrs. Isabel Carr in Bishop-Auckland, Mr. Michael Pudsey in Bernard-Castle, Mr. John Thompson in Kirby-Staven, Mr. Birkhead in Kendal, Mr. Bradley in Appleby, Mr. Bramwell in Penrith, Mr. Cook in Carlisle, Mr. Dixon in Hexham, Mr. Robert Mitford in Morpeth, and Mr. Bunian in Alnwick. . . . [By 12 Jan 1723]: Newcastle, Printed and Sold by John White [but later issues in 1723 have long list of distributors]. [By 30 Sep 1732]: Newcastle upon Tyne: Printed and Sold by John White, next Door to the Quaker's Meeting-House in Pilgrim Street. [By 3 Jul 1742]: Newcastle upon Tyne: Printed and Sold by John White, in Pilgrim Street. [By 8 May 1756]: Printed and sold by John White, at his Printing-Office, in Pilgrim-Street, Newcastle-upon-Tyne.

Newcastle Reference Library: nos. 2 (4 Aug 1711) to 157 (30 Jul 1712), with supplement to no. 96 (10 Mar 1712) and many duplicates; nos. 163 (13 Aug 1712) to 171 (1 Sep 1712); no. 223 (31 Dec 1712); no. 284 (25 May 1713); no. 309 (25 Jul 1713); nos. 493 (25 Sep 1714) to 495 (29 Sep 1714); no. 499 (9 Oct 1714); nos. 781 (28 Jul 1716) to 783 (1 Aug 1716); no. 805 (22 Sep 1716); no. 836 (3 Dec 1716); no. 925 (29 Jun 1717); no. 929 (8 Jul 1717); no. 930 (10 Jul 1717); no. 1136 (3 Nov 1718); no. 1137 (5 Nov 1718); no. 16 (8 Oct 1720); no. 22 (19 Nov 1720); nos. 32 (28 Jan 1721) to 254 (24 Apr 1725), nearly complete, with some duplicates; nos. 1 (1 May 1725) to 381 (12 Aug 1732), nearly complete, with many duplicates; no. 388 (30 Sep 1732); no. 391 (25 Nov 1732); no. 396 (25 Nov 1732); no. 398 (9 Dec 1732); nos. 403 (13 Jan 1733) to 553 (29 Dec 1735), lacking six issues; nos. 558 (3 Jan 1736) to 830 (21 Mar 1741), lacking four issues; nos. 2468 (4 Apr 1741) to 4396 (27 Dec 1760), nearly complete, + .

Newcastle Society of Antiquaries: no. 298 (9 Jan 1731); nos. 2612 (14 Jan 1744) to 2639 (21 Jul 1744); nos. 2641 (4 Aug 1744) to 2662 (29 Dec 1744); nos. 2767 (3 Jan 1747) to 2797 (1 Aug 1747); nos. 2799 (15 Aug 1747) to 2818 (26 Dec 1747); nos. 2873 (14 Jan 1749) to 2923 (30 Dec 1749), lacking two issues; nos. 2976 (5 Jan 1751) to 3027 (28 Dec 1751); nos. 3081 (20 Jan 1753) to 4031 [*sic*] (29 Dec 1753), many issues missing; nos. 4032 (5 Jan 1754) to 4396 (27 Dec 1760), nearly complete, + .

Newcastle Literary and Philosophical Society: no. 2529 (12 Jun 1742); no. 2897 (1 Jul 1749); no. 2995 (18 May 1751).

Ushaw College, Durham: nos. 2509 (16 Jan 1742) to 2712 (14 Dec 1746), lacking five issues.

Kingston-upon-Hull Museum: no. 22 (25 Sep 1725).

National Library of Scotland: no. 2707 (9 Nov 1745).

Office of Berrow's Newspapers Ltd., Worcester: no. 209 (26 Apr 1729).

Bodleian Library: nos. 2703 (12 Oct 1745) to 2737 (7 Jun 1746), fourteen issues only.

British Museum: no. 208 (26 Nov 1712), fac. rep. (1887); nos. 692 (2 Jan 1716) to 743 (30 Apr 1716); nos. 213 (18 Jul 1724) to 254 (24 Apr 1725).

Press Club: nos. 2532 (3 Jul 1742) to 2534 (17 Jul 1742).

University of Reading: nos. 2820 (9 Jan 1748) to 2872 (7 Jan 1749), lacking four issues.

Yale University: no. 2656 (17 Nov 1744); no. 2953 (28 Jul 1750); no. 3064 (23 Sep 1752).

Library of Congress: no. 2713 (21 Dec 1745).

93. The New-Castle Weekly Mercury. [From 27 Apr 1723 con. as]: The New-Castle Weekly Journal.

[No. 1 (14 Jul ? 1722)]—no. 30 (2 Feb 1723)—no. 44 (11 May 1723)—[18 May ? 1723].

Sat; 12 pp.; single col.

New-Castle: Printed and Sold by D. Jones, at the Queen's Head on the Side, by Mr. Akenhead, Bookseller on the Bridge; Mr. Alderman Hall, Bookseller, Carlisle; Mr. William Richardson in Penrith; Mr. John Laidler in Hexham; Mr. Thomas Rennison, in Morpeth; Mr. William Penderton, at Darlington; Mr. Joseph Willen, at Staindrop; Mr. William Sands at Stockton and Gisborough; Mr. Thomas Bunyan, at Alnwick; Mr. J. Smith, at Bishop-Auckland; Mr. James Hamilton at Appleby; Mr. W. Paterson, at West-Auckland; Mr. Edward Atkinson at Brampton; and, at Mr. Alexander Dodds in Berwick. . . . [So in no. 30; slight changes in others.]

Notice in no. 43 (4 May 1723):

> Whereas Mr. Akenhead hath thought fit, for Reasons best known to himself, to decline the Business of Printing, and the rest of the Partners not having Leisure to mind and observe the same, the Affair requiring almost constant Attendance; These are to inform the Publick, That if any Person or Persons, who have Opportunity or Leisure to attend the Business, or desirous of following the same, they will dispose of the Printing Materials to them at reasonable Rates; or if any Person who hath Opportunity to attend it, have a mind to come in as a Partner, the Company will treat with him.
>
> N.B. All who are Indebted to the Company for News, or any Work done, are desired forthwith to send the Money to Mr. Tho. Swinhoe, Glover, on the Tine Bridge, they designing to decline the Business the 18th of this Month.

Newcastle Reference Library: no. 30 (2 Feb. 1723); no. 32 (16 Feb 1723); no. 40 (13 Apr 1723); no. 41 (20 Apr 1723); no. 43 (4 May 1723); no. 44 (11 May 1723).

94.   The North Country Journal: or, the Impartial Intelligencer.

[No. 1 (17 Aug ? 1734)]—no. 17 (7 Dec 1734)—no. 160 (10 Sep 1737)—[1738?]

Sat.

Newcastle upon Tyne: Printed by Isaac Lane and Company, at the Head of the Side, . . . [By 8 Nov 1735]: Newcastle upon Tyne: Printed by Leonard Umphreville, at the Head of the Side, . . . [By 26 Feb 1737]: Newcastle upon Tyne. Printed by Leonard Umphreville and Company, . . . [By 26 Mar 1737]: Newcastle upon Tyne: Printed by —— Umphreville and Company, . . . [By 14 May 1737]: Newcastle upon Tyne: Printed by Thomas Umphreville and Company, . . .

It was announced in no. 65 (8 Nov 1735) that Leonard Umphreville and Isaac Lane had dissolved their partnership.

Notice in the *Newcastle Courant*, no. 714 (30 Dec. 1738):

> All Persons indebted to the Printing-Office, lately carried on by Mr. Leonard Umphreville and Company, are hereby requested immediately to pay their respective Debts to Mr. Wm Rutter, Attorney at Law in Newcastle, who is properly authorized to receive the same, and to no other Person, or they will be prosecuted for the same.

Newcastle Reference Library: nos. 65 (8 Nov 1735) to 160 (10 Sep 1737), thirteen issues only.

American Antiquarian Society, Worcester, Massachusetts: no. 17 (7 Dec 1734); no. 42 (31 May 1735); no. 45 (21 Jun 1735); no. 46 (28 Jun 1735); nos. 48 (12 Jul 1735) to 51 (2 Aug 1735), with duplicate of no. 50 (26 Jul 1735).

95. The Newcastle Journal.

No. 1 (7 Apr 1739)—no. 1127 (27 Dec 1760), + .

Sat.

Under date line: Published by I. Thompson and W. Cuthbert. [From 2 Oct 1742]: Published by I. Thompson and Company. [From 8 Jun 1751]: Printed and Publish'd by I. Thompson and Company.

[Colophon]: Newcastle upon Tyne: Printed by William Cuthbert, on the Head of the Side. [From 3 May 1740]: Newcastle upon Tyne: Printed by William Cuthbert, on the Side; . . . [From 2 Oct 1742]: Newcastle upon Tyne: Printed by John Brown, on the Side, . . . [From 6 Nov 1742]: Newcastle upon Tyne: Printed by John Gooding, on the Side; . . . [By 21 Dec 1745]: Newcastle upon Tyne: Printed by John Gooding, in the Burnthouse Entry on the Side; . . . [From 8 Jun 1751]: At the New Printing-Office on the Side, Newcastle, Subscriptions and Advertisements for this Paper, . . . are taken in.

No. 57 (3 May 1740) has this notice: ☞ This Paper is now printed on the Middle of the Side, where the new Printing-Office will be kept for the future.

No. 184 (9 Oct 1742) has this notice about the dissolution of the Thompson-Cuthbert partnership:

> Whereas an Advertisement has been published by William Cuthbert, and dispersed about the Country, manifestly calculated to abuse and injure my Character and Interest: This is to inform the Publick, that the scandalous Aspersions and Accusations contained in the said Advertisement are all utterly false and groundless, which I am prepared and ready to prove, if any Person will take the trouble of calling upon me at the NEW PRINTING OFFICE where the genuine Newcastle Journal will continue to be published, and all other Printing-Work will be perform'd at the most moderate Prices.
>
> ISAAC THOMPSON.
>
> N.B. All Debts to the late Partnership, ending the 25th of September last, are desired to be paid to the said Isaac Thompson.

No. 234 (24 Sep 1743) has this notice identifying the proprietors:

Newcastle. September 24, 1743.

Whereas Enquiry has frequently been made, to know what Persons are concern'd in the Publication of this Paper, and of late some Mistakes have been made about it: We apprehend it is proper to satisfy the Publick, and do Justice to ourselves in this Particular; and therefore take this Opportunity of assuring our Readers, that we, whose Names are hereunto subscribed, are the only Proprietors of the NEWCASTLE JOURNAL; which, thro' the great Favour of the Publick, is more generally read, and has a larger Circulation thro' the Counties of Durham, York, Lancaster, Westmoreland, Cumberland, and Northumberland, and also the South of Scotland, than any other News Paper; and on that Account, as it must be the Advantage of those who have occasion to advertise in the North to appear in it, so we hope that our Friends will not only continue to oblige us with their own Advertisements, but likewise recommend others to our Paper. Also, whoever has occasion to have any kind of Printing Work perform'd, may be served expeditiously, in the best manner, and at the most moderate Prices, by applying either to John Gooding, Printer, at the New Printing-office in the Burnt-house Entry on the Side, or to any one of us.

ISAAC THOMPSON,
JONATHAN WALKER,
PEREGRINE TYZACK,
ROBERT THORP.

No. 663 (21 Dec 1751) has this notice about John Gooding:

All Persons indebted to John Gooding, Printer in Newcastle, deceased, at the Time of his Death, are desired immediately to pay their respective Debts to Joseph King, Cooper, or to George Bewley, both of Newcastle aforesaid, who are legally empowered to receive the same; . . .

458

Newcastle Reference Library: nos. 1 (7 Apr 1739) to 704 (14 Oct 1752); nos. 706 (28 Oct 1752) to 1065 (29 Sep 1759); nos. 1067 (13 Oct 1759) to 1127 (27 Dec 1760), + .

Newcastle Society of Antiquaries: nos. 248 (7 Jan 1744) to 299 (29 Dec 1744), lacking two issues; nos. 404 (3 Jan 1747) to 434 (1 Aug 1747); nos. 436 (Aug 1747) to 455 (26 Dec 1747); nos. 509 (7 Jan 1749), def., to 1127 (27 Dec 1760), nearly complete, with many duplicates, + .

Ushaw College, Durham: no. 339 (5 Oct 1745).

Kingston-upon-Hull Museum: no. 771 (2 Feb. 1754).

Berrow's Newspapers, Ltd., Worcester: no. 346 (23 Nov 1745).

Bodleian Library: no. 346 (23 Nov 1745); no. 347 (30 Nov 1745); no. 349 (14 Dec 1745); no. 405 (10 Jan 1747); no. 418 (11 Apr 1747); no. 419 (18 Apr 1747); no. [428] (20 Jun 1747).

British Museum: nos. 1 (7 Apr 1739) to 312 (30 Mar 1745); no. 672 (22 Feb 1752).

University of Reading: nos. 456 (2 Jan 1748) to 493 (17 Sep 1748); nos. 495 (1 Oct 1748) to 498 (22 Oct 1748); nos. 500 (5 Nov 1748) to 507 (24 Dec 1748).

Yale University: no. 351 (28 Dec 1745); no. 897 (24 Jul 1756); nos. 921 (8 Jan 1757) to 942 (11 Jun 1757), seven issues only: nos. 1068 (20 Oct 1759) to 1078 (29 Dec 1759); nos. 1089 (15 Mar 1760) to 1126 (20 Dec 1760), fifteen issues only, + .

New York Public Library: no. 364 (29 Mar 1746).

Library of Congress: no. 350 (21 Dec 1745).

96.   The Newcastle Gazette: or, Tyne-Water Journal. [By 13 Nov 1745 con. as]: The Newcastle Gazette.

[No. 1 (20 Jun ? 1744)]—no. 9 (15 Aug 1744)—no. 393 (25 Dec 1751)—[1755?]

Wed.

Printed and Sold by W. Cuthbert in Cutters-Entry in the Close, . . .

Newcastle Reference Library: no. 86 (5 Feb 1746).

Newcastle Society of Antiquaries: no. 9 (15 Aug 1744); nos. 81 (1 Jan 1746) to 185 (30 Dec 1747), lacking ten issues; nos. 238 (4 Jan 1749) to 289 (27 Dec 1749), lacking one issue; nos. 343 (9 Jan 1751) to 393 (25 Dec 1751), lacking one issue.

Bodleian Library: nos. 74 (13 Nov 1745) to 141 (25 Feb 1747); no. 144 (18 Mar 1747); no. 145 (22 Mar 1747).

University of Reading: nos. 186 (6 Jan 1748) to 213 (13 Jul 1748); no. 215 (27 Jul 1748); nos. 218 (17 Aug 1748) to 235 (14 Dec 1748).

97.   The Newcastle Intelligencer.

[No. 1 (15 Oct 1755)]—no. 7 (26 Nov 1755)—no. 190 (30 May 1759).

Wed.

[Under title]: Printed and Publish'd by William Cuthbert and Company. [Colophon]: Printed by William Cuthbert, at his Printing-Office in the Custom-house-Entry. . . .

No. 190 has this announcement:

The Publication of this Paper will, pursuant to former Notice, be discontinued after this Day. . . .

Newcastle Reference Library: nos. 34 (2 Jun 1756) to 178 (7 Mar 1759), ten issues only.

Newcastle Society of Antiquaries: nos. 7 (26 Nov 1755) to 190 (30 May 1759), inc.

NORTHAMPTON

98. Northampton Mercury, or the Monday's Post. Being a Collection of the most Material Occurrences, Foreign & Domestick. Together with An Account of Trade. [From 24 Jul 1721 con. as]: The Northampton Mercury.

Vol. I, no. 1 (2 May 1720)—vol. XLI, no. 40 (29 Dec 1760), + .

Mon; 12 pp.; from 3 May 1725, 4 pp.; single col.; from 28 Aug 1721, 2 cols.; from 1 May 1727, 3 cols.

Northampton: Printed by R. Raikes and W. Dicey, near All Saints Church; . . . [By 20 Nov 1721]: Northampton: Printed by R. Raikes and W. Dicey. . . . [From 24 May 1725]: Northampton: Printed by William Dicey and Robert Raikes, 1725. [From 20 Sep 1725]: Northampton: Printed by William Dicey. . . . [By 4 Apr 1757]: Northampton: Printed by Cluer Dicey. . . . [From 2 Apr 1759]: Printed by Cluer Dicey: And may be had of J. Ellington in Huntingdon, and W. Ward, at Sheffield, in Yorkshire, Booksellers and Stationers. . . .

Northampton Public Library: vol. I, no. 1 (2 May 1720), to vol. XLI, no. 40 (29 Dec 1760), + .

Bodleian Library: vol. III, no. 144 (28 Jan 1723), to vol. IV, no. 266 (1 Jul 1723); vol. IV, no. [298] ([10] Feb 1724), def., to vol. VI, no. 33 (13 Dec 1725), thirteen issues only; vol. VIII, no. 7 (12 Jun 1727), to vol. XVIII, no. 48 (13 Mar 1738), seventeen issues only; vol. XXVI, no. [27] (7 Oct 1745); no. 30 (28 Oct 1745); no. [34] (25 Nov 1745).

Oxford University Press Ephemeral Collection: vol. XI, no. 30 (16 Nov 1730), to vol. XXII, no. 38 (28 Dec 1741), sixteen issues only; vol. XXVI, no. 5 (6 May 1745); vol. XLI, no. 33 (10 Nov 1760).

All Souls' Library, Oxford: vol. I, no. 20. (12 Sep 1720); no. 25 (17 Oct 1725); vol. IV, no. 293 (6 Jan 1724), to vol. V, no. 361 (Sat, 24 Apr 1725); vol. VI, no. 1 (3 May 1725); vol. IX, no. 52 (21 Apr 1729).

Cambridge University Library: vol. XXXVII, no. 12 (21 Jun 1756); vol. XXXVIII, no. 42 (16 Jan 1758).

British Museum: vol. I, nos. 1 (2 May 1720) to 52 (24 Apr 1721); vol. III, nos. 127 (1 Oct 1722) to 151 (18 Mar 1723); vol. XIV, nos. 4 (14 May 1733) to 29 (5 Nov 1733); vol. XXI, no. 11 (30 Jun 1740); vol. XXIV, no. 26 (30 Oct 1743), to vol. XXVIII, no. 45 (8 Feb 1748); vol. XXVIII, no. 47 (22 Feb 1748), to vol. XXIX, no. 24 (12 Sep 1748); vol. XXIX, no. 26 (26 Sep 1748), to vol. XXXII, no. 40 (30 Dec 1751).

Press Club: vol. IX, no. 30 (18 Nov 1728); vol. XXIX, no. 19 (8 Aug 1748).

Yale University: vol. IX, no. 26 (28 Oct 1728).

Library of Congress: vol. III, no. 105 (30 Apr 1722), to vol. IV, no. 282 (21 Oct 1723); vol. IV, no. 284 (4 Nov 1723), to vol. V, no. 310 (4 May 1724).

Wisconsin Historical Society: vol. XI, no. 22 (21 Sep 1730), to vol. XVI, no. 19 (25 Aug 1735), inc.

University of Texas: vol. XXVII, no. 7 (19 May 1746).

99.　Northampton Journal.

[No. 1 (7 Jul 1722)]—[no. 2 (14 Jul 1722)]—?

Sat; 6 or 12 pp. (referred to as "a Sheet and a Half of Waste Paper" by the proprietors of the *Northampton Mercury*); 2 cols.

This paper and its printer, James Pasham, are mentioned disparagingly by Robert Raikes and William Dicey in their *Northampton Mercury*, vol. III, no. 115 (Mon, 9 Jul 1722), and the first two issues are quoted in the *Northampton Mercury* of 23 Jul 1722.

No copy found.

100. Jopson's Coventry and Northampton Mercury, or Weekly Country Journal.

According to an unsigned article, "The Coventry Standard Over Two Centuries," in the *Coventry Standard* of 19 July 1941, a few issues of *Jopson's Coventry Mercury* (item 34 in this Register) were printed in Northampton, the imprint of the issue dated 28 Feb 1743 being: Northampton: Printed by J. Jopson, in Gold Street. By 11 Apr 1743, the paper was again being printed in Coventry.

No copy bearing the Northampton imprint has been found.

NORWICH

101. The Norwich Post: To be Publish'd Weekly: Containing An Account of the most Remarkable Transactions both Foreign and Domestick. [By 19 Feb 1709 con. as]: The Norwich-Post: Publish'd Weekly: Containing the most Remarkable Transactions both Foreign and Domestick. [By Jul 1712 con. as]: The Norwich-Post: With the Freshest Advices, Foreign and Domestick.

[No. 1 (8 Nov ? 1701)]—no. 287 (3 May 1707)—no. 594 (5 Jul 1712)—?

Sat; 2 pp. (?) while Francis Burges was alive (see Hasbart's letter, quoted below); by 3 May 1707, 4 pp.; 2 cols.

[From 1701, printed by Francis Burges]. [By 3 May 1707]: Printed by E. Burges, near the Red-well in Norwich. [By 1 May 1708]: Norwich, Printed by E. Burges, near the Red-Well. 1708. [By 19 Feb 1709]: Norwich, Printed by the Administrator of E. Burges, near the Red-Well, 1709.

This letter was printed in the last column of the *Norwich Gazette,* no. 60 (20 Dec 1707):

Mrs. *Burges,*

THE Printing Business in this Town, as your Husband well experienced, is no more than what One Man can sufficiently perform; You Yourself having given away half the Profit your Husband had by selling a Whole Sheet for a Peny, whereas your Husband never sold a Half Sheet for less: So that 'tis plain, while there are Three of Us, no one can boast of the Gain that is now made. I would be glad to have the Whole in my own Hands, and in order to it do offer you the real Value of what Letter and Stock you have in that Way, and to find Employment for your Man (or Men) into Bargain as soon as you please to discharge them. But as your Husband first set up the Trade here, and left you in Possession of it, you may possibly have taken too great a Liking to the Business to accept of this Offer; if so, I am willing to part with my Materials and Man to you upon the same Terms: If you object that complying with me will do you no Service, there being another still to contend with, who may possibly be rather strengthen'd than weaken'd by my laying down, I farther offer as a Recompense for the Damage you have sustain'd by having Two to contend with all this while, which you are sensible may be made appear was not my Fault at first, let such Friends as you can best confide in name what Method they think most adviseable and likely to bring the other Person to reasonable Terms, and I will be oblig'd to join with you in it: In the mean time, till a more likely Expedient can be found out, I propose this, Let You and I join Partnership for seven Years; (which if we do, I believe no Rational Man will advise that other Person otherwise than to lay down as soon as it be known) and to take off all Jealousie or Apprehension that you or any for you may conceive, that my Design herein should be more for my own private Interest than for yours in the End, I will before we enter into Partnership oblige my self in Bond under what Penalty you please, to lay down the Business wholly when ever you require it of me, you first paying me or giving Security to pay me for my Types, &c. and to provide employ for my Man as above. If you do not think fit to accept of this Proposal, or in a short Time offer a more fair one of your own, you will find the Profit of the Business grow still less by the Example you first set, for there is a Necessity that some of us lay down. I therefore desire you will advise with those you can best trust, whether what I offer be reasonable.

I am Your Friend, *Samuel Hasbart.*

For Mrs. Burges's rejection of this offer, see above, p. 30.

No. 351 (22 May 1708) has this notice:

These are to give Notice, That this Paper begins to be publish'd in Yarmouth this Day, and is to be continu'd weekly. Advertisements are taken in at Yarmouth every Saturday at the Three Wrestlers, where any Person may speak with the Printer about any other Business whatsoever, and shall be reasonable [so] used by him, it being the first Printing-house that ever was in Norwich.

No. 390 (19 Feb 1709) has this notice:

Whereas there has been a Report spread abroad, That the late Widow Burges's Printing-house was to be left off at Michaelmas, This is to satisfy, that it is utterly false, and never was intended; but will be continued with Expedition and Diligence. Where any Person that has occasion to Publish Advertisements in this Paper, or to Print other Things, shall be very reasonably used, and their Business perform'd with Care and Speed.

Norwich Public Library: no. 349 (8 May 1708); no. 351 (22 May 1708); no. 352 (29 May 1708); no. 390 (19 Feb 1709); no. 404 (14 May 1709); no. 413 (23 Jul 1709).

Bridewell Museum, Norwich: no. 594 (5 Jul 1712).

Saffron Walden Museum: no. 287 (3 May 1707).

British Museum: no. 348 (1 May 1708).

102. The Norwich Gazette: or, the Accurate weekly Intelligencer. [From 8 Feb 1707 con. as]: The Norwich Gazette: or, the Loyal Packet. [By 30 Aug 1712 con. as]: The Norwich Gazette Or the Loyal Packet. To be Published Weekly in Norwich and Great Yarmouth. [By 17 Jul 1714 con. as]: The Norwich Gazette or the Loyal Packet. [From 17 Nov 1722 con. as]: The Norwich Gazette.

No. 1 (7 Dec 1706)—vol. XLIII, no. 2236 (30 Dec 1749)—?

Sat; from 5 Mar 1707, Wed and Sat; from 5 Apr 1707, Sat; 2 pp.; from 29 Mar 1707, 4 pp.; from 2 Aug 1712, 6 pp.; by 30 Aug 1712, 2 pp.; by 17 Jul 1714, 6 pp.; from 1 May 1725, 4 pp.; 2 cols.; from 27 Sep 1740, 3 cols.

Norwich: Printed by Hen. Cross-grove, near the Bull-inn, in Magdalen-street, 1706. [From 28 Dec 1706]: Norwich. Printed by Hen. Cross-grove in Magdalen-street, 1706 [etc.] [By 2 Dec 1710]: Norwich: Printed by Henry Cross-grove, 1710. [By 30 Aug 1712]; Norwich: Printed by Henry Cross-grove, living in St. Edmund's, 1712. [By 17 Jul 1714]: Norwich: Printed by Henry Cross-grove, in St. Edmund's, 1714. [From 10 Aug 1717]: Printed by Henry Cross-grove, living in St. Edmund's Parish, 1717. [From 22 Mar 1718]: Norwich: Printed by Henry Cross-grove, living near the Church in St. Giles's Parish; . . . [By 5 Jan 1723]: Norwich: Printed by Henry Cross-grove, in St. Giles's Parish, 1723 [etc.] [From 22 Sep 1744]: Norwich: Printed by Mary Cross-grove and Robert Davy, in St. Giles's Parish, 1744. [From 24 Nov 1744]: Cross-grove's News, printed for R. Davy in St. Giles's Parish in Norwich, 1744. [From 5 Apr 1746]: Cross-grove's News printed for R. Davy, in St. Giles's Parish, 1746; and sold by Mr. Tho. Watson in the Market-Row in Yarmouth, . . . [From 11 Mar 1749 the name of Mr. Woods, School-Master, follows that of Watson.]

In no. 13 (1 March 1707) is this announcement:

> This is to give Notice, That at the Request of several Gentlemen, the NORWICH GAZETTE will be Printed every Wednesday and Saturday, that all Persons who send me Questions may have speedier Answers. And all those Persons that have advertisements put into this News-paper, shall have them Printed as many Wednesdays for nothing, as they pay for Saturdays.

In vol. XII, no. 598 (22 Mar 1718) is this announcement:

> All my loyal Friends and Customers are desir'd to take Notice, that I am now intirely remov'd from where I did live in St. Edmund's Parish, and have actually set up my Printing-Office just by the Church in St. Giles's Parish in this City, where Advertisements are taken in for Cross-grove's News, and at no other Place. Note, that the Fellow with the Crutches sells my News no longer, I having turn'd him out for several Abuses; therefore pray take Care of being deceiv'd.

The death of Henry Cross-grove was announced in the *Norwich Gazette*, vol. XXXVIII, no. 1980 (15 Sep 1744):

> Norwich, September 15. On Wednesday last departed this Life Mr. HENRY CROSS-GROVE, aged 62, Printer of *The Norwich Gazette* and *Magazine* upwards of 38 Years. He was a Man allowed by all Persons of Ingenuity and Learning to be a Man of Learning, Sense, and Spirit. And as his Paper did always appear with the greatest Spirit, Integrity, and Correctness, of any Paper yet extant, so We design (God willing) to continue it in the same Channel, and hope to give the same Satisfaction to all Our good Friends and Customers; and return them Our grateful Thanks, for all their Goodness to the printer now deceased; and are incouraged to hope their Goodness and future Favour will be continued to US his Widow and Son-in-Law, MARY CROSS-GROVE and ROB. DAVY.

For an account of Cross-grove's quarrels and difficulties, see above, pp. 29-30.

Norwich Public Library: [vol. I], no. 1 (7 Dec 1706), to vol. XXXV, no. 1787 (3 Jan 1741), inc., many duplicates; vol. XXXVI, no. 1874 (4 Sep 1742).

Cambridge University Library: vol. XXXV, no. 1787 (3 Jan 1741), to vol. XXXVIII, no. 1944 (7 Jan 1744); vol. XLI, no. 2100 (3 Jan 1747), to vol. XLII, no. 1300 [*sic*] (3 Dec 1748); vol. XLIII, nos. 2190 (11 Feb 1749) to 2236 (30 Dec 1749), three def.

British Museum: vol. VI, no. 276 (19 Jan 1712), def.; no. 277 (26 Jan 1712), def.; vol. VIII, no. [?] (27 Nov 1714), pp. 5-6 only; vol. XIX, no. 969 (1 May 1725), to vol. XXVII, no. 1399 (28 Jul 1733), inc.; vol. XXXV, no. 1811 (20 Jun 1741), to vol. XXXVII, no. 1861 (5 Jun 1742); vol. XXXVIII, no. 1945 (14 Jan 1744), to vol. XLI, no. 2151 (24 Dec 1747), lacking five issues.

Bodleian Library: vol. XL, no. 2058 (15 Mar 1746).

All Souls' Library, Oxford: vol. VIII, no. 406 (17 Jul 1714).

New York Public Library: 4 Mar 1727 and 2 May 1728, fac.

Huntington Library: vol. XXVI, no. 1331 (8 Apr 1732).

103. The Norwich Post-man: with Remarkable Occurrences both Foreign and Domestick, To be continued Weekly.

[No. 1 (28 Dec 1706)]—vol. II, no. 68 (10 Apr 1708)—vol. III, no. 135 (30 Jul 1709)—[no. ? (Feb 1710)]—?

Sat; 2 cols.

Norwich: Printed by W. C. for Tho. Goddard, Bookseller, 1708.

Imprint of an early issue is given by [John Chambers], *A General History of the County of Norfolk* (Norwich: Stacy, 1829), II, 1291, as: "Printed by S. Sheffield, for T. Goddard, Bookseller, Norwich." Publication as late as 1710 is indicated by a letter from a correspondent in the

Norwich Gazette: or, the Loyal Packet, vol. IV, no. 175 (Sat, 11 Feb 1710), beginning:

Mr. Cross-grove,

Yesterday by Chance I saw a News-paper Printed for Tho. Goddard, . . .

Norwich Public Library: vol. II, no. 68 (10 Apr 1708); vol. III, no. 135 (30 Jul 1709).

104. The Norwich Courant: or, Weekly Packet.

[1714?]—[4 Feb 1716]—1718—?

Sat.

It is stated in [John Chambers], *A General History of the County of Norfolk* (Norwich: Stacy, 1829), II, 1291, that the *Norwich Courant, or Weekly Packet* appeared in 1714, "printed by S. Collins, afterwards by John Collins, and then by H. Collins, . . . near the Red Well, St Andrew's," and that the author was a Whig. Dr. Cranfield names Freeman Collins and Edward Cave as responsible for the *Norwich Courant* until, by 1716, it was printed by Mrs. Susannah Collins. An advertisement "which was last Saturday printed in Mrs. Collins's News" was quoted in the *Norwich Gazette,* vol. X, no. 488 (11 Feb 1716). A reference in the *Norwich Gazette,* no. 598 (22 Mar 1718), suggests that the *Norwich Courant* was still appearing in 1718:

One of the witty News Printers in this City having endeavour'd to clear the WHIGG *Weekly Journal* from the Scandal of having *Richard Burridge* for its Author, who has been Twice convicted of speaking horrid Blasphemous Words, by cunningly affirming that he was only Corrector of the said Paper, &c. I cannot but observe, supposing it is as he says, that the WHIGG News-Paper must certainly be horrid Stuff, if they stand in Need of the Correction of a Blasphemer.

No copy found.

105. The Transactions of the Universe: Or the Weekly-Mercury. With Remarkable Occurrences Domestick and Foreign. To be continued Weekly. [By 22 Oct 1722 con. as]: The Weekly-Mercury: or, the Protestant Packet. Containing the most Remarkable Occurrences Foreign and Domestick. [From 12 Feb 1726 con. as]: The Norwich Mercury.

[Vol. I, no. 1 (? 1713)]—vol. II, no. 29 (17 Jul 1714)—20 Oct 1722—27 Dec 1760, + .

Sat; 12 pp.; by 20 Oct 1722, 6 pp.; from 1 May 1725, 4 pp.; single col.; by 20 Oct 1722, 2 cols.; from 20 Sep 1740, 3 cols.

[By 17 Jul 1714]: Printed by W. Chase in the Dove Lane for Tho. Goddard. . . . [By 22 Oct 1722]: Norwich: Printed by W. Chase in the Cockey-Lane, . . . [From 2 Jun 1744]: Norwich: Printed and sold by the Widow of the late W. Chase, in the Cockey-Lane; and also by Mrs. Samuel, Bookseller in Lynn, and Mr. Haliday, Bookseller in Yarmouth; . . . [From 31 Mar 1750]: Norwich: Printed and sold by William Chase, in the Cockey-Lane; also by Mr. Hollingworth, Bookseller in Lynn; and Mr. Campbell, Bookseller in Yarmouth; . . . [From 14 Jul 1753]: Norwich: Printed and sold by W. Chase, in the Cockey-Lane, 1753 [etc.]

The death of William Chase was announced in the *Norwich Mercury* dated 2 Jun 1744:

> On Thursday last after a short Illness, died Mr. William Chase, who had printed the Norwich Mercury for about 30 Years. . . . His Friends will assist the Widow in conducting this Paper, for whose Benefit it will be carried on, depending on the more than ordinary Favour with which it has of late been received by the Publick.

Norwich Public Library: 20 Oct 1722; 24 Nov 1722; 29 Jun 1723, pp. 1-4 only; 1 May 1725 to 26 Oct 1728, with duplicates; 8 Feb 1729 to 27 Dec 1760, + .

Cambridge University Library: 3 Feb 1728, rep.; 16 Sep 1749 to 27 Dec 1760, + .

British Museum: 5 Oct 1728; 31 Mar 1750 to 29 Dec 1753; 9 Jul 1757.

Bodleian Library: 21 Jan 1727 to 11 Mar 1727; 1 Jul 1727; 2 Sep 1727; 16 Sep 1727; 28 Oct 1727; 3 Feb 1728 to 16 Mar 1728; all rep.; 26 Feb 1732 to 18 Mar 1732; no. 422 (27 May 1758).

All Souls' Library, Oxford: vol. II, no. 29 (17 Jul 1714).

University of Chicago Library: fac. rep. of fifty issues from 1727 to 1731, pub. as supp. to *Norwich Mercury* from 9 Jan 1884 to 11 Dec 1889; 28 Jul 1733 to 28 Jul 1759, inc.

Huntington Library: 12 Feb 1732.

106. The Norwich Journal: or, Weekly Intelligencer.

[No. 1 (? 1751)]—vol. III, no. 401 (2 Jun 1753)—?

Sat.

Norwich: Printed and Sold by R. Davy, near St. Giles's Gates: Also Sold at Mr. Dixon's, late Goddard's, and Mr. Goodman's, in the Dove-Lane; and by Messrs. Watson and Woods in Yarmouth: . . .

Although the serial number of the only issue seen implies that the paper had been running for nearly eight years, it is unlikely that the *Norwich Journal* began as early as 1745, since Davy was printing the *Norwich Gazette* as late as December, 1749. If the issue of 2 Jun 1753 is properly reckoned as belonging in the third annual volume, the implication is that the paper began in 1751; but if the serial number 401 is correct, the paper began in 1745.

Norwich Public Library: vol. III, no. 401 (2 Jun 1753).

NOTTINGHAM

107. The Nottingham Post: Being a Faithful Account Of all the Publick News, &c. Impartially Collected from the Best Accounts.

[No. 1 (4 Oct ? 1710)]—no. 42 (18 Jul 1711)—no. 65 (19 [for 14] Dec 1711)—?

Wed; by 14 Dec 1711, Fri; 2 pp.; 2 cols.

Nottingham: Printed and Sold by John Collyer, Bookseller in the Long-Row. And Sold by B. Farnworth in Newark, T. Dickson at his Stall over against the Crown in Mansfield, and John Green Cutler at his Stall in Loughborough. [By 14 Dec 1711]: Nottingham: Printed and Sold by John Collyer in the Long-Row. And Sold by Tho. Sheppard in Derby, and Sam. Gunter in Chesterfield.

Nottingham Central Library: no. 42 (18 Jul 1711).

Nottingham Castle: no. 65 (19 [for 14] Dec 1711).

108. The Weekly Courant Containing a Faithful Account of All Publick Transactions both Foreign and Domestick. Together with Remarks on Trade. [By 1 Jun 1749 con. as]: The Nottingham Weekly Courant. [By 29 Jan 1757 con. as]: Ayscough's Nottingham Courant.

[No. 1 (7 Aug ? 1712)]—vol. IV, no. 21 (22 Dec 1715)— [vol. I, no. 1 (29 Apr ? 1725)]—vol. I, no. 6 (3 Jun 1725) —vol. XXXIV, no. 267 (27 Dec 1760), + .

Thu; by 29 Jan 1757, Sat; 12 pp.; by 3 Jun 1725, 4 pp.; single col.; by 3 Jun 1725, 2 cols.; by 1 Jun 1749, 3 cols.

Nottingham: Printed and sold by William Ayscough, in Bridlesmithgate, and by Mr. Hodges and Mr. Allstree Booksellers in Derby, Mr. Hoyle Brascaster in York, Mr. Sagg Bookseller in York, Mr. Carlton in Gainsborough.

Mr. Dixon in Mansfield. Mr. Unwin in Ashby-de-la-Zouch. Mr. Farnsworth in Newark, William Green in Sheffield. Mr. Bradley in Chesterfield. Mrs. Taylor in Doncaster. and Mr. Swale in Leeds, and at his Shop in Wakefield. . . . [Many additions and changes in subsequent lists of agents.] [By 20 Oct 1720]: Nottingham: Printed and Sold by Anne Ayscough in Bridlesmithgate. . . . [By 2 Jun 1737]: Nottingham, Printed by George Ayscough, in Bridlesmithgate, . . . This Paper is likewise sold by Mr. Allestree, Mr. Roe, and Mr. Trimmer, Booksellers in Derby; Mr. Hardy in Burton upon Trent; R. Tattershall in Ashburn; Mr. Bradley, Bookseller in Chesterfield; Mr. Haxby, Bookseller in Sheffield; Mr. Inman, Bookseller in Doncaster; Mr. Thompson, Bookseller in Gainsborough; J. Hostead in Melton Mowbray; and by Mansfield, Southwell, Newark, and Melton Posts, and by [Mrs. Heathcote Bookseller in Uttoxeter]. . . . [additional names and places in later issues]. [By 1 Jun 1749]: Nottingham: Printed and Sold by George Ayscough in Bridlesmithgate. . . .

Nottingham Central Library: vol. IV, no. 21 (22 Dec 1715), to vol. XII, no. 30 (5 Mar 1724), inc.; vol. III, no. 30 (30 Nov 1727); vol. XXXIII, no. 113 (10 Dec 1757); vol. XXXIV, no. 185 (28 Apr 1759), def.

University of Nottingham Library: vol. IV, no. 24 (12 Jan 1716), to vol. VII, no. 37 (16 Apr 1719), inc.; XXIV, no. 52 (1 Jun 1749), to vol. XXVIII, no. 29 (28 Dec 1752), inc.; vol. XXXIII, no. 139 (10 Jun 1758), to vol. XXXIV, no. 267 (27 Dec 1760), inc., + .

Private Library of T. F. Potter, Esq., Nottingham: vol. I, no. 6 (3 Jun 1725), to vol. V, no. 34 (18 Dec 1729), inc.; vol. VI, no. 48 (25 Mar 1730), to vol. XVIII, no. [?] (30 Dec 1742), eighteen issues only; vol. XXXII, no. 68 (29 Jan 1757); vol. XXXIV, no. 199 (4 Aug 1759).

Office of *Nottingham Guardian-Journal:* vol. XXVI, no. 17 (27 Sep 1750).

York Minster Library: vol. IV, no. 29 (16 Feb 1716), to vol. VII, no. 20 (11 Dec 1718); vol. X, no. 27 (15 Feb 1722), to vol. XIII, no. 19 (10 Dec 1724).

Oxford University Press Ephemeral Collection: vol. XXXII, no. 76 (26 Mar 1757), def.; vol. XXXIV, no. 253 (20 Sep 1760).

New York Public Library; vol. VI, no. 28 (6 Feb 1718).

Yale University: vol. XXVIII, no. 30 (4 Jan 1753), to vol. XXIX, no. 36 (14 Feb 1754); vol. XXX, nos. 30 (2 Jan 1755) to 48 [mis-numbered 46] (8 May 1755).

109. The New Mercury, &c. [From 16 Dec 1715 con. as]: The Nottingham Mercury: or A General View of the Affairs of Europe, but more particularly of Great Britain. [From 13 Jan 1716 title sometimes appears as]: The Nottingham Mercury, &c. [From 21 Mar 1717 con. as]: The Nottingham Mercury: or A General View of the Affairs of Europe, but more particularly of Great Britain. Being a Weekly Account of News. [From 12 Feb 1719 con. as]: The Nottingham Mercury: or, a General View of the Affairs of Europe, But More particularly of Great-Britain: being a Weekly Account of News. With Extracts and Abridgments of Books [from 7 May 1719 last six words of this title were omitted]. [By 23 Feb 1727 con. as]: The Nottingham Mercury.

[No. 1 (1 Jan ? 1714)]—no. 18 (30 Apr 1714)—no. 4 (16 Mar 1727)—?

Fri; by 1 Mar 1716, Thu; 12 pp.; from 22 Mar 1716 to 8 Jun 1721 some issues have 14 pp.; by Feb, 1727, 4 pp.; single col.; by Feb, 1727, 2 cols.

Nottingham: Printed and Sold by John Collyer in the Long-row. And Henry Allystree Bookseller in Derby. [13 Jan 1716]: Nottingham: Printed by J. Collyer in the Long-Row. [22 Mar 1716]: Nottingham: Printed by J. Collyer in the Long-row, and Sold by Henry Allestry in

Derby, P. Davy in Leicester, John Slater in Coventry, Jos. Kemp in Hinkley, D. Watson in Ashbydelazouch, B. Farnworth in Newark, T. Dixon in Mansfield, Mrs. Singleton in Redford, W. Green in Sheffield and T. Carver in Melton. . . . [Other names substituted or added in subsequent issues.] [23 Apr 1719]: Nottingham: Printed by John Collyer, at the Sheep-Pens, . . . [From 15 Jun 1721]: Printed by John Collyer at the Hen-Cross, near the Old Booksellers Shop. . . .

Nottingham Central Library: no. 18 (30 Apr 1714), to 16 Mar 1727, thirty-five issues only.

University of Nottingham Library: 13 Jan 1716 to 24 Sep 1719, twenty-three issues only.

Private Library of T. F. Potter, Esq., Nottingham: 8 Feb; 12 Dec 1723; 30 Jan 1724.

Derby Borough Library: 3 Sep 1719; 10 Nov 1720; 9 Jan 1724.

York Minster Library: 22 Mar 1716 to 26 Apr 1722.

Oxford University Press Ephemeral Collection: 20 Jan 1716, def.

British Museum: 18 Nov 1715 to 17 Dec 1719, inc.; 30 Jun 1720; 28 May 1724.

110. The Nottingham Post.

[No. 1 (Jan ? 1730)]—vol. IX, no. 449 (3 Aug 1738)— vol. XII, no. 617 (24 Oct 1741)—?

Thu.

Printed and Sold by Tho. Collyer, near the Hen-Cross. . . . This Paper may be had of S. Simmons in Sheffield and J. Slater in Chesterfield, Booksellers, . . . [By 30 Jul 1741]: Printed for and Sold by Tho. Collyer, near the Hen-Cross, Nottingham: . . . This Paper [etc., as before].

Private Library of T. F. Potter, Esq., Nottingham: vol. IX, no. 449 (3 Aug 1738); vol. XII, nos. 586 (19 Mar 1741) to 617 (24 Oct 1741), sixteen issues only.

111. The Leicester and Nottingham Journal.

No. 132 (8 Nov 1755)—1756?

Sat.

Printed for J. Gregory, Bookseller, in Leicester; and S. Creswell, Bookseller, in Nottingham.

This is the paper described as item 68 in this Register. It is doubtful that any copies were printed in Nottingham; but in number 132, Gregory and Creswell announced that they were "determined to publish this Weekly Paper early every Saturday Morning, at their respective Shops in Leicester and Nottingham." Presumably this arrangement continued until January, 1756, when Creswell began to print his own paper in Nottingham (item 112 in this Register).

Nottingham Reference Library: no. 132 (8 Nov 1755).

112. Creswell's Nottingham Journal. [Nottingham Central Library copy of no. 49 (11 Dec 1756) has title set thus]: Journal. Nottingham; Creswell's.

[No. 1 (10 Jan ? 1756)]—no. 5 (7 Feb 1756)—vol. II, no. 57 (5 Feb 1757)—[end of 1760]—?

Sat.

Nottingham: Printed by Samuel Creswell, Bookseller under the New-Change, and Sold by Mrs. Monk Bookseller in Mansfield, Mr. Streeton Bookseller in Grantham, Mr. Hill Bookseller in Newark upon Trent, Mr. Doubleday Peruke-maker at Southwell, Mr. Isaac Potter Grocer at Wirksworth, Mr. John Sturtevant Grocer at Ollerton, and Joseph Lee, Sutton Carrier, . . .

Nottingham Central Library: vol. I, no. 49 (11 Dec 1756).

Office of *Nottingham Guardian-Journal:* vol. I, nos. 5 (7 Feb 1756), 11 (20 Mar 1756), 17 (1 May 1756), 24 (19 Jun 1756), 25 (26 Jun 1756), 29 (24 Jul 1756), 33 (21 Aug 1756), 35 (4 Sep 1756), 39 (2 Oct 1756); vol. II, no. 57 (5 Feb 1757), + .

Private Library of W. B. Morrell, Esq., London: vol. I, no. 47 (27 Nov 1756).

OXFORD

113. The Oxford Journal: Or The Tradesman's Intelligencer.

Probably printed in London; advertised in *Queen Anne's Weekly Magazine,* no. 11 (24 Jan 1736), according to James R. Sutherland, "Lost Journals," *Periodical Post Boy,* no. 6 (Mar, 1950), p. 3.

No copy found.

114. The Oxford Flying Weekly Journal, and Cirencester Gazette.

[No. 1 (6 Sep 1746)]—vol. II, no. 71 (11 Jan 1748)— vol. II, no. 79 (7 Mar 1748)—Jun, 1749.

Sat; by 11 Jan 1748, Mon.

Printed by Richard [doubtless in error for Robert] Walker and William Jackson at the new printing office in St. Clements Parish, near St Magdalenes Bridge; . . . [By 11 Jan 1748]: Oxford: Printed by R. Walker, and W. Jackson, at the New Printing-Office near Carfax Conduit, in the High-Street; . . .

Bodleian MS. Top. Oxon. d. 247, fol. 97, has a transcription of the title, imprint, and other matter in no. 1. The name of the partner is there given twice as Richard, but undoubtedly Robert was intended; as Cyprian Blagden has pointed out in *The Library*, Ser. 5, XII (1957), 125, the local civic records show that between Michaelmas, 1746, and Michaelmas, 1747, the Oxford City Council granted to Robert Walker and William Jackson of the parish of All Saints a license to place a sign over their premises. The writer of MS. Top. Oxon. d. 247 noted in the margin that in no. 3 of the *Oxford Flying Weekly Journal* (20 Sep 1746) the proprietors announced that they had removed to premises near the Market Cross in High Street.

This announcement was in the *Oxford Gazette: and Reading Mercury*, no. 189 (19 Jun 1749), and following issues:

> Whereas the Proprietors of the Flying Weekly Journal, lately printed at Oxford, have discontinued that Paper, This is to inform their Customers that we have agreed with most of their Newsmen to carry the Oxford Gazette and Reading Mercury, which we hope they will take instead of the said Journal, assuring them of our Endeavours to procure the best and earliest Intelligence, as we have hitherto done, and that they shall be serv'd in a regular Manner.
>
> C. Micklewright, & Co.

> Advertisements will be taken in by W. Jackson near Carfax-Conduit in Oxford; which it is desir'd may be sent to him on or before every Thursday Night, otherwise he will not be able to transmit them to Reading soon enough to be inserted in the next Paper.

Bodleian Library: vol. II, no. 79 (7 Mar 1748).

Yale University: vol. II, no. 71 (11 Jan 1748).

115. Jackson's Oxford Journal.

No. 1 (5 May 1753)—no. 400 (27 Dec 1760), + .
Sat.

Printed by W. Jackson in the High-street, Oxford . . . .
[By 13 Nov 1756]: Published by W. Jackson in the
High-Street, Oxford; and R. Bond, Printer and Book-
seller, in the Westgate-street, Glocester. . . .

No. 1 (5 May 1753), which has above its title the words
"News, Boys, News! Election News," was preceded by
two facetious papers: *News, Boys, News! or the Elec-
tioneering Journal. Numb. 1. To be continued. By an
Impartial Hand* (11 Apr 1753) and *News, Boys, News!
More and More News! Or, The Electioneering Journal
with Improvements. Numb. 2. To be continued. By an
Impartial Hand* (25 Apr 1753).

Bodleian Library: nos. 1 (5 May 1753) to 370 (31 May
1760); nos. 398 (13 Dec 1760) to 400 (27 Dec 1760),
+ , with many duplicates.

Oxford Public Library: no. 1 (5 May 1753); nos. 6 (9
Jun 1753) to 57 (1 Jun 1754); nos. 59 (15 Jun 1754) to
69 (24 Aug 1754); nos. 74 (28 Sep 1754) to 113 (28
Jun 1755).

British Museum: nos. 1 (5 May 1753) to 400 (27 Dec
1760), +; also *News, Boys, News!* . . . (11 Apr 1753).

Press Club: no. 66 (3 Aug 1754); no. 185 (13 Nov 1756).

Yale University: nos. 1 (5 May 1753) to 130 (25 Oct
1755); also *News, Boys, News!* . . . (11 Apr 1753) and
(25 Apr 1753).

New York Public Library: no. 69 (24 Aug 1754); no. 71
(7 Sep 1754); no. 75 (5 Oct 1754).

University of Chicago: nos. 1 (5 May 1753) to 139 (27
Dec 1755).

PLYMOUTH

116. The Plymouth Weekly-Journal: or, General-Post; Containing an Impartial Account Of all the most Material Occurrences Foreign and Domestick.

[No. 1 (3 Jan ? 1718)]—no. 36 (5 Sep 1718)—vol. I, no. 9 (1 Dec 1721)—vol. I, no. 139 (31 Jul 1724)— vol. II, no. 1 (7 Aug 1724)—vol. II, no. 32 (12 Mar 1725)—?

Fri; 6 pp.; 2 cols.

Plymouth, Printed by W. Kent, in Southside-Street, near the New-Key, . . . [By 25 Nov 1720]: Plymouth, Printed by E. Kent for W. Kent, in Southside-Street, near the New-Key, . . . [From 15 Dec 1721]: Plymouth, Printed by E. Kent, in Southside-Street, near the New-Key, . . .

Plymouth Public Library: vol. I, no. 9 (1 Dec 1721), def., to no. 14 (5 Jan 1722); no. 19 (9 Feb 1722); nos. 21 (23 Feb 1722) to 71 (8 Feb 1723), lacking eleven issues.

Plymouth Proprietary Library: vol. I, nos. 134 (26 Jun 1724) to 139 (31 Jul 1724); vol. II, nos. 1 (7 Aug 1724) to 32 (12 Mar 1725), lacking six issues, some issues def.

British Museum: nos. 36 (5 Sep 1718) to 97 (30 Dec 1720), eleven issues only, all but one def.; vol. I, no. 10 (8 Dec 1721), to no. 119 (3 Jan 1724), seven issues only, all but two def., plus three fragments.

117. The Plymouth Gazette.
[No. 1 (? 1759)]—before 14 Jan 1760.

Printed by [Orion?] Adams.

The imprint of the *Western Flying-Post; or, Sherborne and Yeovil Mercury,* no. 569 (14 Jan 1760), names "Mr.

Adams, at the Printing-Office in Plymouth, late Printer of the Plymouth Paper." In no. 574 of the *Western Flying-Post* (18 Feb 1760), the proprietor thanks the gentlemen of Exeter and Plymouth and in the rest of Devonshire and Cornwall "for their so effective Support of his Paper, that the *Plymouth Gazette* . . . has been obliged to cease."

No copy found.

118. Plymouth and Exeter Gazette

?—1760—?

Mon.

A newspaper bearing this title is listed (with the abbreviation P.E.G.) among the papers cited in the *Public Ledger*, no. 1 (12 Jan 1760), and the next five issues; but the actual references in the *Public Ledger* are identified by the initials E.G. (for *Exeter Gazette?*), not P.E.G. One such reference is "a Tenement with good Wine Vaults at Exeter, see E.G. Jan 7"; another is "The Chandler's Arms at Plymouth-Dock, see E.G. Jan. 7." In no. 2 of the *Public Ledger* (14 Jan 1760), the abbreviation given for the *Plymouth and Exeter Gazette* is P.G. The paper referred to may be the *Plymouth Gazette* [item 117 in this Register] reported in the *Western Flying-Post*, no. 574 (18 Feb 1760), as no longer published.

No copy found.

PORTSMOUTH

119. The Portsmouth and Gosport Gazette, and Salisbury Journal.

[?]—vol. XVII, no. 736 (24 Feb 1752)—no. 768 (13 Nov 1752)—?

Mon.

Salisbury: Printed by Benjamin Collins, at the Printing-Office, and Booksellers Shop on the New Canal, . . .

This is a local edition of the *Salisbury Journal* [item 129 in this Register] unchanged except in title. But the composite title implies the earlier existence of a separate paper called the *Portsmouth and Gosport Gazette*.

Bodleian Library: vol. XVII, no. 736 (24 Feb 1752); no. 737 [misnumbered 736] (2 Mar 1752); no. 742 (20 Apr 1752); no. 747 (25 May 1752); no. 751 (22 Jun 1752); no. 760 (31 Aug 1752); no. 761 (18 Sep, N.S., 1752); no. 763 (9 Oct 1752); no. 768 (13 Nov 1752).

PRESTON

120. Preston Weekly Journal. With News both Foreign and Domestick. [By 17 Sep 1742 con. as]: The Preston Journal. With News both Foreign and Domestick. [By 22 Jun 1744 con. as]: The Preston Journal. [By 23 Aug 1745 con. as]: Smith's Preston Journal. [By 18 Oct 1745 con. as]: Preston Journal.

[No. 1 (3 Oct ? 1740)]—no. 16 (16 Jan 1741)—no. 307 (5 Sep 1745)—?

Fri.

Printed, and sold by W. Smith, at the Printing Office in Church Street, Preston, . . . [Imprint in no. 204 (24 Aug 1744) names William Smith and Anthony Devis as "Partners"]: At the Printing-Office, which is remov'd opposite the White Bull, in Church-Street, Preston; . . . [By 18

Oct 1745]: Preston: Printed by W. Smith, at the Printing-Office in Church-Street; . . .

Harris Public Library, Preston: no. 16 (16 Jan 1741); no. 103 (17 Sep 1742); no. 104 (24 Sep 1742); no. [?] (10 Feb 1744); no. 195 (22 Jun 1744); no. 281 (7 Mar 1746).

British Museum: no. 307 (5 Sep 1746).

Private library of Kenneth Monkman, Esq., London: no. 204 (24 Aug 1744); no. 205 (31 Aug 1744); no. 256 (23 Aug 1745); no. 257 (30 Aug 1745); no. 264 (18 Oct 1745); no. 265 (25 Oct 1745); no. 267 (8 Nov 1745); no. 268 (15 Nov 1745); no. 270 (22 Nov to 20 Dec 1745); no. 271 (27 Dec 1745); no. 273 (10 Jan 1746); no. 278 (14 Feb 1746); nos. 280 (28 Feb 1746) to 282 (14 Mar 1746); nos. [284] (28 Mar 1746) to 288 (25 Apr 1746); no. 290 (9 May 1746); no. 293 (30 May 1746).

Private library of Richmond P. Bond, University of North Carolina: no. 120 (14 Jan 1743); no. 123 (4 Feb 1743); no. 159 (14 Oct 1743); no. 182 (23 Mar 1744); nos. 192 (1 Jun 1744) to 195 (22 Jun 1744); nos. 197 (6 Jul 1744) to 203 (17 Aug 1744); nos. 206 (7 Sep 1744) to 213 (26 Oct 1744); nos. 215 (9 Nov 1744) to 224 (11 Jan 1745), def.; no. 225 (18 Jan 1745); no. 227 (1 Feb 1745); no. 228 (8 Feb 1745); no. 231 (1 Mar 1745); no. 233 (15 Mar 1745); no. 234 (22 Mar 1745); no. 236 (5 Apr 1745); nos. 238 (19 Apr 1745) to 243 (23 May 1745); no. 247 (21 Jun 1745); no. 249 (5 Jul 1745); no. 250 (12 Jul 1745); no. 254 (9 Aug 1745).

121. The True British Courant: Or, Preston Journal. With News both Foreign and Domestick. [By 20 Sep 1745 con. as]: The True British Courant Or, Preston Journal.

[No. 1 (11 Jan ? 1745)]—no. 11 (22 Mar 1745)—no. 414 (26 Jan 1753)—?

Fri.

Preston: Printed by Robert Moon, . . . [Under date line, 20 Sep 1745]: Printed by Robert Moon, at the New Printing-Office in the Cheap-Side, Preston. [By 11 Mar 1748]: Printed for James Stanley and John Moon, at the Printing-Office in the Market-Place, Preston.

Harris Public Library, Preston: no. 11 (22 Mar 1745); no. 22 (7 Jun 1745); no. [37] (20 Sep 1745); no. 278 (8 Jun 1750); nos. 287 (10 Aug 1750) to 289 (24 Aug 1750); no. 313 (8 Feb 1751); no. 314 (15 Feb 1751); no. 399 (13 Oct 1752); no. 414 (26 Jan 1753), def.

Private Library of Kenneth Monkman, Esq., London: no. 14 (12 Apr 1745); no. 39 (4 Oct 1745); no. 43 (1 Nov 1745); no. 161 (11 Mar 1748).

READING

122. The Reading Mercury, or, Weekly Entertainer. [By 10 Jul 1727 con. as]: The Reading Post: Or, The Weekly Mercury. [By 23 Jun 1729 con. as]: The Reading Post: Or, Weekly Mercury. [From 30 Aug 1736, according to announcement in the *London Evening Post*, no. 1370 (28 Aug 1736), con. as]: The Reading Mercury: Or, The London Spy. [By 21 Feb 1737 con. as]: The Reading Mercury: Or, London Spy. [By 6 Feb 1738 con. as]: The Reading Mercury: or, Weekly Post. [From 21 Oct 1745 con. as]: The Reading Mercury: and Oxford Gazette. [From 18 Nov 1745 con. as]: The Oxford Gazette: and Reading Mercury.

No. 1 (8 Jul 1723)—no. [?] (29 Dec 1760), + .

Mon; by 1 Feb 1724, Sat; by 10 Jul 1727, Mon.; 12 pp.; by 1 Feb 1724, 8 pp.; by 5 Jun 1725, 4 pp.; 2 cols.; by 23 Jun 1729, 3 cols.

Reading: Printed by W. Parks, and D. Kinnier, next Door to the Saracen's Head, in High-street. [From 1 Feb 1724]: Reading: Printed by D. Kinnier, . . . [By 13 Mar 1725]: Reading. Printed by D. Kinnier, in London-street over against Mill-lane: . . . [By 10 Jul 1727]: Reading, Printed by W. Ayers in the Filber-Row; . . . [By 29 Apr 1728]: Reading: Printed, by W. Ayers, in Minster Street, . . . [By 26 May 1735]: Reading: Printed by W. Ayers in the Market-Place: . . . [By 21 Feb 1737]: Reading: Printed by W. Carnan, at the Printing-Office in the Market-Place; and sold by A. Pote, over-against the College in Eton; Mr. Ellot, in Newbury; by Judith [?] Titheridge, in Basingstoke, William Prier, in Winchester; Edward Easton, in Sarum, and by the Newsmen. . . . [By 2 Apr 1739]: Reading: Printed by Mary Carnan in the Market-Place: . . . [By 30 Apr 1739]: Reading: Printed by M. Carnan and Company in the Market-Place; . . . [By 30 Jul 1739]: Reading: Printed by J. Carnan and Comp. in the Market-Place; . . . [By 18 Aug 1739]: Reading: Printed by J. Carnan, near the Bible and Crown in the Market-Place: . . . [By 5 Nov 1739]: Reading: Printed by J. Carnan, for J. Newbery at the Bible and Crown in the Market-Place. . . . [By 2 Mar 1741]: Reading, Printed by J. Newbery and C. Micklewright, at the Bible and Crown in the Market-Place. . . . [By 9 Dec 1745]: Reading, Printed by C. Micklewright and Comp. at the Bible and Crown in the Market-Place. . . . [By 26 Nov 1753]: Reading: Printed by C. Micklewright at the Bible and Crown in the Market-Place. . . . [From 3 Nov 1755]: Reading, Printed by M. Micklewright at the Bible and Crown in the Market-Place. . . . [From 26 Jan 1756]: Reading, Printed by C. Pocock at the Bible and Crown in the Market-Place.

Reading Reference Library: vol. II, no. 90 (13 Mar 1725); vol. III, no. 7 (5 Jun 1725); no. 277 (21 Dec

1730); no. 570 (5 Jan 1736); no. 581 (22 Mar 1736); no. 629 (21 Feb 1737); no. 669 (28 Nov 1737); nos. 4 (6 Feb 1738) to 72 (21 May 1739), eight issues only; no. 217 (25 Jan 1742); nos. 367 (20 Nov 1752) to 400 (9 Jul 1753), ten issues only; nos. 471 (11 Nov 1754) to 486 (24 Feb 1755), ten issues only; no. 591 (28 Feb 1757), def.

Office of the *Reading Mercury:* vol. I, no. 31 (1 Feb 1724); nos. 106 (7 Jan 1740) to 582 (27 Dec 1756), inc., some duplicates; nos. 697 (1 Jan 1759) to 748 (24 Dec 1759).

University of Reading Library: no. 200 (23 Jun 1729).

Private library of Powys Lybbe, Esq., Amersham: nos. 96 (10 Jul 1727) to 538 (19 [for 26] May 1735), nine issues only; nos. 65 (2 Apr 1739) to 558 (12 Jul 1756), fifty-four issues only.

Bodleian Library: vol. I, nos. 1 (8 Jul 1723) to 13 (30 Sep 1723), with some duplicates; no. 629 (21 Feb 1737); no. 204 (26 Oct 1741); nos. 323 (13 Feb 1744) to 134 (6 Jun 1748), lacking eight issues; no. 733 (10 Sep 1759); no. 750 (7 Jan 1760); no. 768 (12 May 1760), +.

British Museum: vol. I, no. 1 (8 Jul 1723), fac.; vol. I, no. 31 (1 Feb 1724), fac.; nos. 420 (26 Nov 1753) to 623 (3 Oct 1757), inc.

Yale University: vol. I, no. 1 (8 Jul 1723), fac.; no. 379 (4 Dec. 1732).

Private library of R. M. Wiles: no. 16 (3 Mar 1746).

123. The Reading Journal. [By 23 Jul 1744 con. as]: The Reading Journal; or Weekly Review. [By 10 Mar 1746 con. as]: Henry's Reading Journal; or Weekly Review.

[No. 1 (27 Sep ? 1736)]—no. 128 (5 Mar 1739)—no. 231 (15 Feb 1748)—?

Mon.

Reading: Printed by D. Henry, in Frier-street, . . . [By 23 Jul 1744]: Printed by D. Henry, and publish'd at his House in Frier-Street, Reading, and at his Office the Upper End of the Church yard in Winchester, . . . and also by Mr. Prior Bookseller, . . . [By 10 Mar 1746]: Reading: Printed by D. Henry, and publish'd at his House in Frier-street; and Sold at his Office at the Upper End of the Church-Walk at Winchester. . . . This Paper is Sold likewise by Mr. Wise, Bookseller at Newport in the Isle of Wight, . . . Also by Mr. Prior, Bookseller at Winchester. . . .

A Winchester edition of this paper, differing only in title, was issued in 1746. See item 141 in this Register.

Reading Reference Library: nos. 128 (5 Mar 1739) and 130 (19 Mar. 1739); nos. 42 (23 Jul 1744) to 231 (15 Feb 1748), thirty-two issues only.

ST. IVES

124. The St. Ives Post. Containing An Impartial Collection of all News, Foreign and Domestick: with The Most Material Occurrences.

[No. 1 (18 Mar 1717)]—vol. II, no. 1 (20 Jan 1718)—vol. II, no. 36 (16 Feb 1719)—?

Mon; 12 pp.; single col.

St. Ives in Huntingdonshire: Printed by J. Fisher, . . .

Bodleian Library: vol. II, nos. 1 (20 Jan 1718) to 17 (19 May 1719); nos. 19 (2 Jun 1718) to 21 (16 Jun 1718).

125. St. Ives Post Boy: or, the Loyal Packet. Being A Collection of the most Material Occurrences, Foreign and Domestick. Together with an Account of Trade.

[No. 1 (16 Jun 1718]—no. 2 (23 Jun 1718)—no. 36 (16 Feb 1719)—?

Mon; 12 pp.; single col.

A notice in number 2 (23 June 1718) ends thus: ". . . I have alter'd the Form of my Paper from Folio, to Quarto, I being inform'd by some, that they have been used to that Method."

St. Ives in Huntingdonshire: Printed by R. Raikes. [By 19 Jan 1719]: St. Ives in Huntingdonshire: Printed by R. Raikes, in Water-Lane, near the Bridge, . . .

Bodleian Library: vol. I, nos. 2 (23 June 1718) to 11 (25 Aug 1718); nos. 13 (8 Sep 1718) to 26 (8 Dec 1718); nos. 28 (22 Dec. 1718) to 32 (19 Jan 1719); no. 35 (9 Feb 1719); no. 36 (16 Feb 1719).

126. St. Ives Mercury: or, the Impartial Intelligencer, being A Collection of the most Material occurrences, Foreign and Domestick. Together with An Account of Trade.

[No. 1 (12 Oct ? 1719]—no. 6 (16 Nov 1719)—?

Mon; 12 pp.; single col.

St. Ives, in Huntingdonshire: Printed by William Dicey, near the Bridge, . . .

Norris Library and Museum, St. Ives: vol. I, no. 6 (16 Nov 1719).

SALISBURY

127. The Salisbury Post Man: or, Packet of Intelligence, from France, Spain, Portugal, &c.

No. 1 (27 Sep 1715)—[no. 40 (1 Mar 1716)]—?

Mon, Thu, and Sat; 6 pp.; 2 cols.

Printed by Sam. Farley, at his office adjoyning to Mr. Robert Silcocks, on the Ditch in Sarum, Anno 1715.

It should be noted that, although the title page of no. 1 is dated Saturday, 27 September 1715, that date was not Saturday but Tuesday. Possibly the date of no. 1 should be Saturday, 17 September 1715, or Saturday, 24 September 1715.

No. 40 (1 Mar 1716) was mentioned by Robert Benson and Henry Hatcher, *Old and New Sarum, or Salisbury* (London: Nichols, 1843), p. 509, as then in existence.

Office of *Salisbury and Winchester Journal:* no. 1 (27 Sep 1715), title page and verso (blank) only; no. [?] (24 Nov ? 1715), pp. 3, 4 only, containing news from the *St. James's Evening Post* and other London newspapers dated Tuesday, 22 November 1715.

128. The Salisbury Journal Containing the most Material Occurrences both Foreign and Domestick.

[No. 1 (2 Jun ? 1729]—no. 58 (6 Jul 1730).

Mon.

Sarum: Printed by Charles Hooton at the Printing-Office in Milford-Street, . . .

This notice appeared in no. 58 (6 Jul 1730):

> N.B. This Paper not being encouraged according to Expectation: I shall from this Time decline it; [but] all other Printing Business will be perform'd after the best Manner.
>
> By Yours, &c. Charles Hooton.

Office of *Salisbury and Winchester Journal:* no. 58 (6 Jul 1730).

129. The Salisbury Journal Containing the most Material Occurrences both Foreign and Domestick. [From 4 Dec

1736 con. as]: The Salisbury Journal. [From 27 Feb 1739 con. as]: The Salisbury Journal; or, Weekly Advertiser. [From 11 Jun 1750 con. as]: The Salisbury Journal.

No. 1 (27 Nov 1736)—vol. XXV, no. 1182 (29 Dec 1760), +.

Sat; from 31 Jan 1737, usually Mon, occasionally Sat; from 27 Feb 1739, Tue; by 2 Jul 1746, Mon. This note appeared in no. 43 (19 Sep 1737);

> The publishing this Paper as usual, on Saturday Evening, being attended with many Inconveniences, the same will be published, after the last day of this Month, on every Tuesday Morning, so that the freshest Intelligence by Monday's Post will by that means be inserted, and the same sooner and better Conveyed to our Readers.

But the paper continued to bear Monday dates until 27 February 1739.

Sarum: Printed for William Collins Book-seller in Silver-Street, . . . [From 27 Feb 1739]: Printed by William Collins and Comp. at the Printing-Office on the Ditch in Salisbury; . . . [From 12 Aug. 1740]: Salisbury: Printed by B. Collins and Comp. at the Printing-Office on the Ditch. . . . [From 9 May 1748]: Salisbury: Printed by Benjamin Collins, and Comp. at the Printing-Office, and Booksellers Shop on the New Canal.

This notice appeared in no. 195 (20 Oct 1741):

> *.* Benjamin Collins, Bookseller and Stationer, at the Bible and Crown in Silver Street, is remov'd higher up, into the Corner Shop, fronting the Poultry Cross (last in the Occupation of Mr. Thomas Smith, Apothecary), . . .

This notice appeared in no. 539 (9 May 1748):

> This is to acquaint the Public, that the Printing-Office, Stamp-Office, and Booksellers Shop, By Benjamin Collins, Which Were at the Corner House opposite to the Poultry-Cross, in this City, are now

moved from thence to the New-Canal, (☞ formerly call'd the Ditch) and into the House late in the Possession of Messieurs Tatum and Still, Apothecaries; being the same which Mr. Rawlins Hillman, Apothecary, deceas'd, formerly liv'd in. . . .

For Portsmouth and Gosport edition of this paper, see item 119 in this Registrar.

Office of the *Salisbury and Winchester Journal*: vol. XVII, no. 730 (13 Jan 1752), to vol. XXV, no. 1178 (1 Dec 1760), inc., + .

Salisbury and Wiltshire Museum, Salisbury: vol. IX, no. 389 (2 Jul 1745), to vol. XIX, no. 851 (26 Aug 1754), five issues only.

Private library of Donald Mulcock, Esq., Salisbury: nos. 51 (15 Jan 1739) to 205 (29 Dec 1741), inc.; odd issues for 1742, 1743, 1745, 1747-50, 1758-60, and later.

Wiltshire Archaeological and Natural History Society, Devizes: nos. 427 (24 Mar 1746) to 597 (19 June 1749).

Bath Reference Library: vol. XXI, no. 969 (29 Nov 1756); vol. XXIII, no. 1044 (8 May 1758), to vol. XXIV, no. 1095 (30 Apr 1759); vol. XXV, nos. 1152 (2 Jun 1760) to 1182 (29 Dec 1760), lacking thirteen issues, + .

Bristol Reference Library: vol. XI, no. 404 (15 Oct. 1745), to vol. XIX, no. 859 (21 Oct 1754), seven issues only.

British Museum: vol. VII, no. 324 (10 Apr 1744); vol. IX, no. 372 (12 Mar 1745); no. 373 (19 Mar 1745); vol. XV, no. 577 (30 Jan 1749), def.; no. 633 (26 Feb 1750) to vol. XIX, no. 829 (25 Mar 1754), inc.

Press Club: vol. II, no. 76 (10 Jul 1739); no. 96 (27 Nov 1739).

Yale University Library: no. 1 (27 Nov 1736) to vol. XXV, no. 1182 (29 Dec 1760), + .

SHEFFIELD

130. Lister's Sheffield Weekly Journal. [By 20 Jan 1756 con. as]: Sheffield Weekly Journal: Or, Doncaster Flying-Post.

[No. 1 (23 Apr 1754)]—no. 42 (18 Feb 1755)—no. 172 (16 Aug 1757)—?

Tue.

Colophon of no. 42 (18 Feb 1755): Subscriptions and Advertisements for this Paper are taken in, By Mr. Simmon's, in Sheffield; Mr. Richard Eyre, in Rotherham; Mr. Inman, in Doncaster; Mr. J. Smith, in Barnslley; Mr. Stringer, in Wakefield; Messrs. Edwards and Binns, in Halifax; Mr. Topham, in Bradford; Mr. Birkbeck, in Settle; Mr. Crowther, in Skipton; Mr. Parker, in Keighley; Mr. Brooke, in Huddersfield; Mr. A. Frith, the Halifax Carrier; Mr. Haigh, in Peniston; Mr. Hallam, in Stoney-Middleton; Mr. Bromwell, the Tideswell Carrier; Mr. John Cooper, at Eyam, and at his Shop in Tideswell; Mr. Hallgate, the Buxton Carrier; Mr. Roe, the Bakewell and Wirksworth Carrier; Mr. Frith, in Chesterfield; Mr. Monk, in Mansfield, and at his Shop in Worksop every Wednesday; Mr. William Mycock, the Doncaster Post; and by F. Lister, Printer, opposite the Cross-Daggers, in Sheffield. . . .

Colophon of no. 90 (20 Jan 1756): Subscriptions and Advertisements are taken in at the Printing Office, in Doncaster; Mr. Simmons, Bookseller, in Sheffield; Mr. Richard Whipp, Peruke maker, in Halifax[;] Mr. Brooke, Bookseller, in Huddersfield; Mr. Stringer, Bookseller, and Mr. Robert Parker, in Wakefield; Mr. Richard Topham, in Bradford; Mr. Birbeck [so], in Settle; Mr. Crowther,

Bookseller, in Skipton; Mr. Parker in Keighley; Mr. Haigh, in Peniston; Mr. John Cooper, in Eyam, and at his Shop in Tiddeswall; Mr. Frith, Dyer, and Mr. S. Lee, in Chesterfield; Mr. Joseph Heath, Bookseller, in Nottingham, and at his Shop in Mansfield, every market-day; Mr. William Wilson, Perukemaker, in Rotherham; Thomas Battersby, at Anston; Mr. Saunderson, in Bawtry; Mr. Colson, in Retford; Mr. Saunderson, Bookseller, in Pontefract; Mr. Joseph Smith, in Barnsley, and Revel Homfray's Printing-Office, opposite to the Cock, in the High-Street, Sheffield, and the Persons who carry this News. . . . [Slight changes in later issues.]

Under title of no. 90 and later issues: Printed by Revel Homfray, in High-Street.

Manuscript note, perhaps contemporary, on copy of prospectus at Central Public Library, Halifax, gives 23 Apr 1754 as starting date, though a reckoning back from no. 42 (18 Feb 1755) indicates 7 May 1754 as probable date of the first issue.

In August, 1755, this paper and the *Doncaster Flying-Post* (item 39 in this Register) were consolidated.

This notice appeared in no. 98 (16 Mar 1756):

> All Persons indebted to the Effects of the late Francis Lister, Printer, deceas'd, are hereby required to pay them before the 16th Day of April next, to Margaret Lister, of Sheffield, the Widow and Administratrix of the said Deceased. . . .

Central Library, Sheffield: no. 149 (8 Mar 1757); no. 172 (16 Aug 1757).

Central Public Library, Halifax: prospectus.

York Minster Library: No. 42 (18 Feb 1755); no. 90 (20 Jan 1756); no. 94 (17 Feb 1756); no. 98 (16 Mar. 1756).

131. The Public Advertiser (Sheffield).

[No. 1 (29 Apr ? 1760]—no. 11 (8 Jul 1760)—no. 35 (23 Dec 1760), + .

Tue.

Sheffield: Printed by W. Ward, and sold in the Towns of Rotherham, Barnsley, Wakefield, Leeds, Halifax, Huthersfield, Settle, Skipton, Pontefract, Thorne, Snaith, Howden, Hull, Barton, Patrington, Haydon, Burlington Beverley, Doncaster, Tickhill, Blith, Bawtry, Worksop, Chesterfield, Bakewell [,] Gainsborough, and all the adjacent Villages. Subscriptions and Advertisements, are taken in by the Printer, and by the Persons who deliver the Papers.

Colophon of no. 21 (16 Sep 1760): Sheffield: Printed by William Ward, by whom Advertisements are taken in. Advertisements are also taken in, and the Paper may be had of Mr. Darby in Halifax; Mr. Bull, in Wakefield, Mr. Rawson, in Hull, Beverley, and Howden; Mr. Eyre, in Thorne; Mr. Hodgson, in Doncaster; Mr. Bower, in Bawtry, Tickhill, and Blyth; Mr. Thompson, in Gainsbro'; Mr. Batterby, in Worksop; Mr. Stavely, in Chesterfield; Mr. Wilson in Rotherdam; Mr. Bent, in Barnsley; Mr. Nutter, in Bradford; Mr. Binns, in Huthersfield; Mr. Dearden, at Cullingworthgate; Mr. Parker, in Keighly; Mr. Kidd, in Pontefract; Mr. Toothil, in Bakewell, and Tideswell; at 2s. 6d. the Quarter.

Under title of no. 11 (8 Jul 1760) in Central Library, Sheffield: Printed for, and Sold by, J. Bull, in Wakefield; where Advertisements are taken in for this Paper.

Under title of no. 21 (16 Sep 1760) and later issues in York Minster Library: Printed: for and sold by P. Darby, in Halifax, where Advertisements are taken in for this Paper.

Central Library, Sheffield: no. 11 (8 Jul 1760).

York Minster Library: nos. 21 (16 Sep 1760) to 35 (23 Dec 1760).

SHERBORNE

132. The Sherborne Mercury, or Weekly Advertiser; Containing the freshest Accounts of all Publick Transactions both at Home and Abroad. [From 30 Jan 1749, upon amalgamation with *The Western Flying Post, or Yeovil Mercury,* con. with new numbering as]: The Western Flying-Post; or, Sherborne and Yeovil Mercury.

[No. 1 (21 Feb 1737)]—no. 16 (7 Jun 1737)—vol. XII, no. 623 (23 Jan 1749)—vol. I, no. 1 (30 Jan 1749)—vol. XII, no. 622 (29 Dec 1760), + .

Mon; by 7 Jun 1737, Tue; from 3 Feb 1746, Mon.

Printed at Sherborne by W. Bettinson and G. Price. . . . [By 1 Jan 1740]: Printed at Sherborne, by William Bettinson, from London, . . . [On 1 Sep 1746]: Printed at Sherborne, by J. Bettinson and Comp. from London. [From 8 Sep 1746]: Printed at Sherborne, by H. Bettinson and Comp. from London. . . . [From 30 Jan 1749]: Printed at Sherborne, by R. Goadby and Comp. from London. [By 4 Aug 1755]: Sherborne: Printed by R. Goadby, . . .

The advertisement, dated 19 Feb 1737, announcing that the *Sherborne Mercury* would begin on Monday, 21 Feb 1737, and giving the full title (as at the head of this item) is reprinted in part by L. E. J. Brooke, Esq., in *Somerset Newspapers 1725-1960* (privately printed in Yeovil, 1960), p. 62 f.

This announcement was printed under the date line of vol. XII, no. 623 (23 Jan 1749):

The Proprietors of the SHERBORNE MERCURY, or WEEKLY ADVERTISER, and of the WESTERN FLYING-POST, or YEOVIL MERCURY, beg leave to inform the Publick, that they have agreed to unite the said Papers, to begin the Sixth of February and to print and publish them at *Sherborne*, under the Title of the SHERBORNE and YEOVIL MERCURY, which, by means of this Union, will be render'd the most numerous and extensive Paper in *Great Britain.* All Persons therefore who may have Occasion to advertise in the said *Sherborne* and *Yeovil Mercury*, are desired to send their Advertisements to R. GOADBY and Company, at the Printing-Office in *Sherborne* aforesaid; where Printing Business of every Sort is perform'd in the neatest Manner, and on the most reasonable Terms.

> *H. Bettinson*
> *R. Goadby.*

N. B. The Printing-Office is remov'd from *Yeovil* to *Sherborne,* and the Printing business carried on there only.

A note under the title in vol. V, no. 250 (10 Dec 1753), begins thus:

This Paper is distributed every Week, in great Numbers, in all the CITIES, TOWNS, VILLAGES, PARISHES, &c. of the four GREAT Western Counties, *so noted for their Populousness,* Viz. *Dorset, Somerset, Devon,* and *Cornwall,* in which *no other Paper* is circulated; besides Part of Wiltshire. . . .

Office of the *Western Gazette,* Yeovil: vol. III, no. 150 (1 Jan 1740), to vol. XII, no. 622 (29 Dec 1760), inc., + .

Exeter Public Library: vol. XI, no. 545 (27 Jul 1747), to vol. XII, no. 617 (12 Dec 1748), eleven issues only; vol. VIII, no. 385 (12 Jul 1756), to vol. IX, no. 416 (7 Feb 1757), nine issues only; vol. X, no. 470 (20 Feb 1758); no. 506 (6 Nov 1758); vol. XI, no. 516 (15 Jan 1760), to vol. XII, no. 583 (21 Apr 1760), seven issues only, + .

Bodleian Library: no. 16 (7 Jun 1737); no. 535 (18 May 1747).

Oxford University Press Ephemeral Collection: vol. VII, no. 350 (1 Nov 1743); no. 362 (24 Jan 1744); no. 363 (31 Jan 1744); nos. 365 (14 Feb 1744) to 396 (18 Sep 1744).

British Museum: vol. IX, no. 482 (12 May 1746), def.; vol. XII, no. 588 (23 May 1748); vol. VII, no. 316 (17 Mar 1755); no. 330 (23 Jun 1755); no. 336 (4 Aug 1755); no. 338 (18 Aug 1755).

SHREWSBURY

133. [A Collection of all the Material News]

1705?

2 pp.

[Printed and sold by Thomas Jones at his house in Hill's Lane, near Mardol.]

The title and imprint here given are those recorded by T. W. Hancock in "The First Shrewsbury Newspaper," *Bye-Gones, relating to Wales and the Border Counties 1880-1* (Oswestry: Caxton Works, n.d.), p. 240. From the single issue which he had seen, Hancock quoted a paragraph of news concerning the Duke of Marlborough's visit to Woodstock "to give his last instructions about building his palace, being to go immediately to Holland, on the French army's moving on the Rhine." This indicates that the date of the Shrewsbury paper was some time between Parliament's granting of the Woodstock property to Marlborough on 14 March 1705 and the Duke's departure for Holland on Friday, 30 March 1705; but the Duke was in England again from Saturday, 30 December 1705, to Friday, 12 April 1706, and the report may belong to March or April, 1706.

No copy found.

STAMFORD

134. The Stamford-Post, Or an Account of the most Material News, Foreign and Domestick, to which is added the Weekly Miscellany. [By 17 Jul 1712 con. as]: The Stamford-Post, Or an Account of the most Material News, Foreign and Domestick.

[No. 1 (8 Jun ? 1710)]—[no. 82 (3 Jan 1712)]—[no. 97 (17 Apr 1712)]— no. 112 (31 Jul 1712)—?

Thu; 2 pp. (but see note below; complete copy may have had 4 pp.)

Printed at Stamford, Lincolnshire.

Title of issues not seen are here taken from the *Lincoln, Rutland and Stamford Mercury* of 4 May 1860, which quotes the following paragraph from the front page of no. 97:

> Whereas this Paper is designed to be continued for the future on a whole Sheet viz. The News on the one half Sheet and a Miscellany on the other, consisting of the Heads of any material, pamphlet, or paper that is published in London, and several other useful and diverting subjects. These are therefore to give notice to such Gentlemen as are willing either to instruct or divert the public, if they please to send any subject prose or verse: It shall be thankfully received and carefully incerted.

See Jos. Phillips, "A Pioneer Newspaper," *Notes and Queries*, Ser. 8, VI (24 Nov 1894), 418, and notes by

C. L. Exley now in the Lincolnshire Archives office, Exchequer Gate, Lincoln (Ex. 16).

All Souls' College Library, Oxford: no. 110 (17 Jul 1712); no. 112 (31 Jul 1712).

135. The Stamford Mercury. Being Historical and Political Observations on the Transactions of Europe. Together with Remarks on Trade. The Whole being a Miscellany of Various Subjects, Prose and Verse. [From 9 Sep 1714 con. as]: Stamford Mercury. Being Historical and Political Observations on the Transactions of Europe. Together with Remarks on Trade. [From 11 Jul 1728 con. as]: Stamford Mercury. [From 2 Jan 1729 con. as]: Stamford Mercury. Being Historical and Political Observations on the Transactions of Europe. Together with Remarks on Trade. [By 1 Jul 1731 con. as]: Stamford Mercury.

[No. 1 (? 1713)]—vol. III, no. 43 (13 May 1714)—vol. XXXIX, no. 9 (2 Mar 1732)—[vol. XL (?), no. (?) (13 Jul 1732)]—?

Thu; 12 pp.; by 4 Jan 1728, 8 pp.; single col., except advertisements, which from 1728 are in two columns.

Printed by Tho. Baily and Will. Thompson, at Stamford in Lincolnshire, 1714. [By 22 Apr 1725]: Printed by William Thompson and Thomas Baily at Stamford in Lincolnshire, 1725. [From 18 Jan 1728]: Printed by Will. Thompson and Tho. Baily at Stamford in Lincolnshire, 1727-8. [By 24 Feb 1732]: Printed by W. Thompson and T. Baily, at Stamford in Lincolnshire, 1731-2.

A minute in the Corporation records of Stamford, transcribed by H. L. Evans (editor of the *Lincoln, Rutland and Stamford Mercury* from 1920 to 1950) in his pamphlet, *History of the "Stamford Mercury"* (n.d.), refers to Baily and Thompson as "printers liveing in Saint Martin's in the County of North'ton" and indicates that they were "admitted to be free of this Corporation" on condition that they came to live in the borough before the following Michaelmas, that for the next seven years they printed the official forms used by the Corporation, that for the distributing of their newspaper they employed only such poor persons as were recommended to them by the mayor, and that they gave security "to save the Towne harmless from their respective charges." The minute is dated 15 January 1714, though the two men had apparently been printing the *Stamford Mercury* for some months before that date.

For the relation between this paper and *Howgrave's Stamford Mercury* [item 136 in this Register], see A. Adcock, *Notes and Queries*, Ser. 11, VII (14 June 1913), 471-72. Letters from the 6 July and 13 July issues of this paper, reprinted in the *Northampton Mercury*, vol. XIII, no. 13 (17 Jul 1732), indicate that the Baily-Thompson newspaper continued to appear for several weeks after Howgrave's paper was established. *Howgrave's Stamford Mercury* cannot be regarded as a continuation of the *Stamford Mercury* which started its life in 1713.

This notice is in vol. VII, no. 3 (19 Jan 1716):

> Whereas there has been a Report spread about the Country that the Printers hereof would not be permitted to print this Mercury any more, this is to satisfy the Publick that the said Report is altogether false and groundless, and the said Printers will continue to give an impartial Account of such Publick and Private Occurrences as they shall find published in the most reputable Prints and Letters.

Lincoln, Rutland and Stamford Mercury office: vol. III, no. 43 (13 May 1714), to vol. XXIV, no. 17 (15 Oct 1724), inc., with many duplicates; vol. XXV, no. 16 (22 Apr [1729]), to vol. XXXVII, no. 1 (7 Jan 1731), five issues only; vol. XXXVIII, nos. 1 (1 Jul [1731]) to 26 (30

Dec [1731]), lacking one issue; vol. XXXIX, nos. 8 (24 Feb 1732) and 9 (2 Mar 1732).

Lincolnshire Archives Office, Lincoln: vol. XXXI, no. 3 (18 Jan [1728]), to vol. XXXIII, no. 16 (17 Apr [1729]), lacking eight issues.

Bodleian Library: vol. XXI, no. 23 (6 Jun 1723).

All Souls' College Library, Oxford: vol. VI, no. 2 (7 Jul 1715); vol. VII, no. 25 (21 Jun 1716), to vol. VIII, no. 10 (30 Aug 1716), six issues only; vol. XI, no. 11 (13 Mar 1718); vol. XVI, no. 14 (29 Sep 1720).

Office of Berrow's Newspapers, Ltd., Worcester: vol. XVI, no. 26 (29 Dec 1720).

British Museum: vol. XI, nos. 21 (22 May 1718) to 24 (12 Jun 1718); vol. XX, no. 1 (28 Jun 1722); no. 2 (5 Jul 1722); nos. 9 (23 Aug 1722) to 27 (27 Dec 1722); vol. XXXI, no. 1 (4 Jan [1728]), to vol. XXXII, no. 25 (26 Dec [1728]).

Private library of W. B. Morrell, Esq., London: vol. IV, no. 23 (21 Oct 1714); no. 24 (28 Oct 1714); vol. XI, no. 7 (13 Feb 1718).

Private library of Kenneth Monkman, Esq., London: vol. XVI, no. 24 (8 Dec 1720), def.; no. 26 (29 Dec 1720).

136. Howgrave's Stamford Mercury. [From 22 Apr 1736 con. as]: The Stamford Mercury.

No. 1 (15 Jun [1732])—end of 1760, + .

Thu.

Printed by Francis Howgrave at Stamford in Lincolnshire.

Lincoln, Rutland and Stamford Mercury office: nos. 44 (12 Apr 1733) to 213 (8 Jul 1736), twelve issues only; nos. 217 (5 Aug 1736) to 812 (4 Jun 1747), lacking one issue; no. 945 (28 Dec 1749); no. 1193 (10 Oct 1754).

Lindsey and Holland County Library, Lincoln: nos. 1 (15 Jun 1732) to 200 (8 Apr 1736); nos. 202 (22 Apr 1736) to 392 (27 Dec. 1739).
Bodleian Library: no. 26 (6 Dec 1732).

Yale University Library: no. 93 (21 Mar 1734); nos. 302 (6 Apr 1738) to 346 (8 Feb 1739), eight issues only.

STRATFORD-UPON-AVON

137. The Stratford, Shipston, and Aulcester Journal. [By 9 Mar 1752 con. as]: Keating's Stratford and Warwick Mercury; or, Cirencester Shipston and Alcester Weekly Journal.

Vol. I, no. 1 (5 Feb 1750)—vol. IV, no. 210 (12 Nov 1753).

Mon.

Stratford upon Avon, Printed by J. Keating: Printer, and Bookseller, opposite the Cross; . . . [By 23 Mar 1752]: Stratford upon Avon Printed by J. Keating, at the Printing Office, and Booksellers Shop opposite the Cross. Where Advertisements are taken in, and at his Shops, at Shipston and Alcester: and by the Men who distribute this Paper. . . .

Under imprint in no. 1:

> *.* As an Encouragement to Advertise in this Paper, the Public are desired to take Notice, that it is now Substituted in the Room of the Oxford and Cirencester Flying Posts, and Circulated in Warwickshire, Gloucestershire, Oxfordshire, and Worcestershire and deliver'd for 30 Miles round, and at Oxford the same Day.

By 23 Mar 1752 this notice ends thus: . . . Oxfordshire; and delivered at Oxford, Cirencester, Worcester, Warwick, Birmingham and their neighbouring Villages, &c.

Shakespeare Memorial Library, Stratford-upon-Avon: vol. I, no. 1 (5 Feb 1750); vol. III, no. 114 (9 Mar 1752); no. 116 (23 Mar 1752); vol. IV, no. 178 (9 Apr 1753); no. 189 (18 Jun 1753); no. 210 (12 Nov 1753).

TAUNTON

138. The Taunton-Journal. [From 10 Dec 1725 con. as]: Norris's Taunton-Journal.

[No. 1 (21 May ? 1725)]—20th week (1 Oct 1725)— 138th week (5 Jan 1728)—?

Tue and Fri, issues overlapping in contents; 2 cols.; from 9 Jun 1727, 3 cols.

Printed in Taunton, by William Norris. [From 14 Jul 1727]: Printed in Taunton, by William Norris. And Publish'd every Tuesday and Friday.

Somerset Archaeological and Natural History Society, Taunton: Friday issues: 20th week (1 Oct 1725); 30th week (10 Dec 1725); 31st week (17 Dec 1725); 45th week (25 Mar 1726) to 53rd week (20 May 1726); 56th week (10 Jun 1726) to 85th week (30 Dec 1726); 98th week (31 Mar 1727) to 106th week (26 May 1727); 108th week (9 Jun 1727) to 112th week (7 Jul 1727); 113th [mis-numbered 112th] week (14 Jul 1727); 121st week (8 Sep 1727); 122nd week (15 Sep 1727); 124th week (29th Sep 1727) to 126th week (13 Oct 1727); 137th week (29 Dec 1727); 138th week (5 Jan 1728). Tuesday issues: 113th week (11 Jul 1727); 114th week (18 Jul 1727).

WARRINGTON

139. Eyres's Weekly Journal, or, the Warrington Advertiser.

[No. 1 (23 Mar ? 1756)]—no. 7 (4 May 1756)—no. 19 (27 Jul 1756)—?

Tue.

Warrington: Printed by Thomas and William Eyres, . . .

The actual wood block used in printing one of the two cuts flanking the title is at the Warrington Museum.

Warrington Municipal Library: nos. 7 (4 May 1756) to 9 (18 May 1756); nos. 15 (29 Jun 1756) to 17 (13 Jul 1756); no. 19 (27 Jul 1756).

WHITEHAVEN

140. The Whitehaven Weekly Courant Containing the most Material Advices Both Foreign and Domestick.

[No. 1 (16 Dec ? 1736)]—[no. 6 (20 Jan 1737)]—?

Thu.

Whitehaven, Printed and Sold by Thomas Cotton. Also sold at Mr. Edward Holms Shop in Kendal. . . .

Title, date, and imprint of no. 6 given here are taken from notes made in 1884 by William Jackson and now at the Carlisle Public Library. An advertisement transcribed in those notes indicates that a popular elixir was sold by Cotton "at his Printing House in James Street, next door but two to the Meeting-house, and near the Market Place in Whitehaven." See *Transactions of the Cumber-*

land and Westmorland Antiquarian & Archaeological Society, XIV (1897).

No copy found; but excerpts from no. 6 are reprinted in the *Cumberland Pacquet* of 21 November 1848.

WINCHESTER

141. Henry's Winchester Journal; or Weekly Review.

[No. 1 (31 Oct ? 1743)]—[no. 84 (3 Jun 1745)]—no. 128 (31 Mar 1746)—no. 166 (8 Dec 1746)—?

Mon.

Reading: Printed by D. Henry, and publish'd at his House in Frier-street, and Sold at his Office at the Upper End of the Church Walk at Winchester, . . . This Paper is Sold likewise also by Mr. Wise, Bookseller in the Isle of Wight, . . .

This paper is a local edition of *Henry's Reading Journal; or Weekly Review* [item 123 in this Register], unchanged except in title. No. 84 (3 Jun 1745) is included by F. A. Edwards in "A List of Hampshire Newspapers," *Hampshire Antiquary and Naturalist,* I (1891), 94-97.

Reading Reference Library: no. 166 (8 Dec 1746).

Yale University Library: no. 128 (31 Mar 1746); no. 142 (30 Jun 1746).

WORCESTER

142. The Worcester Post-Man: containing The Heads of all the Remarkable Occurrences, both Foreign and Domes-

tick. [By 24 Aug 1722 con. as]: The Worcester Post. Or, Western Journal. With the most Material Occurrences Foreign and Domestick. [By 30 Apr 1725 con. as]: The Weekly Worcester-Journal. With the most Material Occurrences Foreign and Domestick. [By 14 Apr 1748 con. as]: The Worcester Journal. [From 11 Oct 1753 con. as]: Berrow's Worcester Journal.

[No. 1 (17 Jun ? 1709)]—no. 85 (2 Feb 1711)—no. 185 (9 Jan 1713)—no. 2681 (25 Dec 1760), + .

Fri; from 14 Apr 1748, Thu; 2 pp.; by 9 Jan 1713, 6 pp.; from 30 Apr 1725, 4 pp.; single col.; from 30 Apr 1725, 2 cols.; by Nov. 1732, 3 cols.

[By 2 Feb 1711]: VVorcester: Printed by S. Bryan. 1711. [By 30 Apr 1725]: Worcester: Printed by Stephen Bryan. . . . [14 Apr 1748]: Worcester: Printed by H. Berrow, at the Printing Office late Mr. Bryan's, . . . [From 21 Apr 1748]: Worcester: Printed by H. Berrow, at the Printing-Office in Goose-Lane, near the Cross; . . . [From 11 Oct 1753]; Printed at his Office in Goose-Lane, near the Cross.

It has been asserted that this paper, or a predecessor of this paper, was established as early as 1690. The only basis for that assertion appears to be a passage in Valentine Green, *The History and Antiquities of the City and Suburbs of Worcester* (2 vols.; London: Bulmer, 1796), a passage which is not in Green's earlier work, *A Survey of the City of Worcester* . . . (Worcester: J. Butler for S. Gamidge, 1764). On pages 25 and 26 of the second 1796 volume, Green recorded a conjecture made more than a century after the alleged event, but he presented no evidence:

> From the best information, it is conjectured that a public paper was established in Worcester as early as the commencement of the Revolution. . . . This was, doubtless, the period that gave birth to the

Worcester Weekly Paper. . . . It is uncertain, however, in what order of succession these publications
were first issued, whether monthly or weekly, on
what day of the month or week or in what form,
folio, quarto, or otherwise; but in June, 1709, they
assumed a regular and orderly appearance, in a
small folio, containing six pages, which formed a
weekly number, published every Friday, and were
printed by Stephen Bryan, under the title of "the
Worcester Postman".

Green gave no hint of what he meant by "the best information." The earliest Worcester newspaper he had seen,
he said, was no. 339 of the *Worcester Post-Man*, dated
23 Dec 1715. He had no actual knowledge—nor, apparently, has anyone else—of a Worcester newspaper
printed in the seventeenth century.

It is worth noting that in the *Gloucester Journal*, no.
53 (8 Apr 1723), the assertion is made that the news in
that paper was fresher than that in the *Worcester Post-
Man*, "which has been publish'd at least 14 Years." This
remark does not prove anything; but it is to be supposed
that in directing attention to their rival's longer period
of experience the publishers of the Gloucester paper
would have gone as far as the facts permitted. Certainly
Stephen Bryan's *Worcester Post-Man* did not begin
before 1709. When his death was announced in the
Worcester Journal on 23 Jun 1748, reference was made
to his having been the printer of the paper "near Forty
Years."

Worcester Public Library: nos. 185 (9 Jan 1713) to 641
(6 Oct 1721), nearly complete; nos. 746 (11 Oct 1723)
to 756 (20 Dec 1723); no. 820 (12 Mar 1725); nos. 827
(30 Apr 1725) to 914 (30 Dec 1726); nos. 1281 (11
Jan 1734) to 1453 [*sic*] (23 Jul 1736), lacking fifteen
issues; nos. 1431 (26 Nov 1736) to 1566 (29 Jun 1739),
nine issues only; nos. 1699 (22 Jan 1742) to 1748 (31
Dec 1742), nineteen issues only; nos. 1801 (6 Jan 1744)

to 1851 (28 Dec 1744), lacking nine issues; nos. 1904 (3 Jan 1746) to 2680 (18 Dec 1760), nearly complete.

Office of Berrow's Newspapers, Ltd.: nos. 394 (11 Jan. 1717) to 496 (26 Dec 1718); no. 761 (24 Jan 1724); nos. 1203 (14 Jul 1732) to 1278 (21 Dec 1733); nos. 1573 (17 Aug 1739) to 1685 (16 Oct 1741); no. 1688 (6 Nov 1741); nos. 1699 (22 Jan 1742) to 1955 (26 Dec. 1746); nos. 2021 (14 Apr 1748) to 2526 (29 Dec 1757).

University of Reading Library: nos. 292 (28 Jan 1715) to 334 (18 Nov 1715), def., lacking three issues; no. 1551 (16 Mar 1739).

Birmingham Public Library: no. 2386 (24 Apr 1755).

Bodleian Library: no. 1355 (13 Jun 1735).

Oxford University Press Ephemeral Collection: no. 291 (21 Jan 1715); no. 687 (24 Aug 1722).

British Museum: no. 85 (2 Feb 1711); nos. 339 (23 Dec 1715) to 422 (26 Jul 1717), def., lacking eight issues; no. 924 (10 Mar 1727); no. 942 (14 Jul 1727); no. 961 (24 Nov 1727).

New York Public Library: no. 1274 (23 Nov 1733).

143. The New Worcester Journal.
[No. 1 (Nov ? 1753)]—?

Wed.

Berrow's Worcester Journal, no. 2310 (8 Nov 1753), has a declaration of opposition to "the Publication of a News-Paper (on a Wednesday) by a Person who has not the least Right to exercise the Art of Printing, he having serv'd no Apprenticeship at all thereto, nor hath otherwise had an Opportunity of acquainting himself with the Nature thereof." Satiric verses in *Berrow's Worcester Journal,* no. 2316 (20 Dec 1753), addressed "To the New Printer (as he calls himself)" identify him as Richard ["Brother Dick"] Lewis.

No copy found.

YARMOUTH

144. The Yarmouth Gazette.

May ? 1707—1712?

The existence of a paper with this title is established by an announcement which appeared in Henry Cross-grove's *Norwich Gazette* [item 102 in this Register], no. 29 (24 May 1707), and later issues:

> This is to give Notice, That there is a Newspaper Publisht Weekly at Yarmouth, Intituled the YAR-MOUTH GAZETTE, and for the Benefit of the Publick, all Persons that put Advertisements into the NORWICH GAZETTE, Printed by Henry Cross-grove in Magdalen-street, shall have them put into the YARMOUTH GAZETTE for Nothing, and that as often as they put them in the Norwich Gazette, if they desire it.

This *Yarmouth Gazette* may have been the regular *Norwich Gazette* with the place name changed in the title. With no. 31 (7 Apr 1707) the announcement printed above was modified to begin thus:

> This is to give Notice, That there is a Newspaper Published and Sold Weekly in the Town of Yarmouth, every Market-day, intituled the Yarmouth Gazette, . . .

By August, 1712, the title of the *Norwich Gazette Or the Loyal Packet* was followed by the words, "To be Published Weekly in Norwich and Great Yarmouth," a phrase which would be equally appropriate whether some copies were printed with "Yarmouth" instead of "Norwich" in the title or not. The *Norwich Gazette* of 30 Apr 1712 has title blocks representing (on the left) the arms of Norwich and (on the right) the arms of Yarmouth.

No copy found.

145. [The Yarmouth Post].

[No. 351 (22 May 1708)]—?

Sat; 2 cols.

Norwich, Printed by E. Burges, near the Red-Well, . . .

Evidence that Elizabeth Burges, printer of the *Norwich Post,* issued a Yarmouth edition, probably with special title but otherwise unchanged from the regular edition, is in the notice printed in the *Norwich Post,* no. 351 (22 May 1708). See item 101 in this Register.

No copy found.

YEOVIL

146. The Western Flying Post, or Yeovil Mercury. [From 30 Jan 1749, upon amalgamation with the *Sherborne Mercury, or Weekly Advertiser,* con., with new numbering, as]: The Western Flying-Post; or, Sherborne and Yeovil Mercury [item 132 in this Register].

[No. 1 (30 Jul ? 1744)]—vol. V, no. 213 (22 Aug 1748) —23 Jan 1749.

Mon.

Printed by R. Goadby, at the Printing Office in Yeovil.

Office of the *Western Gazette* Co., Ltd., Yeovil: vol. V, no. 213 (22 Aug 1748).

YORK

147. York Mercury: Or a General View of the Affairs of Europe, But more particularly of Great-Britain: With

Useful Observations on Trade. [From 23 Nov 1724 con. as]: York Journal: Containing The Most Remarkable Passages and Transactions at Home and Abroad. [By 11 Jan 1725 con. as]: York Journal or the Weekly Courant, With Advices Foreign and Domestick. Being a General View of the Affairs of Europe. [By 13 Jun 1727 con. as]: The Original York Journal: or, Weekly Courant. [From 2 Jan 1728 con. as]: The Original Mercury, York Journal: or, Weekly Courant.

Vol. I, no. 1 (23 Feb 1719)—no. 1 (23 Nov 1724)—no. 327 (16 Nov [1731])—?

Mon; by 13 Jun 1727, Tue; 12 pp.; from 23 Nov 1724, 6 pp.; by 21 Dec 1724, 8 pp.; by 1 Feb 1725, 12 pp.; by 13 Jun 1727, 4 pp.; single col.; from 23 Nov 1724, 2 cols.; from 21 Dec 1724, single col.; by 13 Jun 1727, 2 cols.; from 10 Dec 1728, 3 cols.

York: Printed and Sold by Gr. White, and Tho. Hammond, Jun. Bookseller, and by Mr. Body in Whitby, Mr. Clarkson in Scarborough, Mr. Hewitt in Stoxley, Mr. Walker in Thirsk, Mr. Dunn in North-Allerton, Mr. Ferraby Bookseller in Hull, Mr. Mennel in Malton, Mr. Sherwood in Beverley, Mr. Walton in Darlington, Mr. Wilson in Easingwold, Mr. Austin Bookseller in Rippon, and at his Shop in Richmond, Mr. Husband in Stockton, Mr. Plaxton in Kirby, Mr. Cross in Pocklington, Mr. Walker in Wetherby, Zacheus Canby in Selby, Mr. Holmes in Skipton, Mr. Newsom of Burrowbridge, Mr. Rusholm in Howden, Mr. Lawrence in Casselton, Mr. Holtby in Yarm, Mr. Staveley in Hunnanby, Mr. Hawsom in Glaisdale, Mr. Ayrton in Knarsborough, Mr. Skirrow in Settle; . . . [From 13 Feb 1721]: York: Printed and Sold by Charles Bourne, and Tho. Hammond, jun. Bookseller. . . . [From 27 Jul 1724]: York: Printed and Sold by Alice Bourne, and Tho. Hammond, jun. Bookseller, . . . [From 23 Nov 1724]: Printed by Thomas

Gent: And are to be Sold at the Printing-Office in Coffee-House-Yard, York, . . . [By 13 Jun 1727]: York: Printed by Thomas Gent, in Coffee-Yard, over against the Star in Stone-Gate, . . .

This announcement is in vol. II, no. 50 (30 Jan 1721):

> Whereas Grace White, Widow, the late printer of this paper, is now dead, and Charles Bourne being now settled in the Printing-house lately belonging to her: This is therefore to give notice to all gentlemen and others that the said Charles Bourne intends to carry on the said trade of printing in the house situate within the Coffee-Yard within the said city of York: . . .

York Reference Library: vol. IV, no. 28 (27 Aug 1722); vol. VI, no. 16 (1 Jun 1724); fragments of some issues of 1722-25.

York Minster Library: vol. I, no. 1 (23 Feb 1719), to vol. II, no. 52 (13 Feb 1721); vol. III, no. 18 (19 Jun 1721); vol. V, no. 17 (10 Jun 1723), to vol. VI, no. 30 (7 Sep 1724), five issues only; no. 1 (23 Nov 1724); no. 18 (22 Mar 1725); nos. 96 (13 Jun 1727) to 275 (17 Nov [1730]), lacking ten issues.

Kingston-upon-Hull Museum: no. 252 (9 Jun [1730]).

Newcastle Reference Library: vol. VI, no. 3 (2 Mar 1724).

Office of Berrow's Newspapers, Ltd., Worcester: no. 281 (29 Dec [1730]); no. 327 (16 Nov [1731]).

British Museum: vol. I, no. 18 (22 Jun 1719), to vol. VI, no. 36 (19 Oct 1724), scattered issues, many def.; no. 5 (21 Dec 1724); no. 8 (11 Jan 1725); no. 11 (1 Feb 1725).

Private library of Kenneth Monkman, Esq., London: no. 266 (15 Sep [1730]); no. 325 (2 Nov [1731]).

148. The York Courant.

[No. 1 (14 Sep ? 1725)]—no. 171 (17 Dec 1728)—no.
1836 (30 Dec 1760), + .

Tue.

[By 17 Dec 1728]: York: Printed and Sold by John
White, at the Sign of the Printing Press, nigh St. Helen's
Church in Stonegate, and Mr. Ryles at his Shops in Hull
and Beverley, . . . [By 20 Apr 1731]: York, Printed by
Sarah Coke, at the Sign of the Printing Press in Stone-
gate; and Sold by Mr. Ryles at Hull, Mr. Godson at
Beverley, Mr. Mennel at Malton, Mr. Bland at Scar-
borough, Mr. Oldfield at Hallifax, Mr. Robinson Post-
Master of Whitby, Mr. Hill at Snaith, Zacheus Canby at
Selby, Mr. Watson at Pontefract, and Mr. Rose at Knares-
borough; . . . [From 30 Nov 1731]: York: Printed by
John White at the Sign of the Printing-Press in Stonegate: And Sold by . . . [From 1 Oct 1734]: York, Printed
by John Gilfillan, at the Sign of the Printing-Press, at the
Foot of Stonegate. . . . [By 8 Nov 1737]: York: Printed
by Alexander Staples, at the Printing-Press, in Coney-
Street; and Sold by . . . [From 16 Jan 1739]: York:
Printed and Sold by Ward and Chandler, Booksellers, at
the Shop late Mr. Manchlin's in Coney-street, . . . [By
24 Jun 1740]: York: Printed for Caesar Ward, Bookseller
in Coney-Street, . . . [From 25 Jun 1745]: Publish'd by
Richard Bucktrout, late Servant to Caesar Ward, in
Coney-Street. [From 4 Feb 1746]: Publish'd by Caesar
Ward, in Coney-Street, for the Proprietor. [By 23 Jun
1747]: Printed by Caesar Ward, in Coney-Street. . . .
[By 1 May 1759]: Printed by A. Ward, in Coney Street.

These announcements are in no. 470 (10 Sep 1734) and
following issues:

Whereas the Property of my Printing Press at
York is now Sold to John Gilfillan, the Printer of this

Paper, who has served me faithfully above Seven
Years; This is to desire all Persons indebted to me
on Account of this Paper, or otherwise, to pay their
Money to Mr. Edward Seller, in Jubbergate, York,
or to Mrs. Sarah Coke, at the Printing Press in
Stonegate, at or before Michaelmas next.

J. White.

Sept. 4. 1734.

To the kind Encouragers of this Paper.

Gentlemen,

Being in a short Time to set up for my self, I
shall hope for a Continuance of your Favours. You
may depend upon it, that all Care will be taken to
raise the Credit of this Paper, to which end a Set
of curious Types are sent for; and the News will be
impartially collected from all the best and most
authentick News Papers in the Kingdom.

John Gilfillan.

This announcement is in no. 692 (16 Jan 1739):

As the York Courant, by Mr. Staples's leaving off
Trade, is now fallen into other Hands, it may not
be improper to inform our Readers, that We shall
endeavour to compile it in so concise a Manner, as
to give, every Tuesday, the Substance of all that is
material, in the several London Prints of the three
foregoing Posts. . . .

This announcement is in no. 1028 (25 Jun 1745):

Having lately had the Misfortune to lose a very
large Sum of Money by being engag'd with my
Brother-in-Law, who died Insolvent, I have been
oblig'd to sell the Printing-House towards the Satisfaction of my Creditors. The Amount thereof, with
all other my Effects, shall be honestly and faithfully
deliver'd up for their Advantage; and I think myself
in Conscience bound to do all that lies in my Power
towards their Assistance in Recovering my Debts.
Those who know Me will, I am confident, so far be
my Advocates as to acknowledge, that few Men
have been more Industrous and none less Expensive.
I can't help therefore expressing my Hopes, that my

514

Failure will be imputed to the Real and True Cause
—The being answerable for another Man's Actions.
Caesar Ward.

The Publick may be assur'd, that effectual Care
will be taken, by the present Proprietors of the Printing House, to carry on the York Courant with the
same Spirit, and upon the same Principles, which
have hitherto render'd this Paper generally Agreeable. The Printing Business will also be carried on
by the same Hands, and at the same Place as usual,
where Advertisements will be taken in. No Care
nor Expence will be wanting that can any wise tend
to the Service and Entertainment of the Publick.
Rich. Bucktrout.

This letter addressed "To the Public" is in the *Leedes
Intelligencer,* no. 262 (1 May 1759):

Notwithstanding the great, and, to me, unfortunate
Loss of my late Husband, I can assure his Customers, and all Others, That

The YORK COURANT

will be carried on with the same Diligence and
Impartiality as before; under the Conduct of the
same Person, who, for some Years last past, has had
the principal Management of it; Mr. Ward's own
Time being mostly taken up in carrying on a large
Work of another Nature: I humbly hope, therefore,
for the Continuance of your Favours; which will
greatly oblige and encourage,
Your most obedient humble Servant,
ANN WARD

All Manner of Printing-Work will be perform'd
as before.

York Reference Library: nos. 171 (17 Dec 1728) to 488
(14 Jan 1735), nearly complete; nos. 692 (16 Jan 1739)
to 950 (27 Dec 1743), with many duplicates and some
variant issues; nos. [995?] (6 Oct [i.e., Nov] 1744) to 1471
(25 Dec 1753), nearly complete, with many duplicates;
nos. 1474 (15 Jan 1754) to 1626 (21 Dec 1756); no.

1772 (9 Oct 1759); nos. 1784 (1 Jan 1760) to 1836 (30 Dec 1760), + .

York Minster Library; nos. 286 (2 Mar 1731) to 297 (18 May 1731), lacking one issue; nos. 635 (8 Nov 1737) to 669 (18 Jul 1738), many covered with clippings from later newspapers; nos. 671 (1 Aug 1738) to 676 (5 Sep 1738); no. 835 (13 Oct 1741); no. 837 (27 Oct 1741); no. 992 (16 Oct 1744); nos. 1132 (23 Jun 1747) to 1578 (20 Jan 1756), nearly complete; nos. 1784 (1 Jan 1760) to 1817 (19 Aug 1760), lacking five issues; nos. 1828 (4 Nov 1760) and 1829 (11 Nov 1760), + .

Leeds Reference Library: no. 200 (8 Jul 1729); no. 796 (13 Jan 1741), def.; no. 925 (5 Jul 1743); no. 926 (12 Aug 1743); no. 913 [sic] (30 Aug 1743), def.; no. [1044] (15 Oct 1745); no. [1049] (19 Nov 1745); no. [1050] (26 Nov 1745); no. 1055 (31 Dec 1745); no. 1228 (25 Apr 1749); no. 1412 (7 Nov 1752), def.; no. 1445 (26 Jun 1753); no. 1774 (23 Oct 1759), def.

Office of Berrow's Newspapers, Ltd., Worcester: no. 719 (24 Jul 1739).

Oxford University Press Ephemeral Collection: no. 1636 (1 Mar 1757).

Private library of Kenneth Monkman, Esq., London: no. 717 (10 Jul 1739); no. 734 (6 Nov 1739); no. 735 (13 Nov 1739); no. 753 (18 Mar 1740); no. 873 (6 Jul 1742); no. 874 (13 Jul 1742); no. 877 (3 Aug 1742); no. 880 (24 Aug 1742); no. 882 (7 Sep 1742); no. 885 (28 Sep 1742); no. 889 (26 Oct 1742); no. 906 (22 Feb 1743); no. 956 (7 Feb 1744); no. 1028 (25 Jun 1745); nos. 1171 (22 Mar 1748) to 1211 (27 Dec 1748), lacking one issue; no. 1228 (25 Apr 1749); nos. 1264 (2 Jan 1750) to 1419 (26 Dec 1752), lacking two issues; no. 1449 (10 Jul 1753); no. 1487 (16 Apr 1754); no. 1521 (10 Dec 1754), def.; no. 1593 (4 May 1756); no. 1620 (9 Nov 1756); no. 1621 (16 Nov 1756); no. 1749 (1 May 1759).

Yale University Library: nos. 740 (18 Dec 1739) to 790 (2 Dec 1740).

New York Public Library: no. 1073 (6 May 1746).

Library of Congress: no. 846 (29 Dec 1741).

University of Texas Library: no. 875 (20 Jul 1742).

149. The York Gazetteer. [By 1 Mar 1743 con. as]: The York
Gazeteer. With News both Foreign and Domestick.
[No. 1 (10 Mar ? 1741)]—no. 41 (14 Dec 1741)—no.
222 (14 May 1745)—1752.

Tue.

York: Printed by John Jackson in Grape-Lane, . . . This
Paper is also Sold, and Advertisements taken in, by Mr.
Joseph Smith in Barnsley, Mr. Romans and Mr. Baker
in New-Malton, Mr. Richard Parkinson, Grocer, in Pickering, Mr. George Dinmoor in Hull; Mr. Henry Stockton
at Kirbymoorside, Mr. John Bland at Scarborough and
Newil Hodgson at Knaresburgh. [By 4 Jan 1743]: York:
Printed by John Jackson in Grape-Lane, . . . This Paper
is distributed, and Advertisements taken in, by Mr. Joseph Smith in Barnsley, Mr. Romans in Malton, Mr. Richard Parkinson, Grocer, in Pickering, Mr. George Dinmoor
and Mr. Hewit in Hull, Mr. Henry Stockton at Kirbymoorside, Mr. John Bland at Scarbrough, Mr. Watson at
Pontefract, Mr. Lord in Wakefield, Mr. Austin in Ripon,
Mr. Richmond Bainbridge at Richmond and Barnicastle,
Mr. Dowson at Northallerton, Mr. Lofthouse at Otley,
Mr. Nicholson at Sheffield and Rotherham, Mr. Bell at
Beverley, Mr. Haworth at Preston and Skipton, Mr. Rock-
cliff at Leeds and Bradford, and Mr. Sampson at Bridlington. N. B. Great Numbers of these Papers are distributed Weekly in the City of York, and in London,
Lincolnshire, and most parts of Yorkshire. [By 31 May
1743 colophon has]: . . . N. B. This Paper is the most
Advantageous to Advertise in, great Numbers being distributed in the West, North, and East Ridings of Yorkshire; and a great Part of Lincolnshire, Nottinghamshire,
and the Bishoprick of Durham.

End noted in *York Courant* of 4 August 1752: "The Late Publisher of the *York Gazeteer* being advised, by several of his Friends, to desist from carrying on the said Paper, has complied with their Advice. . . ."

York Minster Library: no. 41 (15 Dec 1741).

York Reference Library: nos. 209 (12 Feb 1745) to 212 (5 Mar 1745); no. 214 (19 Mar 1745).

Office of H. Morley and Sons Ltd., York: no. 136 (4 Oct 1743).

Kingston-upon-Hull Museum: no. 222 (14 May 1745).

Private Library of Kenneth Monkman, Esq., London: nos. 97 (4 Jan 1743) to 114 (3 May 1743); nos. 133 (13 Sep 1743) to 135 (27 Sep 1743); nos. 137 (11 Oct 1743) to 142 (15 Nov 1743); nos. 144 (22 Nov 1743) to 149 (27 Dec 1743).

New York Public Library: no. 88 (9 Nov 1742).

150. The York Journal: or, The Weekly Advertiser. [From 10 Dec 1745 con. as]: York Journal: or, The Weekly Advertiser. [From 25 Mar 1746 con. as]: York Journal: or, The Protestant Courant. [By 12 Dec 1749 con. as]: The Protestant York Courant.

No. 1 (26 Nov 1745)—no. 383 (3 Apr 1753)—?

Tue.

York: Printed by John Gilfillan, in Coffee-Yard. [From 11 Feb 1746]: York: Printed by John Gilfillan, in Coffee-Yard; and Sold by Mr. Inman in Doncaster, Mr. Bland in Scarborough, Mr. Lord at Wakefield and Barnsley, Mr. Watson at Pontefract, Mr. Donaldson at Leeds, Mr. Milner at Halifax, Mr. Northrop at Bradford, Mr. Macaulay at Huthersfield, Mr. Watson at Sheffield, Mr. Munby at Hull, Mr. Godson of Beverley, Mr. Parkinson of Pickering, Mr. Dale at Malton, Mr. Newby at Helmsly, Mr. Affleck at Thirsk, Mr. Thompson at Northallerton,

Mr. Garnet at Yarm, Mr. Dent at Richmond, Mr. North at Bedale, Mr. Austin at Ripon, and Mr. North at Boroughbridge; by whom Advertisements and Letters to the Printer are taken in. [Changes in subsequent issues.] [From 24 Mar 1752]: York: Printed for I. Gilfillan, in Coffee-Yard; Sold by . . . .

A notice at the top of the first column in nos. 1 and 2 of this paper begins thus:

Having Advertis'd on the 24th of September last, That I intended to Publish this Paper with all convenient Speed, for the Service of the Public at this Critical Juncture, I take this first Opportunity to Return my Subscribers Thanks for the Encouragement they have been pleased to give me; . . .

In no. 17 (18 Mar 1746) a correspondent requested the printer to alter the subtitle from *The Weekly Advertiser* to *The Protestant Courant.*

This notice is in no. 331 (24 Mar 1752):

Isabella Gilfillan

Takes this Method of returning her sincere Thanks to the Public for the many Favours done to her late Husband, and assures them, that the Printing Business will be carefully carried on, and no Care or Pains will be wanting to merit the Continuance of their Favours.

York Reference Library: nos. 3 (10 Dec 1745) to 383 (3 Apr 1753), lacking two-thirds of the issues.

York Minster Library: no. 126 (19 Apr 1748); no. 165 (17 Jan 1749); no. 260 (13 Nov 1750); no. 262 (27 Nov 1750); no. 291 (18 Jun 1751).

National Library of Scotland: no. 25 (13 May 1746).

Private library of Kenneth Monkman, Esq., London: nos. 1 (26 Nov 1745) to 77 (12 May 1747); no. 78 (19 May 1747), lacking first leaf; nos. 79 (26 May 1747) to 120 (8 Mar 1748).

Bibliography

Bibliography

THE NEWSPAPERS listed in the Register of English Provincial Newspapers, 1701-1760 (Appendix C above) are the chief source of the information set forth in the eight chapters of this book. References have been made in footnotes to other material found to be of use.

Listed below are selected bibliographical works, finding lists, histories of journalism, and special studies of background which may be consulted with profit. No attempt is made to compile a complete catalogue of books and articles which have a bearing on the subject of early journalism.

A. *Publications Listing Early Newspapers*

BRITISH MUSEUM. *Catalogue of Printed Books,* s.v. "Periodical Publications."

CRANE, R. S.; KAYE, F. B.; and PRIOR, M. E. *A Census of British Newspapers and Periodicals 1620-1800.* Chapel Hill, N.C.: University of North Carolina Press, 1927.

CRANFIELD, G. A. *A Hand-List of English Provincial Newspapers and Periodicals 1700-1760.* Cambridge: Bowes & Bowes, for the Cambridge Bibliographical Society, 1952.

————. "Handlist of English Provincial Newspapers and Periodicals, 1700-1760: Additions and Corrections," *Transactions of the Cambridge Bibliographical Society,* II (1956), 269-74.

GABLER, ANTHONY J. *Check List of English Newspapers and Periodicals before 1801 in the Huntington Library.* Reprinted from the *Huntington Library Bulletin,* No. 2 (November, 1931).

GREGORY, WINIFRED (ed.). *Union List of Serials in Libraries of the United States and Canada.* 2nd ed. New York: Wilson, 1943; also Supplement, 1945, ed GABRIELLE E. MALIKOFF, and 2nd Supplement, 1953, ed. MARGA FRANCK.

LAUGHTON, GEORGE E., and STEPHEN, LORNA R. *Yorkshire Newspapers: A Bibliography with Locations.* [Harrogate?]: Yorkshire Branch of the Library Association, 1960.

MILFORD, R. T., and SUTHERLAND, D. M. *A Catalogue of English Newspapers and Periodicals in the Bodleian Library, 1622-1800.* London: Oxford University Press, for the Oxford Bibliographical Society, 1936.

[MUDDIMAN, JOSEPH GEORGE]. *Tercentenary Handlist of English & Welsh Newspapers, Magazines & Reviews.* London: *The Times,* 1920.

PARSONS, HENRY S. *A Check List of Foreign Newspapers in the Library of Congress.* Washington, D.C.: U. S. Government Printing Office, 1929.

"Provincial Newspapers, 1701-1800," *Cambridge Bibliography of English Literature,* ed. F. W. BATESON. London: Cambridge University Press, 1940, II, 720-30.

ROUPELL, MARION G. *Union Catalogue of the Periodical Publications in the University Libraries of the British Isles.* London: National Central Library, 1937.

SCHWEGMANN, GEORGE A., JR. *Newspapers on Microfilm.* 3rd ed. Washington, D.C.: Library of Congress, 1957.

STEWART, ANDREW. *Catalogue of an Exhibition Illustrating the History of the English Newspaper through Three Centuries, from the Library of the Press Club.* London: Bumpus, 1932.

STEWART, JAMES D.; HAMMOND, MURIEL E.; and SAENGER, ERWIN. *British Union-Catalogue of Periodicals. A Record of the Periodicals of the World, from the Seventeenth Century to the Present Day, in British Libraries.* 4 vols. London: Butterworths Scientific Publications, 1955-58; also Supplement, 1962.

STEWART, POWELL. *A Descriptive Catalogue of a Collection at the University of Texas: British Newspapers and Periodicals 1632-1800.* Austin: University of Texas, 1950.

WILES, ROY MCKEEN. "Further Additions and Corrections to G. A. Cranfield's *Handlist of English Provincial Newspapers and Periodicals 1700-1760*," *Transactions of the Cambridge Bibliographical Society,* II (1958), 385-89.

B. *Books and Articles about Newspapers*

Most useful of all bibliographical publications listing secondary works dealing with early journalism in the United Kingdom is *Studies of British Newspapers and Periodicals from their Beginning to 1800: A Bibliography,* by Katherine Kirtley Weed and Richmond P. Bond, published as *Studies in Philology,* Extra Series, No. 2 (December, 1946). In this valuable compilation are listed many special articles on provincial newspapers, including the series headed "The Provincial Press" in *Effective Advertising,* the series headed "The Oldest Newspapers" in *Newspaper World,* numerous articles in *Notes and Queries,* and many similar articles accessible only in the publications of local antiquarian societies. See also the appropriate sections of *The Cambridge Bibliography of English Literature,* particularly II, 689-700.

ANDREW, J. D. "*The Derbyshire Newspaper Press 1720-1855.*" Unpublished Master's thesis, University of Reading, in Derby Borough Library.

ANDREWS, ALEXANDER. *The History of British Journalism, from the Foundation of the Newspaper Press in England to the Repeal of the Stamp Act in 1855.* 2 vols. London: Richard Bentley, 1859.

ASPINALL, ARTHUR. "Statistical Accounts of the London Newspapers in the Eighteenth Century," *English Historical Review,* LXIII (1948), 201-32.

AUSTIN, ROLAND. "The Cirencester Flying-Post," *Notes and Queries,* Ser. 11, X (1914), 325-26.

————. "Robert Raikes, the Elder, & the 'Gloucester Journal,' " *The Library*, Ser. 3, VI (1915), 1-24.

————. " 'Gloucester Journal,' 1722-1922," *Notes and Queries*, Ser. 12, X (1922), 261-64, 283-85.

Axon, Geoffrey R. "A Note on the First Manchester Newspaper," *Transactions of the Lancashire and Cheshire Antiquarian Society*, XLI (1924), 137-38.

————. "A Further Note on the First Manchester Newspaper 1719-1725," *Transactions of the Lancashire and Cheshire Antiquarian Society*, LXVIII (1958), 146-47.

Axon, William E. "Newspapers in 1738-39," *Echoes of Old Lancashire*. London: Andrews, 1899. Pp. 61-71.

Beckett, Arthur. "The First Sussex Newspaper," *Sussex County Magazine*, XV (1941), 247-54.

[Beckwith, Frank]. "The Leeds Intelligencer 1754-1866," *Publications of the Thoresby Society*, XL, Part 3, No. 101 (1953), [i]-lxi.

Berkeley, Mrs. R. "A Sketch of Early Provincial Journalism," *Reports and Papers Read at the Meetings of the Architectural Societies of the Counties of Lincoln and Nottingham, . . . Diocese of Worcester, and County of Leicester*, XXIV (1898), [550]-73.

Berrow's Worcester Journal, No. 12,888 (28 December 1940) (special anniversary issue).

Bicentenary, Gloucester Journal. Gloucester: Chance & Bland, 1922.

Bleyer, Willard Grosvenor. "The Beginnings of English Journalism," *Journalism Quarterly*, VIII (1931), 317-28.

Bourne, H. R. Fox. *English Newspapers. Chapters in the History of Journalism*. 2 vols. London: Chatto and Windus, 1887.

Brushfield, Thomas N. "Andrew Brice and the Early Exeter Newspaper Press," *Report and Transactions of the Devonshire Association for the Advancement of Science, Literature, and Art*, XX (1888), 163-214.

BURTON, K. G. *The Early Newspaper Press in Berkshire (1723-1855)*. Reading: [Published by the author], 1954.

CHOPE, R. PEARSE. "The First Devonshire Newspaper," *Devon and Cornwall Notes and Queries*, IX (1916-17), 243-47.

CLARKE, W. J. *Early Nottingham Printers and Printing*. Nottingham: Forman, 1942; 2nd ed., 1953.

COCK, F. WILLIAM. "The Kentish Post or the Canterbury News Letter," *The Library*, Ser. 3, IV (1913), 285-90.

CRANFIELD, G. A. *The Development of the Provincial Newspaper 1700-1760*. Oxford: Clarendon Press, 1962.

————. "The First Cambridge Newspaper," *Proceedings of the Cambridge Antiquarian Society*, XLV (1952), [5]-16.

DAVIES, ROBERT. *A Memoir of the York Press, with Notices of Authors, Printers, and Stationers, in the Sixteenth, Seventeenth, and Eighteenth Centuries*. Westminster: Nichols, 1868.

DIBBLEE, G. BINNEY. *The Newspaper*. London: Williams & Norgate, n.d.

EVANS, H. L. *The Cradle of the British Press: A Distinction Held by a Lincolnshire Journal*. *"Stamford Mercury"—Our Oldest Paper*. Reprinted from the *Lincolnshire Magazine*, August, 1938.

EWALD, WILLIAM BRAGG. *The Newsmen of Queen Anne*. Oxford: Blackwell, 1956.

FRANK, JOSEPH. *The Beginnings of the English Newspaper 1620-1660*. Cambridge, Mass.: Harvard University Press, 1961.

GALLOP, D. F. "Chapters in the History of the Provincial Newspaper Press 1700-1855." Unpublished Master's thesis, Bristol Reference Library.

GRANT, JAMES. *The Newspaper Press: Its Origin—Progress—and Present Position*. 3 vols. London: Tinsley, 1871-[72].

GRIFFITHS, IVOR. *Berrow's Worcester Journal. An Examination of the Antiquity of Britain's Oldest Newspaper*. Worcester: George Williams & Berrow's Ltd., 1941.

HADLEY, W. W. *The Bi-Centenary Record of the Northampton Mercury. . . .* Northampton: *Mercury* Press, [1920].

HAIG, ROBERT L. *The Gazetteer 1735-1797: A Study in the Eighteenth-Century English Newspaper.* Carbondale, Ill.: Southern Illinois University Press, [1960].

HANSON, LAURENCE. "English Newsbooks, 1620-1641," *The Library,* Ser. 4, XVIII (1937-38), 355-84.

HEWINS, G. S. "Early Newspapers," *Notes and Queries,* CLXXXI (1941), 20.

HERD, HAROLD. *The March of Journalism: The Story of the British Press from 1622 to the Present Day.* London: Allen & Unwin, [1952].

HUNT, F. KNIGHT. *The Fourth Estate: Contributions towards a History of Newspapers, and of the Liberty of the Press.* 2 vols. London: Bogue, 1850.

JEWITT, LLEWELLYN. "An Historical and Descriptive Note on the First Derby Newspaper," *Reliquary,* XXI (1881), 225-34.

LEARY, FREDERICK. *History of the Manchester Periodical Press containing Historical Notices of Newspapers, Journals. . . .* Manuscript volume in Manchester Local History Library; Preface dated 28 May 1889.

MORGAN, WILLIAM THOMAS, and MORGAN, CHLOE SINER. *A Bibliography of British History (1700-1715) with Special Reference to the Reign of Queen Anne.* Vol. III. Bloomington, Ind.: Publisher Not Named, 1939. Pp. 224-335.

MORISON, STANLEY. *Ichabod Dawks and his News-Letter with an Account of the Dawks Family of Booksellers and Stationers 1635-1731.* London: Cambridge University Press, 1931.

———. *The English Newspaper: Some Account of the Physical Development of Journals Printed in London between 1662 and the Present Day.* London: Cambridge University Press, 1932.

———. "The Newspaper," *Johnson's England,* ed. A. S. TURBERVILLE. Vol. II. Oxford: Clarendon Press, 1933. Pp. 331-67.

MUDDIMAN, JOSEPH GEORGE. *The King's Journalist 1659-1689*. London: Bodley Head, 1923.

NICHOLS, JOHN. *Literary Anecdotes of the Eighteenth Century*. 9 vols. London: Nichols, 1812-15. See especially "Of Publick News and Weekly Papers," IV, 33-97.

[PAYNE, MERVYN]. *The Norwich Post: Its Contemporaries and Successors*. Norwich: [Norfolk News Co., Ltd.], 1951.

PLOMER, HENRY ROBERT. "James Abree, Printer and Bookseller, of Canterbury," *The Library*, Ser. 3, IV (1913), 46-56.

READ, DONALD. "Manchester News-Letter," *Manchester Review*, VIII (Spring, 1957), 1-5. Reprinted from *Manchester Guardian*, 31 August 1956.

———. "North of England Newspapers (*c.* 1700-*c.* 1900) and Their Value to Historians," *Proceedings of the Leeds Philosophical Society (Literary and Historical Section)*, VIII (1957), 200-215.

RICHARDSON, MRS. HERBERT. *The Old English Newspaper*. (English Association Pamphlet, No. 86.) London: Oxford University Press, 1933.

SHAABER, MATTHIAS A. "The History of the First English Newspaper," *Studies in Philology*, XXIX (1932), 551-87.

———. *Some Forerunners of the Newspaper in England 1476-1622*. Philadelphia: University of Pennsylvania Press, 1929.

The Story of the Salisbury and Winchester Journal 1729 to 1939. Salisbury: *Salisbury and Winchester Journal*, 1939.

TAYLOR, HENRY. "Chester's Oldest Newspaper," *Chester and North Wales Archaeological and Historic Society Journal*, N. S., XXI (1915), 25-29.

VARLEY, FREDERICK J. *Mercurius Aulicus*. Oxford: Blackwell, 1948.

WILES, ROY MCKEEN. "Freshest Advices, Foreign and Domestick," *Dalhousie Review*, XXXVIII (1958), [8]-17.

WILLIAMS, FRANCIS. *Dangerous Estate: The Anatomy of Newspapers*. London: Longmans, Green, [1957].

"Williams, J. B." [i.e., Joseph George Muddiman]. *A History of English Journalism to the Foundation of the Gazette.* London: Longmans, Green, 1908.

――――. "Henry Cross-grove, Jacobite, Journalist and Printer," *The Library,* Ser. 3, V (1914), 206-19.

――――. "The First English Provincial Newspaper," *Notes and Queries,* Ser. 12, II (1916), 81-82, 216-17, 292.

――――. "The Beginnings of English Journalism," *Cambridge History of English Literature.* Vol. VII. London: Cambridge University Press, 1932. Pp. [343]-65.

C. *Related Studies*

Allnutt, W. H. "English Provincial Presses, III," *Bibliographica,* II (1896), 276-308.

Ashton, T. S. *An Economic History of England: The 18th Century.* London: Methuen, [1955].

Axon, Geoffrey R. "Roger and Orion Adams, Printers," *Transactions of the Lancashire & Cheshire Antiquarian Society,* XXXIX (1921), 108-24.

Beveridge, William Henry, *et al. Prices and Wages in England from the Twelfth to the Nineteenth Century.* Vol. I. London: Longmans, Green, [1939].

Chaney, J. B. "The Historical Value of Newspapers," *Minnesota Historical Society Collections,* VIII (1898), III-19.

Clyde, William M. *The Struggle for the Freedom of the Press from Caxton to Cromwell.* London: Humphrey Milford, 1934.

Coleman, D. C. *The British Paper Industry, 1495-1860.* London: Oxford University Press, 1958.

Collet, Collet Dobson. *History of the Taxes on Knowledge: Their Origin and Repeal.* London: Watts, [1933].

Ellis, Aytoun. *The Penny Universities: A History of the Coffee-Houses.* London: Secker & Warburg, 1957.

FRASER, PETER. *The Intelligence of the Secretaries of State & Their Monopoly of Licensed News 1660-1688.* London: Cambridge University Press, 1956.

GRAYLAND, EUGENE CHARLES. *The Value of Newspaper Sources for Historical and Other Research.* Auckland: Colenso Press, [1948].

HANDOVER, PHYLLIS MARGARET. *Printing in London: From 1476 to Modern Times.* Cambridge, Mass.: Harvard University Press, 1960.

HANSON, LAURENCE. *Government and the Press, 1695-1763.* London: Oxford University Press, 1936.

HARLAND, JOHN. *Collectanea Relating to Manchester and its Neighbourhood,* . . . Vol. II. [Manchester]: For the Chetham Society, 1876. Pp. 102-30.

HOWE, ELLIC. *The London Compositor: Documents Relating to Wages, Working Conditions and Customs of the London Printing Trade, 1785-1900.* London: Bibliographical Society, 1947.

HYETT, FRANCIS ADAMS, and BAZELEY, WILLIAM. *The Bibliographer's Manual of Gloucestershire Literature.* . . . 3 vols. Gloucester: Publisher Not Named: 1895-97.

LAPRADE, WILLIAM THOMAS. *Public Opinion and Politics in Eighteenth-Century England to the Fall of Walpole.* New York: Macmillan Co., 1936.

"MARFORIO." *An Historical View of the Principles, Characters, Persons, &c. of the Political Writers in Great Britain.* . . . London: Webb, 1740. (Also published as "Augustan Reprint Society Publication," No. 69, with Introduction by ROBERT HAIG. Los Angeles: William Andrews Clark Memorial Library, 1958.)

MORISON, STANLEY. "The Bibliography of Newspapers and the Writing of History," *The Library,* Ser. 5, IX (1954), 153-75.

PLOMER, HENRY ROBERT, et al. *A Dictionary of the Printers and Booksellers Who Were at Work in England, Scotland and Ireland from 1668 to 1725.* London: Oxford University Press, for the Bibliographical Society, 1922.

——. BUSHNELL, G. H.; and DIX, E. R. McC. *A Dictionary of the Printers and Booksellers Who Were at Work in England, Scotland and Ireland from 1726 to 1775.* London: Oxford University Press, for the Bibliographical Society, 1932 (for 1930).

POLLARD, GRAHAM. "Notes on the Size of the Sheet," *The Library,* Ser. 4, XXII (1941-42), 120-28.

SALMON, LUCY MAYNARD. *The Newspaper and the Historian.* New York: Oxford University Press, 1923.

SHORTER, A. H. *Paper Mills and Paper Makers in England, 1495-1800.* Hilversum, Netherlands: Paper Publications Society, 1957.

SIEBERT, FREDRICK SEATON. *Freedom of the Press in England 1476-1776: The Rise and Decline of Government Controls.* Urbana, Ill.: University of Illinois Press, 1952.

STEVENS, D. H. *Party Politics and English Journalism, 1702-42.* Menasha, Wis.: Banta, 1936.

STEWART-BROWN, R. "The Stationers, Booksellers and Printers of Chester to about 1800," *Transactions of the Historic Society of Lancashire and Cheshire,* LXXXIII (1931), 101-52.

SUTHERLAND, JAMES R. "The Circulation of Newspapers and Literary Periodicals, 1700-1730," *The Library,* Ser. 4, XV (1934), 110-24.

TIMPERLEY, CHARLES HENRY. *Encyclopædia of Literary and Typographical Anecdote; Being a Chronological Digest of the Most Interesting Facts Illustrative of the History of Literature and Printing. . . .* London: Bohn, 1842.

TURNER, SYDNEY R. *The Newspaper Tax Stamps of Great Britain. The First Issue 1712-1757.* [London]: Sydney R. Turner, [1936].

UPDIKE, DANIEL BERKELEY. *Printing Types: Their History, Forms, and Use: A Study in Survivals.* 2nd ed. Cambridge, Mass.: Harvard University, 1951.

WALCOTT, ROBERT. *English Politics in the Early Eighteenth Century.* Cambridge, Mass.: Harvard University Press, 1956.

WALLIS, ALFRED. "A Sketch of the Early History of the Printing Press in Derbyshire," *Journal of the Derbyshire Archaeological and Natural History Society*, III (1881), 137-56.

WELFORD, RICHARD. "Early Newcastle Typography, 1639-1800," *Archaeologia Aeliana: or Miscellaneous Tracts. . . . Published by the Society of Antiquaries of Newcastle upon Tyne*, Ser. 3, III (1907), 1-134.

WELSH, CHARLES. *A Bookseller of the Last Century. Being Some Account of the Life of John Newbery. . . .* London: Griffith, Farran, Okeden & Welsh, 1885.

WORTH, R. N. "Notes on the History of Printing in Devon," *Report and Transactions of the Devonshire Association for the Advancement of Science, Literature and Art*, XI (1879), 497-515.

Index

Index

Omitted from this index are (a) initial articles, both definite and indefinite, in titles of newspapers and books; (b) all details preceding page 3; (c) modern works of history and criticism, and their authors, mentioned in the text or notes or listed in the Bibliography; (d) names of distributors and places served by them, for which see "Agents, lists of" and "Places served"; (e) casual references to other persons and places; (f) the libraries, public and private, where the newspapers, books, and records are now to be found. It will be useful to observe that references falling within pages 377-519 are to the Register.